Litigating Child Restraint Cases

By

Joseph William Moch, Esq.
&
Arthur Borja

Lawyers & Judges Publishing Co.

This publication is designed to provide accurate and authoritative information in regard to the subject matter covered. It is sold with the understanding that the publisher is not engaged in rendering legal, accounting, or other professional service. If legal advice or other expert assistance is required, the services of a competent professional person should be sought.

—From a *Declaration of Principles* jointly adopted by a Committee of the American Bar Association and a Committee of Publishers and Associations.

Lawyers & Judges Publishing Co.
P.O. Box 30040
Tucson, AZ 85751-0040
(602) 751-1500
FAX - (602) 751-1202

ISBN 0-88450-094-2
Printed in the United States of America
10 9 8 7 6 5 4 3 2 1

DEDICATION

The authors would like to thank, first of all, their wives, Sherry and Betsy for their continued support throughout the making of this work. Also, their children: Joe and Courtney Moch, Alexander, William, and Ricky Borja. It is for them that this work was written.

A special note of thanks to our colleague, Teresa Hendricks, for her ingratiating efforts to cover our schedules and court room appointments. Her efforts allowed the authors the luxury of engaging in the lofty academic pursuits involved in creating this work.

Finally, the authors would like to express their endless gratitude to the skillful editing of our secretaries, Cindy and Alisha, without whose help this work would not have been possible. The authors would also like to show their appreciation to Steve Weintraub, the publisher of this work.

Table of Contents

Preface

This book is intended as a guide to the new attorney, a reference tool for the consumer advocate, and as a bible for the seasoned child restraint litigator. Whatever the level of expertise of the reader, this book has valuable information in a quick reference format.

This work came about as a result of the many cases in the area of passive protection and automotive safety that have come through our doors. After reviewing those cases, we noticed that we had compiled a vast amount of information that would be useful to an attorney handling similar cases. The natural next step, of course, was compiling that information and condensing it into book format.

This work is logically divided into sections which are intended to guide the new attorney or consumer advocate through all facets of the child restraint litigation case.

First of all, the work starts with an introduction to child restraints. It explains what child restraint devices are, how they are used, designs that have been used in the past, available technology in the field, and an introduction into some of the defects associated with the restraints. From this beginning, the authors guide the reader through the legislation, litigation, and social and economic aspects of child restraints.

The work covers federal and state laws that regulate child restraint devices and preemption issues concerning state action. The legislative section is very valuable because it includes information concerning statutes from all 50 states and the District of Columbia. The different statutes are evaluated in terms of their effectiveness. The statutes are also compared and contrasted for requirements and exemptions to child restraint use.

Of special note to the reader is Appendix A which contains a list of terms used throughout this work which may be unfamiliar to the reader. We have tried to make this book a complete reference. Readers can use the bibliographies, appendixes and state sections to supplement their own research. However, the reader is cautioned that the information contained in this book may become outdated due to the state of flux of the subject area.

It is the authors' sincere hope that this book will be useful to the consumer advocates who are in most instances, the last resort of hope for those children who are killed or injured as a result of defective child restraint devices.

Chapter 1

Introduction To Child Restraint Devices

Imagine your car being clipped by a truck and then going out of control. The car rolls over three times and slides down the highway upside down. After recovering from the initial shock, you regain your senses and then a dreadful feeling runs through your body. You remember having placed your child in her car seat in the rear seat. You are afraid to look behind you, but suddenly you hear a familiar joyful sound. Slowly you turn around from the awkward position and see your daughter dangling upside down in her seat laughing from the excitement of the ride. Tears run down your face and you realize that buying that car seat was the wisest investment you ever made.

Unfortunately, the above scenario does not always have the desired ending, and thousands of children are severely injured due to defective child restraint devices. The authors use the term "child restraint devices" as an all inclusive term to cover: child safety seats (CSS), car seats, booster seats, convertible seats, integrated seats, and other terms that refer to devices designed, marketed and sold to protect children passengers in motor vehicles and aircraft.

Historical Analysis

The evolution of the child restraint has barely kept pace with the number of automobiles that are on the road today. Between 1980 and 1990 the number of registered motor vehicles has increased by over 30 million vehicles, from 161.5 million in 1980 to over 194.5 million in 1990. During the same period, the number of licensed drivers increased from 145.3 million in 1980 to over 165 million in 1990.

As the number of cars on the road increases, so does the number of children traveling who need the protection of safe child restraints. Undoubtedly, the quality and the design of child restraints have significantly improved in the last decade.

Reports from the early seventies on the crash worthiness of child car seats showed that most car seats were poor at best. In 1972 a series of sled crash tests showed that only five of all child restraint systems tested were acceptable, and only one car seat received a "good" rating. The improvements are due in part to federal standards such as FMVSS 213 and the many state laws.

All fifty states and the District of Columbia have enacted child passenger restraint laws (Chapter 4 provides complete coverage of the current child passenger laws in all states). Additionally, correct use of child restraints has reduced the number of motor vehicle fatalities involving infants by approximately 70%.

In spite of more than two decades of federal and state legislation aimed at preventing or reducing accidents, parents are still buckling their children up for death. At a lecture in Lansing, Michigan on February 6, 1993, consumer advocate, Ralph Nader, stated that the motor vehicle laws enacted in 1966 have saved over 300,000 lives, however Mr. Nader also pointed out that it has taken 19 years for car manufacturers years to implement their promise of air bags in all cars. Mr. Nader pointed out that 10,000 air-bag equipped cars existed in 1973 when the program was cancelled. Mr. Nader said: "...now there are ads for cars with airbags ...where have they been for 19 years?"

Most of the legislation involving child restraints involved important questions of policy. The pros and cons of mandating the use of passive restraint devices have been thoroughly debated by the Federal government (in the form of Congress and agencies); the state legislatures; consumer advocate groups and the public. The overriding policy, is of course, effective occupant protection.

Studies have shown that without mandatory restraint laws, motorists are not likely to use restraint devices. It has only been after decades of efforts by consumer advocate groups that legislatures have enacted proper statutes that in some cases are useful, but frequently, fall far below the goal of protecting vehicle occupants.

It seems that three decades of legislative battles and political debate are finally paying off. The passive restraint requirements under the Federal Motor Vehicle Safety Standard 208 are being implemented by automobile manufacturers. Installation of passive restraints in automobiles is becoming a standard practice. Automatic safety belts and air bags, allow passengers to remain passive in terms of protecting themselves. Nevertheless, there are still many loopholes to be worked out, but implementation of the policy is taking place.

Many car manufacturers are including passive restraint devices not only for the driver of the vehicle, but also for the passenger. Formerly, passive protection for the passenger consisted solely of automatic seat belts, but now more car manufacturers are including air bags as a standard feature in their cars. Mandatory use of seat belts laws have been enacted in one form or another in all states. The same holds true for child restraint laws.

In spite of legislative progress, many vehicle occupants continue to ignore the laws. Moreover, enforcement of the laws is often difficult due to the way the laws have been written. Although there is varied technology for occupant protection, studies have not taken place to compare the benefits and drawbacks of different occupant protection devices. This is especially true in the case of child restraint devices in newer model cars.

This chapter serves as a background of the technical aspects of child restraint devices. In writing this book the authors have assumed that the reader has no knowledge of the field and therefore have explained all of the concepts involved in child restraints. The readers who have some knowledge can skip this introductory chapter and go on to the other chapters. This chapter was written to facilitate understanding of the chapters that follow.

What Are Child Restraint Devices?

Child restraint devices (CRD's) are referred to by various other names. The names include: child safety seats (CSS), baby car seats, car seats, toddler seats, booster seats, convertible seats, infant seats, and many other names. Although some names are less technical than others, the meaning and definition that they convey does not necessarily define a child restraint device. The authors define child restraint devices as a device intended to protect children riding in automobiles, passenger motor vehicles, or commercial airplanes.

Child restraint devices must meet minimum criteria set forth in Federal Motor Vehicle Safety Standard 213. FMVSS 213 will be covered at length in the federal legislation chapter.

Child restraint devices have been around for over three decades. Although the evolution of the child restraint has lead to safer designs and reduced the number of deaths and injurys, it has been slow at best.

Unfortunately, the child restraint industry in this country is based on a "cookie cutter" approach. Innovative designs are only implemented once one of the manufacturers adds a change to its child restraint line.

Federal and state legislation has also been useful in improving the designs of child restraint devices. If left to their own choices, the manufacturers would still be producing the death traps that were produced in the 50's, 60's and 70's.

Types of Child Restraints

There are various designs of child restraint devices classified according to the age and size of the child using the device. All child restraint devices consist of a hard plastic shell, a soft cushioned liner and straps or a shield designed to protect the child.

The prices between similar types of restraints may vary widely, and yet the protection afforded by the restraints may be the same. When comparing child restraint devices, the attorney must overlook all the bells and whistles and concentrate on the basic design of the restraint. Many parents will be victims of marketing strategies designed to influence their buying decision by appealing to their aesthetic senses. Because of this, it is important that the attorney obtain all advertising (newspapers, media, parents' magazines) on the child restraint that was published at or around the time that the child restraint was purchased. From the advertisement the attorney can determine what express and implied warranties have been made to consumers by the manufacturer.

Infant Carriers

There are five basic types of child restraints. The first child restraint device is intended for newborns to one-year-olds. This type of child restraint device is known as an infant car seat. Some people use the term "infant carrier." However, the term "infant carrier" should never be associated with an infant car seat.

The difference is that an infant carrier is simply just that, an infant carrier or "carry cradle," a basket for transporting a child by hand. On the other hand, an infant car seat is designed to transport an infant in a motor vehicle safely. Infant car seats must comply with federally mandated testing requirements, where on the other hand infant carriers do not.

Though at first glance the distinction between infant carriers and infant car seats may appear petty, the following pictures show that it is more than that. It is often difficult to distinguish between the two types of devices. Unwary parents may strap their child in an infant carrier, not designed for car use, and essentially buckle

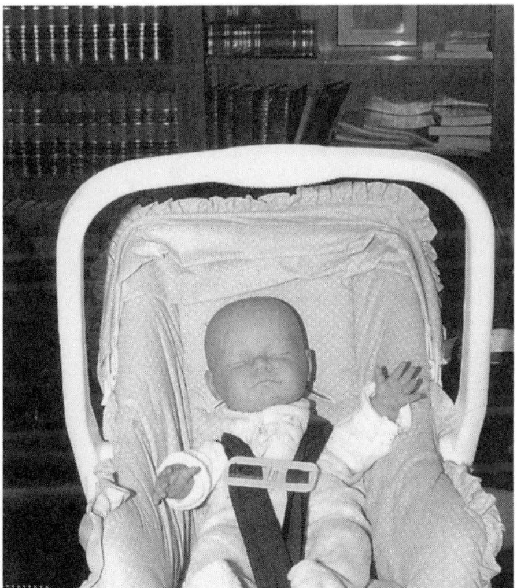

Exhibit 1-1 *Infant carrier front view; note that chest clasp is secured.*

Exhibit 1-2 *Some child restraints are designed to accomodate the growing child. Notice the strap slots.*

their child for death. Many infant carriers do not have warning labels, or have labels that do not adequately warn consumers against the use of infant carriers in vehicles.

Infant seats are designed to fit snugly around an infant from birth up to 20 pounds. The shell must be installed in the rear-facing position to protect the infant adequately. An infant's muscles and bones are not developed enough to absorb the shock of a sudden stop or crash. In particular, an infant's neck muscles like the occipitalis, splenius capitis, semispinalis capitis and the eventrapezius, are not as developed as an adult's muscles. Therefore infants must be provided with additional padding to prevent their heads from violently jerking during a sudden stop. A rolled-up towel or sheet can provide the added stability and protection. Compressible materials like foam, pillows and cushions must never be used. Such materials do not provide adequate protection and fly off during impact.

An infant's head, like the rest of his bones, is soft and weak and needs protection. The anatomy of infants makes them top heavy.

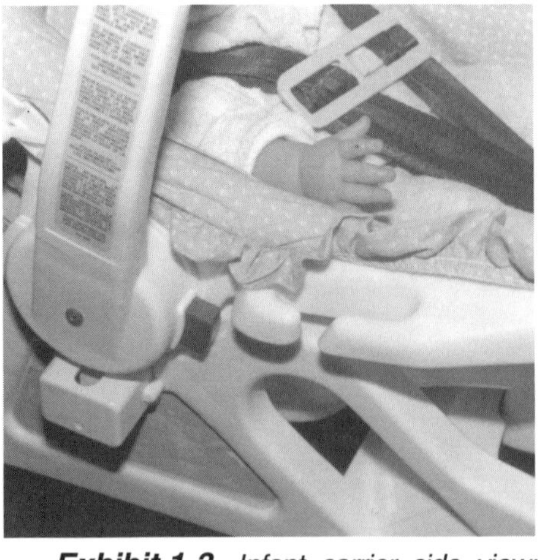

Exhibit 1-3 *Infant carrier side view; note "C" clasps for seat belt attachment.*

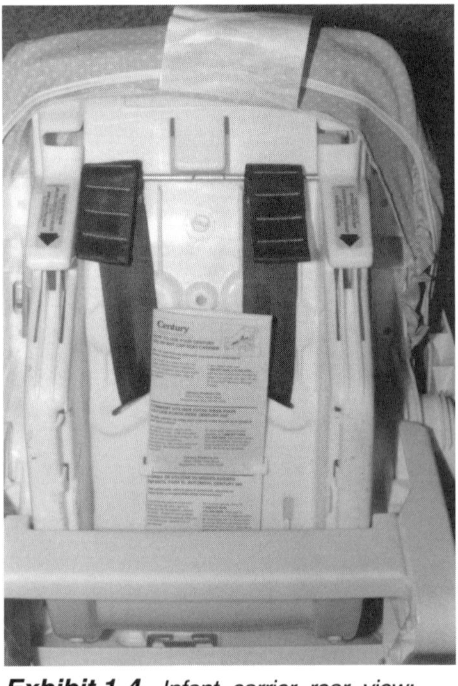

Exhibit 1-4 *Infant carrier rear view; note that metal bar is used to adjust straps. as child grows.*

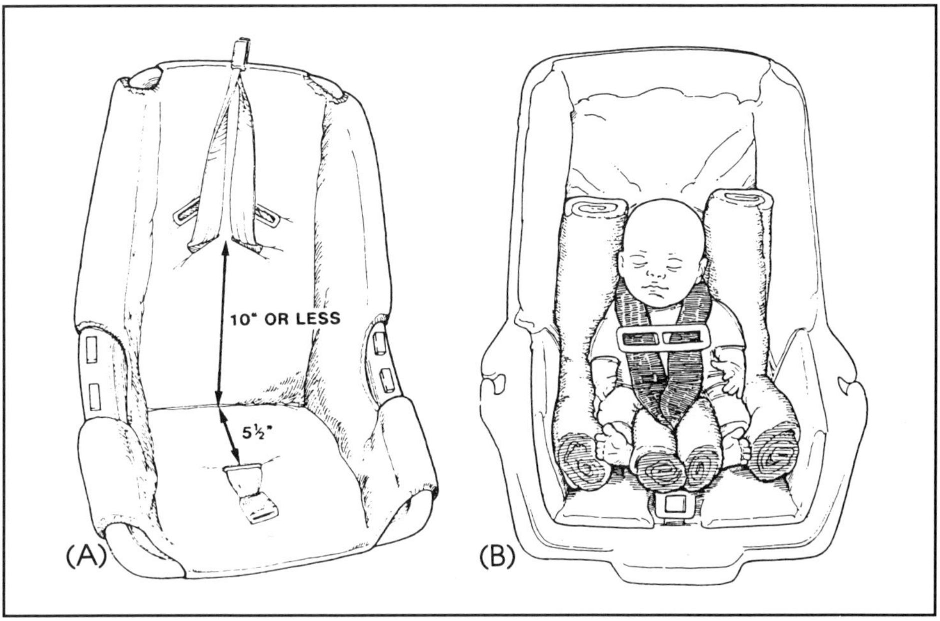

Exhibit 1-5 *(A) Infant seat with maximum harness dimensions for correct fit over a small baby. (B) Small infant secured with additional padding to insure snug fit. Padding should be noncompressible (ie. no foam or pillows).*

Their heads are much larger in proportion to the rest of their bodies. The back of the shell and the harness provides restraint protection to the infant by spreading the collision forces across the infant's back. Placing an infant in a rear-facing position also protects the child from flying debris that may enter the passenger compartment during a collision. If the infant car seat is placed in a forward position, the crash forces tend to concentrate on the child's head and abdomen. The resulting injuries can be tragic and fatal.

Convertible Car Seats

Convertible car seats are a hybrid between an infant car seat and a toddler child restraint or toddler car seats. This design is intended to save the parent money by allowing the parent to use the same car seat for a child from birth up to forty pounds, or more.

Convertible car seats vary in design. Some convertibles combine the use of straps and shields to provide protection to the child. The shield can be either a "T" shield or a bar that rests across the front of the child. The best designs are those that incorporate five-point shoulder harnesses and a shield. Since "harness and shield" restraints require that both the straps and shield are used to ensure adequate protection, the attorney must look for strap designs that are physically attached to the shield. In other words, when the child is secured by the straps, the shield must automatically come down in front of the child. There are many older car seats in use in which the shield is independent of the straps. The momentary inconvenience of securing the child with both straps and shield can prevent either a fatality or a lifetime of pain and suffering. The

Exhibit 1-6 *Sled test; failure to use straps in shield equipped restraint.*

following picture graphically illustrates what happens when only the shield is used in a 30 mph crash.

The potential for misuse of convertibles is high, specially when a small infant is involved. Common misuse includes using the seat in a forward position for an infant. Another example of misuse is when a small infant is placed in a convertible seat without proper

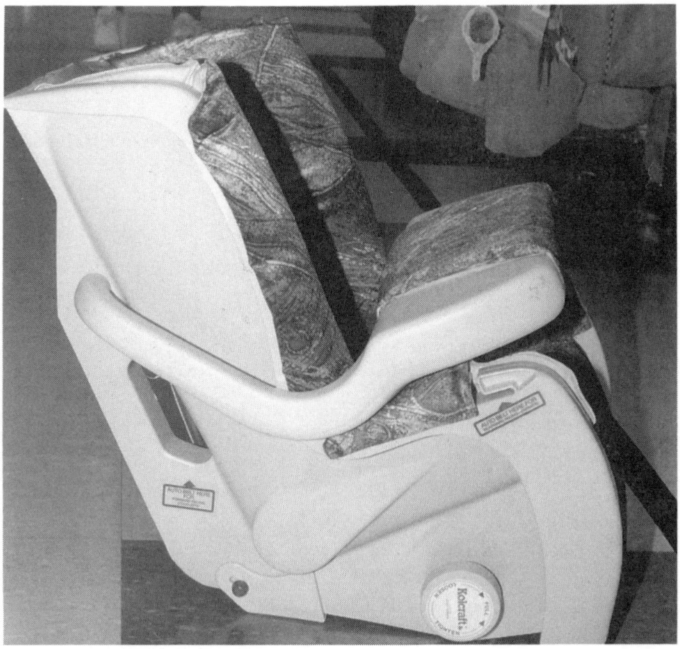

Exhibit 1-7 *Kolcraft convertible seat with "knob" strap adjustment.*

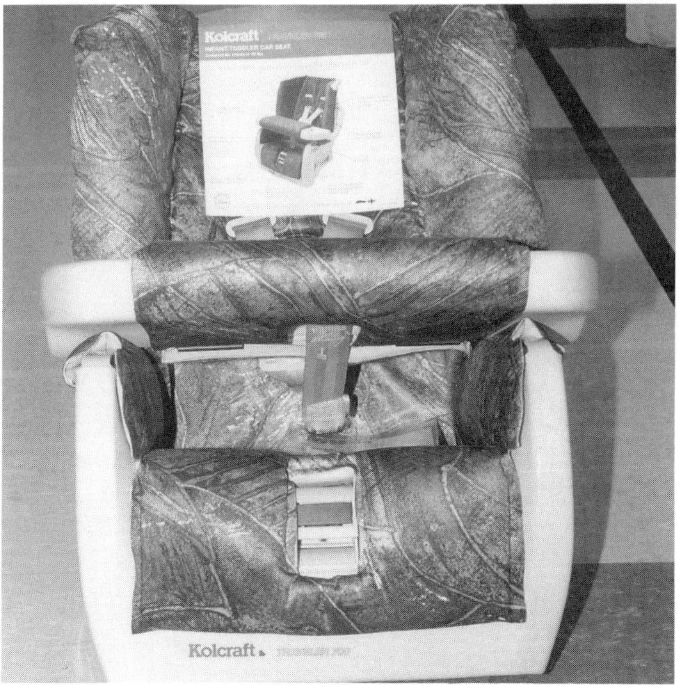

Exhibit 1-8 *Kolcraft convertible seat with full shield.*

padding. See the Chapter on Use and Misuse for proper restraining methods of infants.

Toddler Car Seats or Child Restraints

Child restraint devices designed with a toddler in mind are designed for children who weigh more than 20 pounds. However, the Federal Standard only requires testing for child restraints that are used for children who weigh up to fifty pounds. The standard therefore neglects many children that use child restraints, in particular special needs children who weigh over 50 pounds.

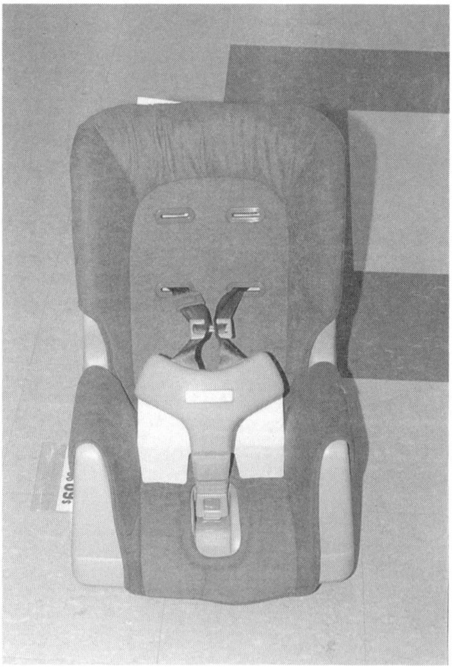

Exhibit 1-9 *Toddler restraint with "T" shield; note slots in shell to accomodate growing child.*

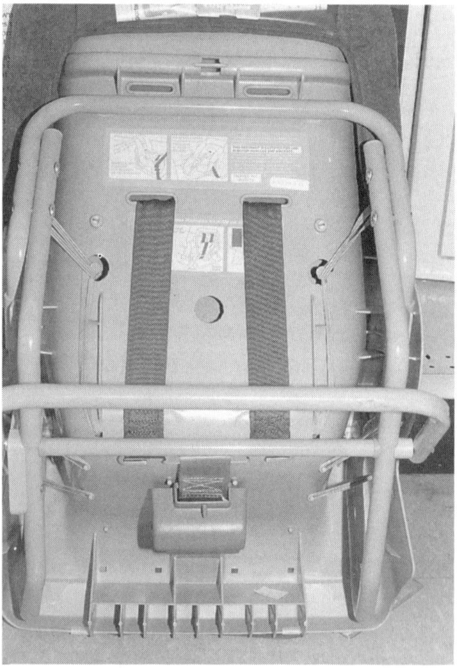

Exhibit 1-10 *Toddler restraint with "T" shield rear view; note one step adjustment for shoulder straps. Both shoulder straps are connected to a single adjustment strap (bottom center).*

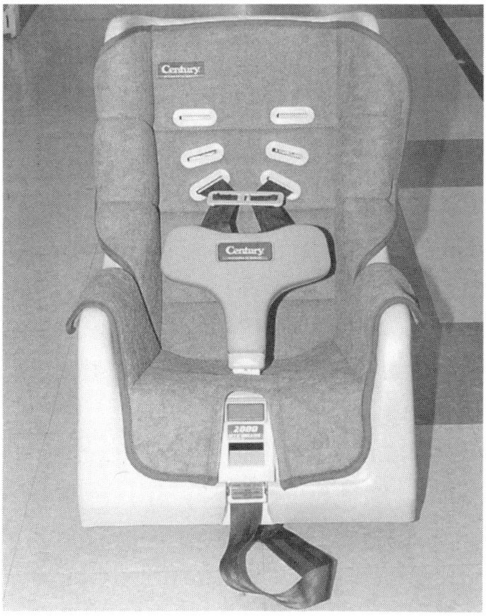

Exhibit 1-11 *Century 2000 STE toddler child restraint with "T" shield.*

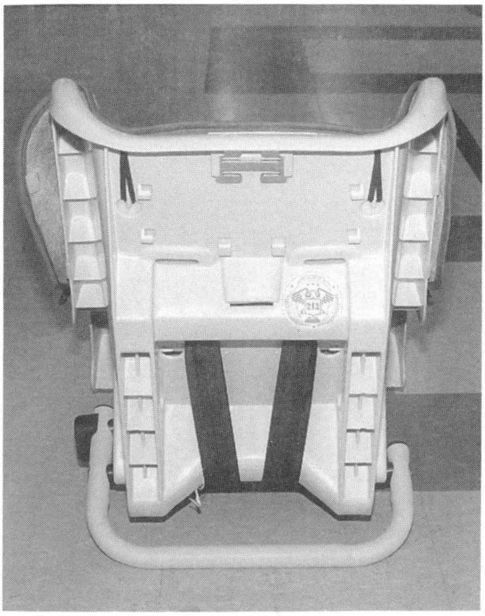

Exhibit 1-12 *Back view of Century 2000 STE seat. Note "FMVSS 213" compliance sticker and locking clip storage.*

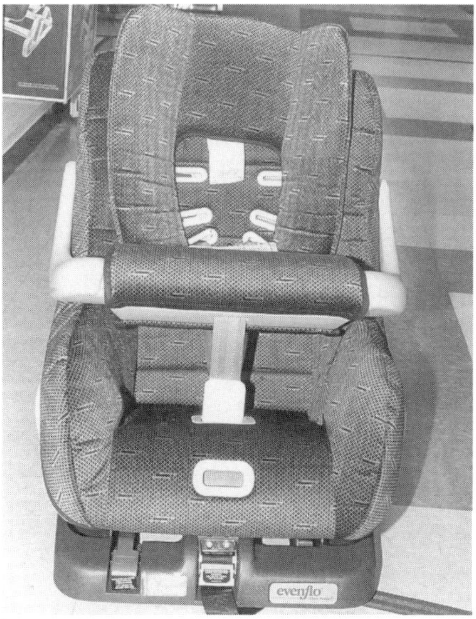

Exhibit 1-13 *Evenflo toddler restraint with full frontal shield and integrated strap. Note one-step adjustment in lower front*

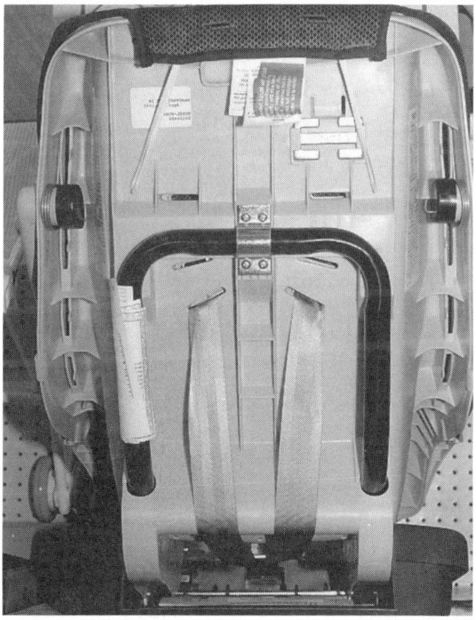

Exhibit 1-14 *Toddler child restraint; side view.*

Booster Car Seats

What are booster seats? Boosters are small car seats that do not have the back and lateral support provided by regular child restraint seats. Boosters consist of a hard plastic shell or platform lined with foam and covered with cloth or vinyl.

Child booster seats have been around for over three decades. Seats of this type are generally used by older children. The National Highway and Traffic Safety Administration has recommended the use of booster seats for children weighing from 40 pounds up to sixty and seventy pounds. Some companies, however, in the past, have marketed their boosters for children weighing as little as twenty pounds.

Until about 1984, booster seats were merely designed to elevate children so that they could use lap and shoulder belts correctly. Elevating the child also allowed the child to see out the window, resulting in a better behaved child in the car environment. The basic use of boosters has changed little since 1984. Most models simply elevate the child and let the seat belts do the restraining. Some models offer additional protection by using a shield to provide added protection.

Throughout the design and development of booster seats, tests have revealed that booster child restraints offer questionable protection to the child passenger. Early designs of booster seats included installation of a tether strap when boosters were only used with a lap belt. The tether strap was to be bolted to a hole drilled in the so-called "package" area, located directly behind the rear seat. The other end of the tether was secured to a safety harness worn by the child. However, studies show that only 10% of all child restraint devices that require the installation of the tether strap are used correctly. Given this statistic, it is clear that the misuse is due to a problem with the design of the child restraint.

The Calspan Corporation tested most of the booster seats available on the market in 1987. The results that the test provided are quite dramatic. Six of eleven booster seats tested failed the test. Child dummies were ejected from six of the eleven booster seats tested.

The test procedures used followed FMVSS 213. However, one difference with the testing consisted of modifying the test dummies so that abdominal pressure could be measured. Calspan used test dummies, which represented children aged nine months, three years and six years. The forces measured in the dummies included the head, chest and abdominal regions at speeds of thirty miles per hour. Although the boosters initially held the dummies in place, the dummies were ejected in the rebound stage. Another issue of concern in the testing was the amount of excursion or head movement during testing. FMVSS 213 required a maximum excursion of no more than 32 inches for a three-year-old child dummy. Five of the eleven boosters tested failed this requirement. When the six-year-old dummy was used, ten out of eleven boosters failed this test.

Modern booster seats have been dramatically improved since the late eighties. The basic design remains the same, but the means through which the booster spreads abdominal pressure has changed. The new boosters used use shields or t-wings to spread the pressure evenly. Moreover, some more modern booster seats provide lateral support. Century Corporation will be unveiling a

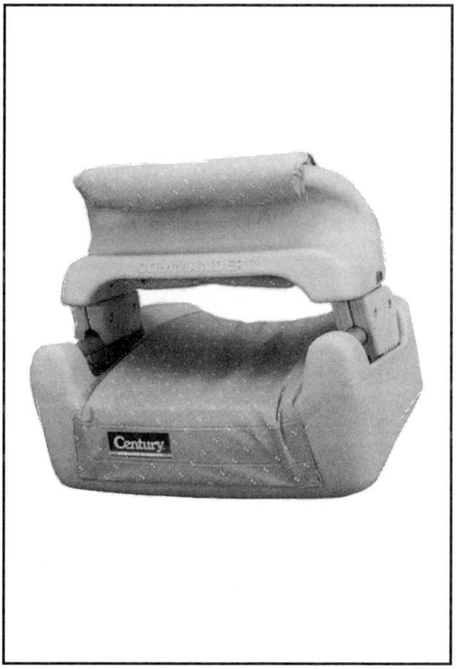

Exhibit 1-15 *Century Booster Car Seat (CR-3), note that the shield is permanently attached to the base and is hinged to allow removal of child.*

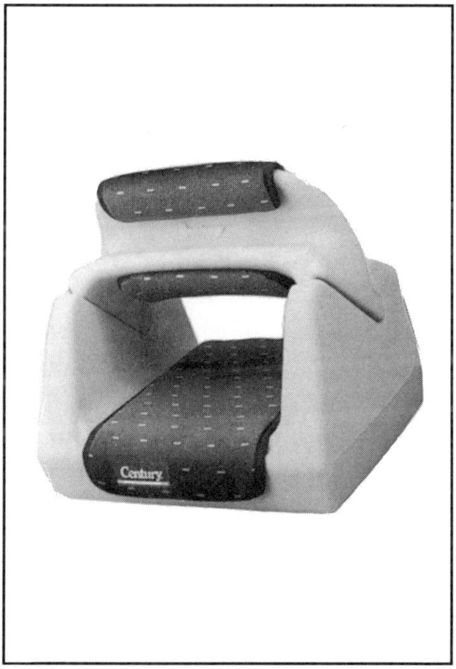

Exhibit 1-16 *Century Booster Car Seat (Commander), shield is not permanently attached to the base; it may come loose if the seat belt is not tightly fastened.*

new type of booster for older children in late summer 1993. The new booster will provide protection to the child from the abdominal region up to the head area.

Integrated Car Seats

A new concept has been introduced in the child passenger arena. The first company to use integrated car seats was the Volvo Company of North America. Volvo was a pioneer in introducing an integrated child restraint to its sedans and station wagons. The design involves use of the middle armrest in the rear of the car as a child restraint. The armrest folds down and provides an integrated booster cushion for children 50 to 80 pounds.

Following the European lead, American companies developed blueprints and marketing to introduce American customers to the idea of integrated child restraints. Yet, it seems that American auto manufacturers are not interested in safety until it becomes a selling point.

Chrysler, a front runner in implementing changes to their line, added integrated child safety seats to its 1992 minivans. The new integrated car seats fold out from the back seat cushion and have five-point straps to secure the child. When not in use, the seat folds into the back of the regular seat. The integrated seats are offered as options in the Chrysler minivans. The cost of the seats is included as an option for about $200.

Other American manufacturers are scrambling to follow Chrysler's lead, and foreign competitors will likely follow the trend. The use of integrated seats enhances the interaction between child restraint system and automobile even more.

Integrated child restraints will likely reduce non-use and misuse of child restraints. Integrated seats are also likely to reduce injuries in side collisions. The "built-in" aspect of the seat will provide greater protection to the child's head and neck in side impacts.

The authors believe that integrated seats will become more common as manufacturers jump on the bandwagon and exploit the safety conscious consumer of the 90's. Integrated seats could bridge the gap and close the exemptions from mandatory child restraint legislation of emergency vehicles, taxis, rental cars.

Summary

All these types of child restraint devices have one goal in common: to protect children traveling on our nation's roads and highways.

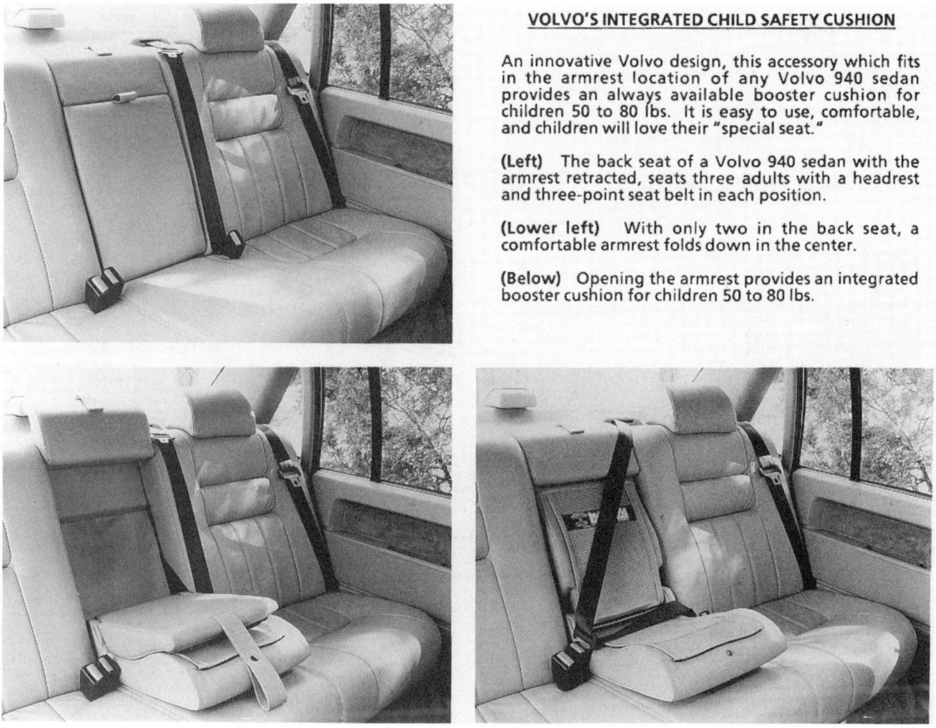

Exhibit 1-17 *Volvo Integrated child seat.*

However, not all child restraint devices succeed in meeting this expectation. Although no child restraint device can be 100% effective 100% of the time, consumers expect that products sold to them will perform as represented to them by the manufacturer.

Chapter 2

Use, Misuse, and Defects Associated with Child Restraint Devices

How Are Child Restraints Used?

How are child restraints used? This section is intended to provide a basic knowledge of the use of child restraint devices to an attorney handling child restraint litigation. It is also a good source of basic information for consumer advocates and others involved in child passenger issues. This section is important from a legal aspect because it may alert the attorney handling a child restraint case to possible misuse of a child restraint device by his client. It must be noted here that misuse of a child restraint device does not necessarily bar a claim against a manufacturer and distributor of a child restraint. If that misuse is pervasive, then it can be shown that the design of that particular child restraint device was defective.

Child restraint use has been studied ever since child restraints were first marketed. The most important study was a study conducted by the National Highway Traffic and Safety Administration in 1988. This study is commonly known as the NHTSA's 19 City Survey. The survey looked not only at seat belt use and helmet use, but it also looked at child restraint use. Based on the survey, use of child restraint devices was estimated at 80% in 1988. This was five years after the first mandatory child restraint law went into effect in Tennessee.

A major finding of this study was that use of child restraint is based upon social, economic and demographic characteristics. In Michigan, use of child restraints was found to be more common among white, affluent families. Use of child restraints was also greater in married couples, than single-parent families. The statistics from other cities in other states were consistent with the sample data.

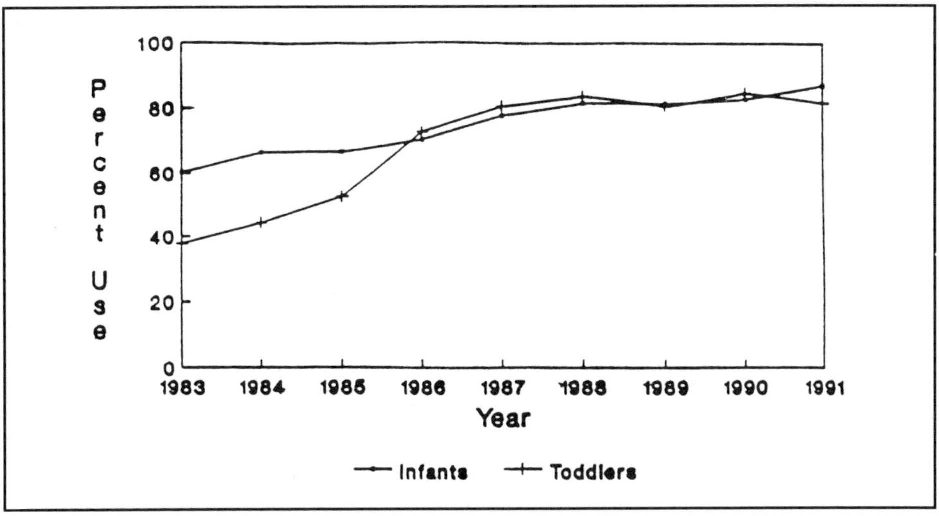

Exhibit 2-1 Child restraint use has increased steadily over the years. Additional use increases and elimination of defects and misuse can save thousands of lives and prevent unnecessary injuries.

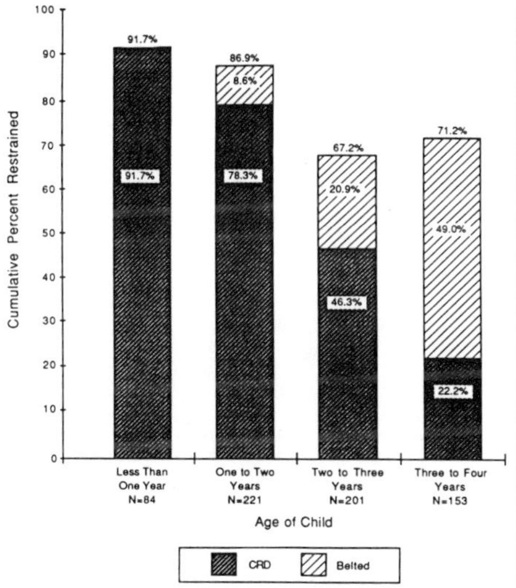

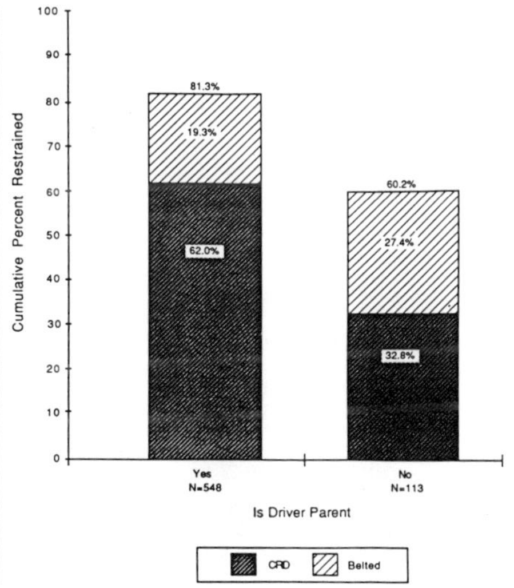

Exhibit 2-2 *Child restraint use by age of child.*

Exhibit 2-3 *Child restraint use by relationship of driver to child.*

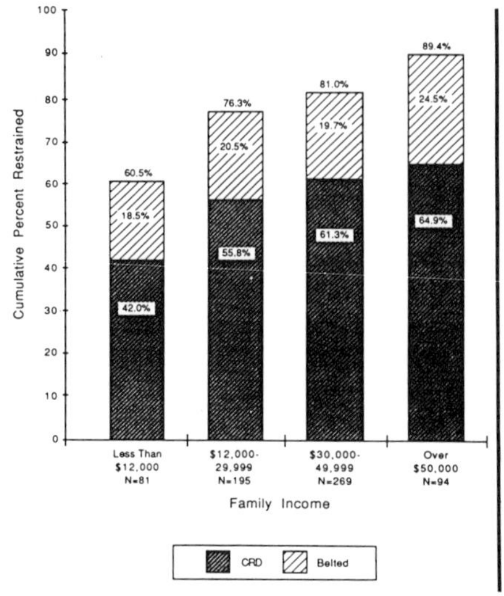

Exhibit 2-4 *Child restraint use by family income.*

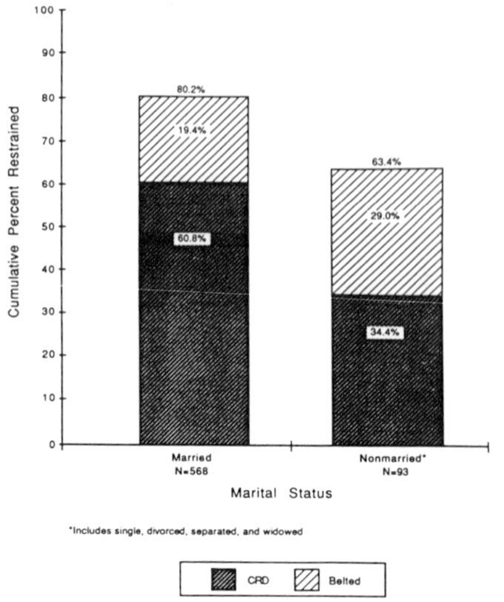

Exhibit 2-5 *Child restraint use by marital status.*

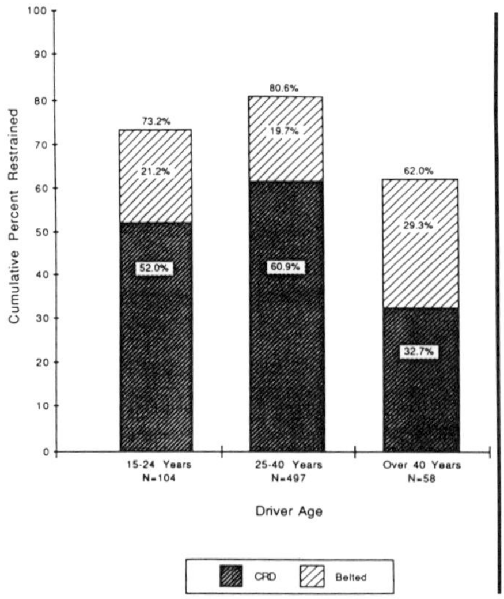

Exhibit 2-6 *Child restraint use by age of driver.*

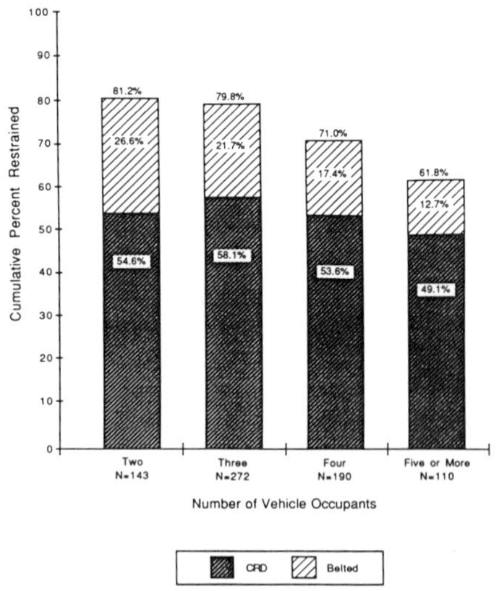

Exhibit 2-7 *Child restraint use by number of vehicle occupants.*

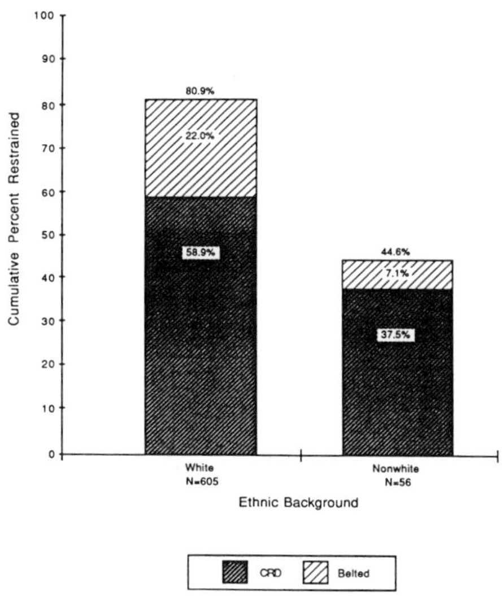

Exhibit 2-8 *Child restraint use by ethnic background.*

The 80% use of child restraints found in the study proves that mandatory legislation does in fact have an affect the general population. Nevertheless, the study also found a high rate of misuse. The study found that one in four child restraints is misused in one form or another. In some cases that misuse is drastic enough to nullify the benefits of placing a child in a child restraint. Misuse of child restraints can also be more harmful than placing a child in a vehicle without any protection at all.

Three Point Versus Five Point Child Restraint Systems

Clearly, five point child restraint systems offer greater protection to a child passenger. However, when five point harness systems first entered the market there were concerns that the greater constraint of the child in child restraint systems would tend to cause injuries. In spite of this, many studies revealed that the safety features of a five point harness system did not increase the likelihood of injury to a child.

In a study conducted at Wayne State University by Dr. Schreck and Dr. Patrick, researchers found that five point harness systems are safe when properly used and provide greater safety than three point harness systems. The study used juvenile chimpanzees for testing, due to their close approximation to the human child. It must be noted here that great care was taken to protect the animals from unnecessary injuries during testing. For example, the child restraints with the animals were only tested on the sled after first using a dummy on an initial run. This was done to prevent possible unnecessary injury that could be caused by equipment malfunction.

Also to protect the animals, non-invasive means of testing for injury were used. In other words, no surgery took place. Indirect methods were used to collect data, such as x-rays, blood enzyme tests, EKG's, and direct observation of the animal's behavior.

The study consisted of observing the performance of the five point restraint system in eleven sled tests. Five of the sled tests were conducted with dummies and seven with the use of the chimpanzees.

The purpose of this study was to determine the potential of injury by five point child restraint systems on specific areas of the child's body. In particular, the study looked at injury to the crotch region, increased abdominal pressure, bone fractures that may be caused by the hip straps, and neck and head injuries, due to hyperflexion of the neck.

The test results conclusively proved that five point child restraint systems do not in any way harm the occupants. Out of eleven tests, there was only one minor injury. The injury consisted of a shoulder burn on one animal. This condition was not permanent and did not require treatment.

The animals were subjected to deceleration at 20, 25 and 30 miles per hour. Observation after the testing occurred showed no side effects, such as whip lash. In conclusion, the five point child restraint system proved to be superior to conventional three point harness systems.

Children differ greatly from adults in their size and skeletal anatomy. Specifically of interest to child restraint systems is the child's pelvic bone anatomy. The pelvis in a child has not yet developed the forward protrusions that adults have in their pelvis. These protrusions, known as the superior and inferior interior iliac spines, help adults to engage the lap belt in a crash and prevent the belt from causing excessive pressure to the abdominal region.

Another major difference between adults and children is the way that the shoulder belt fits. Shoulder belts are designed for adult passengers. The design is too high to provide adequate protection to the child's chest in a crash. It must be noted here that a recent invention known as the ChildSafer™, which is discussed in the Chapter on Innovations, modifies the position of the shoulder harness to protect the child better.

Exhibit 2-9 *ChildSafer™ in use. Note how this simple device repositions shoulder belt to fit across toddler's chest.*

Testing of Child Restraints

NHTSA has required manufacturer's of child safety restraint devices to certify their products by passing federally mandated crash tests. The tests had been conducted since 1981.

In a typical test the child restraint holding a 33 pound dummy is placed on a sled and then accelerated to a speed of 30 miles per hour. The sled is then abruptly stopped to simulate a head on collision. During this testing the seat must remain intact and keep the dummy's head from moving too far forward. This forward movement is known as excursion. NHTSA also tests a 17 1/2 pound dummy using similar conditions.

The standard fails to test for rear, side, or roll over collision. The standard does not address the problem of misuse when the wrong size of child restraint is used.

Typical testing of child restraints includes using an accelerator to conduct the sled test portion. A force gauge is used to determine the force required to release the buckle on the restraint. A head excursion standard is used to find the amount of head movement during the crash and during the rebound phase of the crash.

In a typical sled test of a child restraint, the child restraint is mounted on a bench-type seat. The dummy is then placed in the child restraint. It must be noted here that attorneys testing specific child restraints for specific cases must ensure that the individuals carrying out the tests are testing according to the manufacturer's

Exhibit 2-10 *Sled Test A. Note 1960's bench-type seat used.*

instructions. They must also allow for foreseeable misuse of the child restraint. For example, if the manufacturer calls for a tether strap, then the child restraint should be tested with and without the tether strap.

Testing of child restraint devices is carried out according to the specifications of the Federal Motor Vehicle Safety Standard. Calspan Corporation at its Calspan Advanced Technology Center in Buffalo, New York tests most of the child restraints for the federal government and the manufacturers. As of 1992 the federal government requires that all child restraints available on the market be tested on a yearly basis. They must be tested in all configurations that they are likely to be used whether or not in accordance with the manufacturer's instructions.

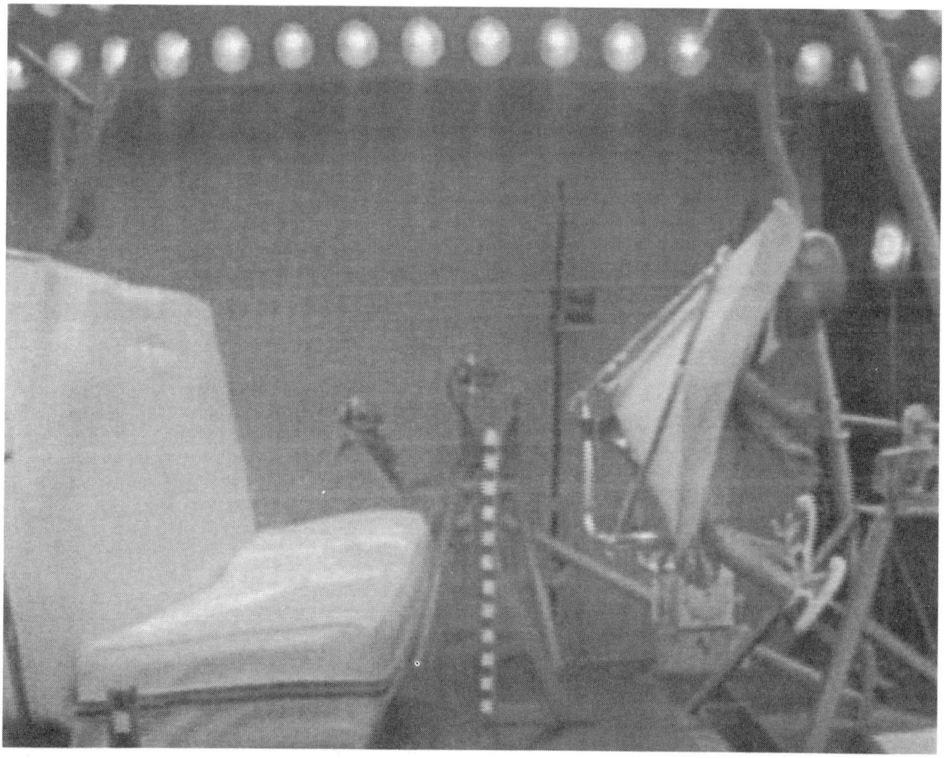

Exhibit 2-11 *Sled Test B. Failure to properly strap a restraint with the seat belt can create a hazard for all automobile occupants.*

How the Testing Sled Works

The sled is a simple apparatus that consists of a minimum number of moving parts. The device consists of a driving mechanism composed of two long tubes. The tube in the front, which is closest to the sled platform, is the low pressure volume.

The rear tube contains high pressure air and is designated as Chamber B. Both chambers contain floating pistons so that the volume can be changed. In the middle of the driving mechanism, where the two tubes are bolted together, there is another small chamber designated as Chamber C. During the firing sequence, Chamber A is pressurized with nitrogen gas to a press selected value of several hundred pounds per square inch. Chamber B is then loaded to a much higher pressure, in the range of 2,000 pounds per square inch of air. To fire the sled, pressurized air from a small externally mounted tank and controlled by a celanoid valve, is submitted into Chamber C. This pressure unseats the O ring that is located between the main piston and orifice plate which then exposes the entire main piston area to the high pressure air forced in from Chamber B. The rate at which the high pressure air is applied to the piston is controlled by the throttling or metering of the airflow through the orifice by means of the metering pin.

Once Chamber B. is open, the thrust column pushes forward at the driving head and accelerates the sled platform rearward along the rails. The amount of force applied to the sled, as it begins to move, is dependent on the shape of the metering pin, the volumes, and the gas pressures in the two main chambers. At the end of the acceleration stroke, the sled is at its maximum velocity. The sled glides along the steel rails on 12 phenolic paths with 8 additional paths mounted at the platform corners to guide it in yaw. Yaw refers to the left-right motions. The sled is allowed to coast, after the acceleration phase, for approximately 7 feet and then the on board brakes are applied. These air operated brakes are initiated by a celanoid valve, which opens at a pre-determined time to apply air pressure to 16 two and a half inch diameter brake pads. The pads are squeezed against the rails to decelerate the sled to a stop. The total distance traveled by the sled during a typical 30 mile per hour run is approximately 45 feet.

Data on the motion of the sled, known as kinematic data is normally obtained through the use of high speed motion picture cameras. The test area is illuminated by 270 overhead 1,000 watt spotlights that permit high quality pictures to be obtained at camera speeds in excess of 2,000 frames per second. The cameras can be either mounted on the sled or stationary. The sled can hold up to 14 on board cameras for better views of the test subjects. The standard position of the cameras, when testing two dummies on board the sled, is to have two direct left side and two right side cameras looking perpendicular to the dummy motion. There are also two high mounted cameras, two lower mounted cameras, three floor mounted rear view cameras, and three front view cameras, as well as one camera directly in front of each dummy, and one on the sled centerline.

Testing of child restraints is a very costly proposition. An alternative is to check with the various companies and agencies that test child restraints to see if a video exists of testing on the particular child restraint of interest to the attorney's case.

Child restraint systems are usually tested on a sled to simulate frontal collisions at 30 mph, rear crashes, and lateral crashes of sixty

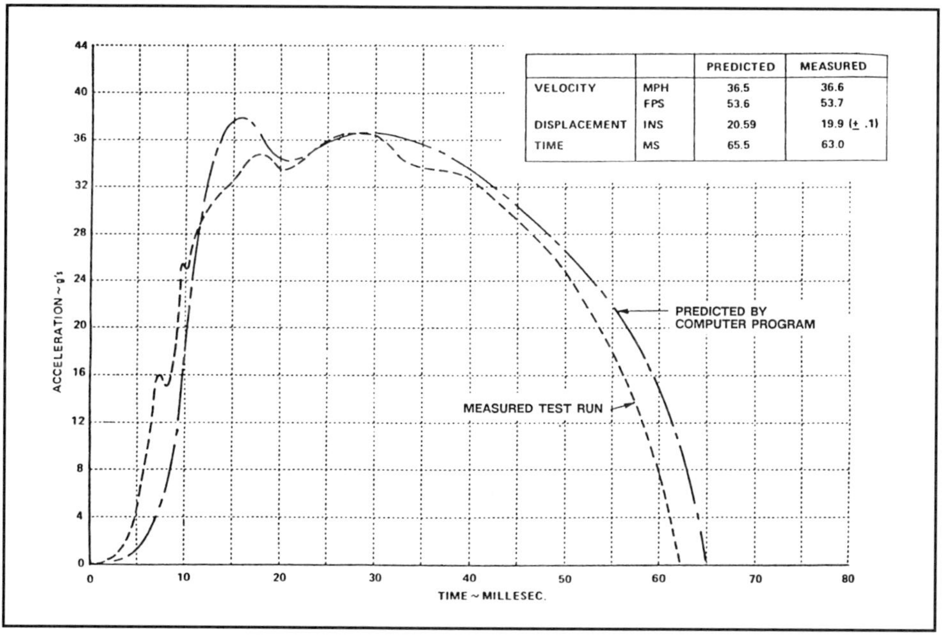

Exhibit 2-12 *Comparison of predicted and actual sled performance.*

degrees. Before the dynamic testing of a child restraint takes place, comparison of the physical characteristics of the particular child restraint must be made with other available child restraints. This comparison can provide valuable information as to the existing state of the art.

The attorney should also gather all of the instruction information provided with the child restraint. Allowances should be made for the child restraints that were obtained through a garage sale or bought second hand. In cases where the child restraint has been obtained second-hand the instructions may be obtained from the manufacturer itself. If the instructions and warning labels are no longer on the restraint, the permanence of the labeling on the restraint may be an issue. In all cases, a careful review of the labels on the child restraint itself should be made to determine what warning, if any, the parents received and how useful and effective those warnings were. In cases where the straps fail to secure the child, even though all procedures and instructions were followed, stretch tests of the webbing of the straps should be carried out.

The dummies used in testing often contain sensors in the neck, head and abdominal regions to measure the forces acting on those areas of the child's body. The dummies are calibrated between tests.

Misuse of Child Restraints

Late one afternoon, a baby strapped in her child safety seat was involved in a crash. The car in which she was riding spun out of control on a slush-covered Indiana road and hit a tree. She was breathing normally 15 minutes after the crash and her only obvious signs of injury were some superficial wounds on her head.

Yet this 3-month-old baby died of internal bleeding on the way to the hospital. An autopsy found that the bleeding came from a severely cut liver—damage that could only have been caused by pressure on her abdomen during the crash.

Was this tragedy that happened *despite* the use of a child safety seat, or *because* of it? Neither. The baby was unprotected because she was placed in the CSS *incorrectly*. The mother, who survived the crash, later described the way she had "restrained" her baby.

"I placed both shoulder straps under her arms and across her belly, holding the straps together with the plastic clip that came with the seat ... because the straps were too big for her shoulders. I did not fasten the buckle that was between her legs because the blanket was bunched around her ... The seat was facing toward the front of the car."

The above example illustrates several examples of misuse. The mother placed the shoulder straps under her daughter's arms instead of over. She failed to fasten the buckle, and she placed the seat in the forward-facing position, instead of the rear facing position recommended for infants.

Use of child restraints not only protects the child in the event of a frontal crash, but a secondary benefit is the creation of a safer environment. Studies have shown that a quarter of all injuries sustained by children in automobiles are the result of non-crash events. The child who is restrained solely by a seat belt is likely to roam about the passenger compartment and distract the driver. Many accidents are caused by drivers who are distracted by children who are not restrained. The use of a restraint device results in better behaved children. In a restraint children are able to see out of the windows of the car and are less likely to become restless.

The key word is "restraint." Studies have shown that parents are unable to control their children's behavior and their automobiles at the same time. In 1978, 44% of the victims that fell from automobiles were unrestrained children. Of the unrestrained children that fell out of their cars, 35% were in the front seat with the driver.

Owning and using a child restraint is not enough. Currently, rear-facing, convertible and booster seats are approved for use in the United States. The rear-facing restraints are intended for newborns and infants up to 20 lb or 27" tall. Convertible seats can be changed from rear-facing seats once the child grows beyond the limits for those seats. The convertible type seat can be used until the child is 40 pounds. Finally, booster seats are designed for children who weigh between 30 to 50 pounds. The booster is designed to complement seat-belt use for children who may not be big enough to ride safely with a seat belt alone.

An education program must also be geared to educate the parents on how to secure their child properly in the child seat. Although child restraint use is up from 1982, many children in those restraints are not properly fastened. Up to 30% of the child re-

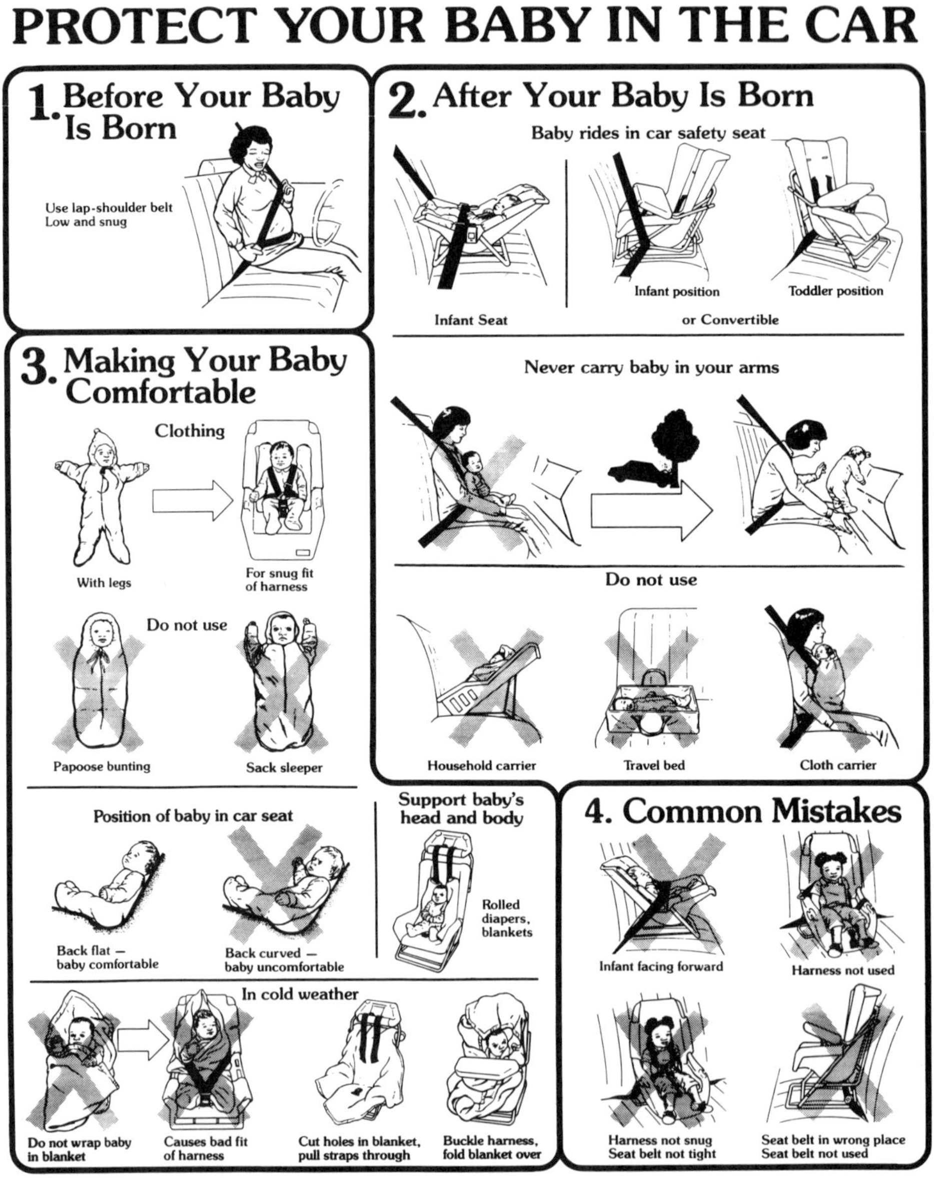

Exhibit 2-13 *This chart illustrates the most common misuses of child restraints. Note that tubular support child restraint devices are no longer recommended.*

straints designed to be used in the rear facing position are used in the forward position. This misuse can be prevented by better designs and warnings from the manufacturers. According to the nineteen city survey undertaken by NHTSA, as many as 80 to 92% of all child restraints are misused in one form or another. Given that statistic, misuse is clearly foreseeable by the manufacturers and creates a duty to warn consumers.

Rear-facing restraints are misused by using them in the forward position. During a luncheon address at a Child Passenger Summit held on March 13-17, 1993 in Chicago, Secretary of Transportation, Frederico Pena, admitted that he buckled his newborn daughter in the forward-facing position when the family left the hospital. Under the glare of public scrutiny, and with his wife providing instruction, Mr. Pena corrected his error.

The restraint placed in the forward-facing position cannot distribute the impact forces along the child's back. The forward position concentrates the force on the neck, head and abdomen of the infant or child resulting in unnecessary injuries and fatalities.

Infant carriers, not designed for automobile use, are often used as child restraints causing death or severe injuries to the infant. Convertible seats are another type of child restraint that are commonly misused. Convertible seats are designed to be used by an infant or a child who weighs up to 50 lb depending on the model of convertible seat. These restraints must be used in the rear facing position with infants and in the forward position once the child reaches 20 pounds. Due to their multiple roles convertible seats are often over priced and subject to misuse.

Manufacturers must be required to improve their designs to reduce child restraint misuse. The problem is two-fold: (1) incompatibility of child restraints with seat belts and (2) inadequate instructions or failure by the parents to follow the instructions. The automobile and child restraint manufacturers should consider the feasibility of designing a universal child restraint/belt system. Another alternative is the creation of a "user performance standard." The standard would require that manufacturers show that a high proportion of parents would properly install the child restraint in various vehicles. Clearly, adequate designs, labeling and education can prevent misuse, save lives and taxpayer dollars that are spent because of preventable deaths and injuries.

Selecting a Child Restraint

It is important for an attorney who is unfamiliar with child restraints to know how to "select" and use an appropriate child restraint for different aged children. A common form of misuse of car seats occurs when the parents use them after the children have outgrown them. Placing a toddler in an infant car seat can have disastrous consequences. Even if a child is "appropriately" fastened in the child restraint, the child can suffer fatal injuries. The following paragraphs describe what to look for in a child restraint. The information is useful for clients who are prospective parents or who have small children. Moreover, the information serves as a check-list for the attorney handling a child restraint case. An under-standing of the use of child restraints can help the attorney determine what his client's safety habits are. The defense will often use poor automotive safety habits on the part of the parents to bolster their arguments of misuse of the restraint device.

The best child restraint is one that fits the child according to the child's age, size and weight; fits in the car, and is easy to use. Infants and low birth weight babies must fit snugly into their infant child restraints. The prospective restraint must meet the federal standard (FMVSS 213) and must have a label that certifies compliance with the standard.

Similar child restraints may vary in price due to the "extras" that are offered with the higher priced model. Remember that both

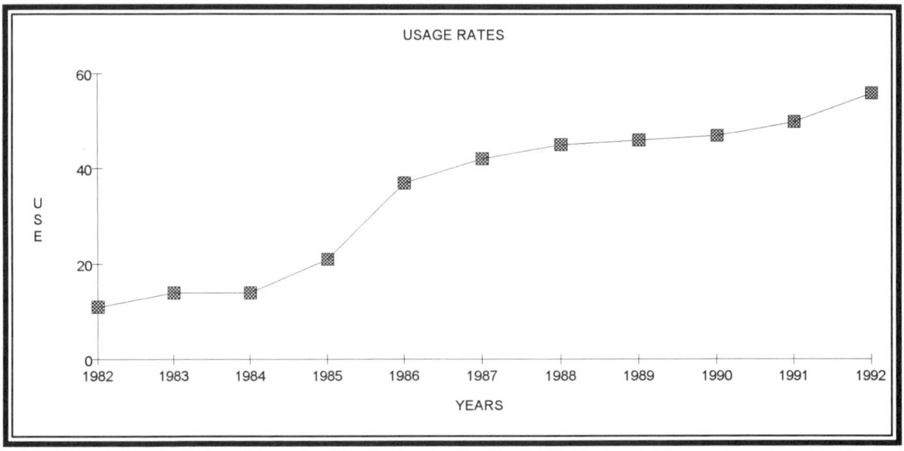

***Exhibit 2-14** A dramatic increase in child restraint use has taken place as a result of mandatory legislation.*

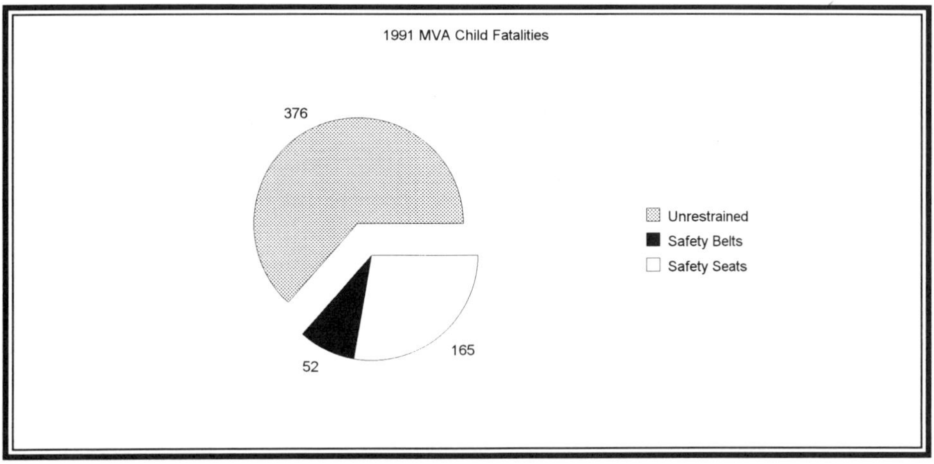

Exhibit 2-15 *Motor vehicle accident fatalities for 1991 in Michigan were greatest among unrestrained children. Fatalities for children in car seats could have been dramatically reduced through correct use and by eliminating defective seats from the market.*

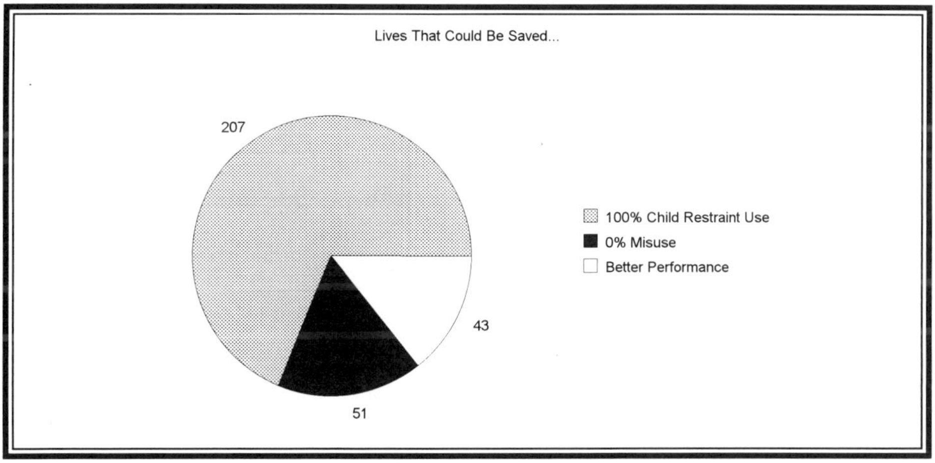

Exhibit 2-16 *Lives that could be saved in Michigan with 100% use of child restraint devices, 0% misuse, and improved performance.*

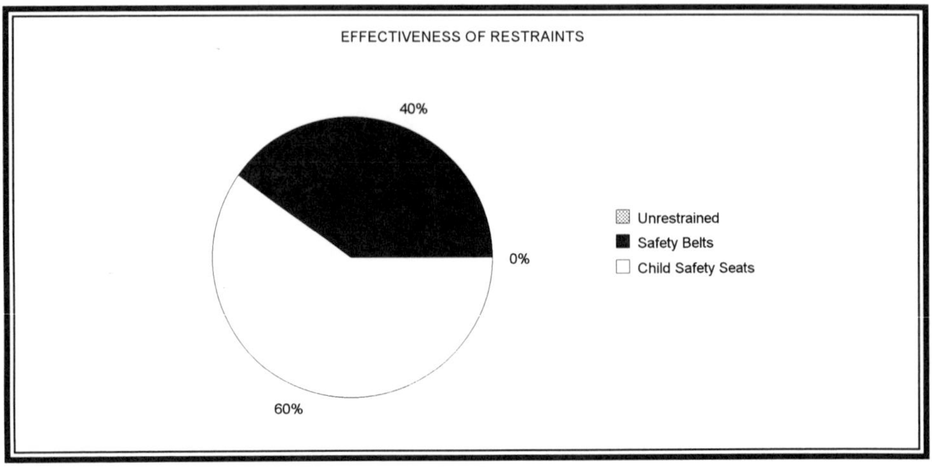

Exhibit 2-17 *Effectiveness of restraints. Child restraint devices are more effective in protecting children than seat belts alone.*

seats may provide the same level of protection in a crash, but the higher priced model may include options that make that restraint easier to use than the lower-priced model.

Formula for Effective Child Restraint in Vehicles

Besides proper legislation, a comprehensive plan requires adequate public education and effective enforcement. Moreover, interaction between legislative, enforcement, and consumer groups with child restraint manufacturers and automobile manufacturers is critical in ensuring the effectiveness of child restraints. One such plan could be used to protect the children who are most at risk: children from birth to six months.

Infants spend less time in automobiles than older children, yet the death and injury rates for infants are proportionately higher for this age group. The problem is due to the lack of public education dealing with the transportation of infants. Parents of infants will often carry the child in their arms in the front of the car. Another factor is that young children often become restless and cry when their needs are not met. Parents are prone to yielding to the infant's cries by taking the child from the safety of the child restraint. The state legislatures have compounded the problem by providing "nursing" exemptions from child restraint law coverage to children being fed in an automobile.

The initial phase of an education program, mandated by federal or state legislation and sponsored by consumer groups and manufacturers, could take place at hospitals to educate new parents on how to protect their newborn child. The National Easter Seal Society through its KARS (Kids Are Riding Safe) program provides information to hospitals regarding a hospital-based model on child restraint education.

It is ironic that hospitals discharge patients by wheeling them out in wheelchairs to their car. However, once the newborn reaches the car, the new parents are sometimes seen transporting their brand new bundles of joy in their automobiles without any protection. A study showed that over 90% of infants leaving hospitals were held in their mother's arms. Such practices can result in baby's first ride being baby's last ride.

***Exhibit 2-18** Failure to restrain an infant can have disasterous consequences.*

1993 SHOPPING GUIDE TO CAR SEATS

All Products listed meet current Federal Motor Vehicle Safety Standard 213. New models in italics

Manufacturer/ Name	Harness Type	Safety Features	Price Range
INFANT SEATS		(Birth to 20lbs unless noted)	
Century 565 series	3-pt. harness	Correct recline indicator; labels in Eng./Sp./Fr.; harness adjustor located on back of seat	$35-50
Century 590 series	3-pt. harness	Detachable base; used without base in second car; correct recline indicator; labels in Eng/Sp/Fr; harness adjustor located on back of seat	$50-70
Cocso Dream Ride	3-pt. harness	To 17lbs only; use as car bed side-facing; use as car seat rear-facing, harness adjustor located on back of seat	$49
Cosco TL-C	3-pt. harness	Harness adjustor located on front of seat	$25
Evenflo Dyn-O-Mite	3-pt. harness	Shoulder belt wraps around front of seat, harness adjustor located on back of seat	$20-30
Evenflo Joy Ride	3-pt. harness	Shoulder belt wraps around front of seat, harness adjustor located in compartment behind seat	$25-40
Evenflo Travel Tandem	3-pt. harness	Detachable base; used without base in second car, harness adjustor located in compartment behind seat	$35-65
Fisher-Price Infant Car Seat	T-shield	Correct recline indicator, padded shield, less suitable for very small infants, harness adjustor located on back of seat	$49
Gerry Guard With Glide	3-pt. harness	Use as glider in house; must be converted to in-car position; harness adjustor located on back of seat	$49-59
Kolcraft Rock N' Ride	3-pt. harness	To 18lbs only; no harness height adjustment; optional detachable base; used without base in second car	$29-50
Playschool Infant Car Seat (Kolcraft)	3-pt. harness	To 18lbs only; inflatable pump head support; harness adjustor located on back of seat	$50-60
CONVERTIBLE SEATS		(Birth up to approximately 40lbs)	
Babyhood Mfg. Baby Sitter	5-pt. harness	Harness adjustors located on sides of base; previously called "Wonda Chair"	$89
Century 1000 STE	5-pt. harness	One-strap harness adjustor located on front of base, labels in Eng/Sp/Fr; adjustable crotch buckle position	$50-90
Century 2000 STE	T-Shield	One-strap harness adjustor located on front of base; labels in Eng/Sp/Fr; adjustable crotch buckle position	$60-90
Century 3000 STE	Tray Shield	One-strap harness adjustor located on front of base; labels in Eng/Sp/Fr; adjustable crotch buckle position	$70-100
Century 5000 STE	Tray Shield	One-strap harness adjustor located on front of base; labels in Eng/Sp/Fr; adjustable crotch buckle position	$70-100
Cosco 5-pt. Luxury 5-pt.	5-pt. harness	One-strap harness adjustor located in front of seat	$49-79

Exhibit 2-19 *The American Academy of Pediatrics 1993 List of Recommended Child Safety Seats.*

Cosco Comfort Ride	Tray Shield	One-strap harness adjustor located in front of seat	$69-89
Cosco Soft Shield	T-Shield	One-strap harness adjustor located in front of seat	$69
Evenflo Champion	Tray Shield	Optional tether available; one-strap harness adjustor located on front of base	$45-75
Evenflo Scout	T-Shield/5 pt. harness	Comes in either 5-pt. or T-Shield; optional tether available; one-strap harness adjustor located on front of base	$39-60
Evenflo Seven Year Car Seat	Tray Shield	Converts to booster (see Evenflo booster); optional tether available; two separate harness adjustors located beneath shield	$90-120
Evenflo Ultara I, Premier	Tray Shield	One-strap harness adjustor located on front of base	$65-95
Evenflo Ultara V Premier	5-pt. harness	One-strap harness adjustor located on front of base	$99
Fisher-Price Bolster, Deluxe Bolster	Tray Shield	Automatic harness adjustment	$90-100
Fisher-Price Car Seat, Comfort Plus Car Seat	T-shield	Automatic harness adjustment	$80-90
Gerry Guard with Securelock	Tray Shield	Automatic harness adjustment; buckle on stalk that opens forward	$69-89
Kolcraft Auto-Mate	Tray Shield	Comes with either 5-pt. or T-Shield; harness adjustment knobs on both sides; requires 2-handed operation	$50-80
Kolcraft Traveler 700	Tray Shield	Harness adjustment knobs on both sides; requires 2-handed operation	$50-100
Renolux GT 2000	5-pt. harness	Harness adjustors on back of seat	$60
Renolux GT 3000	5-pt. harness	Harness adjustors on back of seat	$80
Renolux GT 4000	5-pt. harness	Harness adjustors on back of seat	$70
Renolux GT 5000 5500 Turn-a-Tot	5-pt. harness	Harness adjustors on back of seat; seat swivels on base	$100-110
Safeline Sit 'N Stroll	5-pt. harness	New version of seat originally designed for infants only; birth to 32lbs; rear facing with height limit; 20lbs (and 1 year) to 40lbs, forward facing; belts in forward facing position wrap around front of seat; harness adjustors located on back of seat; labels in Eng/Sp/Fr/Jpn converts to stroller	$159
<u>VESTS AND INTEGRAL SEATS</u>		<u>(20-25 LBS AND UP)</u>	
Little Cargo Auto Safety Vest (25-40lbs)	5-pt. harness	Simplified strap-buckle system; auto lap belt attached through padded stress plate	$39-49
Chrysler Integral Child Seat (20-40lbs; Booster 40 + lbs)	5-pt. harness	Two build-in seats optional in minivans, one converts to a belt-positioning booster for larger child; one seat] available in some sedans, converts to belt-positioning booster	$100-200

E-Z On Vest (25+lbs)	4-pt. harness	Tether strap must be installed in vehicle	$62
BOOSTER SEATS*	BELT POSITION	(Use after convertible/toddler seat is outgrown)	
Century Commander	Wrap around	Shield for use with lab belt, labels in Eng/Sp/Fr	$20-25
Century CR-3	Wrap around	Removable shield for use as a **Belt Positioning Booster Seat** with a lap/shoulder belt; shield for use with lap belt	$30-40
Cosco Explorer	Wrap around	Shield for use with lap belt, two seat heights	$25-35
Evenflo Booster Car Seat	Wrap around or through base	Split shield for use with lap belt; belt through base for short child; internal crotch strap	$35-65
Evenflo Sightseer	Wrap around	Shield for use with lap belt	$20-40
Fisher-Price T-Shield Car Seat	Wrap around	Removable shield for use as a **Belt Positioning Booster Seat** with a lap/shoulder belt, 30-60 lbs; shield with crotch post for use with a lap belt, 40-60 lbs.	$40
Gerry Double Guard	Belt through base when used with shield	Removable shield for use as a **Belt Positioning Booster Seat** with a lap/shoulder belt; shield for use with lap belt, internal lap strap with shield	$45-55
Kolcraft Tot Rider II	Wrap around	Removable shield for use as **Belt Positioning Booster Seat** with a lap/shoulder belt; shield with crotch post that opens forward for use with a lap belt	$25-35

*Belt-positioning boosters without shields for children over 50lbs not listed.

The authors contend that the proposed primary child restraint education offered in hospitals is part of the standard of care that must be offered by all hospitals and health care providers. Health professionals must not only determine if a child restraint is being used, but also encourage the parents to read the instructions and warn them of the consequences of misuse. Health professionals are in a unique position to influence parents concerning child passenger safety issues. Doctors and nurses that treat children are in constant contact with children. The parents seek advice and rely on the health providers' expertise when it comes to the child's health.

Manufacturers and consumer groups could provide hospitals with materials that inform parents which restraints are best for infants. Many of the inexpensive car seats that are available provide the same level of protection as the more expensive models that have all the frills, i.e., padding and gadgets. The secret to the safety of a car seat is in the construction of the shell and the method for securing the child to the seat. Although many hospitals have in-house child restraint programs, many hospitals are reluctant to start education loaner programs due to unfounded concerns of liability. As more hospitals participate, the liability will clearly fall on hospitals that do not have organized programs.

If parents do not have the resources to purchase an infant car seat, hospitals should provide "loaner" car seats to the parents in exchange for a deposit. Wisconsin, for example, has a child restraint loaner program in effect at more than 75% of its hospitals. In addition the loaner program is complemented by an effective education program. Some insurance companies have taken the initiative and provide car seats to their customers at no or reduced cost. League Central, a Michigan Insurance Company provides free car seats to their customers with small children. USAA, a national insurance company provides a Century model car seat at 50% of the cost.

In promoting access to child restraints, many private companies have also started child restraint loaner programs to provide car seats at a reduced cost to their customers. In May 1993, 1800 Midas dealers across the nation will provide Century 1000 STE car seats for $42. Once the seat is no longer needed Midas will accept them and provide $42 in repair services to the parent returning the car seat. The used restraints will then be provided to low-income programs. Once the child outgrows the car seat, the restraint can be returned in exchange for services from the merchant. Other companies have safety programs for their employees that include child restraint education. Allstate for example, through its "Buckle-Up Baby Program," offers infant seats to their employees when their baby is born.

Safety Booster Seat Checkup Form

Checkup Form B

Instructions for parent or driver of vehicle: Please fill in the box below before your checkup. When you are asked to drive to the checkup area, have your child buckled up as usual.

Please Print.

Adult's Name______________ Address______________

City______________ State____ Zip________ Phone (______)______________

Vehicle: Make ______________ Model ______________ Year ________ Passenger air bag?______

Child's Age______yrs. ______ mos. Child's approx. weight______lbs. Sits unassisted? ______

Safety Seat: Mfr. Name______________ Model Name and/or #______________ Date made______________

Does seat have sticker stating it meets vehicle safety standards?______________

This safety seat was: ☐ purchased new ☐ used by older sibling ☐ borrowed or purchased used.

Has it ever been used in a crash? Explain:______________

I found out about this checkup from:______________

Instructions for safety seat checker:
Use this form to check booster seats only. Use one form for each booster. For seats for infants only, convertible seats (fit up to 40 lbs.), or special restraints, use Forms I, C, or S, respectively. **IMPORTANT!** Find manufacturer's instructions before you start the checkup. The instructions for boosters are usually on a sticker glued to the bottom of the seat. However, check for a booklet with details on correct use, particularly for removable-shield boosters.

Check one: ☐ Found instructions on booster ☐ Used our file copy of instructions
☐ Used (complete) instruction label glued to bottom of booster

After you have obtained the instructions, start the checkup.

Checklist:	**Misuse Observed:**
A. Check the Safety Seat Note: Check belt before loosening. 1. Verify owner's info above by looking at safety seat. Mfr. name__________ Model #/name ________ Date __/__/__ 2. Find sticker stating seat meets motor vehicle safety standards. ☐ Found federal vehicle sticker ☐ No sticker; used mfr. instr. 3. Check list of recalled seats. ☐ Not on recall list ☐ On list, corrected	* ☐ Made before 1981 ☐ Restaurant booster ☐ Pillow or cushion ☐ On recall list; not corrected (give copy of list to owner)
Check for correct use Child's age ____ Child's weight ____ Location of booster in car ☐ rear seat ☐ front seat Upper body restrained by: ☐ Shoulder/lap belt, no shield ☐ Shoulder/lap belt with shield ☐ Lap belt with shield ☐ Harness with tether ☐ Head and neck are supported OR →	☐ Small shield used for child under 40 lbs. ☐ No shield or harness used ☐ Safety belt too loose ☐ Shldr. belt,wrong location ☐ Lap belt, wrong location ☐ Harness not tethered/wrong ☐ Head above vehicle seat

*Other: ______________

Safety seat checker: Review form before turning it in, please. After you have filled in the checklist, make sure the parent has completed the box at the top of the page. Sign and date the form.

Parent requests information to be mailed regarding: ______________

Name of checker (print)______________ Date ______________

Signature of checker ______________ Phone (______)______________

P. O. Box 553. Altadena, CA 91003 (310) 673-2666

Exhibit 2-20 *Sample child restraint device check-up forms.*

Convertible Safety Seat Checkup Form | Checkup Form C | Side 1

Instructions for parent or driver of vehicle: Please fill in the box below before your checkup. When you are asked to drive to the checkup area, have your child buckled up as usual.

Please Print.

Adult's Name__________ Address__________

City__________ State_____ Zip_______ Phone (_____)__________

Vehicle: Make __________ Model __________ Year _______ Passenger air bag?_____

Child's Age_____yrs. _____ mos. Child's approx. weight_____lbs. Sits unassisted? _____

Safety Seat: Mfr. Name__________ Model Name and/or #__________ Date made_______

Does seat have sticker stating it meets vehicle safety standards?__________

This safety seat was: ☐ purchased new ☐ used by older sibling ☐ borrowed or purchased used.

Has it ever been used in a crash? Explain:__________

I found out about this checkup from:__________

Instructions for safety seat checker:
Use this form to check convertible (birth to 40 lbs.) safety seats only. Use one form for each safety seat. For infant-only seats, boosters, or special restraints, use Forms I, B or S, respectively.

IMPORTANT! Find manufacturer's instruction booklet before you start the checkup!
Check one: ☐ Found instruction booklet with seat ☐ Used our file copy of instruction booklet

After you have obtained the instruction booklet, turn to Side 2 and start the checkup.

P. O. Box 553, Altadena, CA 91003 (310) 673-2666

Exhibit 2-21 *Sample child restraint device check-up forms.*

Convertible Seat Checkup Form

Checkup Form C | Side 2

Checklist:	Misuse Observed:
A. Check the Safety Seat Note: Check belt before loosening.	
1. Verify owner's info on side 1 by looking at safety seat.	
Mfr. name________ Model #/name ________ Date __/__/__	☐ Made before 1981
2. Find sticker stating seat meets motor vehicle safety standards.	☐ No identification found
☐ Found federal vehicle sticker ☐ No sticker; found mfr. instr	☐ Illegal seat
3. Check list of recalled seats. ☐ Not on recall list	
☐ On list (give copy of list to owner) ☐ Already corrected	☐ On recall list; not corrected

Checklist:	Misuse Observed:
B. Check Position of Child and Safety Seat	☐ Infant facing front of car
4. Safety seat faces toward ☐ front of car ☐ back of car.	☐ Seat too small
5. Safety seat ☐ fits child comfortably ☐ does not fit	☐ Seat too big
6. Safety seat is adjusted ☐ nearly upright ☐ reclined halfway	☐ Thick pad used under child
☐ reclined more than halfway back	☐ Infant reclined over 45°
7. Child is riding in ☐ back seat, center ☐ back seat, side	☐ Infant upright or slumped
☐ front seat, center ☐ front seat, right	☐ Forward-facing, reclined

Checklist:	Misuse Observed:
C. Check Harness System	
8. Harness system is ☐ complete and in working order OR→	☐ Harness incomplete/broken
9. Harness threading ☐ matches diagram in instructions OR→	☐ Harness threaded wrong
☐ harness straps "locked" into slides OR →	☐ Straps not locked, could slip
10. Top tether strap required? (check instructions)	☐ Top tether needed, not used
☐ required ☐ not required	☐ Top tether installed wrong
11. Check if child is harnessed per instructions, including:	**Harness Errors**
☐ Harness snug, but comfortable	☐ Harness too loose
☐ Forward-facing: top strap slots used	☐ Slots too low
☐ Rear-facing: lowest strap slots used	☐ Slots too high
☐ Crotch strap short so lap straps are low over hips	☐ Crotch strap too long
☐ Crotch strap/stalk routed between legs	☐ Crotch strap placed wrong
☐ Buckle fastened securely (passes "yank" test)	☐ Buckle not firmly latched
☐ Shoulder straps routed over shoulders, not arms	☐ Straps on or under arms
☐ Retainer clip/strap used, if required (see instructions)	☐ No retainer clip, if required
☐ Retainer clip/strap, if required, at armpit level	☐ Retainer clip placed wrong

Checklist:	Misuse Observed:
D. Check Vehicle Safety Belt	
12. Belt type used to secure safety seat (check one box only)	
Continuous shoulder/lap belt: **Separate lap belt:**	
☐ passive belt or ☐ manual or	☐ Passive belt used
☐ automatic locking ☐ automatic locking or	☐ Needs locking clip
☐ emergency locking or ☐ emergency locking	☐ Locking clip incorrect
☐ locking latchplate	
☐ switchable retractor	
13. Check if belt is fastened tightly.	
☐ Belt was tight ☐ Made belt tight ☐ Couldn't get belt tight	☐ Safety belt not attached
☐ Locking clip installed by parent ☐ l.c. installed by SBS	☐ Safety belt too loose
14. Check belt location and compare with instructions.	☐ Lap belt in wrong location
☐ Belt location OK ☐ Corrected belt location ☐ Belt won't fit	☐ Shoulder belt placed wrong

Other:________________________________

Safety seat checker: Review form before turning it in, please. After you filled in Sections A-D, make sure the parent has completed the first box on side 1. Sign and date the form.

Parent requests information to be mailed regarding: ____________________

Name of checker (print)____________________ Date __________

Signature of checker ____________________ Phone (____)__________

Exhibit 2-22 *Sample child restraint device check-up forms.*

Chapter 3

Federal Legislation

Background

Motor vehicle accidents are the number one cause of traumatic epilepsy and are associated with mental retardation and spinal cord injuries. The leading cause of death for individuals between the ages of 1 to 34 is the everyday automobile accident. The emotional and economic costs associated with automobile accidents justify changes in education, enforcement, legislation and litigation concerning child restraints. In 1990, 926 children under age 5 died in automobile crashes in the United States. Tens of thousands of children are injured annually on our roads. The federal standards enacted to protect our children have failed to provide adequate guidelines concerning the testing and use of child restraints. The standard only applies to children weighing up to 50 pounds. The standard fails to recognize that many special needs children who weigh in excess of 50 lbs. require special child restraint systems.

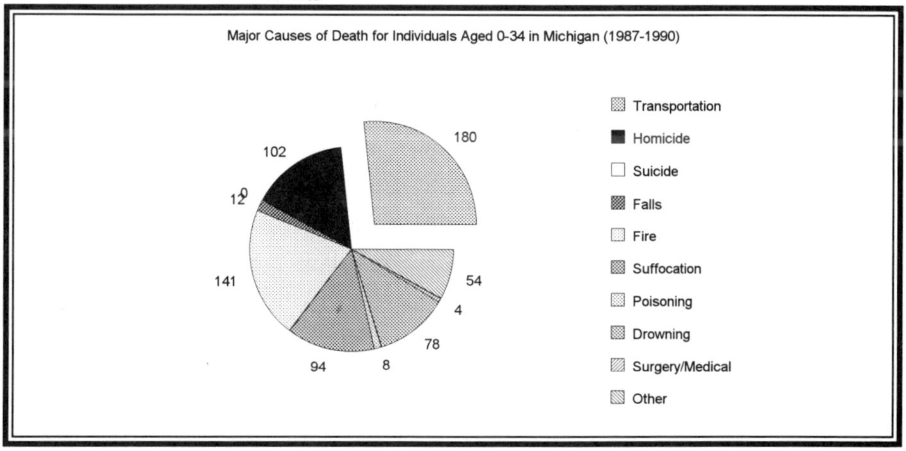

Exhibit 3-1

As early as 1972, the industry has been aware that child restraint systems performed poorly in crash worthiness tests. In a series of sled crash-tests, only five child restraint systems were found acceptable and only one device was rated "good". In the wake of an overwhelming number of fatalities, the National Highway Traffic Safety Administration (NHTSA) adopted Federal Motor Vehicle Standard 213. FMVSS 213 was the result of a series of changes to requirements first published by NHTSA in the *Federal Register* in 1970.

FMVSS 213 became effective on April 1, 1971 and has subsequently been modified. Standard 213 (FMVSS 213) regulates both, the design of child restraints and the accompanying instruction manuals. Since 1981, all child restraints manufactured in the United States must meet crash-test requirements, and must have a label that has the date of manufacture, warnings and a statement of compliance with the federal standard. The standard was first enacted in 1971, but only cars seats manufactured after January 1, 1981 must comply with the standard.

Nevertheless, Standard 213 fails to consider the different age groups, physical characteristics and special needs of children that may use a particular child restraint. The standard simply specifies requirements for child restraints to be used by children who weigh 50 pounds or less. Special needs children face special hardships when traveling in automobiles to school, clinics or any other place. Often, well-meaning parents resort to using restraints that have not met the minimal certification provided under FMVSS 213. But even those children who are able to use certified child restraints may not be safe, because the testing is not comprehensive and is flawed.

The sled tests, under the federal standard, consist of placing the child restraint on a 1960's bench type back seat. The dynamic testing of child restraints has been conducted in the past by the Highway Safety Research Institute (HSRI), Calspan, General Motors and the DOT-NHTSA Safety Research Laboratory. The dynamic test measures horizontal movement of a block torso when subjected to a force of 1000 lbs. in a forward position or 500 lbs. in a rearward direction to simulate a 30 mph impact. A 33-pound dummy is used to represent a three-year-old, and a 17-pound dummy is used to represent a one-year-old. After securing the child restraint with the appropriate dummy, the sled is then accelerated to 30 mph and abruptly stopped to simulate a head-on collision. See Testing of Child Restraints section in Chapter 2.

The major flaw with the test is that it fails to consider side, rear impacts and roll over accidents. Crash protection standards in Europe in the form of ECE 44 provide for three different masses to be tested to simulate three different age groups. The testing includes an overturning test designed to simulate a roll-over accident. The test consists of rotating the restrained dummy 360 degrees in longitudinal and lateral directions.

Furthermore, the testing under FMVSS 213 provides no data regarding the interaction of the restraint with more modern, bucket-style seats and the smaller passenger compartments in modern cars. Currently all fifty states and the District of Columbia have enacted child restraint statutes. Use of restraints has increased by 82%.

Exhibit 3-2 *Due to the federal legislation enacted in the form of FMVSS 213, many lives have been saved. In spite of this legislation, accidents like the one illustrated above are not always preventable.*

Federal Motor Vehicle Safety Standards

In the sixties the U.S. Congress authorized the creation of NHTSA to implement and oversee federal standards to protect motor vehicle occupants. The overall goal was to increase safety and reduce injuries and fatalities on the highways. Many standards are now in place that regulate automobile and passenger safety. Two of those standards are included in this chapter for quick reference and as a source to the practitioner/advocate.

Standard No. 208: Occupant crash protection.

NHTSA's Federal Motor Vehicle Standard 208 is part of the federal legislation introduced in the 1960's to curtail the number of deaths taking place on our nation's roads and highways. The standard was amended in 1984 to require that all passenger cars sold after September 1, 1989 be equipped with airbags or automatic seat belts. In 1991, the requirement for airbags or automatic seat belts was extended to pick up trucks and vans. This latest requirement is to be phased in by the automotive industry for cars manufactured in 1995 to 1998.

The federal standard prompted the state legislatures to pass many automotive safety laws. Mandatory seat belt laws are a prime example of such laws. Federal standards like standard 208 and the various state laws have shown that automotive safety laws reduce crashes and save lives. NHTSA concluded that the risk of death in cars equipped with airbags is 23% lower than in cars equipped with manual seat belts.

A thorough understanding of Standard 208 is critical for attorneys handling motor vehicle accident cases where a defect in the vehicle may have been responsible for the injuries or deaths of the attorney's clients.

49 CFR 571.208

§1. Scope. This standard specifies performance requirements for the protection of vehicle occupants in crashes.

§2. Purpose. The purpose of this standard is to reduce the number of deaths of vehicle occupants, and the severity of injuries, by specifying vehicle crash worthiness requirements in terms of forces and accelerations measured on anthropomorphic dummies in test crashes, and by specifying equipment requirements for active and passive restraint systems.

§3. Application. This standard applies to passenger cars, multipurpose passenger vehicles, trucks, and buses. In addition, §9., Pressure vessels and explosive devices, applies to vessels designed to contain a pressurized fluid or gas, and to explosive devices, for use in the above types of motor vehicles as part of a system designed to provide protection to occupants in the event of a crash.

§4. General requirements.

§4.1 Passenger cars.

§4.1.1 Passenger cars manufactured from January 1, 1972, to August 31, 1973. Each passenger car manufactured from January 1, 1972, to August 31, 1973, inclusive, shall meet the requirements of §4.1.1.1, §4.1.1.2, or §4.1.1.3. A protection system that meets the requirements of §4.1.1.1, or §4.1.1.2 may be installed at one or more designated seating positions of a vehicle that otherwise meets the requirements of §4.1.1.3.

§4.1.1.1 First option—complete passive protection system. The vehicle shall meet the crash protection requirements of §5. by means that require no action by vehicle occupants.

§4.1.1.2 Second option—lap belt protection system with belt warning. The vehicle shall —

(a) At each designated seating position have a Type 1 seat belt assembly or a Type 2 seat belt assembly with a detachable upper torso portion that conforms to §7.1 and §7.2 of this standard;

(b) At each front outboard designated seating position, have a seat belt warning system that conforms to §7.3; and

(c) Meet the frontal crash protection requirements of §5.1, in a perpendicular impact, with respect to anthropomorphic test devices in each front outboard designated seating position restrained only by Type 1 seat belt assemblies.

§4.1.1.3 Third option—lap and shoulder belt protection system with belt warning.

§4.1.1.3.1 Except for convertibles and open-body vehicles, the vehicle shall—

(a) At each front outboard designated seating position have a Type 2 seat belt assembly that conforms to @ 571.209 and §7.1 and §7.2 of this standard, with either an integral or detachable upper torso portion, and a seat belt warning system that conforms to §7.3;

(b) At each designated seating position other than the front outboard positions, have a Type 1 or Type 2 seat belt assembly that conforms to @ 571.209 and to §7.1 and §7.2 of this standard; and

(c) When it perpendicularly impacts a fixed collision barrier, while moving longitudinally forward at any speed up to and including 30 m.p.h., under the test conditions of §8.1 with anthropomorphic test devices at each front outboard position restrained by Type 2 seat belt assemblies, experience no complete separation of any load-bearing element of a seat belt assembly or anchorage.

§4.1.1.3.2 Convertibles and open-body type vehicles shall at each designated seating position have a Type 1 or Type 2 seat belt assembly that conforms to @ 571.209 and to §7.1 and §7.2 of this standard, and at each front outboard designated seating position have a seat belt warning system that conforms to §7.3.

§4.1.2 Passenger cars manufactured on or after September 1, 1973, and before September 1, 1986. Each passenger car manufactured on or after September 1, 1973, and before September 1, 1986, shall meet the requirements of §4.1.2.1, §4.1.2.2 or §4.1.2.3. A protection system that meets the requirements of §4.1.2.1 or §4.1.2.2 may be installed at one or more designated seating positions of a vehicle that otherwise meets the requirements of §4.1.2.3.

§4.1.2.1 First option—frontal/angular automatic protection system. The vehicle shall:

(a) At each front outboard designated seating position meet the frontal crash protection requirements of §5.1 by means that require no action by vehicle occupants;

(b) At the front center designated seating position and at each rear designated seating position have a Type 1 or Type 2 seat belt assembly that conforms to Standard No. 209 and to §7.1 and §7.2; and

(c) Either. (1) Meet the lateral crash protection requirements of §5.2 and the roll-over crash protection requirements of §5.3 by means that require no action by vehicle occupants; or

(2) At each front outboard designated seating position have a Type 1 or Type 2 seat belt assembly that conforms to Standard No. 209 and §7.1 through §7.3, and that meets the requirements of §5.1 with front test dummies as required by §5.1, restrained by the Type 1 or Type 2 seat belt assembly (or the pelvic portion of any Type 2 seat belt assembly which has a detachable upper torso belt) in addition to the means that require no action by the vehicle occupant.

§4.1.2.2 Second option—head-on automatic protection system. The vehicle shall —

(a) At each designated seating position have a Type 1 seat belt assembly or Type 2 seat belt assembly with a detachable upper torso portion that conforms to §7.1 and §7.2 of this standard.

(b) At each front outboard designated seating position, meet the frontal crash protection requirements of §5.1, in a perpendicular impact, by means that require no action by vehicle occupants;

(c) At each front outboard designated seating position, meet the frontal crash protection requirements of §5.1, in a perpendicular impact, with a test device restrained by a Type 1 seat belt assembly; and

(d) At each front outboard designated seating position, have a seat belt warning system that conforms to §7.3.

§4.1.2.3 Third option—lap and shoulder belt protection system with belt warning.

§4.1.2.3.1 Except for convertibles and open-body vehicles, the vehicle shall—

(a) At each front outboard designated seating position have a seat belt assembly that conforms to §7.1 and §7.2 of this standard, and a seat belt warning system that conforms to §7.3. The belt assembly shall be either a Type 2 seat belt assembly with a non detachable shoulder belt that conforms to Standard No. 209 (@ 571.209), or a Type 1 seat belt assembly such that with a test device restrained by the assembly the vehicle meets the frontal crash protection requirements of §5.1 in a perpendicular impact.

(b) At any center front designated seating position, have a Type 1 or Type 2 seat belt assembly that conforms to Standard No. 209 (@ 571.209) and to §7.1 and §7.2 of this standard, and a seat belt warning system that conforms to §7.3; and

(c) At each other designated seating position, have a Type 1 or Type 2 seat belt assembly that conforms to Standard No. 209 (@ 571.209) and §7.1 and §7.2 of this standard.

§4.1.2.3.2 Convertibles and open-body type vehicles shall at each designated seating position have a Type 1 or Type 2 seat belt assembly that conforms to Standard No. 209 (@ 571.209) and to §7.1 and §7.2 of this standard, and at each front designated seating position have a seat belt warning system that conforms to §7.3.

§4.1.3 Passenger cars manufactured on or after September 1, 1986, and before September 1, 1989.

§4.1.3.1 Passenger cars manufactured on or after September 1, 1986, and before September 1, 1987.

§4.1.3.1.1 Subject to §4.1.3.1.2 and §4.1.3.4, each passenger car manufactured on or after September 1, 1986, and before September

1, 1987, shall comply with the requirements of §4.1.2.1, §4.1.2.2 or §4.1.2.3. A vehicle shall not be deemed to be in noncompliance with this standard if its manufacturer establishes that it did not have reason to know in the exercise of due care that such vehicle is not in conformity with the requirement of this standard.

§4.1.3.1.2 Subject to §4.1.3.4 and §4.1.5, the amount of passenger cars, specified in §4.1.3.1.1 complying with the requirements of §4.1.2.1 shall be not less than 10 percent of:

(a) The average annual production of passenger cars manufactured on or after September 1, 1983, and before September 1, 1986, by each manufacturer, or

(b) The manufacturer's annual production of passenger cars during the period specified in §4.1.3.1.1.

§4.1.3.1.3 A manufacturer may exclude convertibles which do not comply with the requirements of §4.1.2.1, when it is calculating its average annual production under §4.1.3.1.2(a) or its annual production under §4.1.3.1.2(b).

§4.1.3.2 Passenger cars manufactured on or after September 1, 1987, and before September 1, 1988.

§4.1.3.2.1 Subject to §4.1.3.2.2 and §4.1.3.4, each passenger car manufactured on or after September 1, 1987, and before September 1, 1988, shall comply with the requirements of §4.1.2.1, §4.1.2.2 or §4.1.2.3. A vehicle shall not be deemed to be in noncompliance with this standard if its manufacturer establishes that it did not have reason to know in the exercise of due care that such vehicle is not in conformity with the requirement of this standard.

§4.1.3.2.2 Subject to §4.1.3.4 and §4.1.5, the amount of passenger cars specified in §4.1.3.2.1 complying with the requirements of §4.1.2.1. shall be not less than 25 percent of:

(a) The average annual production of passenger cars manufactured on or after September 1, 1984, and before September 1, 1987, by each manufacturer, or

(b) The manufacturer's annual production of passenger cars during the period specified in §4.1.3.2.1.

§4.1.3.2.3 A manufacturer may exclude convertibles which do not comply with the requirements of §4.1.2.1, when it is calculating its average annual production under §4.1.3.2.2(a) or its annual production under §4.1.3.2.2(b).

§4.1.3.3 Passenger cars manufactured on or after September 1, 1988, and before September 1, 1989.

§4.1.3.3.1 Subject to §4.1.3.3.2 and §4.1.3.4, each passenger car manufactured on or after September 1, 1988, and before September 1, 1989, shall comply with the requirements of §4.1.2.1, §4.1.2.2 or §4.1.2.3. A vehicle shall not be deemed to be in noncompliance with this standard if its manufacturer establishes that it did not have reason to know in the exercise of due care that such vehicle is not in conformity with the requirement of this standard.

§4.1.3.3.2 Subject to §4.1.3.4 and §4.1.5, the amount of passenger cars specified in §4.1.3.3.1 complying with the requirements of §4.1.2.1 shall be not less than 40 percent of:

(a) The average annual production of passenger cars manufactured on or after September 1, 1985, and before September 1, 1988, by each manufacturer or

(b) The manufacturer's annual production of passenger cars during the period specified in §4.1.3.3.1.

§4.1.3.3.3 A manufacturer may exclude convertibles which do not comply with the requirements of §4.1.2.1, when it is calculating its average annual production under §4.1.3.3.2(a) or its annual production under §4.1.3.3.2(b).

§4.1.3.4 Calculation of complying passenger cars.

(a) For the purposes of calculating the numbers of cars manufactured under §4.1.3.1.2, §4.1.3.2.2, or §4.1.3.3.2 to comply with §4.1.2.1:

(1) Each car whose driver's seating position complies with the requirements of §4.1.2.1(a) by means not including any type of seat belt and whose front right seating position will

comply with the requirements of §4.1.2.1(a) by any means is counted as 1.5 vehicles, and

(2) Each car whose driver's seating position complies with the requirements of §4.1.2.1(a) by means not including any type of seat belt and whose right front seat seating position is equipped with a manual Type 2 seat belt is counted as one vehicle.

(b) For the purposes of complying with §4.1.3.1.2, a passenger car may be counted if it:

(1) Is manufactured on or after September 1, 1985, but before September 1, 1986, and

(2) Complies with §4.1.2.1.

(c) For the purposes of complying with §4.1.3.2.2, a passenger car may be counted if it:

(1) Is manufactured on or after September 1, 1985, but before September 1, 1987,

(2) Complies with §4.1.2.1, and

(3) Is not counted toward compliance with §4.1.3.1.2

(d) For the purposes of complying with §4.1.3.3.2, a passenger car may be counted if it:

(1) Is manufactured on or after September 1, 1985, but before September 1, 1988,

(2) Complies with §4.1.2.1, and

(3) Is not counted toward compliance with §4.1.3.1.2 or §4.1.3.2.2.

§4.1.3.5 Passenger cars produced by more than one manufacturer.

§4.1.3.5.1 For the purposes of calculating average annual production of passenger cars for each manufacturer and the amount of passenger cars manufactured by each manufacturer under §4.1.3.1.2, §4.1.3.2.2 or §4.1.3.3.2, a passenger car produced by more than one manufacturer shall be attributed to a single manufacturer as follows, subject to §4.1.3.5.2:

(a) A passenger car which is imported shall be attributed to the importer.

(b) A passenger car manufactured in the United States by more than one manufacturer, one of which also markets the vehicle, shall be attributed to the manufacturer which markets the vehicle.

§4.1.3.5.2 A passenger car produced by more than one manufacturer shall be attributed to any one of the vehicle's manufacturers specified by an express written contract, reported to the National Highway Traffic Safety Administration under 49 CFR Part 585, between the manufacturer so specified and the manufacturer to which the vehicle would otherwise be attributed under §4.1.3.5.1.

§4.1.4 Passenger cars manufactured on or after September 1, 1989.

§4.1.4.1 Except as provided in §4.1.4.2, each passenger car manufactured on or after September 1, 1989 shall comply with the requirements of §4.1.2.1. Any passenger car manufactured on or after September 1, 1989 and before September 1, 1993 whose driver's designated seating position complies with the requirements of §4.1.2.1(a) by means not including any type of seat belt and whose right front designated seating position is equipped with a manual Type 2 seat belt so that the seating position complies with the occupant crash protection requirements of §5.1, with the Type 2 seat belt assembly adjusted in accordance with §7.4.2, shall be counted as a vehicle complying with §4.1.2.1. A vehicle shall not be deemed to be in noncompliance with this standard if its manufacturer establishes that it did not know in the exercise of due care that such vehicle is not in conformity with this standard.

§4.1.4.2 (a) Each passenger car, other than a convertible, manufactured before December 11, 1989 may be equipped with, and each passenger car, other than a convertible, manufactured on or after December 11, 1989 and before September 1, 1990 shall be equipped with a Type 2 seat belt assembly at every forward-facing rear outboard designated seating position. Type 2 seat belt assemblies installed pursuant to this provision shall comply with Standard No. 209 (49 CFR 571.209) and with §7.1.1 of this standard.

(b) Except as provided in §4.1.4.2.1 and §4.1.4.2.2, each passenger car, other than a convertible, manufactured on or after September 1, 1990 and each convertible passenger car manufactured on or after September 1, 1991 shall be equipped with an integral Type 2 seat belt assembly at every forward-facing rear outboard designated seating position. Type 2 seat belt assemblies installed in compliance with this requirement shall comply with Standard No. 209 (49 CFR 571.209) and with §7.1 an §7.2 of this standard. If a Type 2 seat belt assembly installed in compliance with this requirement incorporates any webbing tension-relieving device, the vehicle owner's manual shall include the information specified in §7.4.2(b) of this standard for the tension relieving device, and the vehicle shall comply with §7.4.2(c) of this standard.

(c) As used in this section, "rear outboard designated seating position" means any "outboard designated seating position" (as that term is defined at 49 CFR 571.3) that is rearward of the front seat(s), except any designated seating position adjacent to a walkway that is located between the seat and the near side of the vehicle and is designed to allow access to more rearward seating positions.

§4.1.4.2.1 Any rear outboard designated seating position with a seat that can be adjusted to be forward-facing and to face some other direction shall either:

(i) Meet the requirements of §4.1.4.2 with the seat in any position in which it can be occupied while the vehicle is in motion; or

(ii) When the seat is in its forward-facing position, have a Type 2 seat belt assembly with an upper torso restraint that conforms to §7.1 and §7.2 of this standard and that adjusts by means of an emergency locking retractor that conforms with Standard No. 209 (49 CFR 571.209), which upper torso restraint may be detachable at the buckle, and, when the seat is in any position in which it can be occupied while the vehicle is in motion, have a Type 1 seat belt or the pelvic portion of a Type 2 seat belt assembly that conforms to §7.1 and §7.2 of this standard.

§4.1.4.2.2 Any rear outboard designated seating position on a readily removable seat (that is, a seat designed to be easily removed and replaced by means installed by the manufacturer for that purpose) in a vehicle manufactured on or after September 1, 1992 shall meet the requirements of §4.1.4.2 and may use an upper torso belt that detaches at either its upper or lower anchorage points, but not both anchorage points, to meet those requirements. The means for detaching the upper torso belt may use a push-button action.

§4.1.5 Mandatory seat belt use laws.

§4.1.5.1 If the Secretary of Transportation determines, by not later than April 1, 1989, that state mandatory safety belt usage laws have been enacted that meet the criteria specified in §4.1.5.2 and that are applicable to not less than two-thirds of the total population of the 50 states and the District of Columbia (based on the most recent Estimates of the Resident Population of States, by Age, Current Population Reports, Series P-25, Bureau of the Census), each passenger car manufactured under §4.1.3 or §4.1.4 on or after the date of that determination shall comply with the requirements of §4.1.2.1, §4.1.2.2. or §4.1.2.3.

§4.1.5.2 The minimum criteria for state mandatory safety belt usage laws are:

(a) Require that each front seat occupant of a passenger car equipped with safety belts under Standard No. 208 has a safety belt properly fastened about his or her body at all times when the vehicle is in forward motion.

(b) If waivers from the safety belt usage requirement are to be provided, permit them for medical reasons only.

(c) Provide for the following enforcement measures:

(1) A penalty of not less than $ 25.00 (which may include court costs) for each occupant of a car who violates the belt usage requirement.

(2) A provision specifying that the violation of the belt usage requirement may be used to mitigate damages with respect to any person who is involved in a passenger car accident while violating the belt usage requirement and who seeks

in any subsequent litigation to recover damages for injuries resulting from the accident. This requirement is satisfied if there is a rule of law in the State permitting such mitigation.

(3) A program to encourage compliance with the belt usage requirement.

(d) An effective date of not later than September 1, 1989.

§4.2 Trucks and multipurpose passenger vehicles with GVWR of 10,000 pounds or less.

§4.2.1 Trucks and multipurpose passenger vehicles with a GVWR of 10,000 pounds or less, manufactured on or after January 1, 1976 and before September 1, 1991. Each truck and multipurpose passenger vehicle, with a gross vehicle weight rating of 10,000 pounds or less, manufactured before September 1, 1991, shall meet the requirements of §4.1.2.1, or at the option of the manufacturer, §4.1.2.2 or §4.1.2.3 (as specified for passenger cars), except that forward control vehicles manufactured prior to September 1, 1981, convertibles, open-body type vehicles, walk-in van-type trucks, motor homes, vehicles designed to be exclusively sold to the U.S. Postal Service, and vehicles carrying chassis-mount campers may instead meet the requirements of §4.2.1.1 or §4.2.1.2.

§4.2.1.1 First option—complete automatic protection system. The vehicle shall meet the crash protection requirements of §5 by means that require no action by vehicle occupants.

§4.2.1.2 Second option—belt system. The vehicle shall have seat belt assemblies that conform to Standard 209 installed as follows:

(a) A Type 1 or Type 2 seat belt assembly shall be installed for each designated seating position in convertibles, open-body type vehicles, and walk-in van-type trucks.

(b) In all vehicles except those for which requirements are specified in §4.2.1.2(a), a Type 2 seat belt assembly shall be installed for each outboard designated seating position that includes the windshield header within the head impact area, and a Type 1 or Type 2 seat belt assembly shall be installed for each other designated seating position.

§4.2.2 Trucks and multipurpose passenger vehicles with a GVWR of 8,500 pounds or less and an unloaded vehicle weight of 5,500 pounds or less, manufactured on or after September 1, 1991 and before September 1, 1997. Except as provided in §4.2.4, each truck and multipurpose passenger vehicle with a gross vehicle weight rating of 8,500 pounds or less and an unloaded vehicle weight of 5,500 pounds or less, manufactured on or after September 1, 1991 and before September 1, 1997, shall meet the requirements of §4.1.2.1, or at the option of the manufacturer, §4.1.2.2 or §4.1.2.3 (as specified for passenger cars), except that convertibles, open-body type vehicles, walk-in van-type trucks, motor homes, vehicles designed to be exclusively sold to the U.S. Postal Service, and vehicles carrying chassis-mount campers may instead meet the requirements of §4.2.1.1 or §4.2.1.2. Each Type 2 seat belt assembly installed in a front outboard designated seating position in accordance with §4.1.2.3 shall meet the requirements of §4.6.

§4.2.3 Trucks and multipurpose passenger vehicles manufactured on or after September 1, 1991 with either a GVWR or more than 8,500 pounds but not greater than 10,000 pounds or with an unloaded vehicle weight greater than 5,500 pounds and a GVWR of 10,000 pounds or less. Except as provided in §4.2.4, each truck and multipurpose passenger vehicle manufactured on or after September 1, 1991, that has either a gross vehicle weight rating which is greater than 8,500 pounds, but not greater than 10,000 pounds, or has an unloaded vehicle weight greater than 5,500 pounds and a GVWR of 10,000 pounds or less, shall meet the requirements of §4.1.2.1, or at the option of the manufacturer, §4.1.2.2 or §4.1.2.3 (as specified for passenger cars), except that convertibles, open-body type vehicles, walk-in van-type trucks, motor homes, vehicles designed to be exclusively sold to the U.S. Postal Service, and vehicles carrying chassis-mount campers may instead meet the requirements of §4.2.1.1 or §4.2.1.2.

§4.2.4 Rear outboard seating positions in trucks and multipurpose passenger vehicles manufactured on or after September 1, 1991 with a GVWR of 10,000 pounds or less. Except as provided in

§4.2.4.2 and §4.2.4.3, each truck and each multipurpose passenger vehicle, other than a motor home, manufactured on or after September 1, 1991 that has a gross vehicle weight rating of 10,000 pounds or less shall be equipped with an integral Type 2 seat belt assembly at every forward-facing rear outboard designated seating position. Type 2 seat belt assemblies installed in compliance with this requirement shall comply with Standard No. 209 (49 CFR 571.209) and with §7.1 and §7.2 of this standard. If a Type 2 seat belt assembly installed in compliance with this requirement incorporates any webbing tension-relieving device, the vehicle owner's manual shall include the information specified in §7.4.2(b) of this standard for the tension relieving device, and the vehicle shall comply with §7.4.2(c) of this standard.

§4.2.4.1 As used in this section—

(a) Motor home means a motor vehicle with motive power that is designed to provide temporary residential accommodations, as evidenced by the presence of at least four of the following facilities: cooking; refrigeration or ice box; self-contained toilet; heating and/or air conditioning; a potable water supply system including a faucet and a sink; and a separate 110-125 volt electrical power supply and/or an LP gas supply.

(b) Rear outboard designated seating position means any "outboard designated seating position" (as that term is defined at 49 CFR 571.3) that is rearward of the front seat(s), except any designated seating positions adjacent to a walkway located between the seat and the side of the vehicle, which walkway is designed to allow access to more rearward seating positions.

§4.2.4.2 Any rear outboard designated seating position with a seat that can be adjusted to be forward-facing and to face some other direction shall either:

(i) Meet the requirements of §4.2.4 with the seat in any position in which it can be occupied while the vehicle is in motion; or

(ii) When the seat is in its forward-facing position, have a Type 2 seat belt assembly with an upper torso restraint that conforms to §7.1 and §7.2 of this standard and that adjusts by means of an emergency locking retractor that conforms with Standard No 209 (49 CFR 571.209), which upper torso restraint may be detachable at the buckle, and, when the seat is in any position in which it can be occupied while the vehicle is in motion, have a Type 1 seat belt or the pelvic portion of a Type 2 seat belt assembly that conforms to §7.1 and §7.2 of this standard.

§4.2.4.3 Any rear outboard designated seating position on a readily removable seat (that is, a seat designed to be easily removed and replaced by means installed by the manufacturer for that purpose) in a vehicle manufactured on or after September 1, 1992 shall meet the requirements of §4.2.4 and may use an upper torso belt that detaches at either its upper or lower anchorage point, but not both anchorage points, to meet those requirements. The means for detaching the upper torso belt may use a push-button action.

§4.2.5 Trucks, buses, and multipurpose passenger vehicles with a GVWR of 8,500 pounds or less and an unloaded vehicle weight of 5,500 pounds or less manufactured on or after September 1, 1994, and before September 1, 1997.

§4.2.5.1 Trucks, buses, and multipurpose passenger vehicles with a GVWR of 8,500 pounds or less and an unloaded vehicle weight of 5,500 pounds or less manufactured on or after September 1, 1994, and before September 1, 1995.

§4.2.5.1.1 Subject to §4.2.5.1.2 and §4.2.5.5 and except as provided in §4.2.4, each truck, bus, and multipurpose passenger vehicle, other than walk-in van-type trucks and vehicles designed to be exclusively sold to the U.S. Postal Service, with a GVWR of 8,500 pounds or less and an unloaded vehicle weight of 5,500 pounds or less that is manufactured on or after September 1, 1994 and before September 1, 1995, shall comply with the requirements of §4.1.2.1, §4.1.2.2, or §4.1.2.3 (as specified for passenger cars). A vehicle shall not be deemed to be in noncompliance with this standard if its manufacturer establishes that it did not have reason to know in the exercise of due care that such vehicle is not in conformity with the requirement of standard.

§4.2.5.1.2 Subject to §4.2.5.5, the amount of trucks, buses, and multipurpose passenger vehicles specified in §4.2.5.1.1 complying with §4.1.2.1 (as specified for passenger cars) shall be not less than 20 percent of:

(a) The average annual production of trucks, buses, and multipurpose passenger vehicles with a GVWR of 8,500 pounds or less and an unloaded vehicle weight of 5,500 pounds or less manufactured on or after September 1, 1991, and before September 1, 1994, by each manufacturer that produced such vehicles during each of those annual production periods, or

(b) The manufacturer's total production of trucks, buses, and multipurpose passenger vehicle with a GVWR of 8,500 pounds or less and an unloaded vehicle weight of 5,500 pounds or less during the period specified in §4.2.5.1.1.

§2.5.2 Trucks, buses, and multipurpose passenger vehicles with a GVWR of 8,500 pounds or less and an unloaded vehicle weight of 5,500 pounds or less manufactured on or after September 1, 1995 and before September 1, 1996.

§4.2.5.2.1 Subject to §4.2.5.2.2 and §4.2.5.5 and except as provided in §4.2.4, each truck, bus, and multipurpose passenger vehicle, other than walk-in van-type trucks and vehicles designed to be exclusively sold to the U.S. Postal Service, with a GVWR of 8,500 pounds or less and an unloaded vehicle weight of 5,500 pounds or less that is manufactured on or after September 1, 1995 and before September 1, 1996, shall comply with the requirements of §4.1.2.1, §4.1.2.2, or §4.1.2.3 (as specified for passenger cars). A vehicle shall not be deemed to be in noncompliance with this standard if its manufacturer establishes that it did not have reason to know in the exercise of due care that such vehicle is not in conformity with the requirement of this standard.

§4.2.5.2.2 Subject to §4.2.5.5, the amount of trucks, buses, and multipurpose passenger vehicles specified in §4.2.5.2.1 complying with §4.1.2.1 (as specified for passenger cars) shall be not less than 50 percent of:

(a) The average annual production of trucks, buses, and multipurpose passenger vehicles with a GVWR of 8,500 pounds or less and an unloaded vehicle weight of 5,500 pounds or less manufactured on or after September 1, 1992, and before September 1, 1995, by each manufacturer that produced such vehicles during each of those annual production periods, or

(b) The manufacturer's total production of trucks, buses, and multipurpose passenger vehicles with a GVWR of 8,500 pounds or less and an unloaded vehicle weight of 5,500 pounds or less during the period specified in §4.2.5.2.1.

§4.2.5.3 Trucks, buses, and multipurpose passenger vehicles with a GVWR of 8,500 pounds or less and an unloaded vehicle weight of 5,500 pounds or less manufactured on or after September 1, 1996 and before September 1, 1997.

§4.2.5.3.1 Subject to §4.2.5.3.2 and §4.2.5.5 and except as provided in §4.2.4, each truck, bus, and multipurpose passenger vehicle, other than walk-in van-type trucks and vehicles designed to be exclusively sold to the U.S. Postal Service, with a GVWR of 8,500 pounds or less and an unloaded vehicle weight of 5,500 pounds or less that is manufactured on or after September 1, 1996 and before September 1, 1997, shall comply with the requirements of §4.1.2.1, §4.1.2.2, or §4.1.2.3 (as specified for passenger cars). A vehicle shall not be deemed to be in noncompliance with this standard if its manufacturer establishes that it did not have reason to know in the exercise of due care that such vehicle is not in conformity with the requirement of this standard.

§4.2.5.3.2 Subject to §4.2.5.5, the amount of trucks, buses, and multipurpose passenger vehicles specified in §4.2.5.3.1 complying with §4.1.2.1 (as specified for passenger cars) shall be not less than 90 percent of:

(a) The average annual production of trucks, buses, and multipurpose passenger vehicles with a GVWR of 8,500 pounds or less and an unloaded vehicle weight of 5,500 pounds or less manufactured on or after September 1, 1993, and before September 1, 1996, by each manufacturer that produced such vehicles during each of those annual production periods, or

(b) The manufacturer's total production of trucks, buses, and multipurpose passenger vehicles with a GVWR of 8,500 pounds or less and an unloaded vehicle weight of 5,500 pounds or less during the period specified in §4.2.5.3.1.

§4.2.5.4 Alternative phase-in schedule. A manufacturer may, at its option, comply with the requirements of this section instead of complying with the requirements set forth in §4.2.5.1, §4.2.5.2, and §4.2.5.3.

(a) Except as provided in §4.2.4, each truck, bus, and multipurpose passenger vehicle, other than walk-in van-type trucks and vehicles designed to be exclusively sold to the U.S. Postal Service, with a GVWR of 8,500 pounds or less and an unloaded vehicle weight of 5,500 pounds or less that is manufactured on or after September 1, 1994 and before September 1, 1995, shall comply with the requirements of §4.1.2.1, §4.1.2.2, or §4.1.2.3 (as specified for passenger cars).

(b) Except as provided in §4.2.4, each truck, bus, and multipurpose passenger vehicle, other than walk-in van-type trucks and vehicles designed to be exclusively sold to the U.S. Postal Service, with a GVWR of 8,500 pounds or less and an unloaded vehicle weight of 5,500 pounds or less that is manufactured on or after September 1, 1995 shall comply with the requirements of §4.1.2.1 (as specified for passenger cars) of this standard. A vehicle shall not be deemed to be in noncompliance with this standard if its manufacturer establishes that it did not have reason to know in the exercise of due care that such vehicle is not in conformity with the requirement of this standard.

(c) Each truck, bus, and multipurpose passenger vehicle with a GVWR of 8,500 pounds or less and an unloaded vehicle weight of 5,500 pounds or less manufactured on or after September 1, 1995, but before September 1, 1998, whose driver's seating position complies with the requirements of §4.1.2.1(a) of this standard by means not including any type of seat belt and whose right front passenger's seating position is equipped with a manual Type 2 seat belt that complies with §5.1 of this standard, with the seat belt assembly adjusted in accordance with §7.4.2, shall be counted as a vehicle complying with §4.1.2.1.

§4.2.5.5 Calculation of complying trucks, buses, and multipurpose passenger vehicles with a GVWR of 8,500 pounds or less and an unloaded vehicle weight of 5,500 pounds or less.

(a) For the purposes of the calculations required in §4.2.5.1.2, §4.2.5.2.2, and §4.2.5.3.2 of the number of trucks, buses, and multipurpose passenger vehicles with a GVWR of 8,500 pounds or less and an unloaded vehicle weight of 5,500 pounds or less that comply with §4.1.2.1 (as specified for passenger cars):

(1) Each truck, bus, and multipurpose passenger vehicle with a GVWR of 8,500 pounds or less and an unloaded vehicle weight of 5,500 pounds or less whose driver's seating position complies with the requirements of §4.1.2.1(a) by means not including any type of seat belt and whose front right seating position complies with the requirements of §4.1.2.1(a) by any means is counted as 1.5 vehicles, and

(2) Each truck, bus, and multipurpose passenger vehicle with a GVWR of 8,500 pounds or less and an unloaded vehicle weight of 5,500 pounds or less whose driver's seating position complies with the requirements of §4.1.2.1(a) by means not including any type of seat belt and whose right front passenger's seating position is equipped with a manual Type 2 seat belt that complies with §5.1 of this standard, with the seat belt assembly adjusted in accordance with §7.4.2, is counted as one vehicle.

(3) Each truck, bus, and multipurpose passenger vehicle with a GVWR of 8,500 pounds or less and an unloaded vehicle weight of 5,500 pounds or less that is manufactured in two or more stages or that is altered (within the meaning of @ 567.7 of this chapter) after having previously been certified in accordance with Part 567 of this chapter is not subject to the requirements of §4.2.5.1.2, §4.2.5.2.2, and §4.2.5.3.2. Such vehicles may be excluded from all calculations of compliance with §4.2.5.1.2, §4.2.5.2.2, and §4.2.5.3.2.

(b) For the purposes of complying with §4.2.5.1.2, a truck, bus, or multipurpose passenger vehicle with a GVWR of 8,500 pounds or less and an unloaded vehicle weight of 5,500 pounds or less may be counted if it:

(1) Is manufactured on or after September 1, 1992, but before September 1, 1994, and

(2) Is certified as complying with §4.1.2.1 (as specified for passenger cars).

(c) For the purposes of complying with §4.2.5.2.2, a truck, bus, or multipurpose passenger vehicle with a GVWR of 8,500 pounds or less and an unloaded vehicle weight of 5,500 pounds or less may be counted if it:

(1) Is manufactured on or after September 1, 1992, but before September 1, 1995,

(2) Is certified as complying with §4.1.2.1 (as specified for passenger cars), and

(3) Is not counted toward compliance with §4.2.5.1.2.

(d) For the purposes of complying with §4.2.5.3.2, a truck, bus, or multipurpose passenger vehicle with a GVWR of 8,500 pounds or less and an unloaded vehicle weight of 5,500 pounds or less may be counted if it:

(1) Is manufactured on or after September 1, 1992, but before September 1, 1996,

(2) Is certified as complying with §4.1.2.1 (as specified for passenger cars), and

(3) Is not counted toward compliance with §4.2.5.1.2 or §4.2.5.2.2.

§4.2.5.6 Trucks, buses, and multipurpose passenger vehicles with a GVWR of 8,500 pounds or less and an unloaded vehicle weight of 5,500 pounds or less produced by more than one manufacturer.

§4.2.5.6.1 For the purposes of calculating average annual production for each manufacturer and the amount of vehicles manufactured by each manufacturer under §4.2.5.1.2, §4.2.5.2.2, or §4.2.5.3.2, a truck, bus, or multipurpose passenger vehicle with a GVWR of 8,500 pounds or less and an unloaded vehicle weight of

5,500 pounds or less produced by more than one manufacturer shall be attributed to a single manufacturer as follows, subject to §4.2.5.6.2:

(a) A vehicle that is imported shall be attributed to the importer.

(b) A vehicle that is manufactured in the United States by more than one manufacturer, one of which also markets the vehicle, shall be attributed to the manufacturer that markets the vehicle.

§4.2.5.6.2 A truck, bus, or multipurpose passenger vehicle with a GVWR of 8,500 pounds or less and an unloaded vehicle weight of 5,500 pounds or less produced by more than one manufacturer shall be attributed to any one of the vehicle's manufacturers specified in an express written contract, reported to the National Highway Traffic Safety Administration under 49 CFR part 585, between the manufacturer so specified and the manufacturer to which the vehicle would otherwise be attributed under §4.2.5.4.1.

§4.2.6 Trucks, buses, and multipurpose passenger vehicles with a GVWR of 8,500 pounds or less and an unloaded vehicle weight of 5,500 pounds or less manufactured on or after September 1, 1997. Except as provided in §4.2.4, each truck, bus, and multipurpose passenger vehicle with a GVWR of 8,500 pounds or less and an unloaded vehicle weight of 5,500 pounds or less manufactured on or after September 1, 1997 shall comply with the requirements of §4.1.2.1 (as specified for passenger cars) of this standard, except that walk-in van-type trucks and vehicles designed to be exclusively sold to the U.S. Postal Service may instead meet the requirements of §4.2.1.1 or §4.2.1.2. Each truck, bus, and multipurpose passenger vehicle with a GVWR of 8,500 pounds or less and an unloaded vehicle weight of 5,500 pounds or less manufactured on or after September 1, 1997, but before September 1, 1998, whose driver's seating position complies with the requirements of §4.1.2.1(a) of this standard by means not including any type of seat belt and whose right front passenger's seating position is equipped with a manual Type 2 seat belt that complies with @ 5.1 of this standard, with the seat belt assembly adjusted in accordance with §7.4.2., shall be counted as a vehicle complying with §4.1.2.1. A vehicle shall not be deemed to be in noncompliance with this standard if its manufacturer establishes that it did not have reason to know in the exercise of due care that such vehicle is not in conformity with the requirement of this standard.

§4.3 Trucks and multipurpose passenger vehicles, with GVWR of more than 10,000 pounds.

§4.3.1 Trucks and multipurpose passenger vehicles with a GVWR of more than 10,000 pounds, manufactured in or after January 1, 1972 and before September 1, 1990. Each truck and multipurpose passenger vehicle with a gross vehicle weight rating of more than 10,000 pounds, manufactured on or after January 1, 1972 and before September 1, 1990, shall meet the requirements of §4.3.1.1 or §4.3.1.2. A protection system that meets the requirements of §4.3.1.1 may be installed at one or more designated seating positions of a vehicle that otherwise meets the requirements of §4.3.1.2.

§4.3.1.1 First option—complete passenger protection system. The vehicle shall meet the crash protection requirements of §5 by means that require no action by vehicle occupants.

§4.3.1.2 Second option—belt system. The vehicle shall, at each designated seating position, have either a Type 1 or a Type 2 seat belt assembly that conforms to §571.209.

§4.3.2 Trucks and multipurpose passenger vehicles with a GVWR of more than 10,000 pounds, manufactured on or after September 1, 1990. Each truck and multipurpose passenger vehicle with a gross vehicle weight rating of more than 10,000 pounds, manufactured on or after September 1, 1990, shall meet the requirements of §4.3.2.1 or §4.3.2.2. A protection system that meets the requirements of §4.3.2.1 may be installed at one or more designated seating positions of a vehicle that otherwise meets the requirements of §4.3.2.2.

§4.3.2.1 First option—complete passenger protection system. The vehicle shall meet the crash protection requirements of §5 by means that require no action by vehicle occupants.

§4.3.2.2 Second option—belt system. The vehicle shall, at each designated seating position, have either a Type 1 or a Type 2 seat belt assembly that conforms to @ 571.209 of this part and §7.2 of this Standard. A Type 1 belt assembly or the pelvic portion of a dual retractor Type 2 belt assembly installed at a front outboard seating position shall include either an emergency locking retractor or an automatic locking retractor. If a seat belt assembly installed at a front outboard seating position includes an automatic locking retractor for the lap belt or the lap belt portion, that seat belt assembly shall comply with the following:

(a) An automatic locking retractor used at a front outboard seating position that has some type of suspension system for the seat shall be attached to the seat structure that moves as the suspension system functions.

(b) The lap belt or lap belt portion of a seat belt assembly equipped with an automatic locking retractor that is installed at a front outboard seating position must allow at least 3/4 inch, but less than 3 inches, of webbing movement before retracting webbing to the next locking position.

(c) Compliance with §4.3.2.2(b) of this standard is determined as follows:

(1) The seat belt assembly is buckled and the retractor end of the seat belt assembly is anchored to a horizontal surface. The webbing for the lap belt or lap belt portion of the seat belt assembly is extended to 75 percent of its length and the retractor is locked after the initial adjustment.

(2) A load of 20 pounds is applied to the free end of the lap belt or the lap belt portion of the belt assembly (i.e., the end that is not anchored to the horizontal surface) in the direction away from the retractor. The position of the free end of the belt assembly is recorded.

(3) Within a 30 second period, the 20 pound load is slowly decreased, until the retractor moves to the next locking position. The position of the free end of the belt assembly is recorded again.

(4) The difference between the two positions recorded for the free end of the belt assembly shall be at least 3/4 inch but less than 3 inches.

§4.4 Buses.

§4.4.1 Buses manufactured on or after January 1, 1972 and before September 1, 1990. Each bus manufactured on or after January 1, 1972 and before September 1, 1990, shall meet the requirements of §4.4.1.1 or §4.4.1.2.

§4.4.1.1 First option—complete passenger protection system—driver only. The vehicle shall meet the crash protection requirements of §5, with respect to an anthropomorphic test dummy in the driver's designated seating position, by means that require no action by vehicle occupants.

§4.4.1.2 Second option—belt system—driver only. The vehicle shall, at the driver's designated seating position, have either a Type 1 or a Type 2 seat belt assembly that conforms to §571.209.

§4.4.2 Buses manufactured on or after September 1, 1990. Each bus manufactured on or after September 1, 1990, shall meet the requirements of §4.4.2.1 or §4.4.2.2.

§4.4.2.1 First option—complete passenger protection system—driver only. The vehicle shall meet the crash protection requirements of §5, with respect to an anthropomorphic test dummy in the driver's designated seating position, by means that require no action by vehicle occupants.

§4.4.2.2 Second option—belt system—driver only. The vehicle shall, at the driver's designated seating position, have either a Type 1 or a Type 2 seat belt assembly that conforms to @ 571.209 of this part and §7.2 of this Standard. A Type 1 belt assembly or the pelvic portion of a dual retractor Type 2 belt assembly installed at the driver's seating position shall include either an emergency locking retractor or an automatic locking retractor. If a seat belt assembly installed at the driver's seating position includes an automatic locking retractor for the lap belt or the lap belt portion, that seat belt assembly shall comply with the following:

(a) An automatic locking retractor used at a driver's seating position that has some type of suspension system for the seat shall be attached to the seat structure that moves as the suspension system functions.

(b) The lap belt or lap belt portion of a seat belt assembly equipped with an automatic locking retractor that is installed at the driver's seating position must allow at least 3/4 inch, but less than 3 inches, of webbing movement before retracting webbing to the next locking position.

(c) Compliance with §4.4.2.2(b) of this standard is determined as follows:

(1) The seat belt assembly is buckled and the retractor end of the seat belt assembly is anchored to a horizontal surface. The webbing for the lap belt or lap belt portion of the seat belt assembly is extended to 75 percent of its length and the retractor is locked after the initial adjustment.

(2) A load of 20 pounds is applied to the free end of the lap belt or the lap belt portion of the belt assembly (i.e., the end that is not anchored to the horizontal surface) in the direction away from the retractor. The position of the free end of the belt assembly is recorded.

(3) Within a 30 second period, the 20 pound load is slowly decreased, until the retractor moves to the next locking position. The position of the free end of the belt assembly is recorded again.

(4) The difference between the two positions recorded for the free end of the belt assembly shall be at least 3/4 inch but less than 3 inches.

§4.4.3 Buses manufactured on or after September 1, 1991.

§4.4.3.1 Each bus with a gross vehicle weight rating of more than 10,000 pounds shall comply with the requirements §4.4.2.1 or §4.4.2.2.

§4.4.3.2 Except as provided in §4.4.3.2.2 and §4.4.3.2.3, each bus with a gross vehicle weight rating of 10,000 pounds or less, except a school bus, shall be equipped with an integral Type 2 seat belt assembly at the driver's designated seating position and at the front and every rear forward-facing outboard designated seating position, and with a Type 1 or Type 2 seat belt assembly at all other designated seating positions. Type 2 seat belt assemblies installed in compliance with this requirement shall comply with Standard No. 209 (49 CFR 571.209) and with §7.1 and §7.2 of this standard. If a Type 2 seat belt assembly installed in compliance with this requirement incorporates any webbing tension-relieving device, the vehicle owner's manual shall include the information specified in §7.4.2(b) of this standard for the tension relieving device, and the vehicle shall comply with §7.4.2(c) of this standard.

§4.4.3.2.1 As used in this section, a "rear outboard designated position" means any "outboard designated seating position" (as that term is defined at 49 CFR 571.3) that is rearward of the front seat(s), except any designated seating positions adjacent to a walkway located between the seat and the side of the vehicle, which walkway is designed to allow access to more rearward seating positions.

§4.4.3.2.2 Any rear outboard designated seating position with a seat that can be adjusted to be forward-facing and to face some other direction shall either:

(i) Meet the requirements of §4.4.3.2 with the seat in any position in which it can be occupied while the vehicle is in motion; or

(ii) When the seat is in its forward-facing position, have a Type 2 seat belt assembly with an upper torso restraint that conforms to §7.1 and §7.2 of this standard and that adjusts by means of an emergency locking retractor that conforms with Standard No. 209 (49 CFR 571.209), which upper torso restraint may be detachable at the buckle, and, when the seat is in any position in which it can be occupied while the vehicle is in motion, have a Type 1 seat belt or the pelvic portion of a Type 2 seat belt assembly that conforms to §7.1 and §7.2 of this standard.

§4.4.3.2.3 Any rear outboard designated seating position on a readily removable seat (that is, a seat designed to be easily removed and replaced by means installed by the manufacturer for that purpose) in a vehicle manufactured on or after September 1, 1992 shall meet the requirements of §4.4.3.2 and may use an upper torso belt that detaches at either its upper or lower anchorage point, but not both anchorage points, to meet those requirements. The means for detaching the upper torso belt may use a push-button action.

§4.4.3.3 Each school bus with a gross vehicle weight rating of 10,000 pounds or less shall be equipped with an integral Type 2 seat belt assembly at the driver's designated seating position and at the right front passenger's designated seating position (if any), and with a Type 1 or Type 2 seat belt assembly at all other designated seating positions. Type 2 seat belt assemblies installed in compliance with this requirement shall comply with Standard No. 209 (49 CFR 571.209) and with §7.1 and §7.2 of this standard. The lap belt portion of a Type 2 seat belt assembly installed at the driver's designated seating position and at the right front passenger's designated seating position (if any) shall include either an emergency locking retractor or an automatic locking retractor, which retractor shall not retract webbing to the next locking position until at least 3/4 inch of webbing has moved into the retractor. In determining whether an automatic locking retractor complies with this requirement, the webbing is extended to 75 percent of its length and the retractor is locked after the initial adjustment. If a Type 2 seat belt assembly installed in compliance with this requirement incorporates any webbing tension-relieving device, the vehicle owner's manual shall include the information specified in §7.4.2(b) of this standard for the tension-relieving device, and the vehicle shall comply with §7.4.2(c) of this standard.

§4.4.4 Buses with a GVWR of 8,500 pounds or less and an unloaded vehicle weight of 5,500 pounds or less manufactured on or after September 1, 1994. Each bus with a GVWR of 8,500 pounds or less and an unloaded vehicle weight of 5,500 pounds or less manufactured on or after September 1, 1984 shall comply with the requirements of §4.2.5 and §4.2.6 of this standard, as applicable, for front seating positions, and with the requirements of §4.4.3.2 or §4.4.3.3 of this standard, as applicable, for all rear seating positions.

§4.5 Other general requirements.

§4.5.1 Labeling and driver's manual information. Each vehicle shall have a label setting forth the manufacturer's recommended schedule for the maintenance or replacement, necessary to retain the performance required by this standard, of any crash deployed occupant protection system. The schedule shall be specified by month and year, or in terms of vehicle mileage, or by intervals measured from the date appearing on the vehicle certification label provided pursuant to 49 CFR Part 567. The label shall be permanently affixed to the vehicle within the passenger compartment and lettered in English in block capitals and numerals not less than three thirty-seconds of an inch high. Instructions concerning maintenance or replacement of the system and a description of the functional operation of the system shall be provided with each vehicle, with an appropriate reference on the label. If a vehicle owner's manual is provided, this information shall be included in the manual.

§4.5.2 Readiness indicator. An occupant protection system that deploys in the event of a crash shall have a monitoring system with a readiness indicator. The indicator shall monitor its own readiness and shall be clearly visible from the driver's designated seating position. A list of the elements of the system being monitored by the indicator shall be included with the information furnished in accordance with §4.5.1 but need not be included on the label.

§4.5.3 Automatic belts. Except as provided in §4.5.3.1, a seat belt assembly that requires no action by vehicle occupants (hereinafter referred to as an "automatic belt") may be used to meet the crash protection requirements of any option under §4. and in place of any seat belt assembly otherwise required by that option.

§4.5.3.1 An automatic belt that provides only pelvic restraint may not be used pursuant to §4.5.3 to meet the requirements of an option that requires a Type 2 seat belt assembly.

§4.5.3.2 An automatic belt, furnished pursuant to §4.5.3, that provides both pelvic and upper torso restraint may have either a detachable or non detachable upper torso portion, notwithstanding provisions of the option under which it is furnished.

§4.5.3.3 An automatic belt furnished pursuant to §4.5.3 shall:

(a) Conform to §7.1 and have a single emergency release mechanism whose components are readily accessible to a seated occupant.

(b) In place of a warning system that conforms to §7.3 of this standard, be equipped with the following warning system: At the left front designated seating position (driver's position), a warning system that activates a continuous or intermittent audible signal for a period of not less than 4 seconds and not more than 8 seconds and that activates a continuous or flashing warning light visible to the driver for not less than 60 seconds (beginning when the vehicle ignition switch is moved to the "on" or the "start" position) when condition (A) exists simultaneously with condition (B), and that activates a continuous or flashing warning light, visible to the driver, displaying the identifying symbol for the seat belt telltale shown in Table 2 of Standard No. 101 (49 CFR 571.101), or, at the option of the manufacturer if permitted by Standard No. 101, displaying the words "Fasten Seat Belts" or "Fasten Belts," for as long as condition (A) exists simultaneously with condition (C).

(A) The vehicle's ignition switch is moved to the "on" position or to the "start" position.

(B) The driver's automatic belt is not in use, as determined by the belt latch mechanism not being fastened, or, if the automatic belt is non-detachable, by the emergency release mechanism being in the released position. In the case of motorized automatic belts, the determination of use shall be made once the belt webbing is in its locked protective mode at the anchorage point.

(C) The belt webbing of a motorized automatic belt system is not in its locked, protective mode at the anchorage point.

§4.5.3.4 An automatic belt furnished pursuant to §4.5.3 that is not required to meet the perpendicular frontal crash protection requirements of §5.1 shall conform to the webbing, attachment hardware, and assembly performance requirements of Standard No. 209.

§4.6 Dynamic testing of manual belt systems.

§4.6.1 Each truck and multipurpose passenger vehicle with a GVWR of 8,500 pounds or less and an unloaded weight of less than 5,500 pounds that is manufactured on or after September 1, 1991, and is equipped with a Type 2 seat belt assembly at a front outboard designated seating position pursuant to §4.1.2.3 shall meet the frontal crash protection requirements of §5.1 at those designated seating positions with a test dummy restrained by a Type 2 seat belt assembly that has been adjusted in accordance with §7.4.2. A vehicle shall not be deemed to be in noncompliance with this standard if its manufacturer establishes that it did not have reason to know in the exercise of due care that such vehicle is not in conformity with the requirement of this standard.

§4.6.2 Any manual seat belt assembly subject to the requirements of §5.1 of this standard by virtue of any provision of this standard other than §4.1.2.1(c)(2) does not have to meet the requirements of §4.2(a)-(f) and §4.4 of Standard No. 209 (@ 571.209).

§4.6.3 Any manual seat belt assembly subject to the requirements of §5.1 of this standard by virtue of §4.1.2.1(c)(2) does not have to meet the elongation requirements of §4.2(c), §4.4(a)(2), §4.4(b)(4), and §4.4(b)(5) of Standard No. 209 (@ 571.209).

§5. Occupant crash protection requirements.

§5.1 Vehicles subject to §5.1 shall comply with either §5.1(a) or §5.1(b), or any combination thereof, at the manufacturer's option; except that vehicles manufactured before September 1, 1993 that comply with the requirements of §4.1.2.1(a) by means not including any type of seat belt or inflatable restraint shall comply with §5.1(a).

(a) Impact a vehicle traveling longitudinally forward at any speed, up to and including 30 mph, into a fixed collision barrier that is perpendicular to the line of travel of the vehicle, or at any angle up to 30 degrees in either direction from the perpendicular to the line of travel of the vehicle under the applicable conditions of §8. The test dummy specified in §8.1.8.1 placed at each front outboard designated seating position shall meet the injury criteria of §6.1.1, 6.1.2., 6.1.3, and 6.1.4.

(b) Impact a vehicle traveling longitudinally forward at any speed, up to and including 30 mph, into a fixed collision barrier that is perpendicular to line of travel of the vehicle, or at any angle up to 30 degrees in either direction from the perpendicular to the line of travel of the vehicle, under the applicable conditions of §8. The test dummy specified in §8.1.8.2 placed at each front outboard designated seating position shall meet the injury criteria of §6.2.1, 6.2.2., 6.2.3, 6.2.4, and 6.2.5.

§5.2 Lateral moving barrier crash test.

§5.2.1 Vehicles subject to §5.2 shall comply with either §5.2.1(a) or §5.2.1(b), or any combination thereof, at the manufacturer's option; except that vehicles manufactured before September 1, 1993 that comply with the requirements of §4.1.2.1(c) by means not including any type of seat belt or inflatable restraint shall comply with §5.2.1(a).

(a) Impact a vehicle laterally on either side by a barrier moving at 20 mph under the applicable conditions of §8. The test dummy specified in §8.1.8.1 placed at the front outboard designated seating position adjacent to the impacted side shall meet the injury criteria of §6.1.2 and §6.1.3.

(b) When the vehicle is impacted laterally under the applicable conditions of §8, on either side by a barrier moving at 20 mph, with a test device specified in §8.1.8.2, which is seated at the front outboard designated seating position adjacent to the impacted side, it shall meet the injury criteria of §6.2.2, and §6.2.3.

§5.3 Roll-over. Subject a vehicle to a roll-over test under the applicable condition of §8 in either lateral direction at 30 mph with either, at the manufacturer's option, a test dummy specified in §8.1.8.1 or §8.1.8.2, placed in the front outboard designated seating position on the vehicle's lower side as mounted on the test platform. The test dummy shall meet the injury criteria of either §6.1.1. or §6.2.1.

§6. Injury criteria.

§6.1 Injury criteria for the Part 572, Subpart B, 50th percentile Male Dummy.

§6.1.1 All portions of the test dummy shall be contained within the outer surfaces of the vehicle passenger compartment throughout the test.

§6.1.2 The resultant acceleration at the center of gravity of the head shall be such that the expression:

$$\left[\frac{1}{(t_2 - t_2)}\int_{t_1}^{t_2} adt\right]^{2\ 3} \quad (t_2 - t_2)$$

shall not exceed 1,000 where a is the resultant acceleration expressed as a multiple of g (the acceleration of gravity), and t_1 and t_2 are any two points in time during the crash of the vehicle which are separated by not more than a 36 millisecond time interval.

§6.1.3 The resultant acceleration at the center of gravity of the upper thorax shall not exceed 60 g's, except for intervals whose cumulative duration is not more than 3 milliseconds.

§6.1.4 The compressive force transmitted axially through each upper leg shall not exceed 2250 pounds.

§6.2 Injury Criteria for the Part 572, Subpart E, Hybrid III Test Dummy.

§6.2.1 All portions of the test dummy shall be contained within the outer surfaces of the vehicle passenger compartment throughout the test.

§6.2.2 The resultant acceleration at the center of gravity of the head shall be such that the expression:

$$\left[\frac{1}{(t_2 - t_2)}\int_{t_1}^{t_2} adt\right]^{2\ 3} \quad (t_2 - t_2)$$

shall not exceed 1,000 where a is the resultant acceleration expressed as a multiple of g (the acceleration of gravity), and t1 and t2 are any two points in time during the crash of the vehicle which are separated by not more than a 36 millisecond time interval.

§6.2.3 The resultant acceleration calculated from the output of the thoracic instrumentation shown in drawing 78051-218, revision R incorporated by reference in Part 572, Subpart E of this chapter shall not exceed 60 g's, except for intervals whose cumulative duration is not more than 3 milliseconds.

§6.2.4 Compression deflection of the sternum relative to the spine, as determined by instrumentation shown in drawing 78051-317, revision A incorporated by reference in Part 572, Subpart E of this chapter, shall not exceed 3 inches.

§6.2.5 The force transmitted axially through each upper leg shall not exceed 2250 pounds.

§7. Seat belt assembly requirements.

§7.1 Adjustment.

§7.1.1 Except as specified in §7.1.1.1 and §7.1.1.2, the lap belt of any seat belt assembly furnished in accordance with §4.1.2 shall adjust by means of any emergency-locking or automatic-locking retractor that conforms to @ 571.209 to fit persons whose dimensions range from those of a 50th percentile 6-year-old child to those of a 95th percentile adult male and the upper torso restraint shall adjust by means of an emergency-locking retractor or a manual adjusting device that conforms to @ 571.209 to fit persons whose dimensions range from those of a 5th percentile adult female to those of a 95th percentile adult male, with the seat in any position, the seat back in the manufacturer's nominal design riding position, and any adjustable anchorages adjusted to the manufacturer's nominal design position for a 50th percentile adult male occupant. However, an upper torso restraint furnished in accordance with §4.1.2.3.1(a) shall adjust by means of an emergency-locking retractor that conforms to @ 571.209.

§7.1.1.1 A seat belt assembly installed at the driver's seating position shall adjust to fit persons whose dimensions range from those of a 5th-percentile adult female to those of a 95th-percentile adult male.

§7.1.1.2 (a) A seat belt assembly installed in a motor vehicle other than a forward control vehicle at any designated seating position other than the outboard positions of the front and second seats shall adjust either by a retractor as specified in §7.1.1 or by a manual adjusting device that conforms to @ 571.209.

(b) A seat belt assembly installed in a forward control vehicle at any designated seating position other than the front outboard seating positions shall adjust either by a retractor as specified in §7.1.1 or by a manual adjusting device that conforms to @ 571.209.

§7.1.1.3 A Type 1 lap belt or the lap belt portion of any Type 2 seat belt assembly installed at any forward-facing outboard designated seating position of a vehicle with a gross vehicle weight rating of 10,000 pounds or less to comply with a requirement of this standard, except walk-in van-type vehicles and school buses, shall meet the requirements of §7.1 by means of an emergency locking retractor that conforms to Standard No. 209 (49 CFR 571.209).

§7.1.1.4 Notwithstanding the other provisions of §7.1—§7.1.1.3, emergency-locking retractors on belt assemblies located in positions other than front outboard designated seating positions may be equipped with a manual webbing adjustment device capable of causing the retractor that adjusts the lap belt to lock when the belt is buckled.

§7.1.2 The intersection of the upper torso belt with the lap belt in any Type 2 seat belt assembly furnished in accordance with §4.1.1 or §4.1.2, with the upper torso manual adjusting device, if provided, adjusted in accordance with the manufacturer's instructions, shall be at least 6 inches from the front vertical center line of a 50th-percentile adult male occupant, measured along the center line of the lap belt, with the seat in its rearmost and lowest adjustable position and with the seat back in the manufacturer's nominal design riding position.

§7.1.3 The weights and dimensions of the vehicle occupants referred to in this standard are as follows:

	50th-percentile 6-year-old child	5th-percentile adult female	50th-percentile adult male	95th-percentile adult male
Weight	47.3 pounds	102 pounds	164 pounds ± 3	215 pounds
Erect sitting height	25.4 inches	30.9 inches	35.7 inches ± .1	38 inches
Hip breadth (sitting)	8.4 inches	12.8 inches	14.7 inches ± .7	16.5 inches
Hip circumference (sitting)	23.9 inches	36.4 inches	42 inches	47.2 inches
Waist circumference (sitting)	20.8 inches	23.6 inches	32 inches ± .6	42.5 inches
Chest depth	———	7.5 inches	9.3 inches ± .2	10.5 inches
Chest circumference:				
(nipple)	———	30.5 inches	———	———
(upper)	———	29.8 inches	37.4 inches ± .6	44.5 inches
(lower)	———	26.6 inches	———	———

§7.2 Latch mechanism. A seat belt assembly installed in any vehicle, except an automatic belt assembly, shall have a latch mechanism —

(a) Whose components are accessible to a seated occupant in both the stowed and operational positions;

(b) That releases both the upper torso restraint and the lap belt simultaneously, if the assembly has a lap belt and an upper torso restraint that require unlatching for release of the occupant; and

(c) That releases at a single point by a push-button action.

§7.3 (a) A seat belt assembly provided at the driver's seating position shall be equipped with a warning system that, at the option of the manufacturer, either—

(1) Activates a continuous or intermittent audible signal for a period of not less than 4 seconds and not more than 8 seconds and that activates a continuous or flashing warning light visible to the driver displaying the identifying symbol for the seat belt telltale shown in Table 2 of FMVSS 101 or, at the option of the manufacturer if permitted by FMVSS 101, displaying the words "Fasten Seat Belts" or "Fasten Belts", for not less than 60 seconds (beginning when the vehicle ignition switch is moved to the "on" or the "start" position) when condition (b) exists simultaneously with condition (c), or that

(2) Activates, for a period of not less than 4 seconds and not more than 8 seconds (beginning when the vehicle ignition switch is moved to the "on" or the "start" position), a continuous or flashing warning light visible to the driver, displaying the identifying symbol of the seat belt telltale shown in Table 2 of FMVSS 101 or, at the option of the manufacturer if permitted by FMVSS 101, displaying the words "Fasten Seat Belts" or "Fasten Belts", when condition (b) exists, and a continuous or intermittent audible signal when condition (b) exists simultaneously with condition (c).

(b) The vehicle's ignition switch is moved to the "on" position or to the "start" position.

(c) The driver's lap belt is not in use, as determined, at the option of the manufacturer, either by the belt latch mechanism not being fastened, or by the belt not being extended at least 4 inches from its stowed position.

§7.4 Seat belt comfort and convenience.

(a) Automatic seat belts. Automatic seat belts installed in any vehicle, other than walk-in van-type vehicles, which has a gross vehicle weight rating of 10,000 pounds or less, and which is manufactured on or after September 1, 1986, shall meet the requirements of §7.4.1, §7.4.2, and §7.4.3.

(b) Manual seat belts.

(1) Vehicles manufactured after September 1, 1986. Manual seat belts installed in any vehicle, other than manual Type 2 belt systems installed in the front outboard seating positions in passenger cars or manual belts in walk-in van-type vehicles, which have a gross vehicle weight rating of 10,000 pounds or less, shall meet the requirements of §7.4.3, §7.4.4, §7.4.5, and §7.4.6.

(2) Vehicles manufactured after September 1, 1989.

(i) If the automatic restraint requirement of §4.1.4 is rescinded pursuant to §4.1.5, then manual seat belts installed in a passenger car shall meet the requirements of §7.1.1.3(a), §7.4.2, §7.4.3, §7.4.4, §7.4.5, and §7.4.6.

(ii) Manual seat belts installed in a bus, multipurpose passenger vehicle and truck with a gross vehicle weight rating of 10,000 pounds or less, except for walk-in van-type vehicles, shall meet the requirements of §7.4.3, §7.4.4, §7.4.5, and §7.4.6.

§7.4.1 Convenience hooks. Any manual convenience hook or other device that is provided to stow seat belt webbing to facilitate entering or exiting the vehicle shall automatically release the webbing when the automatic belt system is otherwise operational and shall remain in the released mode for as long as (a) exists simultaneously with (b), or, at the manufacturer's option, for as long as (a) exists simultaneously with (c) —

(a) The vehicle ignition switch is moved to the "on" or "start" position;

(b) The vehicle's drive train is engaged;

(c) The vehicle's parking brake is in the released mode (non engaged).

§7.4.2 Webbing tension-relieving device. Each vehicle with an automatic seat belt assembly or with a Type 2 manual seat belt assembly that must meet the occupant crash protection requirements of §5.1 of this standard installed at a front outboard designated seating position, and each vehicle with a Type 2 manual seat belt assembly installed at a rear outboard designated seating position in compliance with a requirement of this standard, that has either automatic or manual tension-relieving devices permitting the introduction of slack in the webbing of the shoulder belt (e.g., "comfort clips" or "window-shade" devices) shall:

(a) Comply with the requirements of §5.1 with the shoulder belt webbing adjusted to introduce the maximum amount of slack recommended by the vehicle manufacturer pursuant to §7.4.2(b).

(b) Have a section in the vehicle owner's manual that explains how the tension-relieving device works and specifies the maximum amount of slack (in inches) recommended by the vehicle manufacturer to be introduced into the shoulder belt under normal use conditions. The explanation shall also warn that introducing slack beyond the amount specified by the manufacturer could significantly reduce the effectiveness of the shoulder belt in a crash; and

(c) Have, except for open-body vehicles with no doors, an automatic means to cancel any shoulder belt slack introduced into the belt system by a tension-relieving device. In the case of an automatic safety belt system, cancellation of the tension-relieving device shall occur each time the adjacent vehicle door is opened. In the case of a manual seat belt required to meet §5.1, cancellation of the tension-relieving device shall occur, at the manufacturer's option, either each time the adjacent door is opened or each time the latchplate is released from the buckle. In the case of a Type 2 manual seat belt assembly installed at a rear outboard designated seating position, cancellation of the tension-relieving device shall occur, at the manufacturer's option either each time the door designed to allow the occupant of that seating position entry and egress of the vehicle is opened or each time the latchplate is released from the buckle. In the case of open-body vehicles with no doors, cancellation of the tension-relieving device may be done by a manual means.

§7.4.3 Belt contact force. Except for manual or automatic seat belt assemblies that incorporate a webbing tension-relieving device, the upper torso webbing of any seat belt assembly shall not exert more than 0.7 pounds of contact force when measured normal to and one inch from the chest of an anthropomorphic test dummy, positioned in accordance with either §10 or §11 of this standard in the seating position for which that seat belt assembly is provided, at the point where the center line of the torso belt crosses the midsagittal line on the dummy's chest.

§7.4.4 Latchplate access. Any seat belt assembly latchplate that is located outboard of a front outboard seating position in accordance with §4.1.2 shall also be located within the outboard reach envelope of either the outboard arm or the inboard arm described in §10.6 of this standard and, in the case of a Part 572 Subpart B test dummy, Exhibit 3-3a of this standard, or, in the case of a Part 572 Subpart E test dummy, Exhibit 3-3b of this standard, when the latchplate is in its normal stowed position and any adjustable anchorages are adjusted to the manufacturer's nominal design position for a 50th percentile male occupant. There shall be sufficient clearance between the vehicle seat and the side of the vehicle interior to allow the test block defined in Exhibit 3-4 unhindered transit to the latchplate or buckle.

§7.4.5 Retraction. When tested under the conditions of §8.1.2 and §8.1.3, with anthropomorphic test dummies whose arms have been removed and which are positioned in accordance with either §10 or §11, or any combination thereof, in the front outboard designated seating positions and restrained by the belt systems for those positions, the torso and lap belt webbing of any of those seat belt systems shall automatically retract to a stowed position either when the adjacent vehicle door is in the open position and the seat belt latchplate is released, or, at the option of the manufacturer, when the latchplate is released. That stowed position shall prevent any part of the webbing or hardware from being pinched when the adjacent vehicle door is closed. A belt system with a tension-relieving device in an open-bodied vehicle with no doors shall fully retract when the tension/relieving device is deactivated. For the purpose of the retraction requirement, outboard armrests, which are capable of being stowed, on vehicle seats shall be placed in their stowed positions.

§7.4.6 Seat belt guides and hardware.

§7.4.6.1 (a) Any manual seat belt assembly whose webbing is designed to pass through the seat cushion or between the seat cushion and seat back shall be designed to maintain one of the following three seat belt parts (the seat belt latchplate, the buckle, or the seat belt webbing) on top of or above the seat cushion under normal conditions (i.e., conditions other than when belt hardware is intentionally pushed behind the seat by a vehicle occupant). In addition, the remaining two seat belt parts must be accessible under normal conditions.

(b) The requirements of §7.4.6.1(a) do not apply to: (1) seats whose seat cushions are movable so that the seat back serves a function other than seating, (2) seats which are removable, or (3) seats which are movable so that the space formerly occupied by the seat can be used for a secondary function.

§7.4.6.2 The buckle and latchplate of a manual seat belt assembly subject to §7.4.6.1 shall not pass through the guides or conduits provided for in §7.4.6.1 and fall behind the seat when the events listed below occur in the order specified: (a) The belt is completely retracted or, if the belt is non retractable, the belt is unlatched; (b) the seat is moved to any position to which it is designed to be adjusted; and (c) the seat back, if foldable, is folded forward as far as possible and then moved backward into position. The inboard receptacle end of a seat belt assembly installed at a front outboard designated seating position shall be accessible with the center arm rest in any position to which it can be adjusted (without having to move the armrest).

§8. Test conditions.

§8.1 General conditions. The following conditions apply to the frontal, lateral, and roll-over tests.

§8.1.1 Except as provided in paragraph (c) of §8.1.1, the vehicle, including test devices and instrumentation, is loaded as follows:

(a) Passenger cars. A passenger car is loaded to its unloaded vehicle weight plus its rated cargo and luggage capacity weight, secured in the luggage area, plus the weight of the necessary anthropomorphic test devices.

(b) Multipurpose passenger vehicles, trucks, and buses. A multipurpose passenger vehicle, truck, or bus is loaded to its unloaded vehicle weight plus 300 pounds or its rated cargo and luggage capacity weight, whichever is less, secured in the load carrying area and distributed as nearly as possible in proportion to its gross axle weight ratings, plus the weight of the necessary anthropomorphic test devices. For the purposes of @ 8.1.1, unloaded vehicle weight does not include the weight of work-performing accessories. Vehicles are tested to a maximum unloaded vehicle weight of 5,500 pounds.

(c) Fuel system capacity. With the test vehicle on a level surface, pump the fuel from the vehicle's fuel tank and then operate the engine until it stops. Then, add Stoddard solvent to the test vehicle's fuel tank in an amount which is equal to not less than 92 and not more than 94 percent of the fuel tank's usable capacity stated by the vehicle's manufacturer. In addition, add the amount of Stoddard solvent needed to fill the entire fuel system from the fuel tank through the engine's induction system.

(d) Vehicle test attitude. Determine the distance between a level surface and a standard reference point on the test vehicle's body, directly above each wheel opening, when the vehicle is in its "as delivered" condition. The "as delivered" condition is the vehicle as received at the test site, with 100 percent of all fluid capacities and all tires inflated to the manufacturer's specifications as listed on the vehicle's tire placard. Determine the distance between the same level surface and the same standard reference points in the vehicle's "fully loaded condition." The "fully loaded condition" is the test vehicle loaded in accordance with §8.1.1 (a) or (b), as applicable. The load placed in the cargo area shall be center over the longitudinal center line of the vehicle. The pretest vehicle attitude shall be equal to either the as delivered or fully loaded attitude or between the as delivered attitude and the fully loaded attitude.

§8.1.2 Adjustable seats are in the adjustment position midway between the forward most and rearmost positions, and if separately adjustable in a vertical direction, are at the lowest position. If an adjustment position does not exist midway between the forward most and rearmost positions, the closest adjustment position to the rear of the midpoint is used.

§8.1.3 Place adjustable seat backs in the manufacturer's nominal design riding position in the manner specified by the manufacturer. Place any adjustable anchorages at the manufacturer's nominal design position for a 50th percentile adult male occupant. Place each adjustable head restraint in its highest adjustment position. Adjustable lumbar supports are positioned so that the lumbar support is in its lowest adjustment position.

§8.1.4 Adjustable steering controls are adjusted so that the steering wheel hub is at the geometric center of the locus it describes when it is moved through its full range of driving positions.

§8.1.5 Movable vehicle windows and vents are, at the manufacturer's option, placed in the fully closed position.

§8.1.6 Convertibles and open-body type vehicles have the top, if any, in place in the closed passenger compartment configuration.

§8.1.7 Doors are fully closed and latched but not locked.

§8.1.8 Anthropomorphic test dummies.

§8.1.8.1 The anthropomorphic test dummies used for evaluation of occupant protection systems manufactured pursuant to applicable portions of paragraphs §4.1.2, 4.1.3, and §4.1.4 shall conform to the requirements of Subpart B of Part 572 of this Chapter.

§8.1.8.2 Anthropomorphic test devices used for the evaluation of occupant protection systems manufactured pursuant to applicable portions of paragraphs §4.1.2, §4.1.3, and §4.1.4 shall conform to the requirements of Subpart E of Part 572 of this Chapter.

§8.1.9.1 Each Part 572, Subpart B test dummy specified in §8.1.8.1 is clothed in formfitting cotton stretch garments with short sleeves and mid calf length pants. Each foot of the test dummy is equipped with a size 11EE shoe which meets the configuration size, sole, and heel thickness specifications of MIL-S 131192 and weighs 1.25 X #0.2 pounds.

§8.1.9.2 Each Part 572, Subpart E test dummy specified in §8.1.8.2 is clothed in formfitting cotton stretch garments with short sleeves and mid calf length pants specified in drawings 78051-292 and -293 incorporated by reference in Part 572, Subpart E of this chapter, respectively or their equivalents. A size 11EE shoe specified in drawings 78051-294 (left) and 78051-295 (right) or their equivalents is placed on each foot of the test dummy.

§8.1.10 Limb joints are set at lg., barely restraining the weight of the limb when extended horizontally. Leg joints are adjusted with the torso in the supine position.

§8.1.11 Instrumentation does not affect the motion of dummies during impact or roll-over.

§8.1.12 Temperature of the test dummy.

§8.1.12.1 The stabilized temperature of the test dummy specified by §8.1.8.1 is at any level between 66° F and 78° F.

§8.1.12.2 The stabilized temperature of the test dummy specified by §8.1.8.2 is at any level between 69° F and 72° F.

§8.2 Lateral moving barrier crash test conditions. The following conditions apply to the lateral moving barrier crash test.

§8.2.1 The moving barrier, including the impact surface, supporting structure, and carriage, weighs 4,000 pounds.

§8.2.2 The impact surface of the barrier is a vertical, rigid, flat rectangle, 78 inches wide and 60 inches high, perpendicular to its direction of movement, with its lower edge horizontal and 5 inches above the ground surface.

§8.2.3 During the entire impact sequence the barrier undergoes no significant amount of dynamic or static deformation, and absorbs no significant portion of the energy resulting from the impact, except for energy that results in translational rebound movement of the barrier.

§8.2.4 During the entire impact sequence the barrier is guided so that it travels in a straight line, with no significant lateral, vertical or rotational movement.

§8.2.5 The concrete surface upon which the vehicle is tested is level, rigid and of uniform construction, with a skid number of 75 when measured in accordance with American Society for Testing and Materials Method E-274-65T at 40 m.p.h., omitting water delivery as specified in paragraph 7.1 of that method.

§8.2.6 The tested vehicle's brakes are disengaged and the transmission is in neutral.

§8.2.7 The barrier and the test vehicle are positioned so that at impact—

(a) The vehicle is at rest in its normal attitude;

(b) The barrier is traveling in a direction perpendicular to the longitudinal axis of the vehicle at 20 m.p.h.; and

(c) A vertical plane through the geometric center of the barrier impact surface and perpendicular to that surface passes through the driver's seating reference point in the tested vehicle.

§8.3 Roll-over test conditions. The following conditions apply to the roll-over test.

§8.3.1 The tested vehicle's brakes are disengaged and the transmission is in neutral.

§8.3.2 The concrete surface on which the test is conducted is level, rigid, of uniform construction, and of a sufficient size that the vehicle remains on it throughout the entire roll-over cycle. It has a skid number of 75 when measured in accordance with American Society for Testing and Materials Method E-274-65T at 40 m.p.h. omitting water delivery as specified in paragraph 7.1 of that method.

§8.3.3 The vehicle is placed on a device, similar to that illustrated in Exhibit 3-2, having a platform in the form of a flat, rigid plane at an angle of 23° from the horizontal. At the lower edge of the platform is an unyielding flange, perpendicular to the platform with a height of 4 inches and a length sufficient to hold in place the tires that rest against it. The intersection of the inner face of the flange with the upper face of the platform is 9 inches above the roll-over surface. No other restraints are used to hold the vehicle in position during the deceleration of the platform and the departure of the vehicle.

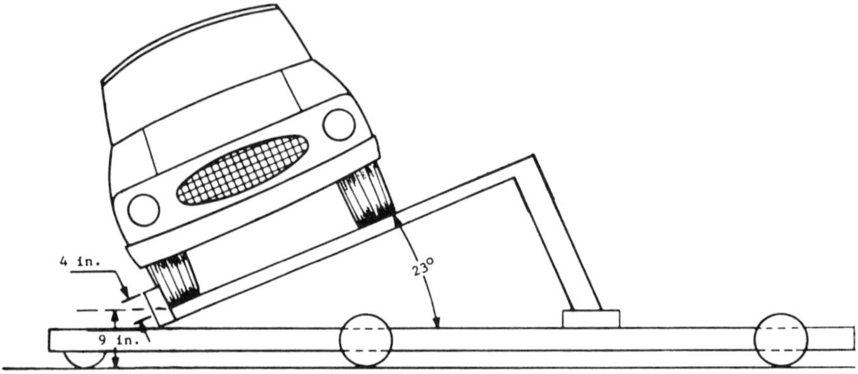

Exhibit 3-3 *Typical device for roll-over test*

§8.3.4 With the vehicle on the test platform, the test devices remain as nearly as possible in the posture specified in §8.1.

§8.3.5 Before the deceleration pulse, the platform is moving horizontally, and perpendicularly to the longitudinal axis of the vehicle, at a constant speed of 30 m.p.h. for a sufficient period of time for the vehicle to become motionless relative to the platform.

§8.3.6 The platform is decelerated from 30 to 0 m.p.h. in a distance of not more than 3 feet, without change of direction and without transverse or rotational movement during the deceleration of the platform and the departure of the vehicle. The deceleration rate is at least 20g for a minimum of 0.04 seconds.

§9. Pressure vessels and explosive devices.

§9.1 Pressure vessels. A pressure vessel that is continuously pressurized shall conform to the requirements of @ 178.65-2, 178.65-

6(b), 178.65-7, 178.65-9 (a) and (b), and 178.65-10 of this title. It shall not leak or evidence visible distortion when tested in accordance with @ 178.65-11(a) of this title and shall not fail in any of the ways enumerated in @ 178.65-11(b) of this title when hydrostatically tested to destruction. It shall not crack when flattened in accordance with @ 178.65-12(a) of this title to the limit specified in @ 178.65-12(a)(4) of this title.

§9.2 Explosive devices. An explosive device shall not exhibit any of the characteristics prohibited by @ 173.51 of this title. All explosive material shall be enclosed in a structure that is capable of containing the explosive energy without sudden release of pressure except through overpressure relief devices or parts designed to release the pressure during actuation.

§10. Test dummy positioning procedures. Position a test dummy, conforming to Subpart B of Part 572 of this chapter, in each front outboard seating position of a vehicle as set forth below in §10 through §10.9. Each test dummy is restrained during the crash tests of §5 as follows:

(a) In a vehicle equipped with automatic restraints at each front outboard designated seating position that is certified by its manufacturer as meeting the requirements of §4.1.2.1 (a) and (c)(1), each test dummy is not restrained during the frontal test of §5.1, the lateral test of §5.2 and the roll-over test of §5.3 by any means that requires occupant action.

(b)(1) In a vehicle equipped with an automatic restraint at each front outbound seating position that is certified by its manufacturer as meeting the requirements of §4.1.2.1 (a) and (c)(2), each test dummy is not restrained during one frontal test of §5.1 by any means that require occupant action. If the vehicle has a manual seat belt provided by the manufacturer to comply with the requirements of §4.1.2.1(c), then a second frontal test is conducted in accordance with §5.1 and each test dummy is restrained both by the automatic restraint system and the manual seat belt, adjusted in accordance with §10.9.

(2) In a vehicle equipped with an automatic restraint only at the driver's designated seating position, pursuant to

§4.1.3.4(a)(2), that is certified by its manufacturer as meeting the requirements of §4.1.2.1(a) and (c)(2), the driver test dummy is not restrained during one frontal test of §5.1 by any means that require occupant action. If the vehicle also has a manual seat belt provided by the manufacturer to comply with the requirements of §4.1.2.1(c), then a second frontal test is conducted in accordance with §5.1 and the driver test dummy is restrained both by the automatic restraint system and the manual seat belt, adjusted in accordance with §10.9. At the option of the manufacturer, a passenger test dummy can be placed in the right front outboard designated seating position during the testing required by this section. If a passenger test dummy is present, it shall be restrained by a manual seat belt, adjusted in accordance with §10.9.

(c) In a vehicle equipped with a manual belt at the front outboard designated seating positions that is certified by its manufacturer to meet the requirements of §4.6, each test dummy is restrained by the manual safety belts, adjusted in accordance with §10.9, installed at each front outboard seating positions.

§10.1 Vehicle equipped with front bucket seats. Place the test dummy's torso against the seat back and its upper legs against the seat cushion to the extent permitted by placement of the test dummy's feet in accordance with the appropriate paragraph of §10. Center the test dummy on the seat cushion of the bucket seat and set its midsagittal plane so that it is vertical and parallel to the center line of the seat cushion.

§10.1.1 Driver position placement. (a) Initially set the knees of the test dummy 14 1/2 inches apart, measured between the outer surfaces of the knee pivot bolt heads, with the left outer surface 5.9 inches from the midsagittal plane of the test dummy.

(b) Rest the right foot of the test dummy on the undepressed accelerator pedal with the rearmost point of the heel on the floor pan in the plane of the pedal. If the foot cannot be placed on the accelerator pedal, set it initially perpendicular to the lower leg and place it as far forward as possible in the direction of the pedal center line with the rearmost point of the heel resting on the floor pan. Except as prevented by contact with a vehicle surface, place the right leg so that the upper and lower leg center lines fall, as close as possible, in a vertical plane without inducing torso movement.

(c) Place the left foot on the toe board with the rearmost point of the heel resting on the floor pan as close as possible to the point of intersection of the planes described by the toe board and the floor pan and not on the wheel well projection. If the foot cannot be positioned on the toe board, set it initially perpendicular to the lower leg and place it as far forward as possible with the heel resting on the floor pan. If necessary to avoid contact with the vehicle's brake or clutch pedal, rotate the test dummy's left foot about the lower leg. If there is still pedal interference, rotate the left leg outboard about the hip the minimum distance necessary to avoid the pedal interference. Except as prevented by contact with a vehicle surface, place the left leg so that the upper and lower leg center lines fall, as close as possible, in a vertical plane. For vehicles with a foot rest that does not elevate the left foot above the level of the right foot, place the left foot on the foot rest so that the upper and lower leg center lines fall in a vertical plane.

§10.1.2 Passenger position placement.

§10.1.2.1 Vehicles with a flat floor pan/toe board. (a) Initially set the knees 11 3/4 inches apart, measured between the outer surfaces of the knee pivot bolt heads.

(b) Place the right and left feet on the vehicle's toe board with the heels resting on the floor pan as close as possible to the intersection point with the toe board. If the feet cannot be placed flat on the toe board, set them perpendicular to the lower leg center lines and place them as far forward as possible with the heels resting on the floor pan.

(c) Place the right and left legs so that the upper and lower leg center lines fall in vertical longitudinal planes.

§10.1.2.2 Vehicles with wheel house projections in passenger compartment. (a) Initially set the knees 11 3/4 inches apart, measured between the outer surfaces of the knee pivot bolt heads.

(b) Place the right and left feet in the well of the floor pan/toe board and not on the wheel house projection. If the feet cannot be placed flat on the toe board, initially set them perpendicular to the lower leg center lines and then place them as far forward as possible with the heels resting on the floor pan.

(c) If it is not possible to maintain vertical and longitudinal planes through the upper and lower leg center lines for each leg, then place the left leg so that its upper and lower center lines fall, as closely as possible, in a vertical longitudinal plane and place the right leg so that its upper and lower leg center lines fall, as closely as possible, in a vertical plane.

§10.2 Vehicle equipped with bench seating. Place the test dummy's torso against the seat back and its upper legs against the seat cushion, to the extent permitted by placement of the test dummy's feet in accordance with the appropriate paragraph of §10.1.

§10.2.1 Driver position placement. Place the test dummy at the left front outboard designated seating position so that its midsagittal plane is vertical and parallel to the center line of the vehicle and so that the midsagittal plane of the test dummy passes through the center of the steering wheel rim. Place the legs, knees, and feet of the test dummy as specified in §10.1.1.

§10.2.2 Passenger position placement. Place the test dummy at the right front outboard designated seating position so that the midsagittal plane of the test dummy is vertical and longitudinal, and the same distance from the vehicle's longitudinal center line as the midsagittal plane of the test dummy at the driver's position. Place the legs, knees, and feet of the test dummy as specified in §10.1.2.

§10.3 Initial test dummy hand and arm placement. With the test dummy at its designated seating position as specified by the appropriate requirements of §10.1 or §10.2, place the upper arms against the seat back and tangent to the side of the upper torso. Place the lower arms and palms against the outside of the upper legs.

§10.4 Test dummy settling.

§10.4.1 Test dummy vertical upward displacement. Slowly lift the test dummy parallel to the seat back plane until the test dummy's buttocks no longer contact the seat cushion or until there is test dummy head contact with the vehicle's headlining.

§10.4.2 Lower torso force application. Apply a rearward force of 50 pounds against the center of the test dummy's lower torso in a horizontal direction. The line of force application shall be 6 1/2 inches above the bottom surface of the test dummy's buttocks.

§10.4.3 Test dummy vertical downward displacement. Remove as much of the 50 pound force as necessary to allow the test dummy to return downward to the seat cushion by its own weight.

§10.4.4 Test dummy upper torso rocking. Apply a 10 to 15 pound horizontal rearward force to the test dummy's lower torso. Then apply a horizontal forward force to the test dummy's shoulders sufficient to flex the upper torso forward until its back no longer contacts the seat back. Rock the test dummy from side to side 3 or 4 times so that the test dummy's spine is at any angle from the vertical in the 14 to 16 degree range at the extremes of each rocking movement.

§10.4.5 Test dummy upper torso force application. While maintaining the 10 to 15 pound horizontal rearward force applied in §10.4.4 and with the test dummy's midsagittal plane vertical, push the upper torso back against the seat back with a force of 50 pounds applied in a horizontal rearward direction along a line that is coincident with the test dummy's midsagittal plane and 18 inches above the bottom surface of the test dummy's buttocks.

§10.5 Belt adjustment for dynamic testing. With the test dummy at its designated seating position as specified by the appropriate requirements of §8.1.2, §8.1.3 and §10.1 through §10.4, place and adjust the safety belt as specified below.

§10.5.1 Manual safety belts. Place the Type 1 or Type 2 manual belt around the test dummy and fasten the latch. Pull the Type 1 belt webbing out of the retractor and allow it to retract; repeat this operation four times. Remove all slack from the lap belt portion of a Type 2 belt.

Pull the upper torso webbing out of the retractor and allow it to retract; repeat this operation four times so that the excess webbing in the shoulder belt is removed by the retractive force of the retractor. Apply a 2 to 4 pound tension load to the lap belt of a single retractor system by pulling the upper torso belt adjacent to the latchplate. In the case of a dual retractor system, apply a 2 to 4 pound tension load by pulling the lap belt adjacent to its retractor. Measure the tension load as close as possible to the same location where the force was applied. After the tension load has been applied, ensure that the upper torso belt lies flat on the test dummy's shoulder.

§10.5.2 Automatic safety belts. Ensure that the upper torso belt lies flat on the test dummy's shoulder after the automatic belt has been placed on the test dummy.

§10.5.3 Belts with tension-relieving devices. If the automatic or dynamically-tested manual safety belt system is equipped with a tension-relieving device, introduce the maximum amount of slack into the upper torso belt that is recommended by the manufacturer for normal use in the owner's manual for the vehicle.

§10.6 Placement of test dummy arms and hands. With the test dummy positioned as specified by §10.4 and without inducing torso movement, place the arms, elbows, and hands of the test dummy, as appropriate for each designated seating position in accordance with §10.6.1 or §10.6.2. Following placement of the arms, elbows and hands, remove the force applied against the lower half of the torso.

§10.6.1 Driver's position. Move the upper and the lower arms of the test dummy at the driver's position to their fully outstretched position in the lowest possible orientation. Push each arm rearward permitting bending at the elbow, until the palm of each hand contacts the outer part of the rim of the steering wheel at its horizontal center line. Place the test dummy's thumbs over the steering wheel rim and position the upper and lower arm center lines as close as possible in a vertical plane without inducing torso movement. The thumbs shall be over the steering wheel rim and are lightly taped to the steering wheel rim so that if the hand of the test dummy is pushed upward by a force of not less than 2 pounds and not more than 5 pounds, the tape shall release the hand from the steering wheel rim.

§10.6.2 Passenger position. Move the upper and the lower arms of the test dummy at the passenger position to the fully outstretched position in the lowest possible orientation. Push each arm rearward, permitting bending at the elbow, until the upper arm contracts the seat back and is tangent to the upper part of the side of the torso, the palm contacts the outside of the thigh, and the little finger is barely in contact with the seat cushion.

§10.7 Repositioning of feet and legs. After the test dummy has been settled in accordance with §10.4, the safety belt system has been positioned, if necessary, in accordance with §10.5, and the arms and hands of the test dummy have been positioned in accordance with §10.6, reposition the feet and legs of the test dummy, if necessary, so that the feet and legs meet the applicable requirements of §10.1 or §10.2.

§10.8 Test dummy positioning for latchplate access. The reach envelopes specified in §7.4.4 are obtained by positioning a test dummy in the driver's seat or passenger's seat in its forward most adjustment position. Attach the lines for the inboard and outboard arms to the test dummy as described in Exhibit 3-3 of this standard. Extend each line backward and outboard to generate the compliance arcs of the outboard reach envelope of the test dummy's arms.

§10.9 Test dummy positioning for belt contact force.

§10.9.1 Vehicles manufactured before September 1, 1987. To determine compliance with §7.4.3 of this standard, a manufacturer may use, at its option, either the test procedure of §10.9.1 or the test procedure of §10.9.2. Position the test dummy in the vehicle in accordance with the appropriate requirements specified in §10.1 or §10.2 and under the conditions of §8.1.2 and §8.1.3. Fasten the latch and pull the belt webbing three inches from the dummy's chest and release until the webbing is within one inch of the test dummy's chest and measure the belt contact force.

§10.9.2 Vehicles manufactured on or after September 1, 1987. To determine compliance with §7.4.3 of this standard, position the test dummy in the vehicle in accordance with the appropriate requirements specified in §10.1 or §10.2 and under the conditions of §8.1.2 and §8.1.3. Close the vehicle's adjacent door, pull either 12 inches of belt webbing or the maximum available amount of belt webbing, whichever is less, from the retractor and then release it, allowing the belt webbing to return to the dummy's chest. Fasten the latch and pull the belt webbing three inches from the test dummy's chest and release until the webbing is within one inch of the test dummies chest and measure the belt contact force.

§11. Positioning Procedure for the Part 572 Subpart E Test Dummy.

§11.1 Head. The transverse instrumentation platform of the head shall be horizontal within 1/2 degree. To level the head of the test dummy, the following sequences must be followed. First, adjust the position of the H point within the limits set forth in §11.4.3.1 to level the transverse instrumentation platform of the head of the test dummy. If the transverse instrumentation platform of the head is still not level, then adjust the pelvic angle of the test dummy within the limits specified in §11.4.3.2 of this standard. If the transverse instrumentation platform of the head is still not level, then adjust the neck bracket of the dummy the minimum amount necessary from the non-adjusted "0" setting to ensure that the transverse instrumentation platform of the head is horizontal within 1/2 degree. The test dummy shall remain within the limits specified in §11.4.3.1 and §11.4.3.2 after any adjustment of the neck bracket.

§11.2.1 The driver's upper arms shall be adjacent to the torso with the center lines as close to a vertical plane as possible.

§11.2.2 The passenger's upper arms shall be in contact with the seat back and the sides of torso.

§11.3 Hands.

§11.3.1 The palms of the driver test dummy shall be in contact with the outer part of the steering wheel rim at the rim's horizontal center line. The thumbs shall be over the steering wheel rim and shall be lightly taped to the steering wheel rim so that if the hand of the test dummy is pushed upward by a force of not less than 2 pounds and not more than 5 pounds, the tape shall release the hand from the steering wheel rim.

§11.3.2 The palms of the passenger test dummy shall be in contact with outside of thigh. The little finger shall be in contact with the seat cushion.

§11.4 Torso.

§11.4.1 In vehicles equipped with bench seats, the upper torso of the driver and passenger test dummies shall rest against the seat back. The midsagittal plane of the driver dummy shall be vertical and parallel to the vehicle's longitudinal center line, and pass through the center of the steering wheel rim. The midsagittal plane of the passenger dummy shall be vertical and parallel to the vehicle's longitudinal center line and the same distance from the vehicle's longitudinal center line as the midsagittal plane of the driver dummy.

§11.4.2 In vehicles equipped with bucket seats, the upper torso of the driver and passenger test dummies shall rest against the seat back. The midsagittal plane of the driver and the passenger dummy shall be vertical and shall coincide with the longitudinal center line of the bucket seat.

§11.4.3 Lower Torso.

§11.4.3.1 H-point. The H-point of the driver and passenger test dummies shall coincide within 1/2 inch in the vertical dimension and 1/2 inch in the horizontal dimension of a point 1/4 inch below the position of the H-point determined by using the equipment and procedures specified in SAE J826 (Apr 80) except that the length of the lower leg and thigh segments of the H-point machine shall be adjusted to 16.3 and 15.8 inches, respectively, instead of the 50th percentile values specified in Table 1 of SAE J826.

§11.4.3.2 Pelvic angle. As determined using the pelvic angle gage (GM drawing 78051-532 incorporated by reference in Part 572,

Subpart E of this chapter) which is inserted into the H-point gaging hole of the dummy, the angle measured from the horizontal on the 3 inch flat surface of the gage shall be 22 1/2 degrees plus or minus 2 1/2 degrees.

§11.5 Legs.

§11.5.1 The legs of the driver and passenger test dummy shall be placed as provided in §11.5.2 or, at the option of the vehicle manufacturer until September 1, 1991, as provided in §10.1.1 for the driver and §10.1.2 for the passenger, except that the initial distance between the outboard knee clevis flange surfaces shall be 10.6 inches for both the driver and the passenger rather than 14 1/2 inches as specified in §10.1.1(a) for the driver and 11 3/4 inches as specified in §10.1.2.1(a) and §10 1.2.2(a) for the passenger.

§11.5.2 The upper legs of the driver and passenger test dummies shall rest against the seat cushion to the extent permitted by placement of the feet. The initial distance between the outboard knee clevis flange surfaces shall be 10.6 inches. To the extent practicable, the left leg of the driver dummy and both legs of the passenger dummy shall be in vertical longitudinal planes. To the extent practicable, the right leg of the driver dummy shall be in a vertical plane. Final adjustment to accommodate placement of feet in accordance with §11.6 for various passenger compartment configurations is permitted.

§11.6 Feet. The feet of the driver test dummy shall be positioned in accordance with §10.1.1 (b) and (c) of this standard. The feet of the passenger test dummy shall be positioned in accordance with §10.1.2.1 (b) and (c) or §10.1.2.2 (b) and (c) of this standard, as appropriate.

§11.7 Test dummy positioning for latchplate access. The reach envelopes specified in §7.4.4 are obtained by positioning a test dummy in the driver's seat or passenger's seat in its forward most adjustment position. Attach the lines for the inboard and outboard arms to the test dummy as described in Exhibit 3-3 of this standard. Extend each line backward and outboard to generate the compliance arcs of the outboard reach envelope of the test dummy's arms.

§11.8 Test dummy positioning for belt contact force. To determine compliance with §7.4.3 of this standard, position the test dummy in the vehicle in accordance with the requirements specified in §11.1 through §11.6 and under the conditions of §8.1.2. and §8.1.3. Pull the belt webbing three inches from the test dummy's chest and release until the webbing is within 1 inch of the test dummy's chest and measure the belt contact force.

§11.9 Manual belt adjustment for dynamic testing. With the test dummy at its designated seating position as specified by the appropriate requirements of §8.1.2, §8.1.3 and §11.1 through §11.6, place the Type 2 manual belt around the test dummy and fasten the latch. Remove all slack from the lap belt. Pull the upper torso webbing out of the retractor and allow it to retract; repeat this operation four times. Apply a 2 to 4 pound tension load to the lap belt. If the belt system is equipped with a tension-relieving device introduce the maximum amount of slack into the upper torso belt that is recommended by the manufacturer for normal use in the owner's manual for the vehicle. If the belt system is not equipped with a tension-relieving device, allow the excess webbing in the shoulder belt to be retracted by the retractive force of the retractor.

Note: The concept of an occupant protection system which requires "no action by vehicle occupants," as that term is used in Standard No. 208, is intended to designate a system which will perform its protective restraining function after a normal process of ingress or egress without separate deliberate actions by the vehicle occupant to deploy the restraint system. Thus, the agency considers an occupant protection system to be automatic if an occupant has to take no action to deploy the system but would normally slightly push the seat belt webbing aside when entering or exiting the vehicle or would normally make a slight adjustment in the webbing for comfort.

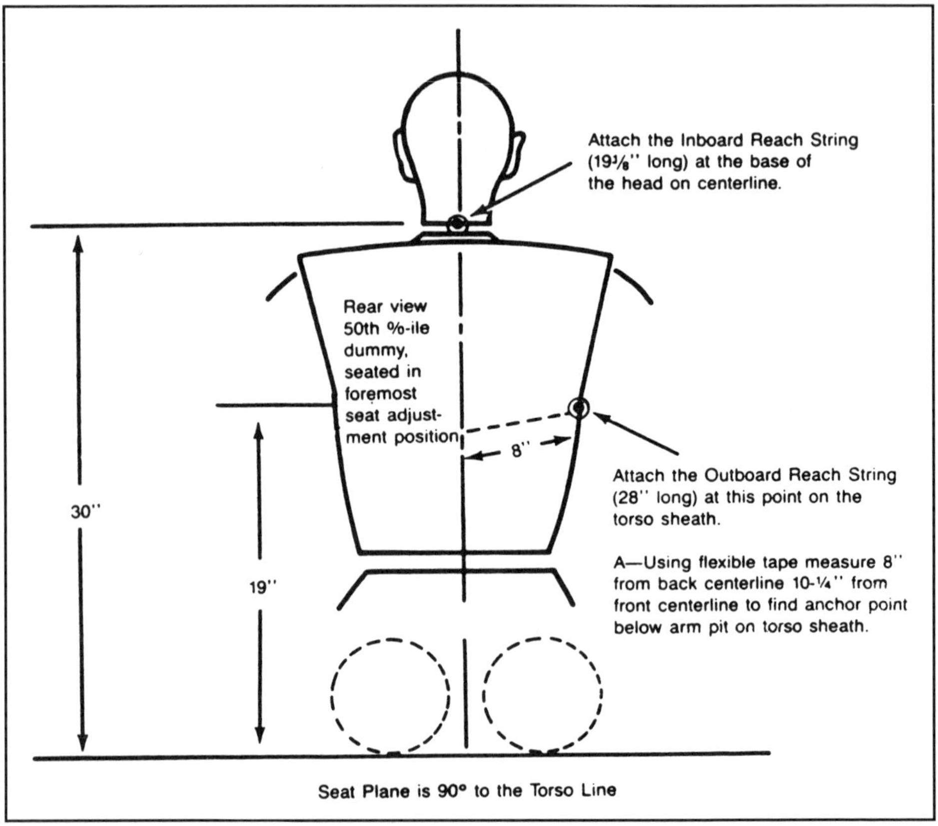

Exhibit 3-4a *Location of anchoring points for latchplate reach limiting chains or strings to test for latchplate accessibility using subpart B test device.*

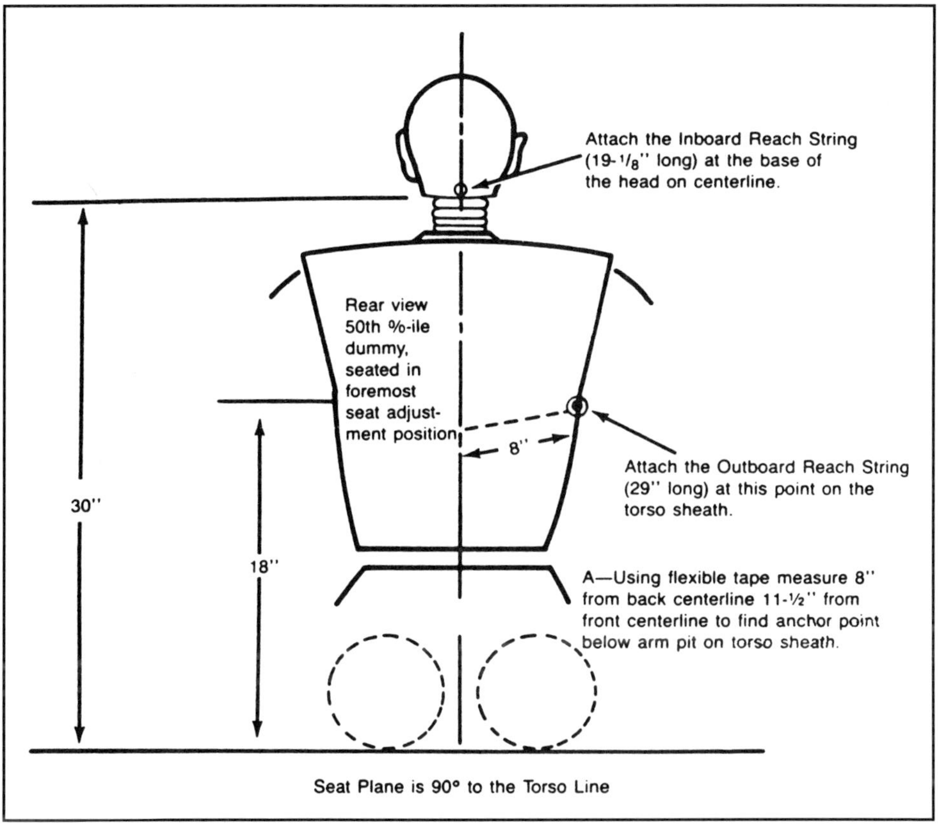

Exhibit 3-3b *Location of anchoring points for latchplate reach limiting chains or strings to test for latchplate accessibility using subpart E test device.*

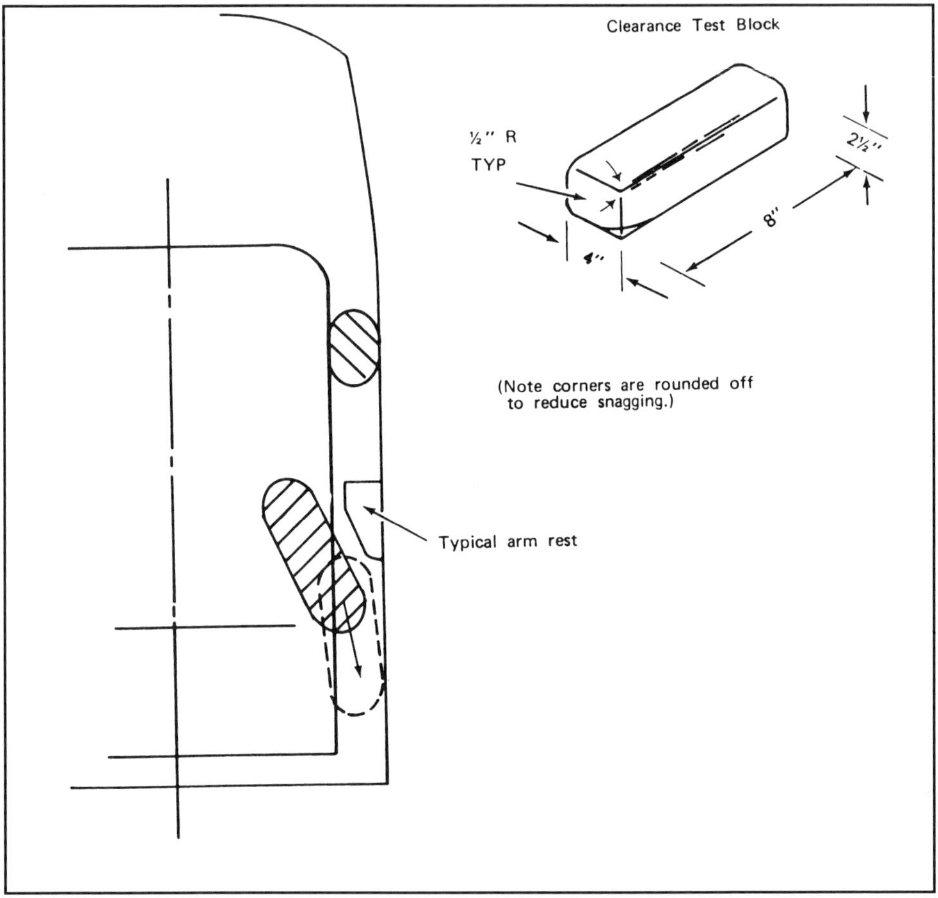

Exhibit 3-5 *Use of clearance test block to determine hand/arm access.*

Federal Preemption of State Common Law Claims

One strategy used by the defense in a child restraint case is to seek summary judgment by raising the issue of preemption. The starting point in this analysis is the underlying statute. In this case, the statute is the National Traffic and Motor Vehicle Safety Act and in particular, FMVSS 213.

In addition to the underlying statute, a careful analysis of congressional intent and previous decisions in this area is necessary to determine whether defective child restraint claims brought in state courts are preempted by federal law. Federal law may preempt state claims in one of three ways: expressly, implicitly by occupying the field, or implicitly through conflict between the state and federal legislation.

In looking at the National Traffic and Motor Vehicle Safety Act (Safety Act), it is quite clear that the most important objective of the Safety Act is to reduce the number of deaths and injuries that take place on our nation's highways and roads. Therefore, any common law which furthers that goal cannot be held to be inconsistent with the congressional intent. If the purpose for which Congress enacted the legislation in the first place is not frustrated, then such state legislation cannot be preempted by the federal law.

Unlike federal preemption in airbag cases, federal child restraint legislation under FMVSS 213, does not allow a manufacturer to chose from several options on how to implement the policies of the act. The airbag cases are different because the underlying federal statute in those cases, FMVSS 208, gives the automobile manufacturers three options in providing for occupant protection. Therefore, airbag cases are essentially preempted from state litigation, since it would be unfair to hold a manufacturer liable from choosing from one of the options provided for in FMVSS 208 and not another.

Federal preemption in child restraint cases has been tested and positively decided in at least one Maryland District Court. The federal district court in Welsh did not find the preemption analysis useful in child restraint cases due to the uniqueness of the regulatory scheme of air bag regulation.

In Welsh, the Plaintiffs relied on the "Savings Clause" of the Safety Act. The plain language of the "Savings Clause" clearly saves claims under state common law by stating: "Compliance with any federal motor vehicle safety standard issued under this subchapter does not exempt any person from any liability under common law." This provision clearly evidences congressional intent with respect to federal preemption of child restraint claims brought under common law. The Court in its analysis of express preemption found that a strong presumption against preemption in tort cases exists, because the subject matter has historically been left to state control.

The defense in the Welsh case argued for preemption based on the Supremacy Clause of the Constitution as it applies through the Safety Act and FMVSS 213. The manufacturer stated that 15 U.S.C. § 1392 (d), in particular, preempted the parents' state tort claim. The savings clause reads in part: "Whenever a Federal motor vehicle safety standard established under this subchapter is in effect, no State or political subdivision of a State shall have any authority either to establish, or to continue in effect, with respect to any motor vehicle or item of motor vehicle any safety standard applicable to the same aspect of performance of such vehicle or item of equipment which is not identical to the Federal standard."The Welsh court found that the preemption clause of the Safety Act did not apply to child restraint cases because standards of care under state law are not "safety standards" within the scope of Section 1392 (d).

Standard No. 213: Child Restraint Systems.

Standard 213 is the governing standard for child restraint devices. NHTSA has recently considered public comments on many of the issues that are not covered or neglected by the standard. The issues include: the interaction of child restraint devices with air-bag equipped vehicles, child seat performance criteria, booster seat performance, and methods for restraining infants and handicapped children.

The standard is useful in determining if the manufacturer has committed any violations in the manufacture, testing or marketing of its child restraints. The standard, although worded in the typical technical language common to these type of rules, also defines many terms for the practitioner. FMVSS 213 is an invaluable guide to the attorney investigating and litigating a child restraint defect case.

49 C.F.R. 571.213

§1. Scope. This standard specifies requirements for child restraint systems used in motor vehicles and aircraft.

§2. Purpose. The purpose of this standard is to reduce the number of children killed or injured in motor vehicle crashes and in aircraft.

§3. Application. This standard applies to child restraint systems for use in motor vehicles and aircraft.

§4. Definitions.

Add-on child restraint system means any portable child restraint system.

Booster seat means a child restraint which consists of only a seating platform that does not extend up to provide a cushion for the child's back or head.

Built-in child restraint system means any child restraint system which is an integral part of a passenger car.

Car bed means a child restraint system designed to restrain or position a child in the supine or prone position on a continuous flat surface.

Child restraint system means any device except Type I or Type II seat belts, designed for use in a motor vehicle or aircraft to restrain, seat, or position children who weigh 50 pounds or less.

Contactable surface means any child restraint system surface (other than that of a belt, belt buckle, or belt adjustment hardware) that may contact any part of the head or torso of the appropriate test dummy, specified in §7, when a child restraint system is tested in accordance with §6.1.

Representative aircraft passenger seat means either a Federal Aviation Administration approved production aircraft passenger seat or a simulated aircraft passenger seat conforming to Exhibit 3-10.

Seat orientation reference line or SORL means the horizontal line through Point Z as illustrated in Exhibit 3-5a.

Specific vehicle shell means the actual vehicle model part into which the built-in child restraint system is fabricated, including the complete surroundings of the built-in system. If the built-in child restraint system is manufactured as part of the rear seat, these surroundings, include the back of the front seat, the interior rear side door panels and trim, the rear seat, the floor pan, the B and C pillars, and the ceiling. If the built-in system is manufactured as part of the front seat, these surroundings include the dashboard; the steering wheel, column, and attached levers and knobs; the "A" pillars; any levers and knobs installed in the floor or on a console; the interior front side door panels and trim; the front seat; the floor pan; and the ceiling.

Torso means the portion of the body of a seated anthropomorphic test dummy, excluding the thighs, that lies between the top of the child restraint system seating surface and the top of the shoulders of the test dummy.

§5 Requirements for child restraint systems certified for use in motor vehicles. Each child restraint system certified for use in motor vehicles shall meet the requirements in this section when, as specified, tested in accordance with §6.1.

§5.1 Dynamic performance.

§5.1.1 Child restraint system integrity. When tested in accordance with §6.1, each child restraint system shall:

(a) Exhibit no complete separation of any load bearing structural element and no partial separation exposing either surfaces with a radius of less than 1/4 inch or surfaces with protrusions greater than 3/8 inch above the immediate adjacent surrounding contactable surface of any structural element of the system;

(b) If adjustable to different positions, remain in the same adjustment position during the testing as it was immediately before the testing; and

(c) If a front facing child restraint system, not allow the angle between the system's back support surfaces for the child and the system's seating surface to be less than 45 degrees at the completion of the test.

§5.1.2 Injury criteria. When tested in accordance with §6.1, each child restraint system that, in accordance with §5.5.2(f), is recommended for use by children weighing more than 20 pounds, shall

(a) Limit the resultant acceleration at the location of the accelerometer mounted in the test dummy head as specified in Part 572 such that the expression:

$$\left[\frac{1}{(t_2 - t_2)}\int_{t_1}^{t_2} adt\right]^{2\ 3} \qquad (t_2 - t_2)$$

shall not exceed 1,000, where a is the resultant acceleration expressed as a multiple of g (the acceleration of gravity), and t_1 and t_2 are any two moments during the impacts.

(b) Limit the resultant acceleration at the location of the accelerometer mounted in the test dummy upper thorax as specified in Part 572 to not more than 60 g's, except for intervals whose cumulative duration is not more than 3 milliseconds.

§5.1.3 Occupant excursion. When tested in accordance with §6.1 and adjusted in any position which the manufacturer has not, in accordance with §5.5.2(i), specifically warned against using in motor vehicles, each child restraint system shall meet the applicable excursion limit requirements specified in §5.1.3.1-§5.1.3.3.

§5.1.3.1 Child restraint systems other than rear-facing ones and car beds. Each child restraint system, other than a rear-facing child restraint system or a car bed, shall retain the test dummy's torso within the system.

(a) In the case of an add-on child restraint system, no portion of the test dummy's head shall pass through a vertical transverse plane that is 32 inches forward of point z on the standard seat assembly, measure along the center SORL (as illustrated in figure 1B), and neither knee pivot point shall pass through a vertical, transverse plan that is 36 inches forward of point z on the standard seat assembly, measured along the center SORL.

(b) In the case of a built-in child restraint system, neither knee pivot shall pass through a vertical, transverse plane that is 36 inches forward of the hinge point of the specific passenger car seat into which the system is built, measured along a horizontal line parallel to the vehicle's longitudinal center line and the center line of the passenger car seat.

§5.1.3.2 Rear-facing child restraint systems. In the case of each rear-facing child restraint system, all portions of the test dummy's torso shall be retained within the system and no portion of the target point on either side of the dummy's head shall pass through the transverse orthogonal planes whose intersection contains, the forward-most and top-most points on the child restraint system surfaces (illustrated in Exhibit 1C).

§5.1.3.3 Car beds. In the case of car beds, all portions of the test dummy's head and torso shall be retained within the confines of the car bed.

§5.1.4 Back support angle. When a rear-facing child restraint system is tested in accordance with §6.1, the angle between the system's back support surface for the child and the vertical shall not exceed 70 degrees.

§5.2 Force distribution.

§5.2.1 Minimum head support surface—child restraints other than car beds.

§5.2.1.1 Except as provided in §5.2.1.2, each child restraint system other than a car bed shall provide restraint against rearward movement of the head of the child (rearward in relation to the child) by means of a continuous seat back which is an integral part of the system and which—

(a) Has a height, measured along the system seat back surface for the child in the vertical longitudinal plane passing through the longitudinal center line of the child restraint systems from the lowest point on the system seating surface that is contacted by the buttocks of the seated dummy, as follows:

Weight n[1] (in pounds)	Height n[2] (in inches)
Less than 20 lbs.	18
20 lbs. or more, but not more than 40 lbs.	20
More than 40 lbs.	22

n[1] When a child restraint system is recommended under §5.5(f) for use by children of the above weights.
n[2] The height of the portion of the system seat back providing head restraint shall not be less than the above.

(b) Has a width of not less than 8 inches, measured in the horizontal plane at the height specified in paragraph (a) of this section. Except that a child restraint system with side supports extending at least 4 inches forward from the padded surface of the portion of the restraint system provided for support of the child's head may have a width of not less than 6 inches, measured in the horizontal plane at the height specified in paragraph (a) of this section.

(c) Limits the rearward rotation of the test dummy head so that the angle between the head and torso of the dummy specified in §7. when tested in accordance with §6.1 is not more than 45 degrees greater than the angle between the head and torso after the dummy has been placed in the system in accordance with §6.1.2.3 and before the system is tested in accordance with §6.1.

§5.2.1.2 A front-facing child restraint system is not required to comply with §5.2.1.1 if the target point on either side of the dummy's head is below a horizontal plane tangent to the top of—

(a) The standard seat assembly, in the case of an add-on child restraint system, when the dummy is positioned in the system and the system is installed on the assembly in accordance with §6.1.2.

(b) the passenger car seat, in the case of a built-in child restraint system, when the system is activated and the dummy is positioned in the system in accordance with §6.1.2.

§5.2.2 Torso impact protection. Each child restraint system other than a car bed shall comply with the applicable requirements of §5.2.2.1 and §5.2.2.2.

§5.2.2.1(a) The system surface provided for the support of the child's back shall be flat or concave and have a continuous surface area of not less than 85 square inches.

(b) Each system surface provided for support of the side of the child's torso shall be flat or concave and have a continuous surface of not less than 24 square inches for systems recommended for children weighing 20 pounds or more, or 48 square inches for systems recommended for children weighing less than 20 pounds.

(c) Each horizontal cross section of each system surface designed to restrain forward movement of the child's torso shall be flat or concave and each vertical longitudinal cross section shall be flat or convex with a radius of curvature of the underlying structure of not less than 2 inches.

§5.2.2.2 Each forward-facing child restraint system shall have no fixed or movable surface—

(a) Directly forward of the dummy and intersected by a horizontal line—

(1) Parallel to the SORL, in the case of the add-on child restraint system, or

(2) Parallel to a vertical plane through the longitudinal center line of the passenger car seat, in the case of the built-in child restraint system, and

(b) Passing through any portion of the dummy, except for surfaces which restrain the dummy when the system is tested in accordance with §6.1.2.1.2, so that the child restraint system shall conform to the requirements of §5.1.2 and §5.1.3.1.

§5.2.3 Head impact protection.

§5.2.3.1 Each child restraint system, other than a child harness, which is recommended under §5.5.2(f) for children weighing less than 20 pounds shall comply with §5.2.3.2.

§5.2.3.2 Each system surface, except for protrusions that comply with §5.2.4, which is contactable by the dummy head when the system is tested in accordance with §6.1 shall be covered with slow recovery, energy absorbing material with the following characteristics:

(a) A 25 percent compression-deflection resistance of not less than 0.5 and not more than 10 pounds per square inch when tested in accordance with §6.3.

(b) A thickness of not less than 1/2 inch for materials having a 25 percent compression-deflection resistance of not less than 1.8 and not more than 10 pounds per square inch when tested in accordance with §6.3. Materials having a 25 percent compression-deflection resistance of less than 1.8 pounds per square inch shall have a thickness of not less than 3/4 inch.

§5.2.4 Protrusion limitation. Any portion of a rigid structural component within or underlying a contactable surface, or any portion of a child restraint system surface that is subject to the requirements of §5.2.3 shall, with any padding or other flexible overlay material removed, have a height above any immediately adjacent restraint system surface of not more than 3/8 inch and no exposed edge with a radius of less than 1/4 inch.

§5.3 Installation.

§5.3.1 Each add-on child restraint system shall have no means designed for attaching the system to a vehicle seat cushion and vehicle seat back and no component (except belts) that is designed to be inserted between the vehicle seat cushion and vehicle seat back.

§5.3.2 When installed on a vehicle seat, each add-on child restraint system, other than child harnesses, shall be capable of being restrained against forward movement solely by means of a Type I seat belt assembly (defined in @ 571.209) that meets Standard No. 208 (@ 571.208), or by means of a Type I seat belt assembly plus one additional anchorage strap that is supplied with the system and conforms to §5.4.

§5.3.3 Car beds. Each car bed shall be designed to be installed on a vehicle seat so that the car bed's longitudinal axis is perpendicular to a vertical longitudinal plane through the longitudinal axis of the vehicle.

§5.4 Belts, belt buckles, and belt webbing.

§5.4.1 Performance requirements. The webbing of belts provided with a child restrain system and used to attach the system to the vehicle or to restrain the child within the system shall —

(a) After being subjected to abrasion as specified in §5.1(d) or §5.3(c) of FMVSS 209 (@ 571.209), have a breaking strength of not less than 75 percent of the strength of the unabraded webbing when tested in accordance with §5.1(b) of FMVSS 209.

(b) Meet the requirements of §4.2 (e) through (h) of FMVSS No. 209 (@ 571.209); and

(c) If contactable by the test dummy torso when the system is tested in accordance with §6.1, have a width of not less than 1 1/2 inches when measured in accordance with §5.4.1.1.

§5.4.1.1 Width test procedure. Condition the webbing for 24 hours in an atmosphere of any relative humidity between 48 and 67 percent, and any ambient temperature between 70° and 77° F. Measure belt webbing width under a tension of 5 pounds applied lengthwise.

§5.4.2 Belt buckles and belt adjustment hardware. Each belt buckle and item of belt adjustment hardware used in a child restraint system shall conform to the requirements of §4.3(a) and §4.3(b) of FMVSS No. 209 (@ 571.209).

§5.4.3 Belt Restraint.

§5.4.3.1 General. Each belt that is part of a child restraint system and that is designed to restrain a child using the system shall be adjustable to snugly fit any child whose height and weight are within the ranges recommended in accordance with §5.5.2(f) and who is positioned in the system in accordance with the instructions required by §5.6.

§5.4.3.2 Direct restraint. Each belt that is part of a child restraint system and that is designed to restrain a child using the system and to attach the system to the vehicle shall, when tested in accordance with §6.1, impose no loads on the child that result from the mass of the system, or

(a) In the case of an add-on child restraint system, for the mass of the seat back of the standard seat assembly specified in §7.3, or

(b) In the case of a built-in child restraint system, from the mass of any part of the vehicle into which the child restraint system is built.

§5.4.3.3 Seating systems. Except for child restraint systems subject to §5.4.3.4, each child restraint system that is designed for use by a child in a seated position and that has belts designed to restrain the child, shall, with the test dummy specified in §7. positioned in the system in accordance with §6.1.2.3 provide:

(a) Upper torso restraint in the form of:

(i) Belts passing over each shoulder of the child, or

(ii) A fixed or movable surface that complies with §5.2.2.1(c), and

(b) Lower torso restraint in the form of:

(i) A lap belt assembly making an angle between 45° and 90° with the child restraint seating surface at the lap belt attachment points, or

(ii) A fixed or movable surface that complies with §5.2.2.1(c), and

(c) In the case of each seating system recommended for children over 20 pounds, crotch restraint in the form of:

(i) A crotch belt connectable to the lap belt or other device used to restrain the lower torso, or

(ii) A fixed or movable surface that complies with §5.2.2.1(c).

§5.4.3.4 Harnesses. Each child harness shall:

(a) Provide upper torso restraint, including belts passing over each shoulder of the child;

(b) Provide lower torso restraint by means of lap and crotch belt; and

(c) Prevent a child of any height for which the restraint is recommended for use pursuant to §5.5.2(f) from standing upright on the vehicle seat when the child is placed in the device in accordance with the instructions required by §5.6.

§5.4.3.5 Buckle Release. Any buckle in a child restraint system belt assembly designed to restrain a child using the system shall:

(a) When tested in accordance with §6.2.1 prior to the dynamic test of §6.1, not release when a force of less than 9 pounds is applied and shall release when a force of not more than 14 pounds is applied;

(b) After the dynamic test of §6.1, when tested in accordance with §6.2.3, release when a force of not more than 16 pounds is applied;

(c) Meet the requirements of §4.3(d)(2) of FMVSS No. 209 (@ 571.209), except that the minimum surface area for child restraint buckles designed for push button application shall be 0.6 square inch;

(d) Meet the requirements of §4.3(g) of FMVSS No. 209 (@ 571.209) when tested in accordance with §5.2(g) of FMVSS No. 209; and

(e) Not release during the testing specified in §6.1.

§5.5 Labeling.

§5.5.1 Each add-on child restraint system shall be permanently labeled with the information specified in §5.5.2 (a) through (l).

§5.5.2 The information specified in paragraphs (a) through (l) of this section shall be stated in the English language and lettered in letters and numbers that are not smaller than 10 point type and are on a contrasting background.

(a) The model name or number of the system.

(b) The manufacturer's name. A distributor's name may be used instead if the distributor assumes responsibility for all duties and liabilities imposed on the manufacturer with respect to the system by the National Traffic and Motor Vehicle Safety Act, as amended.

(c) The statement: "Manufactured in ____," inserting the month and year of manufacture.

(d) The place of manufacture (city and State, or foreign country). However, if the manufacturer uses the name of the distributor, then it shall state the location (city and State, or foreign country) of the principal offices of the distributor.

(e) The statement: "This child restraint system conforms to all applicable Federal motor vehicle safety standards."

(f) One of the following statements, inserting the manufacturer's recommendations for the maximum weight and height of children who can safely occupy the system:

(i) This infant restraint is designed for use by children who weigh ____ pounds or less and whose height is _____ inches or less; or

(ii) This child restraint is designed for use only by children who weigh between ______ and ______ pounds and whose height is ______ inches or less and who are capable of sitting upright alone; or

(iii) This child restraint is designed for use only by children who weigh between ______ and ______ pounds and are between ______ and ______ inches in height.

(g) The following statement, inserting the location of the manufacturer's installation instruction booklet or sheet on the restraint:

WARNING! FAILURE TO FOLLOW EACH OF THE FOLLOWING INSTRUCTIONS CAN RESULT IN YOUR CHILD STRIKING THE VEHICLE'S INTERIOR DURING A SUDDEN STOP OR CRASH.

SECURE THIS CHILD RESTRAINT WITH A VEHICLE BELT AS SPECIFIED IN THE MANUFACTURER'S INSTRUCTIONS LOCATED__.

(h) In the case of each child restraint system that has belts designed to restrain children using them:

SNUGLY ADJUST THE BELTS PROVIDED WITH THIS CHILD RESTRAINT AROUND YOUR CHILD.

(i) In the case of each child restraint system which is not intended for use in motor vehicles at certain adjustment positions, the following statement, inserting the manufacturer's adjustment restrictions.

DO NOT USE THE__ADJUSTMENT POSITION(S) OF THIS CHILD RESTRAINT IN A MOTOR VEHICLE.

(j) In the case of each child restraint system equipped with an anchorage strap, the statement:

SECURE THE TOP ANCHORAGE STRAP PROVIDED WITH THIS CHILD RESTRAINT AS SPECIFIED IN THE MANUFACTURER'S INSTRUCTIONS.

(k) In the case of each child restraint system which can be used in a rear-facing position, one of the following statements:

(i) PLACE THIS CHILD RESTRAINT IN REAR-FACING POSITION WHEN USING IT WITH AN INFANT; or

(ii) PLACE THIS INFANT RESTRAINT IN A REAR-FACING POSITION WHEN USING IT IN THE VEHICLE.

(l) An installation diagram showing the child restraint system installed in the right front outboard seating position equipped with a continuous-loop lap/shoulder belt and in the center rear seating position as specified in the manufacturer's instructions.

(m) Child restraints that are certified as complying with the provisions of section §8 shall be labeled with the statement "THIS RESTRAINT IS CERTIFIED FOR USE IN MOTOR VEHICLES AND AIRCRAFT". This statement shall be in red lettering, and shall be placed after the certification statement required by paragraph (e) of this section.

§5.5.3 The information specified in §5.5.2 (g) through (k) shall be located on the add-on child restraint system so that it is visible when the system is installed as specified in §5.6.1.

§5.5.4 Each built-in child restraint system shall be permanently labeled with the information specified in §5.5.5 (a) through (j), so that it is visible when the system is activated for use as specified in §5.6.2.

§5.5.5 The information specified in paragraphs (a) through (j) of this section shall be stated in the English language and lettered in letters and numbers which are not smaller than 10-point type and are on a contrasting background. This information shall be printed in the vehicle owner's manual.

(a) The model name or number of the system.

(b) The manufacturer's name. A distributor's or dealer's name may be used instead if the distributor or dealer assumes responsibility for all duties and liabilities imposed on the manufacturer with respect to the system by the National Traffic and Motor Vehicle Safety Act, as amended.

(c) The statement: "Manufactured in ______," inserting the month and year of manufacture.

(d) The place of manufacture (city and State, or foreign country). However, if the manufacturer uses the name of the distributor or dealer, then it shall state the location (city and State, or foreign country) of the principal offices of the distributor or dealer.

(e) The statement: "This child restraint system conforms to all applicable Federal motor vehicle safety standards."

(f) One of the following statements, inserting the manufacturer's recommendations for the maximum weight and height of children who can safely occupy the system:

(i) This infant restraint is designed for use by children who weigh ____ pounds or less and whose height is ____ inches or less;

(ii) This child restraint is designed for use only by children who weigh between _____ and _____ pounds and whose height is _____ inches or less and who are capable of sitting upright alone; or

(iii) This child restraint is designed for use by children who weigh between _____ and _____ pounds and are between _____ and _____ inches in height.

(g) The following statement:
WARNING! FAILURE TO FOLLOW THE MANUFACTURER'S INSTRUCTIONS ON THE USE OF THIS CHILD RESTRAINT SYSTEM CAN RESULT IN YOUR CHILD STRIKING THE VEHICLE'S INTERIOR DURING A SUDDEN STOP OR CRASH.

(h) In the case of each built-in child restraint system that has belts designed to restrain children using them:
SNUGLY ADJUST THE BELTS PROVIDED WITH THIS CHILD RESTRAINT AROUND YOUR CHILD.

(i) In the case of each built-in child restraint which can be used in a rear-facing position, the following statement:
PLACE AN INFANT IN A REAR-FACING POSITION IN THIS CHILD RESTRAINT.

(j) A diagram or diagrams showing the fully activated child restraint system in infant and/or child configurations.

§5.6 Printed Instructions for Proper Use.

§5.6.1 Add-on child restraint systems. Each add-on child restraint system shall be accompanied by printed installation instructions in the English language that provide a step-by-step procedure, including diagrams, for installing the system in motor vehicles, securing the system in the vehicles, positioning a child in the system, and adjusting the system to fit the child.

§5.6.1.1 In a vehicle with rear designated seating positions, the instructions shall alert vehicle owners that, according to accident statistics, children are safer when properly restrained in the rear seating positions than in the front seating positions.

§5.6.1.2 The instructions shall specify in general terms the types of vehicles, the types of seating positions, and the types of vehicle safety belts with which the add-on child restraint system can or cannot be used.

§5.6.1.3 The instructions shall explain the primary consequences of not following the warnings required to be labeled on the child restraint system in accordance with §5.5.2 (g) through (k).

§5.6.1.4 The instructions for each car bed shall explain that the car bed should position in such a way that the child's head is near the center of the vehicle.

§5.6.1.5 The instructions shall state that add-on child restraint systems should be securely belted to the vehicle, even when they are not occupied, since in a crash an unsecured child restraint system may injure other occupants.

§5.6.1.6 Each add-on child restraint system shall have a location on the restraint for storing the manufacturer's instructions.

§5.6.2 Built-in Child restraint systems. Each built-in child restraint system shall be accompanied by printed instructions in the English language that provide a step-by-step procedure, including diagrams, for activating the built-in child restraint system, positioning a child in the system, adjusting the restraint and, if provided, the restraint harness to fit the child. This information and the information specified in §5.5.5, shall be included in the vehicle owner's manual.

§5.6.2.1 The instructions shall explain the primary consequences of not following the manufacturer's warnings for proper use of the child restraint system in accordance with §5.5.5(f) through (i).

§5.6.3 The instructions shall explain the primary consequences of noting following the warnings required to be labeled on the child restraint system in accordance with §5.5.2 (g) through (k).

§5.6.4 The instructions for each car bed shall explain that the car bed should position in such a way that the child's head is near the center of the vehicle.

§5.6.5 The instructions shall state that child restraint systems should be securely belted to the vehicle, even when they are not occupied, since in a crash an unsecured child restraint system may injure other occupants.

§5.6.6 Each child restraint system shall have a location on the restraint for storing the manufacturer's instructions.

§5.7 Flammability. Each material used in a child restraint system shall conform to the requirements of §4 of FMVSS No. 302 (571.302). In the case of a built-in child restraint system, the requirements of §4 of FMVSS No. 302 shall be met in both the "in-use" and "stowed" positions.

§6 Test conditions and procedures.

§6.1 Dynamic systems test.

§6.1.1 Test conditions.

§6.1.1.1 (a) The test device for add-on child restraint systems is the standard seat assembly specified in §7.3. The assembly is mounted on a dynamic test platform so that the center SORL of the seat is parallel to the direction of the test platform travel and so that movement between the base of the assembly and the platform is prevented. The test device for built-in child restraint systems is either the specific vehicle shell or the specific vehicle. The specific vehicle shell, if selected for testing, is mounted on a dynamic test platform so that the longitudinal center line of the shell is parallel to the direction of the test platform travel and so that movement between the base of the shell and the platform is prevented.

(b) The platform is instrumented with an accelerometer and data processing system having a frequency response of 60 Hz channel class as specified in Society of Automotive Engineers Recommended Practice J211 JUN80 “Instrumentation for Impact Tests." The accelerometer sensitive axis is parallel to the direction of test platform travel.

(c) For built-in child restraint systems, an alternate test device is the specific vehicle into which the built-in system is fabricated. Activate the system in accordance with the manufacturer’s instructions provided in the vehicle owner’s manual in accordance with §5.6.2. When the complete vehicle traveling longitudinally forward at any speed up to and including 30 mph, impacts a fixed collision barrier that is perpendicular to the line of travel of the vehicle, the built-in child restraint system shall meet the injury criteria of §5.1.2. The following test conditions apply to this alternate test device.

(i) The vehicle is loaded to its unloaded vehicle weight plus its rated cargo and luggage capacity weight, secured in the luggage area, plus the appropriate child test dummy and, at the option of the manufacturer, an anthropomorphic test dummy which conforms to the requirements of Subpart B or Subpart E of Part 572 of this title for a 50th percentile adult male dummy placed in the front outboard seating position. If the built-in child restraint system is installed at one of the seating positions otherwise requiring the placement of a Part 572 test dummy, then in the frontal barrier crash specified in §6.1.1.2, the appropriate child test dummy shall be substituted for the Part 572 test dummy, but only at that seating position. The fuel tank is filled to any level from 90 to 95 percent of capacity.

(ii) Adjustable seats are in the adjustment position midway between the forward-most and rearmost positions, and if separately adjustable in a vertical direction, are at the lowest position. If an adjustment position does not exist midway between the forward-most and rearmost positions, the closest adjustment position to the rear of the midpoint is used.

(iii) Adjustable seat backs are in the manufacturer's nominal design riding position. If a nominal position is not specified, the seat back is positioned so that the longitudinal center line of the child test dummy's neck is vertical, and if an anthropomorphic test dummy is used, the accelerometer surfaces in the test dummy's head and thorax, as positioned in the vehicle, are horizontal. If the vehicle is equipped with adjustable head restraints, each is adjusted to its highest adjustment position.

(iv) Movable vehicle windows and vents are, at the manufacturer's option, placed in the fully closed position.

(v) Convertibles and open-body type vehicles have the top, if any, in place in the closed passenger compartment configuration.

(vi) Doors are fully closed and latched but not locked.

(vii) All instrumentation and data reduction is in conformance with SAE J211 JUN80.

§6.1.1.2 The tests are frontal barrier impact simulations of the test platform or frontal barrier crashes of the specific vehicles as specified in §5.1 (@ 571.208) and for:

(a) Test Configuration I specified in §6.1.2.1.1, are at a velocity change of 30 mph with the acceleration of the test platform entirely within the curve shown in Exhibit 3-6, or for the specific vehicle test with the deceleration produced in 30 mph frontal barrier crash.

(b) Test Configuration II specified in §6.1.2.1.2 are set at a velocity change of 20 mph with the acceleration of the test platform entirely within the curve shown in Exhibit 3-7, or for the specific vehicle test with the deceleration produced in 20 mph frontal barrier crash.

§6.1.1.3 In the case of add-on child restraint systems, Type 1 seat belt assemblies meeting the requirements of Standard No. 209 (@ 571.209) and having webbing with a width of not more than 2 inches are attached, without the use of retractors or reels of any kind, to the seat belt anchorage points (illustrated in Exhibit 3-5b) provided on the standard seat assembly.

§6.1.1.4 Performance tests under §6.1 are conducted at any ambient temperature from 66° to 78° F and at any relative humidity from 10 percent to 70 percent.

§6.1.2 Dynamic test procedure.

§6.1.2.1 Test configuration.

§6.1.2.1.1 Test configuration I. (a) In the case of each add-on child restraint system other than a child harness, a booster seat with a top anchorage strap, or a restraint designed for use by physically handicapped children, install a new add-on child restraint system at the center seating position of the standard seat assembly in accordance with the manufacturer's instructions provided with the system pursuant to §5.6.1, except that the add-on restraint shall be secured to the standard vehicle seat using only the standard vehicle lap belt. A child harness, a booster seat with a top anchorage strap, or a restraint designed for use by physically handicapped children shall be installed at the center seating position of the standard seat assembly in accordance with the manufacturer's instructions provided with the system pursuant to §5.6.1.

(b) In the case of each built-in child restraint system, activate the restraint in the specific vehicle shell or the specific vehicle, in accordance with the manufacturer's instructions provided in the vehicle owner's manual in accordance with §5.6.2.

§6.1.2.1.2 Test configuration II. (a) In the case of each add-on child restraint system which is equipped with a fixed or movable surface described in §5.2.2.2, or a booster seat with a top anchorage strap, install a new add-on child restraint system at the center seating position of the standard seat assembly using only the standard seat lap belt to secure the system to the standard seat.

(b) In the case of each built-in child restraint system which is equipped with a fixed or movable surface described in §5.2.2.2, or a built-in booster seat with a top anchorage strap, activate the system in the specific vehicle shell or the specific vehicle in accordance with the manufacturer's instructions provided in the vehicle owner's manual in accordance with §5.6.2.

§6.1.2.2 Tighten all belts used to attach the add-on child restraint system to the standard seat assembly to a tension of not less than 12 pounds and not more than 15 pounds, as measured by a load cell used on the webbing portion of the belt. Tighten all manual vehicle belts used to secure the built-in child restraint system or a child to the specific vehicle shell or specific vehicle to one of the following tensions:

(a) For a seat equipped with a manual adjuster or automatic locking retractor, not less than 12 pounds and not more than 15 pounds, as measured by a load cell used on the webbing portion of the belt;

(b) For a seat equipped with an emergency locking retractor, as specified in §4.3 of Standard 209.

§6.1.2.3 Place in the child restraint any dummy specified in §7. for testing systems for use by children of the heights and weights for which the system is recommended in accordance with §5.6.

§6.1.2.3.1 When placing the 3-year-old test dummy in add-on or built-in child restraint systems other than car beds, position the test dummy according to the instructions for child positioning provided by the manufacturer with the system in accordance with §5.6.1 or §5.6.2 while conforming to the following:

(a) Holding the test dummy torso upright until it contacts the system's design seating surface, place the test dummy in the seated position within the system with the midsagittal plane of the test dummy head—

(1) Coincident with the center SORL of the standard seating assembly, in the case of the add-on child restraint system, or

(2) Vertical and parallel to the longitudinal center line of the specific vehicle shell or the specific vehicle, in the case of a built-in child restraint system.

(b) Extend the arms of the test dummy as far as possible in the upward vertical direction. Extend the legs of the dummy as far as possible in the forward horizontal direction, with the dummy feet perpendicular to the center line of the lower legs.

(c) Using a flat square surface with an area of 4 square inches, apply a force of 40 pounds, perpendicular to:

(i) The plane of the back of the standard seat assembly in the case of an add-on child restraint system, or

(ii) The back of the vehicle seat in the specific vehicle shell or the specific vehicle in the case of a built-in child restraint system, first against the dummy crotch and then at the dummy thorax in the midsagittal plane of the dummy. For a child restraint system with a fixed or movable surface described in §5.2.2.2, which is being tested under the conditions of test configuration II, do not attach any of the child restraint belts unless they are an integral part of the fixed or movable surface. For all other child restraint systems and for a child restraint system with a fixed or movable surface which is being tested under the conditions of test configuration I, attach all appropriate child restraint belts and tighten them as specified in §6.1.2.4. Attach all appropriate vehicle belts and tighten them as specified in §6.1.2.2. Position each movable surface in accordance with the manufacturer's instructions provided in accordance with §5.6.1 or §5.6.2.

(d) After the steps specified in paragraph (c) of this standard, rotate each dummy limb downwards in the plane parallel to the dummy's midsagittal plane until the limb contacts a surface of the child restraint system or the standard seat assembly in the case of an add-on system, or the specific vehicle shell or specific vehicle in the case of a built-in system, as appropriate. Position the limbs, if necessary, so that limb placement does not inhibit torso or head movement in tests conducted under §6.

§6.1.2.3.2 When placing the 6-month-old dummy in add-on or built-in child restraint systems other than car beds, position the test dummy according to the instructions for child positioning provided with the system by the manufacturer in accordance with §5.6.1 or §5.6.2 while conforming to the following:

(a) With the dummy in the supine position on a horizontal surface, and while preventing movement of the dummy torso by placing a hand on the center of the torso, rotate the dummy legs upward by lifting the feet until the legs contact the upper torso and the feet touch the head, and then slowly release the legs but do not return them to the flat surface.

(b) Place the dummy in the child restraint system so that the back of the dummy torso contacts the back support surface of the system. For a child restraint system which is equipped with a fixed or movable surface described in §5.2.2.2, which is being tested under the conditions of test configuration II, do not attach any of the child restraint belts unless they are an integral part of the fixed or movable surface. For all other child restraint systems and for a child restraint system with a fixed or movable surface which is being tested under the conditions of test configuration I, attach all appropriate child restraint belts and tighten them as specified in §6.1.2.4. Attach all appropriate vehicle belts and tighten them as specified in §6.1.2.2. Position each movable surface in accordance with the manufacturer's instructions provided in accordance with §5.6.1 or §5.6.2. If the dummy's head does not remain in the proper position, it shall be taped against the front of the seat back surface of the system by means of a single thickness of 1/4 -inch-wide paper masking tape placed across the center of the dummy's face.

(c) Position the dummy arms vertically upwards and then rotate each arm downward toward the dummy's lower body until the arm contacts a surface of the child restraint system or the standard seat assembly in the case of an add-on child restraint system, or the specific vehicle shell or the specific vehicle in the case of a built-in child restraint system, ensuring that no arm is restrained from movement in other than the downward direction, by any part of the system or the belts used to anchor the system to the standard seat assembly, the specific vehicle shell, or the specific vehicle.

§6.1.2.3.3 When placing the 6-month-old dummy or 3-year-old dummy in a car bed, place the dummy in the car bed in the supine position with its midsagittal plane perpendicular to the center SORL of the standard seat assembly and position the dummy within the car bed in accordance with instructions for child positioning provided with the car bed by its manufacturer in accordance with §5.6.

§6.1.2.4 If provided, shoulder and pelvic belts that directly restrain the dummy shall be adjusted as follows:

Tighten the belts until a 2-pound force applied (as illustrated in figure 5) to the webbing at the top of each dummy shoulder and to the pelvic webbing two inches on either side of the torso midsagittal plane pulls the webbing 1/4 inch from the dummy.

§6.1.2.5 Accelerate the test platform to simulate frontal impact in accordance with §6.1.1.2(a) or §6.1.1.2(b), as appropriate.

§6.1.2.6 For add-on child restraint systems, measure dummy excursion and determine conformance with the requirements specified in §5.1 as appropriate. For built-in child restraint systems, measure dummy knee excursion and determine conformance with the requirements specified in §5.1 as appropriate.

§6.2 Buckle release test procedure. The belt assembly buckles used in any child restraint system shall be tested in accordance with §6.2.1 through §6.2.4 inclusive.

§6.2.1 Before conducting the testing specified in §6.1, place the loaded buckle on a hard, flat, horizontal surface. Each belt end of the buckle shall be pre-loaded in the following manner. The anchor end of the buckle shall be loaded with a two pound force in the direction away from the buckle. In the case of buckles designed to secure a single latch plate, the belt latch plate end of the buckle shall be pre-loaded with a two pound force in the direction away from the buckle. In the case of buckles designed to secure two or more latch plates, the belt latch plate ends of the buckle shall be loaded equally so that the total load is two pounds, in the direction away from the buckle. For push-button-release buckles, the release force shall be applied by a conical surface (cone angle not exceeding 90 degrees). For push-button-release mechanisms with a fixed edge (referred to in Exhibit 3-11 as "hinged button"), the release force shall be applied at the center line of the button, 0.125 inches away from the movable edge directly opposite the fixed edge, and in the direction that produces maximum releasing effect. For push-button-release mechanisms with no fixed edge (referred to in Exhibit 3-11 as "floating button"), the release force shall be applied at the center of the release mechanism in the direction that produces the maximum releasing effect. For all other buckle release mechanisms, the force shall be applied on the center line of the buckle lever or finger tab in the direction that produces the maximum releasing effect. Measure the force required to release the buckle. Exhibit 3-11 illustrates the loading for the different buckles and the point where the release force should be applied, and Exhibit 3-12 illustrates the conical surface used to apply the release force to push-button-release buckles.

§6.2.2 After completion of the testing specified in §6.1, and before the buckle is unlatched, tie a self-adjusting sling to each wrist and ankle of the test dummy in the manner illustrated in Exhibit 3-8.

§6.2.3 Pull the sling horizontally in the manner illustrated in Exhibit 3-8 and parallel to the center SORL of the standard seat assembly, in the case of an add-on child restraint system, or parallel to the longitudinal center line of either the specific vehicle shell or the specific vehicle, in the case of a built-in child restraint system, and apply a force of 20 pounds in the case of a system tested with a 6-month-old dummy and 45 pounds in the case of a system tested with a 3-year-old dummy.

§6.2.4 While applying the force specified in §6.2.3, and using the device shown in Exhibit 3-12 for push-button-release buckles, apply the release force in the manner and location specified in §6.2.1, for that type of buckle. Measure the force required to release the buckle.

§6.3 Head impact protection—energy absorbing material test procedure.

§6.3.1 Prepare and test specimens of the energy absorbing material used to comply with §5.2.3 in accordance with the applicable 25 percent compression-deflection test described in the American Society for Testing and Materials (ASTM) Standard D1056-73, "Standard Specification for Flexible Cellular Materials—Sponge or Expanded Rubber," or D1564-71 "Standard Method of Testing Flexible Cellular Materials—Slab Urethane Foam" or D1565-76 "Standard Specification for Flexible Cellular Materials—Vinyl Chloride Polymer and Copolymer open-cell foams."

§7 Test dummies.

§7.1 Six-month-old dummy. An unclothed "Six-month-old Size Manikin" conforming to Subpart D of Part 572 of this chapter is used for testing a child restraint system that is recommended by its manufacturer in accordance with §5.6 for use by children in a weight range that includes children weighing not more than 20 pounds.

§7.2 Three-year-old dummy. A three-year-old dummy conforming to subpart C of part 572 of this chapter is used for testing a child restraint that is recommended by its manufacturer in accordance with §5.6 for use by children in a weight range that includes children weighing more than 20 pounds.

(a) Built-in child restraints. When a three-year-old test dummy is used for testing a built-in child restraint, the dummy shall be assembled with the head assembly specified in @ 572.16(a)(1) of this chapter.

(b) Add-on child restraints. (1) Until September 1, 1993, when a three-year-old test dummy is used for testing an add-on child restraint, the dummy shall be assembled using, at the manufacturer's option, either head assembly specified in @ 572.16(a) of this chapter.

(2) Effective September 1, 1993, when a three-year-old dummy is used for testing an add-on child restraint, the dummy shall be assembled with the head assembly specified in @ 572.16(a)(1) of this chapter.

§7.2.1 Before being used in testing under this standard, the dummy is conditioned at any ambient temperature from 66° F to 78° F and at any relative humidity from 10 percent to 70 percent for at least 4 hours.

§7.2.2 When used in testing under this standard, the dummy is clothed in thermal knit waffle-weave polyester and cotton underwear, a size 4 long-sleeved shirt weighing 0.2 pounds, a size 4 pair of long pants weighing 0.2 pounds and cut off just far enough above the knee to allow the knee target to be visible, and size 7M sneakers with rubber toe caps, uppers of dacron and cotton or nylon and a total weight of 1 pound. Clothing other than the shoes is machine-washed in 160° F to 180° F water and machine-dried at 120° F to 140° F for 30 minutes.

§7.3 Standard test devices.

(a) The standard test devices used in testing add-on child restraint systems under this standard are:

(1) For testing for motor vehicle use, a standard seat assembly consisting of a simulated vehicle bench seat, with three seating positions, which is described in Drawing Package SAS-100-1000 (consisting of drawings and a bill of materials); and

(2) For testing for aircraft use, a standard seat assembly consisting of a representative aircraft passenger seat.

(b) The standard test devices used in testing built-in child restraint systems under this standard are either a specific vehicle shell or a specific vehicle.

§8 Requirements, test conditions, and procedures for child restraint systems manufactured for use in aircraft.

Each child restraint system manufactured for use in both motor vehicles and aircraft must comply with all of the applicable requirements specified in Section §5 and with the additional requirements specified in §8.1 and §8.2.

§8.1 Installation instructions. Each child restraint system manufactured for use in aircraft shall be accompanied by printed instructions in the English language that provide a step-by-step procedure, including diagrams, for installing the system in aircraft passenger seats, securing the system to the seat, positioning a child in the system when it is installed in aircraft, and adjusting the system to fit the child. In the case of each child restraint which is not intended for use in aircraft at certain adjustment positions, the following statement, with the manufacturer's restrictions inserted, shall be included in the instructions.

DO NOT USE THE____ADJUSTMENT POSITION(S) OF THIS CHILD RESTRAINT IN AIRCRAFT.

§8.2 Inversion test. When tested in accordance with §8.2.1 through §8.2.5 and adjusted in any position which the manufacturer has not, in accordance with §8.1, specifically warned against using in aircraft, each child restraint system manufactured for use in aircraft shall meet the requirements of S.8.2.1 through §8.2.6. The manufacturer may, at its option, use any seat which is a representative aircraft passenger seat within the meaning of §4.

§8.2.1 A representative aircraft passenger seat shall be positioned and adjusted so that its horizontal and vertical orientation and its seat back angle are the same as shown in Exhibit 3-10.

§8.2.2 The child restraint system shall be attached to the representative aircraft passenger seat using, at the manufacturer's option, any Federal Aviation Administration approved aircraft safety belt, according to the restraint manufacturer's instructions for attaching the restraint to an aircraft seat. No supplementary anchorage belts or tether straps may be attached; however, Federal Aviation Administration approved safety belt extensions may be used.

§8.2.3 In accordance with §6.1.2.3.1 through §6.1.2.3.3, place in the child restraint any dummy specified in §7 for testing systems for use by children of the heights and weights for which the system is recommended in accordance with §5.5 and §8.1.

§8.2.4 If provided, shoulder and pelvic belts that directly restrain the dummy shall be adjusted in accordance with §6.1.2.4.

§8.2.5 The combination of representative aircraft passenger seat, child restraint, and test dummy shall be rotated forward around a horizontal axis which is contained in the median transverse vertical plane of the seating surface portion of the aircraft seat and is located one inch below the bottom of the seat frame, at a speed of 35 to 45 degrees per second, to an angle of 180 degrees. The rotation shall be stopped when it reaches that angle and the seat shall be held in this position for three seconds. The child restraint shall not fall out of the aircraft safety belt nor shall the test dummy fall out of the child restraint at any time during the rotation or the three second period. The specified rate of rotation shall be attained in not less than one half second and not more than one second, and the rotating combination shall be brought to a stop in not less than one half second and not more than one second.

§8.2.6 Repeat the procedures set forth in §8.2.1 through §8. 2.4. The combination of the representative aircraft passenger seat, child restraint, and test dummy shall be rotated sideways around a horizontal axis which is contained in the median longitudinal vertical plane of the seating surface portion of the aircraft seat and is located one inch below the bottom of the seat frame, at a speed of 35 to 45 degrees per second, to an angle of 180 degrees. The rotation shall be stopped when it reaches that angle and the seat shall be held in this position for three seconds. The child restraint shall not fall out of the aircraft safety belt, nor shall the test dummy fall out of the child restraint at any time during the rotation or the three second period. The specified rate of rotation shall be attained in not less than one half second and not more than one second, and the rotating combination shall be brought to a stop in not less than one half second and not more than one second.

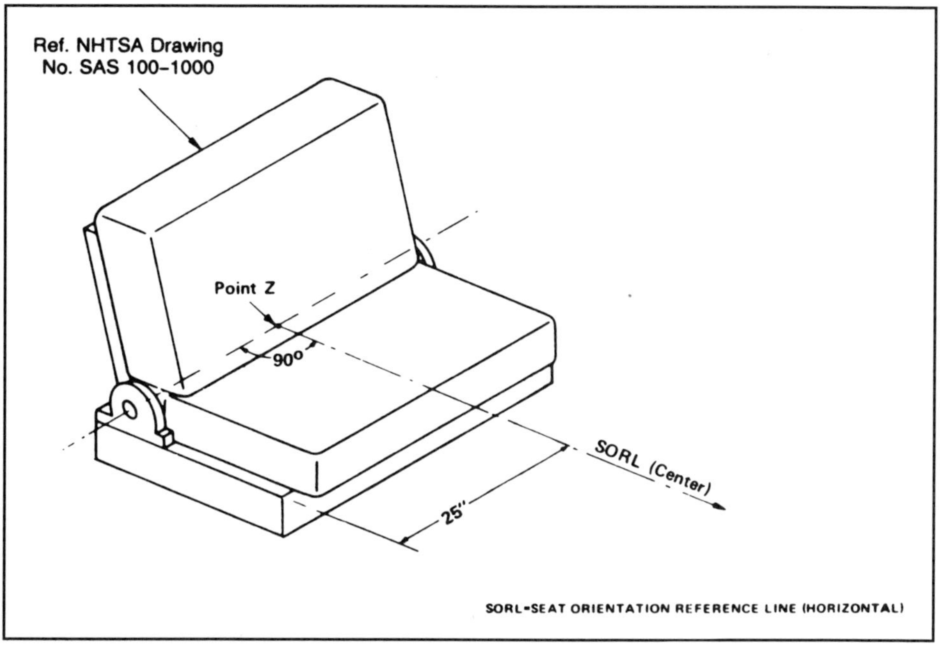

Exhibit 3-6a *SORL location on the standard seat.*

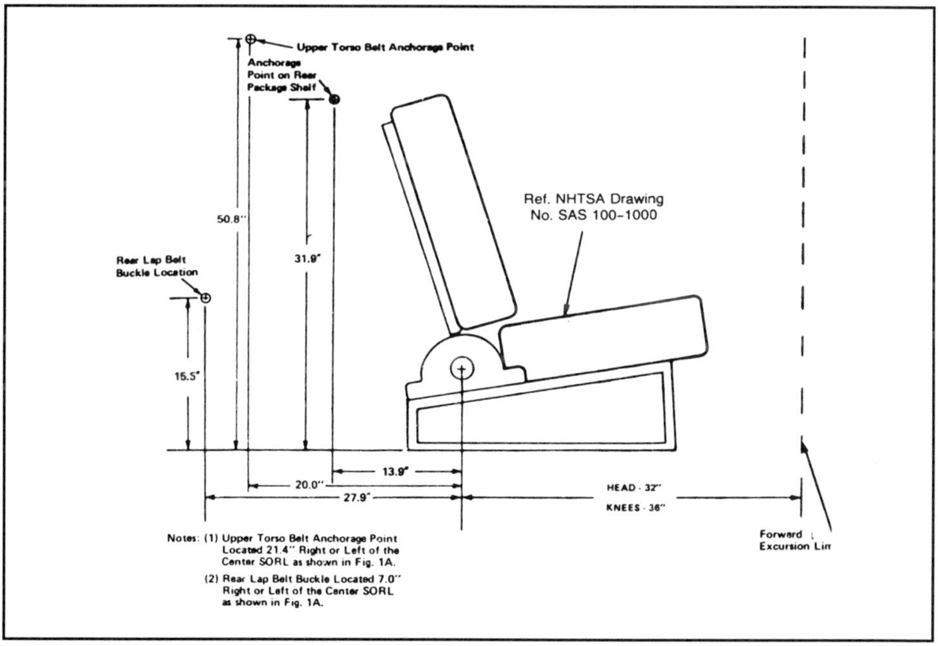

Exhibit 3-6b *Locations of additional belt anchorage points and forward excursion limit.*

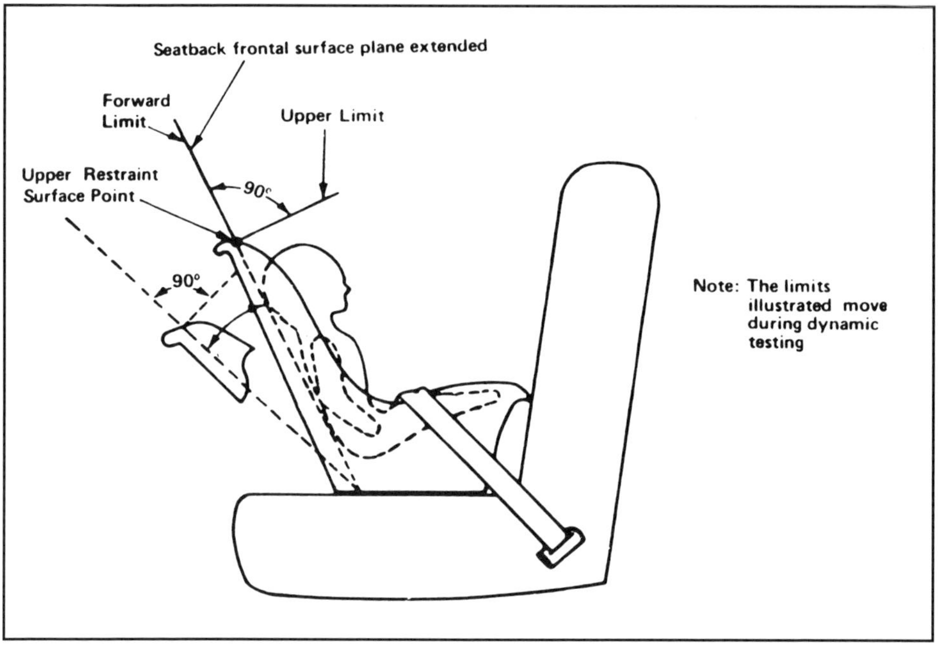

Exhibit 3-6c *SORL location on the standard seat.*

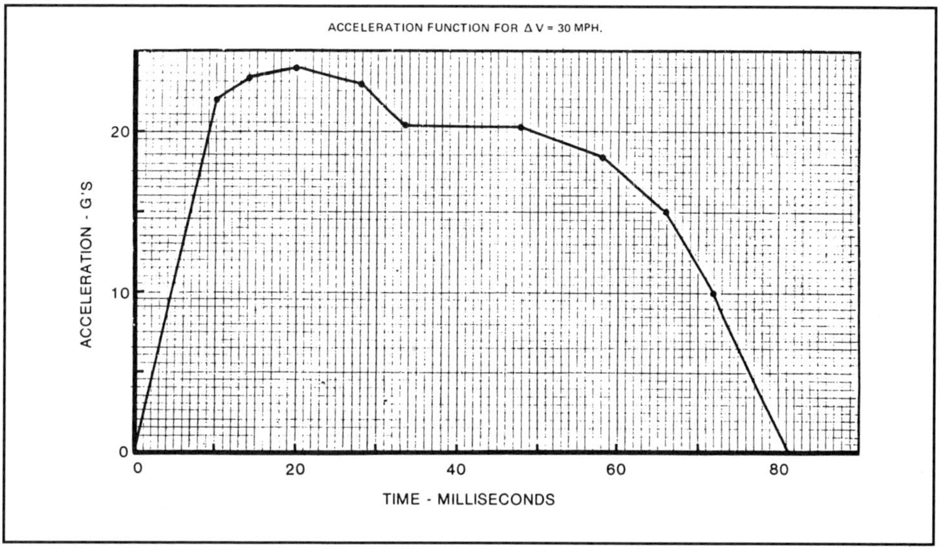

Exhibit 3-7 *Sled Test Acceleration Curve at 30 MPH*

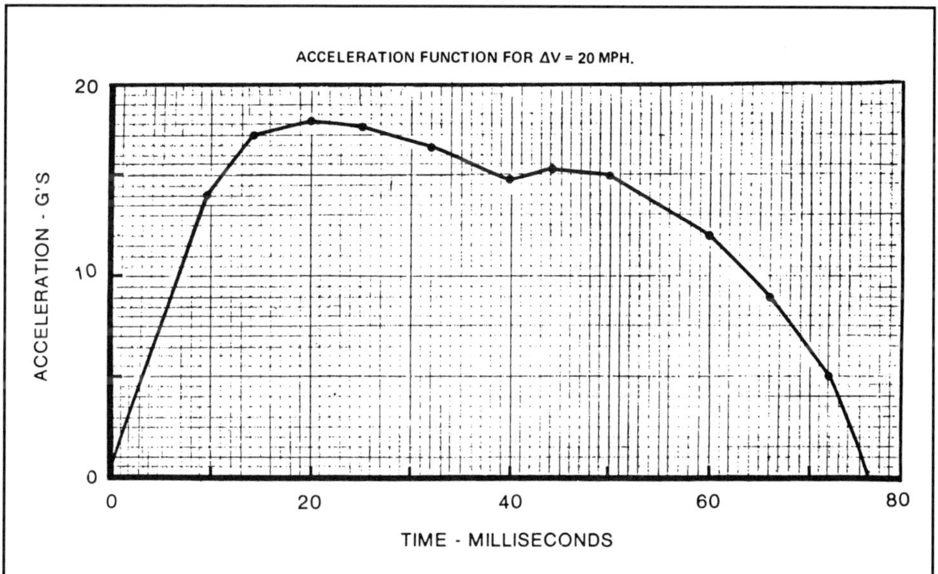

Exhibit 3-8 *Sled Test Acceleration Curve at 20 MPH*

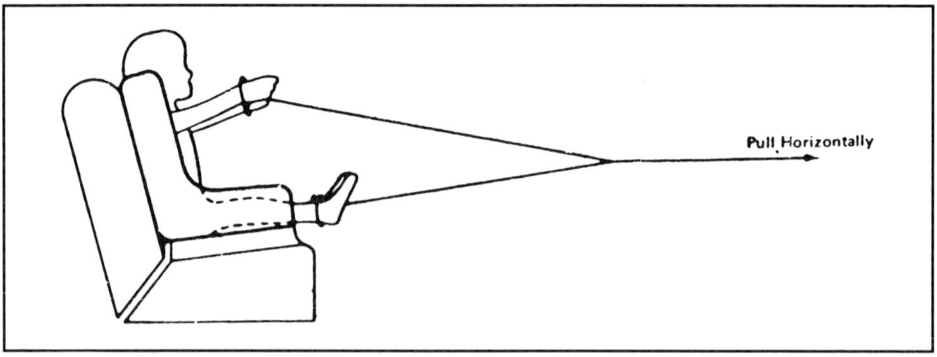

Exhibit 3-9 *Buckle Release Test*

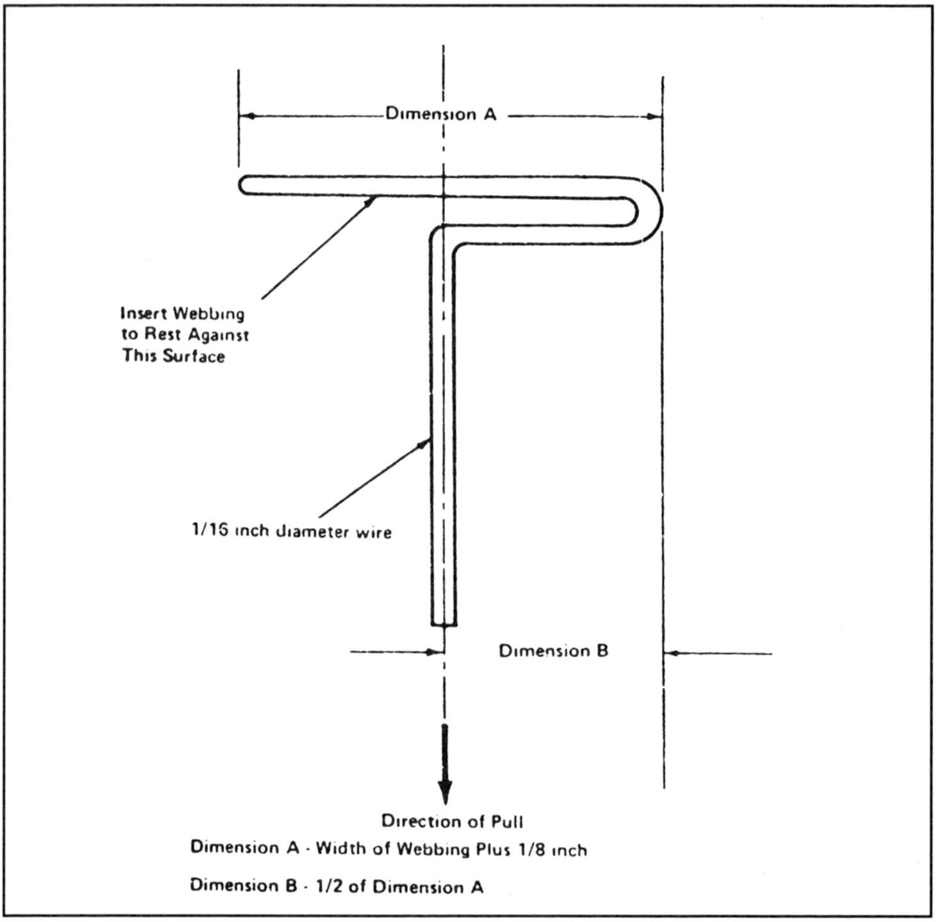

Exhibit 3-10 *Webbing Tension Pull Device*

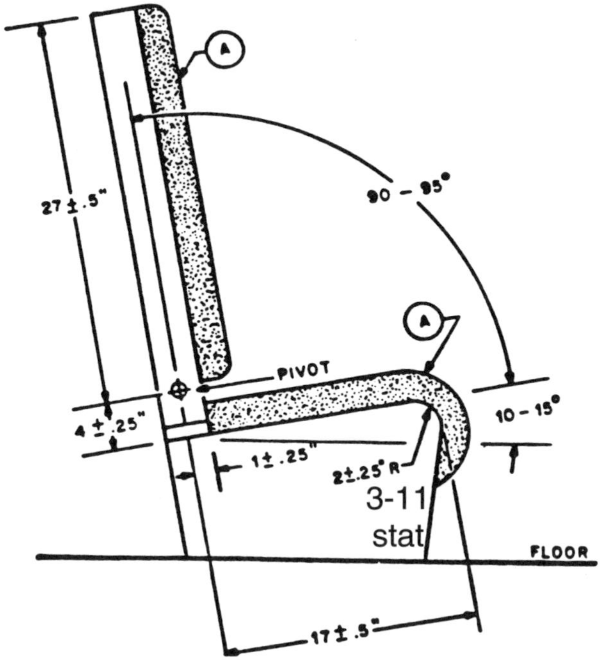

"A" represents a 2- to 3-inch thick polyurethane foam pad, 1.5-2.0 pounds per cubic foot density, over 0.020-inch-thick aluminum pan, and covered by 12- to 14-ounce marine canvas. The sheet aluminum pan is 20 inches wide and supported on each side by a rigid structure. The seat back is a rectangular frame covered with the aluminum sheet and weighing between 14 and 15 pounds, with a center of mass 13 to 16 inches above the seat pivot axis. The mass moment of inertia of the seat back about the seat pivot axis is between 195 and 220 ounce-inch-second^2. The seat back is free to fold forward about the pivot, but a stop prevents rearward motion. The passenger safety belt anchor points are spaced 21 to 22 inches apart and are located in line with the seat pivot axis.

Exhibit 3-11 *Simulated Aircraft Passenger Seat*

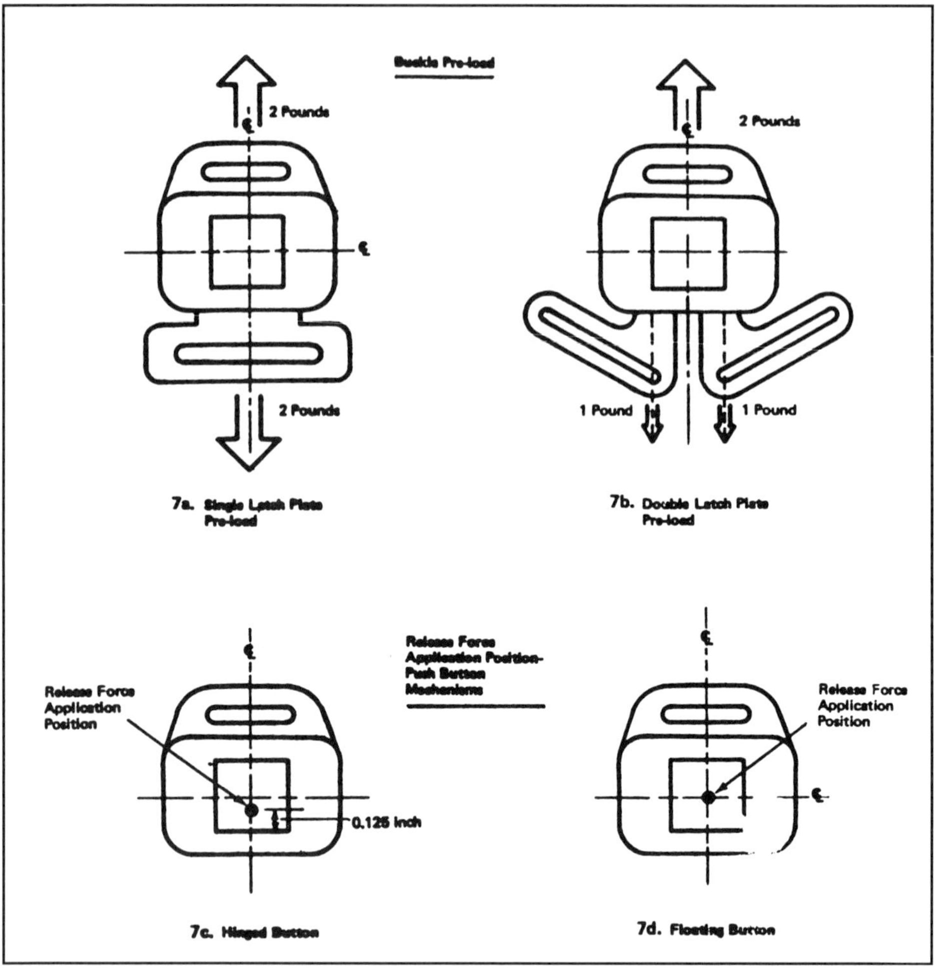

Exhibit 3-12 *Pre-impact Buckle Release Force Test Set-up*

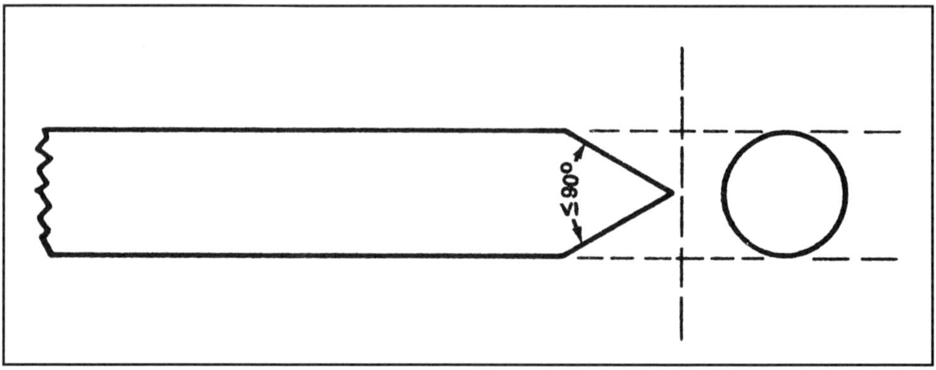

Exhibit 3-13 *Release Force Application Device—Push Button Release Buckles*

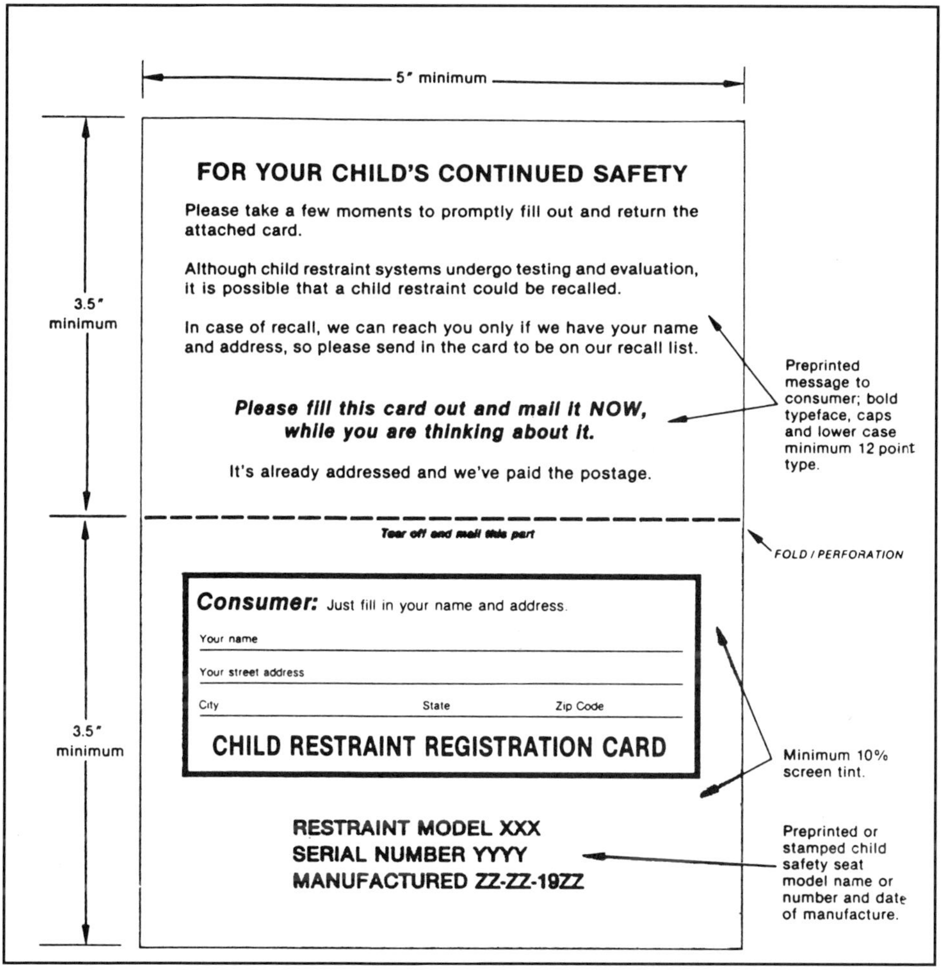

Exhibit 3-14a Registration Form for Child Restraint Systems—Product Identification Number and Purchaser Information Side

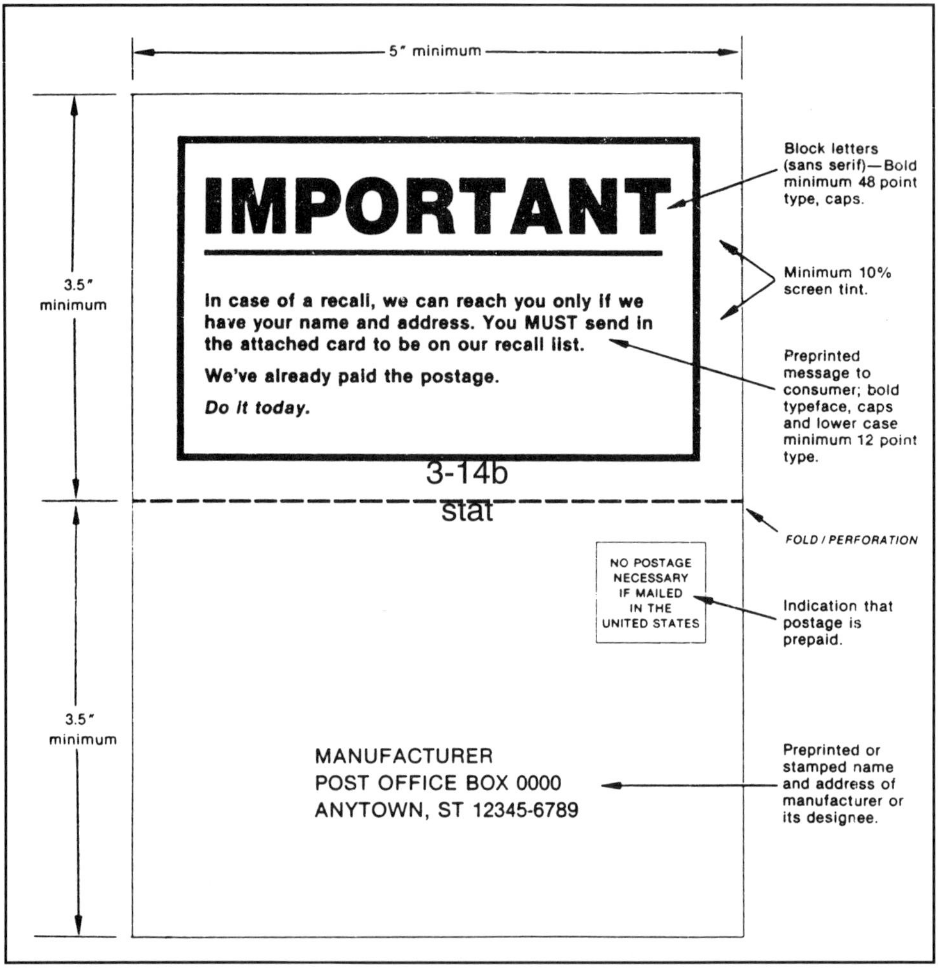

Exhibit 3-14b Registration Form for Child Restraint Systems—Address Side

Alternatives to Current Federal and State Laws

Congress, through its spending power, can condition the receipt of federal funds by the states, on compliance with federal laws. In essence the government can "bribe" the states to perform certain functions as long as the functions are in furtherance of the general welfare. The legislation could be similar to the maximum speed limit provisions currently tied to federal highway funding. Legislation enacted in the early eighties allowed for a reduction in federal highway funding if data submitted by a state showed that more than fifty percent of vehicles exceed the posted speed limit.

Federal incentives could be used to encourage child restraint use by parents. Currently, a bill is pending in the U.S. Senate that would give a tax credit to parents who purchase a child restraint. The bill introduced by Senator Inouye on January 21, 1993 has been referred to the Committee on Finance. The credit is limited to the tax year in which the purchase takes place and is also limited to "qualified" child restraints as defined in FMVSS 213. If approved, the bill would be effective as law for the tax years after December 31, 1992.

The House of Representatives in a bi-partisan effort has also proposed child restraint legislation. The house bill seeks to amend the Federal Aviation Act of 1958 to require the use of child restraints on commercial aircraft. More legislation of this nature is needed to encourage parents to buy and use child restraints. But federal and state legislation must primarily address the quilted patchwork of laws that now govern child restraint use.

Chapter 4

Current State Legislation

Although many states have significantly increased safety by passing child restraint laws, there are many arbitrary exceptions. The state laws create various loopholes and exemptions for children of certain ages, weight, or height. Some states exempt children from using seat belts when all available seat belts are in use.

Many laws refer to "passenger vehicles only" which in effect exempt ambulances, police cars, taxis and school buses and day care vehicles. The fines for offenders vary widely from ten up to five hundred dollars. Most of the states waive the fines for first time offenders upon proof by the offender that a child restraint seat has been obtained. New Hampshire and Indiana provide for the harshest penalties with a maximum amount of $500.00. These loopholes in the legislation make enforcement difficult and have resulted in many unnecessary and senseless deaths. It has been estimated that if child safety seats were used by all children 500 deaths and 53,000 injuries could be prevented each year.

In the past, states have been reluctant to adopt and enforce mandatory legislation concerning the use of seat belts, helmets, passive restraints, and child restraints. The states have used the rationale that an individual's right to privacy is paramount. The policy argument has been that an individual's right to chose their mode of travel should not be dictated by the state government.

However, times have changed the prevailing public policy. Today, more and more states have provisions in their statutes that regulate the use of helmets, passive restraints, seat belts, and child restraints. All states now have mandatory child restraint legislation. The differences in the legislation can first be classified as to the purpose of the litigation. Some statutes cover educational programs as well as mandatory use laws. There are a number of variations from this major two themes.

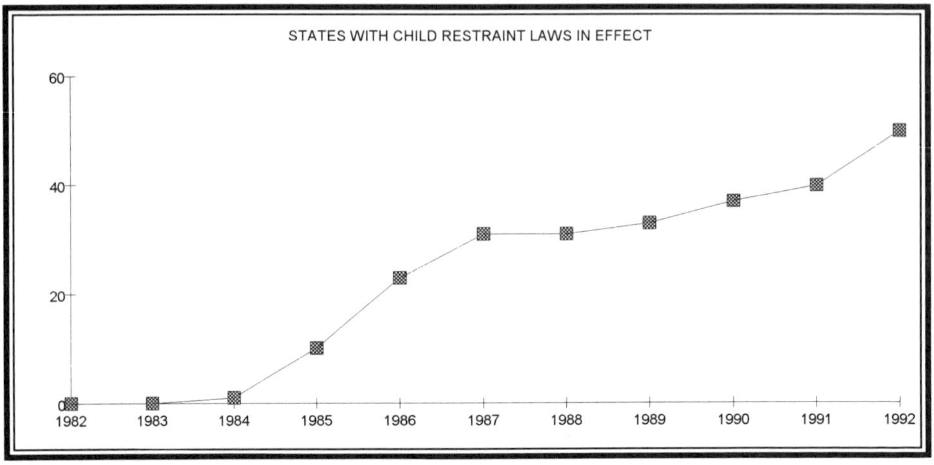

Exhibit 4-1 *All 50 states currently have child restraint laws. However, the exemptions from coverage and loopholes allow many children to die needlessly each year.*

The next major criteria, which can be used to compare and contrast the various state laws, is the age or size of the child, the seating position of the child in the vehicle, the type of restraint, the status of the people who must comply with the statute, and the ownership of the vehicle.

Though imperfect, state legislation has increased safety while decreasing the number of lives lost to tragic vehicular accidents. In Michigan, for example, the use rate for child restraints before the mandatory law took effect was about 30%. After the law took effect on April 1, 1982 police records indicated an 80% use rate. Even though only 6.42% of all children involved in Motor Vehicle Accident's in Michigan in 1991 were not properly restrained, the latest figures compiled suggest that percentage wise more unrestrained children died or were injured. Of those children that were restrained, it is not known what role the child restraint played in the collision. Police officers do not investigate the exact cause of injury and often police accident forms only provide the seating positions and extent of injury to the occupants of a vehicle.

Injuries to Children in MVA's Under Four Year's of Age 1991

	Chidren Properly Restrained	Unrestrained Children
Total # of Children	8861	608
Deaths:	6 (.07%)	4 (.66%)
Injuries:		
A type*	40 (.45%)	34 (5.59%)
B type**	166 (1.87%)	65 (10.69%)
C type***	344 (3.88%)	68 (11.18%)
No Injury	8305 (93.72%)	437 (71.88%)

* Incapacitating injury.
** Bruises, contusions and abrasions.
***Complaint of injury but not visible injury.

The fatality rate has steadily decreased since 1968 when the federal government first implemented legislation in the area of automobile safety. In 1968 the fatality rate involving automobile crashes was 5.2 deaths per 100 million vehicle miles travelled. By 1990 the fatality rate had decreased to 2.1 deaths per million vehicle miles traveled. Still, more lives could be saved by perfecting and standardizing child restraint legislation and by improving the current testing standards.

Tennessee took the lead by enacting the first child restraint law in the United States. Tennessee enacted the Tennessee Child Passenger Protection Act in 1978. The new law decreased the death rates of children four and under. Only two of the children that died in auto accidents during the first five years that the statute was in effect were in car seats. After the Tennessee initiative, many states followed, but the problem persists: How can we adequately protect our children while traveling in automobiles on the nation's roads and highways?

Development of Child Restraint Legislation

The success in Tennessee cannot be credited solely to passage of a child restraint law. Passing an adequate law is only the first step to a successful formula. Tennessee's formula included training and educating the Tennessee Highway Patrol (THP), resulting in a well

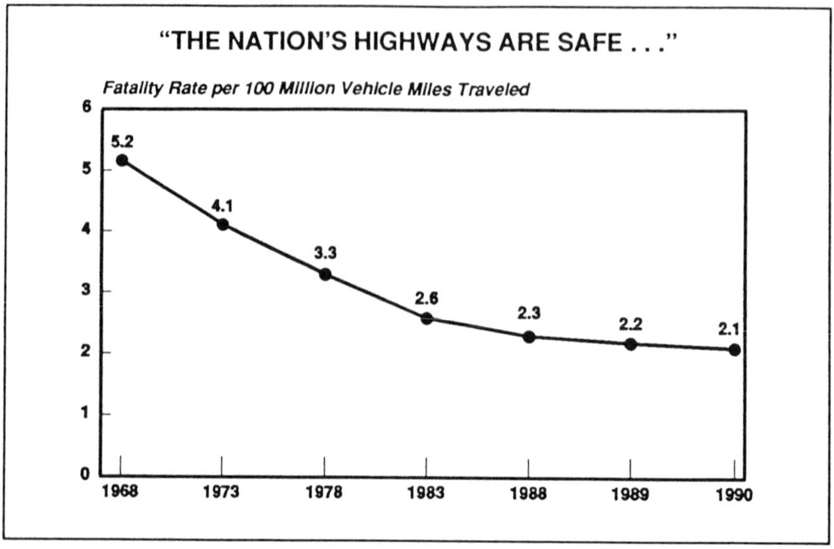

Exhibit 4-3 Fatality rates have declined due to increased use of seat belts and passive protection devices.

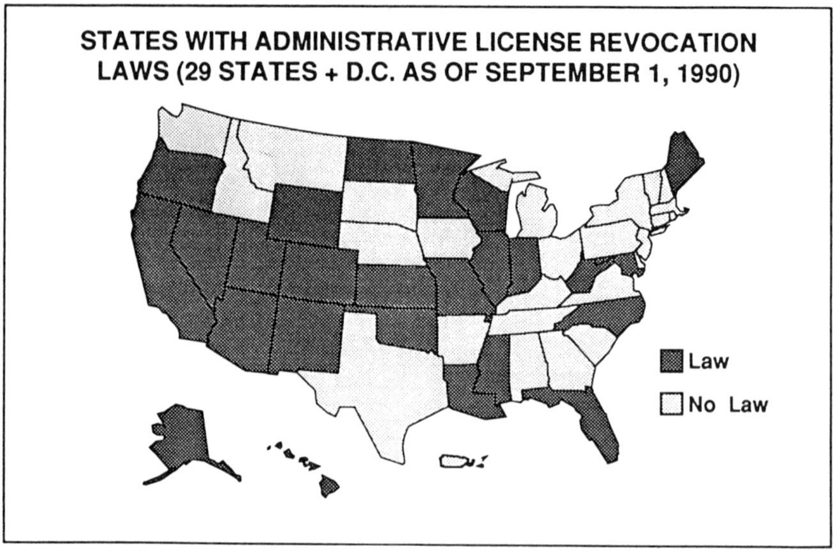

Exhibit 4-2 *revocation laws are a deterrent to repeat offenders*

orchestrated program of enforcement, education and prevention to attain the goals of the legislation.

As part of a highway safety grant, the THP received 800 child restraint seats. THP officers would then cite violators of the law, and place the child in the child restraint provided by the THP. In addition, educational material would be given to the offender. Later, the court had the power to dismiss the charge if the driver returned the child restraint furnished by THP, and showed proof that a child restraint had been purchased after the date of the violation. For those individuals unable to afford a child restraint, the THP would provide them with one from their child restraint donor program.

Child restraint legislation is sometimes perceived as a conflict between individual liberty and the public welfare. The conflicting interests are: 1) the power of the federal government to interfere with individual rights; 2) the power of the states to regulate citizen's rights; 3) the constitutional freedoms of the individual. 4) The right of manufacturers to interfere with legislation designed to protect consumers.

An example of the fourth interest at work, is the bargain struck in 1984 between then Secretary of Transportation, Elizabeth Dole, and the automobile manufacturers. Dole agreed to rescind the federal requirement, that manufacturers install airbags or automatic seatbelts, if states representing two thirds of the population enacted mandatory seat belt use laws. Under pressure from the automobile manufacturers, most states passed seat belt legislation but the laws did not meet the guidelines set out by Dole. As a result, the automobile manufacturers are still required to install airbags or automatic seatbelts in all cars.

Perfecting and Standardizing Child Restraint Legislation

The statistical evidence conclusively proves that the effective means for increasing child restraint use is through mandatory legislation. NHTSA's 19-City Survey shows a direct correlation between use of safety belts and mandatory legislation. Seatbelt use has increased from a low of 11% in 1982 to 49% in 1990. The results of mandatory legislation can be measured both in terms of lives saved and dollars saved. More than 1,500 lives have been saved since 1982. The number of injuries prevented or diminished due to child restraint use is more than ten times that number. However, current legislation makes enforcement difficult due to the differences and loopholes among the states. Most laws cover children under the age of four. Some laws apply only to residents of the state. In a few states, the law is only applicable to the parents of the child.

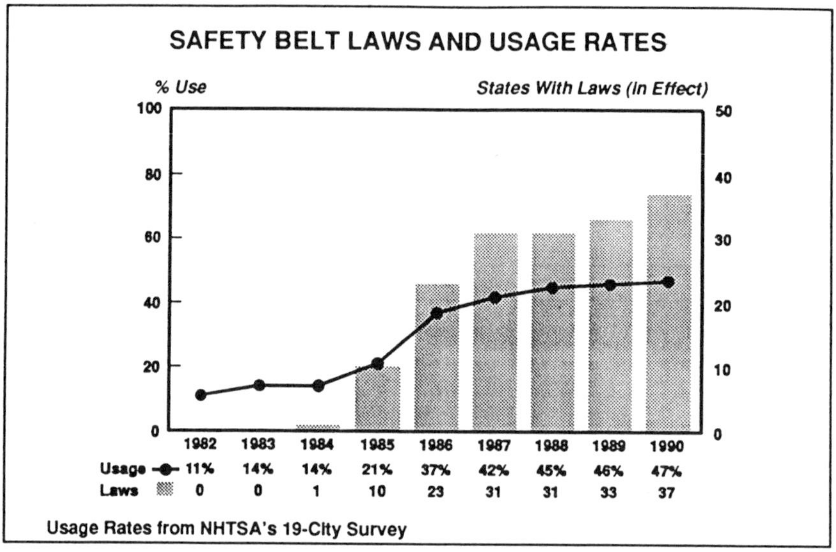

Exhibit 4-4 NHTSA's 19-City Survey shows an increase in seat belt use after the introduction of mandatory legislation in most states.

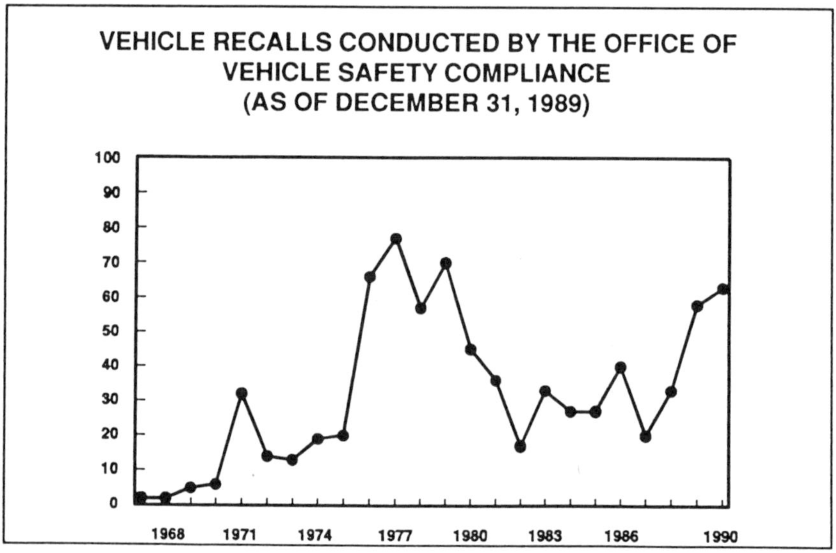

Exhibit 4-5 Recalls of vehicles have peaked at different times. On the other hand, child restraint device recalls have been steadily increasing in the last three years.

CHILD PASSENGER PROTECTION LAWS

November 1991

STATE	EFFECTIVE DATE	AGE	RESTRAINT REQUIREMENT		PENALTY[3]
			SAFETY SEAT REQUIRED	MAY SUBSTITUTE SAFETY BELTS	
Alabama	7/82	Under 6	Under 6	Either 4 or 5	$10
Alaska	6/85	Under 16	Under 4	4 thru 15	$50, 2 pts.
Arizona[1]	8/83	Thru 4[2]	Thru 4[2]	No	$50
Arkansas	8/83	Under 5	Under 3	Between 3 & 5	$10–$25
California	1/83	Under 4[2]	Under 4[2]	No	$100
Colorado	1/84	Under 4[2]	Under 4[2]	No	$25
Connecticut	5/82	Under 4	Under 4	Between 1 &4 in rear seat	$25–$100
Delaware[1]	6/82	Under 4	Under 4	No	$25
Dist. of Columbia	7/83	Under 6	Under 3	Between 3 & 6	$25
Florida	7/83	Under 6	Under 4	Between 4 & 6	$15
Georgia	7/84	Under 5	Under 3	Between 3 & 5	$150, 3 pts.
Hawaii	7/83	Under 4	Under 3	Between 3 & 4	$100 max.
Idaho[1]	1/85	Under 4[2]	Under 4[2]	No	$100 max.
Illinois	7/83	Under 6	Under 4	Between 4 & 6	$25–$50
Indiana	1/84	Under 5	Under 3	Between 3 & 5	$50–$500
Iowa	1/85	Under 6	Under 3	Between 3 & 6	$10
Kansas	1/82	Under 15	Under 4	Between 3 & 14 in front seat	$10
Kentucky[1]	7/82	Under 40"	Under 40"	No	$50
Louisiana	9/84	Under 5	Under 5	Between 3 &5 in rear seat	$25–$50
Maine	9/83	Under 19	Thru 4	Between 1 & 4 if not in parent's car	$25–$50
Maryland	1/84	Under 10[2]	Under 4	Between 3 & 10	$25–$50
Massachusetts	1/82	Thru 12	Under 5	Under 5	$25
Michigan	4/82	Thru 15	Thru 4	1 thru 4 in rear seat	$10
Minnesota	8/83	Under 11	Under 4	4 thru 10 in rear seat	$25
Mississippi	7/83	Under 2	Under 2	No	$25
Missouri	1/84	Under 4	Under 4	Under 4 in rear seat	$25
Montana[1]	1/84	Under 4[2]	Under 2	Between 2 & 4	$10–$25
Nebraska	8/83	Under 5[2]	Under 4[2]	No	$25
Nevada	7/83	Under 5	Under 5	Under 5 in rear seat	$35–$100
New Hampshire	7/83	Under 12	Under 5	Under 5 thru 12	$500 max.

STATE	EFFECTIVE DATE	AGE	RESTRAINT REQUIREMENT		PENALTY[3]
			SAFETY SEAT REQUIRED	MAY SUBSTITUTE SAFETY BELTS	
New Jersey	4/83	Under 5	Under 5	Between 1 1/2 & 5 in rear seat	$10–$25
New Mexico	6/83	Under 11	Under 5	Between 1 & 5 in rear seat	$50
New York	4/82	Under 10	Under 4	Between 4 & 10 in rear seat	$100 max.
North Carolina	7/82	Under 6	Under 3	Between 3 & 6	$25
North Dakota	1/84	Thru 10	Under 3	3 thru 10	$20
Ohio	3/83	Under 4[2]	Under 4[2]	Between 1 & 4 if not in parent's vehicle	$10
Oklahoma	11/83	Under 5	Under 4	Under 4 in rear, 4–5 in front or rear	$25 max.
Oregon	1/84	Under 16	Under 1	Between 1 & 5	$50 max.
Pennsylvania	1/84	Under 4	Under 4	Between 1 & 4 in rear seat	$25
Puerto Rico	1/89	Under 4	Under 4	Over 40 pounds	$10
Rhode Island	7/80	Thru 12	Thru 3	No	$10
South Carolina	7/83	Under 6	Under 4	Between 1 & 6 in rear seat	$25
South Dakota	7/84	Under 5	Under 2	Between 2 & 5	$20
Tennessee	1/78	Under 4	Under 4	No	$25–$50
Texas	10/84	Under 4	Under 2	Between 2 & 4	$25–$50
Utah	7/84	Under 8	Under 2	Between 2 & 8	$20
Vermont	7/84	Thru 12	Under 5	Between 1 & 5 in rear seat	$25
Virginia	1/83	Under 4	Under 3	Between 3 & 4 or over 40 pounds	$25
Washington[1]	1/84	Under 5	Under 1	Between 1 & 5	$30
West Virginia	7/81	Under 9	Under 3	Between 3 & 5	$10–$20
Wisconsin	11/82	Under 4	Under 2	Between 2 & 4	$10–$200
Wyoming	4/85	Under 3[2]	Under 3[2]	No	$25

[1] Law applies only to parents and leagal guardians.
[2] Or less than 40 pounds.
[3] Most states waive fines upon proof of safety seat acquisition.

U.S. Department of Transportation
NATIONAL HIGHWAY TRAFFIC SAFETY ADMINISTRATION

Moreover, a police officer trying to enforce the law has several determinations to make. Depending on the jurisdiction, an officer must determine the child's age, the child's relation to the driver, and that the driver owns the car.

In fourteen states (Alabama, Arizona, Arkansas, Georgia, Indiana, Iowa, Mississippi, Missouri, Nevada, North Carolina, Ohio, Pennsylvania, South Carolina and Washington) the laws only cover children traveling in cars registered in that particular state. Some states only protect children if they are related to the driver. Again, the officer's initial field impressions should be given deference while allowing the driver to rebut such presumptions.

An on the spot determination that a child is protected by child restraint legislation, as a function of his or her age, presents an enforcement problem. The problem can probably be resolved by presuming that the officer's field observations are correct and allowing the alleged violator to rebut the presumption by presenting such evidence to the court. Additionally, some laws require that children be restrained in approved child restraints. "Approval" of a child restraint is in the context of FMVSS 213. The training offered to police officers in the area of child restraints plays a critical role in the officer being able to identify "approved" restraints. The task is not made any easier when the recent number of recalls of various restraints is taken into account.

Moreover, having an approved restraint is only half of the formula, proper use is equally, if not more, important. These requirements and other current legislation make enforcement difficult.

A source for information is NHTSA's 19-City Survey which began in 1979. The survey compiles data concerning the trends in use of seatbelts, helmets, and child restraints by motorists. NHTSA has also funded the Department of Health and Human Services which conducted a survey entitled: "The Survey of Mothers of Young Children." The survey gleaned valuable information on how parents first obtain child restraint information, how parents learn to use child restraints and how parents obtain and follow child restraint instructions.

Standardization based on up-to-date research is needed to aid police officers in enforcing child restraint laws. The federal government could enact legislation to encourage uniformity among the states and increase enforcement of child restraint laws.

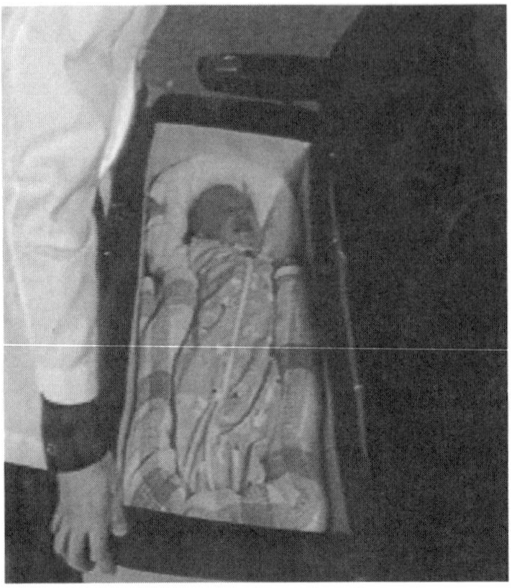

(a)

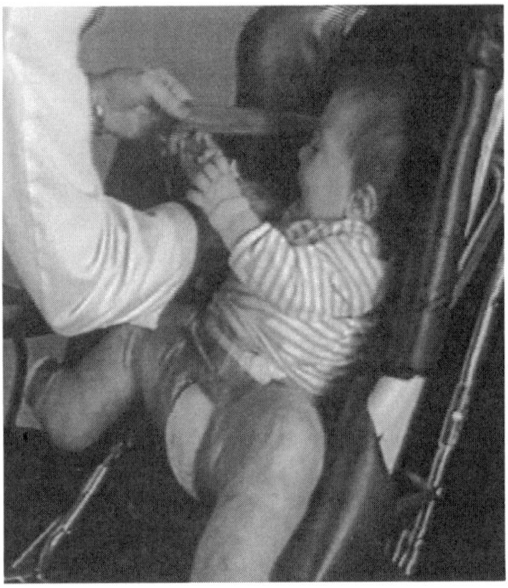

(b)

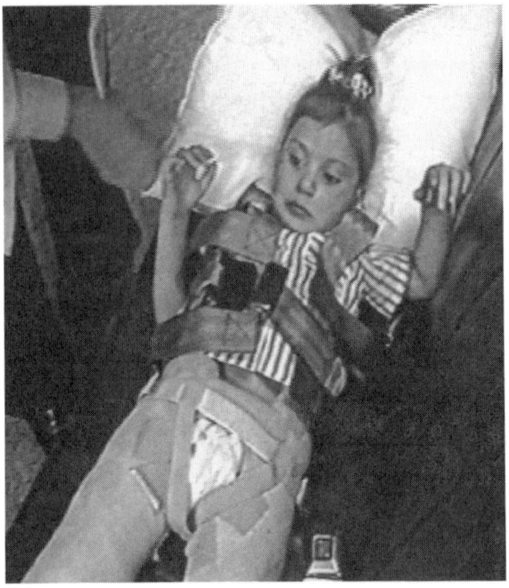

(c)

Exhibit 4-6a-c *Three often overlooked groups of children: (a) infants; (b) injured children; (c) handicapped children.*

Current State Laws

The statutes that follow are a compilation of the latest child restraint laws from all 50 states and the Disctrict of Columbia. This section is intended as a guide for the attorney researching his particular jurisdiction's statute. Attorneys must check their state statutes for the latest changes and amendments. This area of passenger protection is in constant flux and state legislatures consider many bills on child passenger protection every year. This chapter is useful because all the similarities and differences of the different statutes are at the reader's fingertips.

ALABAMA

Code of Ala. 32-5-222 (1992)

Child passenger restraints; required for children under six; penalty

(a) Every person transporting a child under the age of six years in a motor vehicle registered in this state and operated on the roadways, streets, or highways of this state, shall provide for the protection of the child by properly using a child passenger restraint system meeting applicable Federal Motor Vehicle Safety Standards. Provided that, with respect to a child who is either four or five years of age, the term "child passenger restraint system meeting applicable Federal Motor Vehicle Safety Standards" shall be deemed to include seat belts installed by the motor vehicle manufacturer, dealer or owner. Provided that in no event shall failure to wear a child passenger restraint system be considered as contributory negligence. Provided that the term "motor vehicle" as used in this section shall not apply to trucks or buses having tonnage rating of one ton or more.

(b) No provision of this section shall be construed as creating any duty, standard of care, right, or liability between parent and child that is not recognized under the laws of the state of Alabama as they presently exist, or may, at any time in the future, be constituted by statute or decision.

(c) Any person violating the provisions of this section may be fined not more than $10.00 for each offense.

(d) The provisions of this section notwithstanding, nothing contained herein shall be deemed a violation of any law which would otherwise nullify or change in any way the provisions or coverage of any insurance contract.

ALASKA

Alaska Stat. 28.05.095 (1992)

Use of safety devices required

(a) Except as provided in (c) of this section a person

(1) 16 years of age or older may not occupy a motor vehicle while being driven unless restrained by a safety belt; and

(2) may not operate a motor vehicle unless restrained by a safety belt.

(b) Except as provided in (c) of this section, a driver may not transport a child under the age of 16 in a motor vehicle unless the driver has provided and properly secured each child as described in this subsection. If the child is less than four years of age, the child shall be properly secured in a child safety device meeting the standards of the United States Department of Transportation for a child safety device for infants. If the child is four but not yet 16 years of age, the child shall be properly secured in a child safety device approved for a child of that age and size by the United States Department of Transportation or in a safety belt, whichever is appropriate for the particular child.

(c) Subsections (a) and (b) do not apply to

(1) passengers in a school bus, unless the school bus is required to be equipped with seat belts by the United States Department of Transportation or an emergency vehicle;

(2) a vehicle operator acting in the course of employment delivering mail or newspapers from inside the vehicle to roadside mail or newspaper boxes;

(3) a person or class of persons exempted by regulation under AS 28.05.096; or

(4) a person required to be restrained by safety belts under (a) or (b) of this section if the motor vehicle is not equipped with safety belts.

(d) A person may not remove a safety belt from a vehicle solely to be exempted under (c)(4) of this section.

(e) Notwithstanding any other provision of law, a peace officer may not stop or detain a motor vehicle to determine compliance with (a) of this section, or issue a citation for a violation of (a) of this section, unless the peace officer has probable cause to stop or detain the motor vehicle other than for a violation of (a) of this section.

ARIZONA

28-907 (1992)

Child passenger restraint system; special fund for indigents; exemptions; violation; classification; definitions

A. A parent, guardian or custodian of a child four or less years of age or forty or fewer pounds in weight when transporting that child in a noncommercial motor vehicle operated on the highways of this state and registered in this state in the name of the parent, guardian or custodian shall properly secure that child in a child passenger restraint system.

B. The department shall adopt standards, in accordance with Federal Motor Vehicle Standards, for the performance, design and installation of childpassenger restraint systems for use in noncommercial motor vehicles for children four or less years of age or forty or fewer pounds in weight.

C. A person who violates this section is guilty of a petty offense with a maximum fine of fifty dollars, except that no fine may be imposed if a sufficient showing is made by the defendant that the motor vehicle has been subsequently equipped with a child passenger restraint system which meets the standards adopted pursuant to subsection B of this section. A sufficient showing may include a receipt mailed to the appropriate court officer which evidences purchase or acquisition of a child passenger restraint system. Notwithstanding section 13-811 or 22-404 the court imposing and collecting such fine shall transfer the monies, exclusive of any assessments imposed pursuant to section 41-2403, to the state treasurer for deposit in the child passenger restraint fund. The child passenger restraint fund shall not exceed a balance of twenty thousand dollars. All monies collected over the twenty thousand dollar balance shall be deposited into the Arizona highway user revenue fund.

D. In the event that a vehicle is stopped for an apparent violation of this section by a law enforcement officer, such officer shall determine from the driver, or any adult passenger, both of the following:

1. If anyone in the vehicle is the parent, custodian or guardian of the unrestrained child or children in the car.

2. Whether the unrestrained child or children in the vehicle are four or less years of age or less than forty pounds in weight.

E. If the information given to the officer indicates that a violation of this section has not been committed, the officer shall not detain the vehicle any further unless some additional violation is involved. In no event shall the stopping of a vehicle for an apparent or actual violation of this section constitute probable cause for the search or seizure of such vehicle.

F. Prior to the release of any newly born child from a hospital, the hospital in conjunction with the attending physician shall provide the parents of the child with a copy of this section and information with regard to the availability of loaner or rental programs for child passenger restraint devices which may be available in the community where the child is born.

G. A child passenger restraint fund is established in the department of economic security which consists of all fines deposited pursuant to subsection C of this section and any monies donated by the public. The department of economic security shall purchase child passenger restraint systems which meet the requirements of this section from monies deposited in the fund. At the request of a licensed hospital, a public or private agency providing shelter services to victims of domestic violence, a public or private agency providing shelter services to homeless families or a health clinic, but subject to availability, the department of economic security shall distribute child passenger restraint systems to the requesting hospital, public or private agency or health clinic. On the application of any person to a hospital, a public or private agency providing shelter services to victims of domestic violence, a public or private agency providing shelter services to homeless families or a health clinic and a finding by the hospital, public or private agency or health clinic to which the application was made that the applicant is unable to acquire a child passenger restraint system because the person is indigent, the hospital, public or private agency or health clinic shall, subject to availability, loan the applicant a child passenger restraint system at no charge for as long as the applicant has a need to transport a child who is subject to this section.

H. The requirements of this section or evidence of a violation of this section are not admissible as evidence in a judicial proceeding except in a judicial proceeding for a violation of this section.

I. The provisions of this section shall not apply if the motor vehicle was originally manufactured without passenger restraint devices.

J. A parent, guardian or custodian transporting more than one child four or less years of age or forty or fewer pounds in weight in a motor vehicle which because of the restricted size of the passenger area does not provide sufficient area for the required number of child passenger restraint devices shall not be subject to prosecution under this section if at least one child is restrained as required and the parent, guardian or custodian has secured as many of the other children in child passenger restraint devices pursuant to this section as is reasonable given the restricted size of the passenger area and the number of passengers being transported in the motor vehicle.

K. For the purposes of this section:

1. "Custodian" has the same meaning as provided in section 8-201.
2. "Indigent" has the same meaning as provided in section 11-297, subsection B.

L. The provisions of this section do not apply to a motor vehicle which is also a recreational vehicle as defined by section 41-2142. HISTORY: Last year in which legislation affected this section: 1991

ARKANSAS

19-6-443 (1992)

Child Passenger Protection Fund

The Arkansas Child Passenger Protection Fund shall consist of those special revenues as specified in subdivision (67) of @ 19-6-301, and other moneys that may be appropriated, allocated, or donated to such fund, there to be used by the Arkansas Highway Safety Program for the purchase of child passenger safety seats as set out in @ 27-34-101 et seq.

27-34-102 (1992)

Legislative intent

It is the legislative intent that all state, university, county, and local law enforcement agencies, as well as all physicians and hospitals, in recognition of the problems, including death and serious injury associated with unrestrained children in motor vehicles, conduct a continuing safety and public awareness campaign so as to encourage and promote the use of child passenger safety seats.

27-34-103 (1992)

Penalty

(a) Any person who violates this chapter shall, upon conviction, be fined not less than ten dollars ($10.00) nor more than twenty-five dollars ($25.00).

(b) The fine may be waived upon satisfactory proof being presented to the court that the defendant has acquired, purchased, or rented an approved child passenger safety seat as described in @ 27-34-104.

27-34-104 (1992)

Requirements

(a) Every driver who regularly transports a child under the age of five (5) years in a passenger automobile, van, or pickup truck, other than one operated for hire, which is registered in this state shall provide, while the motor vehicle is in motion and operated on a public road, street, or highway of this state, for the protection of the child by properly placing, maintaining, and securing the child in a child passenger safety seat system meeting applicable Federal Motor Vehicle Safety Standards in effect on August 1, 1983.

(b) If a child is three (3) to five (5) years of age, a safety belt shall be sufficient to meet the requirements of this section.

27-34-105 (1992)

Exceptions

The provisions of this chapter shall not apply when any one of the following conditions exist:

(1) The motor vehicle is being used as an ambulance or other emergency vehicle;

(2) When an emergency exists that threatens the life of any person operating a motor vehicle to whom this section otherwise would apply or the life of any child who otherwise would be required to be restrained under this chapter;

(3) If all seating positions equipped with child passenger safety seat systems or seat safety belts are occupied; or

(4) If any child who would otherwise be required to be restrained under this chapter is physically unable because of medical reasons to use a child passenger safety seat system or seat safety belt.

27-34-106.

Effect of noncompliance

(a) The failure to provide or use a child passenger safety seat shall not be considered, under any circumstances, as evidence of comparative or contributory negligence, nor shall failure be admissible as evidence in the trial of any civil action with regard to negligence.

(b) Neither shall the failure to provide or use a child passenger safety seat be considered, under any circumstances, as evidence in any prosecution for negligent homicide.

27-34-107 (1992)

Child Passenger Protection Fund

(a) A special fund is created which shall be known as the Arkansas Child Passenger Protection Fund.

(b) The fund shall consist of all fines which are collected for violations of this chapter and other moneys that may be appropriated, allocated, or donated for the purpose of being placed in the fund.

(c) The Arkansas Highway Safety Program shall purchase child passengersafety seats from the fund established in this section.

(d) The seats purchased by the Arkansas Highway Safety Program shall be loaned or rented to hospitals or other groups or individuals who may loan or rent such seats to others for the purpose of transporting children.

CALIFORNIA

Child Passenger Restraints Requirements

Cal Veh Code 27360 (1993)

Prohibition against failure to use proper seat restraint system

(a) No parent or legal guardian, when present in a passenger vehicle or motortruck of less than 6,001 pounds unladen weight, shall permit his or her child or ward under the age of four years or weighing less than 40 pounds to be transported upon a highway in the motor vehicle without providing and properly using, for each such child or ward, a child passenger restraint system meeting applicable Federal Motor Vehicle Safety Standards.

(b) No driver shall transport on a highway any child under four years of age or weighing less than 40 pounds in a passenger vehicle or motortruck of less than 6,001 pounds unladen weight without providing and properly securing the child in a child passenger restraint system meeting applicable Federal Motor Vehicle Safety Standards. This subdivision does not apply to a driver if the parent or legal guardian of the child is also present in the vehicle and is not the driver.

(c)(1) A first offense under this section is punishable by a fine of one hundred dollars ($ 100), except that the court may waive the fine if the defendant establishes to the satisfaction of the court that he or she is economically disadvantaged and the court, instead, refers the defendant to a child passenger restraint low-cost purchase or loaner program. If the fine is waived, the court shall nevertheless report the conviction to the department pursuant to Section 1803.

(2) A second or subsequent offense under this section is punishable by a fine of one hundred dollars ($ 100), no part of which may be waived by the court.

(d) Notwithstanding any other provision of law, the fines collected for a violation of this section shall be allocated as follows:

(1) Sixty percent to local health departments in the county where the violation occurred, to be used for a child passenger restraint low-cost purchase or loaner program which shall include, but not be limited to, education on the proper installation and use of a child passenger restraint system. The county may contract for the implementation of the program.

Local health departments shall report on an ongoing basis to the Office of Traffic Safety in the Business, Transportation and Housing Agency whenever a child passenger restraint low-cost purchase or loaner program is developed or funded pursuant to subdivision (d). The Office of Traffic Safety shall prepare and distribute to the counties a listing of all child passenger restraint low-cost purchase or loaner programs in the state. Each county shall forward the listing to the courts and county hospitals in that county.

(2) Fifteen percent to the county for the administration of the program.

(3) Twenty-five percent to the city, to be deposited in its general fund except that, if the violation occurred in an unincorporated area, this amount shall be allocated to the county for purposes of paragraph (1).

27361.

Vehicle stop by law enforcement officer

Any law enforcement officer reasonably suspecting a violation of Section 27360 may stop any vehicle transporting a child appearing to the officer to be within the age or weight specified in Section 27360. The officer may issue a notice to appear for a violation of Section 27360.

27362.

Installation of nonconforming seat restraint system; Responsibility for compliance; Penalty for violation

(a) No manufacturer, wholesaler, or retailer shall sell, offer for sale, or install in any motor vehicle any child passenger restraint system not conforming to all applicable Federal Motor Vehicle Safety Standards on the date of sale or installation. Responsibility for compliance with this section shall rest with the individual selling, offering for sale, or installing the system. Every person who violates this section is guilty of a misdemeanor and shall be punished as follows:

(1) Upon a first conviction, by a fine not exceeding four hundred dollars ($ 400) or by imprisonment in the county jail for a period of not more than 90 days, or both.

(2) Upon a second or subsequent conviction, by a fine not exceeding one thousand dollars ($ 1,000) or by imprisonment in the county jail for a period of not more than 180 days, or both.

(b) The fines collected for a violation of this section shall be allocated as follows:

(1) Sixty percent to local health departments in the county where the violation occurred, to be used for a child passenger restraint low-cost purchase or loaner program which shall include, but not be limited to, education on the proper installation and use of a child passenger restraint system. The county may contract for the implementation of the program.

Local health departments shall report on an ongoing basis to the Office of Traffic Safety in the Business, Transportation and Housing Agency whenever a child passenger restraint low-cost purchase or loaner program is developed or funded pursuant to subdivision (b). The Office of Traffic Safety shall prepare and distribute to the counties a listing of all child passenger restraint low-cost purchase or loan programs in the state. Each county shall forward the listing to the courts and county hospitals in that county.

(2) Fifteen percent to the county for the administration of the program.

(3) Twenty-five percent to the city, to be deposited in its general fund except that, if the violation occurred in an unincorporated area, this amount shall be allocated to the

county for purposes of paragraph (1). HISTORY:Added Stats 1982 ch 839 @ 2. Amended Stats 1990 ch 33 @ 5 (SB 1372), effective March 26, 1990; Stats 1991 ch 1223 @ 4 (SB 1073).

27363.

Exemption from requirements of article

(a) The court may exempt from the requirements of this article any class of child by age, weight, or size if it is determined that the use of a child passenger restraint system would be impractical by reason of physical unfitness, medical condition, or size. The court may require satisfactory proof of the child's physical unfitness, medical condition, or size.

(b) In case of an emergency, or when a child is being transported in an authorized emergency vehicle, if there is no child passenger restraint system available, a child may be transported without the use of such a system, but the child shall be secured by a seat belt.

27363.5 (1993)

Provision of information concerning requirement of child passenger restraint systems to parents of hospitalized child

(a) Every public or private hospital shall, at the time of or before the discharge of a child under the age of four years, or weighing less than 40 pounds, provide and discuss information on the law requiring child passenger restraint systems to the parents or the person to whom the child is released.

(b) A public or private hospital shall not be responsible for the failure of the parent or person to whom the child is released to use a child passenger restraint system.

27364.

Legislative intent; Scope of article

It is the intent of the Legislature, in enacting this article, to insure that children, who are, because of their tender years, helpless dependent passengers, are provided with the safest transportation possible. Nothing in this article shall be construed to extend application of these provisions to a class of children other than the class of children herein specified.

27365.

Notice by car rental agency of requirement of use of proper seat restraint system; Requirement that agency provide proper seat restraint systems upon request

(a) (1) Every car rental agency in California shall inform each of its customers of the provisions of Section 27360 by posting, in a place conspicuous to the public in each established place of business of the agency, a notice not smaller than 15 inches by 20 inches which states the following:

"CALIFORNIA LAW REQUIRES ALL CHILDREN UNDER THE AGE OF 4 OR WEIGHING LESS THAN 40 POUNDS TO BE TRANSPORTED IN A CHILD RESTRAINT SYSTEM. THIS AGENCY IS REQUIRED TO PROVIDE FOR RENTAL A CHILD RESTRAINT SYSTEM IF YOU DO NOT HAVE SUCH A SYSTEM YOURSELF."

(2) The posted notice specified in paragraph (1) is not required if the car rental agency's place of business is located in a hotel which has a business policy prohibiting the posting of signs or notices in any area of the hotel. In that case, a car rental agency shall furnish a written notice to each customer which contains the same information as required for the posted notice.

(b) Every such agency shall have available for, and shall, upon request, provide for rental to, adults traveling with children under the age of four or weighing less than 40 pounds, child passenger seat restraint systems meeting applicable Federal Motor Vehicle Safety Standards on the date of the rental transaction, in good and safe condition, with no missing original parts, and not older than five years.

(c) A violation of this section is an infraction punishable by a fine of one hundred dollars ($ 100).

40000.15.

Misdemeanors

A violation of any of the following provisions shall constitute a misdemeanor, and not an infraction:

Sections 23103 and 23104, relating to reckless driving.

Section 23109, relating to speed contests or exhibitions.

Section 23110, subdivision (a), relating to throwing at vehicles.

Section 23152, relating to driving under the influence.

Subdivision (b) of Section 23222, relating to possession of marijuana.

Sections 23237 and 23244, relating to ignition interlock devices.

Section 23253, relating to officers on vehicular crossings.

Section 23332, relating to trespassing.

Section 24011.3, relating to vehicle bumper strength notices.

Section 27150.1, relating to sale of exhaust systems.

Section 27362, relating to child passenger seat restraints.

Section 28050, relating to true mileage driven.

Section 28050.5, relating to nonfunctional odometers.

Section 28051, relating to resetting odometer.

Section 28051.5, relating to device to reset odometer.

CONNECTICUT

14-100a (1990)

Seat safety belts. Child restraint system

(a) No new passenger motor vehicle may be sold or registered in this state unless equipped with at least two sets of seat safety belts for the front and rear seats of the motor vehicle, which belts comply with the requirements of subsection (b) of this section. The anchorage unit at the attachment point shall be of such construction, design and strength as to support a loop load strength of not less than four thousand pounds for each belt.

(b) No seat safety belt may be sold for use in connection with the operation of a motor vehicle on any highway of this state unless it is so constructed and installed as to have a loop strength through the complete attachment of not less than four thousand pounds, and the buckle or closing device shall be of such construction and design that after it has received the aforesaid loop belt load it can be released with one hand with a pull of less than forty-five pounds.

(c) (1) The operator of and any front seat passenger in a private passenger motor vehicle, as defined in subsection (g) of section 38a-363, or a vanpool vehicle equipped with seat safety belts complying with the provisions of the Code of Federal Regulations Title 49, Section 571.209, as amended from time to time, shall wear such seat safety belt while the vehicle is being operated on the highways of this state, except that a child under the age of four years shall be restrained as provided in subsection (d) of this section. Each operator of such vehicle shall secure or cause to be secured in a seat safety belt any front seat passenger four years of age or older and under sixteen years of age. The provisions of this subdivision shall not apply to an operator of or any front seat passenger in any vehicle equipped with air bags complying with the provisions of the Code of Federal Regulations Title 49, Section 571.208, as amended from time to time.

(2) The provisions of subdivision (1) of this subsection shall not apply to any person whose physical disability or impairment would prevent restraint in such safety belt, provided such person obtains a written statement from a licensed physician containing reasons for such person's inability to wear such safety belt and including information concerning the nature and extent of such condition. Such person shall carry the statement on his person or in the motor vehicle at all times when it is being operated.

(3) As used in this subsection, "private passenger motor vehicle" does not mean an authorized emergency vehicle

responding to an emergency call or a motor vehicle operated (A) by a rural letter carrier of the United States postal service while performing his official duties, or (B) by a person engaged in the delivery of newspapers.

(4) Failure to wear a seat safety belt shall not be considered as contributory negligence nor shall such failure be admissible evidence in any civil action.

(5) During the period commencing January 1, 1986, and ending January 31, 1986, any person who violates this subsection shall be issued a verbal warning by law enforcement officers. On and after February 1, 1986, any person who violates the provisions of this subsection shall have committed an infraction and shall be fined fifteen dollars. Points may not be assessed against the operator's license of any person convicted of such violation.

(d) Any person who transports a child under the age of four years in a motor vehicle on the highways of this state shall provide and require the child to use a child restraint system approved pursuant to regulations adopted by the department of motor vehicles in accordance with the provisions of chapter 54. For any child between the ages of one year and four years, a seat safety belt in the rear seat of the motor vehicle which complies with the provisions of subsection (b) of this section may be used in lieu of a child restraint system. As used in this subsection, "motor vehicle" does not mean a recreational vehicle of the truck or van type or a truck or bus having a tonnage rating of one ton or more. Failure to use a child restraint system shall not be considered as contributory negligence nor shall such failure be admissible evidence in any civil action. Violation of this subsection shall be an infraction. The court shall waive any fine imposed on a person who violates this subsection if such person provides proof that he acquired and installed a child restraint system meeting the requirements of this subsection on or before the court appearance date.

(e) The commissioner shall administer the provisions of this section.

DELAWARE

21 Del. C. 4803 (1992)

Child restraint in motor vehicles

(a) Every person shall be responsible, when transporting a child under the age of 4 years and weighing less than 40 pounds in a motor vehicle operated on the roadways, streets or highways of this State, for providing for the protection of the child by properly using a child passenger restraint system meeting the Federal Motor Vehicle Safety Standards. The duty imposed by this subsection shall not apply to any operator or passenger of a motor bus, limousine or taxicab as defined in @ 1801 of Title 2.

(b) The court may, upon presentation of evidence that a violator of this section has purchased or obtained a child passenger restraint system subsequent to the violation, dismiss all charges pursuant to this section.

(c) A violation of this section shall be an offense punishable by a fine of no more than $28.75 for each violation. The failure to provide a child restraint system for more than 1 child in the same vehicle at the same time, as required by this section, shall not be treated as a separate offense.

(d) Failure to wear a child passenger restraint system shall not be considered as evidence of either comparative or contributory negligence in any civil suit arising out of any motor vehicle accident in which a child under 4 is injured, nor shall failure to wear a child passenger restraint system be admissible as evidence in the trial of any civil action.

DISTRICT OF COLUMBIA

D.C. Code 40-1201 (1992)

Findings; purpose

The Council of the District of Columbia finds that:

(1) (A) Nationally, motor vehicle accidents are the leading cause of death of children of less than 6 years of age;

(B) In 1981, over 600 children of less than 6 years of age were reported injured in motor vehicle accidents in the District of Columbia, reflecting an increase of 16% over reported injuries in 1980 and 40% over reported injuries in 1979;

(C) Young children, due to their small size and early skeletal development, are at a much greater risk of serious bodily injury in motor vehicle accidents than are adults;

(D) Proper use of child restraint seats and safety belts has been estimated to reduce by as much as 90% and 67%, respectively, the fatalities and injuries to children resulting from motor vehicle accidents;

(E) Reducing fatalities and injuries to children from motor vehicle accidents through the proper use of child restraint seats and safety belts would result in a significant reduction of the social and economic burdens which these accidents place upon families, insurers, and the public generally;

(F) Project Safe-Child is a cooperative program conducted by the Office of Child Health Advocacy at Children's Hospital National Medical Center and the Transportation Safety Division of the Office of Policy and Program Development in the District of Columbia Department of Transportation which includes a child restraint loaner program for the distribution of child restraints to residents of the District of Columbia; and

(G) Project Safe-Child's public information program and child restraint loaner programs, upon being expanded through greater allocation of federal grant funds from the National

Highway Traffic Safety Administration, can assist the public in complying with this chapter.

(2) It is the purpose of this chapter to require that children of less than 16 years of age be protected by being properly restrained in a child restraint seat or safety belt when riding in a motor vehicle.

40-1202.

Definitions

As used in this chapter the term:

(1) " Child restraint seat" means any motor vehicle restraint system which has been designed to protect children and has been approved pursuant to @ 40-1204.

(2) "Operator" means a person who drives or is in actual physical control of a vehicle.

(3) "Properly restrained," when used in reference to the use of a safety belt, means secured with the lap portion of a safety belt which is provided in a motor vehicle; and when used in reference to the use of a child restraint seat, means secured in a child restraint seat which itself has been fastened to the motor vehicle by a safety belt and in which all securing straps are being used.

(4) "Transport" means to have a child of less than 6 years of age as a passenger in a motor vehicle while the operator is seated in the driver position and the motor vehicle is either parked or in motion.

(5) "Motor vehicle" means any device with more than 3 wheels and a seating capacity of 8 or fewer passengers, exclusive of the operator, which is propelled by an internal-combustion engine, electricity, or steam, and which is designed, used, or maintained for passenger or recreational purposes, or which is designed, used, or maintained for transporting freight, merchandise, or other commercial loads or property.

The term "motor vehicle" does not include any device which is used for livery, sightseeing, taxi, ambulance, funeral, or farm purposes; or any device with more than 3 wheels which is propelled by an internal-combustion engine, electricity, or steam and which has a seating capacity of more than 8 passengers, exclusive of the operator.

40-1203.

Requirements

(a) The operator of a motor vehicle may not transport any child of less than 3 years of age unless the child is properly restrained in a child restraint seat.

(b) The operator of a motor vehicle may not transport any child between 3 years of age and 16 years of age unless the child is properly restrained in an approved child restraint seat or safety belt.

(c) A parent or legal guardian may transport his or her own child without restraint herein if that person is transporting a number of his or her own children of less than 16 years of age which exceeds the number of passenger positions equipped with safety belts in the motor vehicle. However, an unrestrained child may not be transported in the front seat of a motor vehicle.

40-1204.

Seats to conform to federal safety standards

Child restraint seats shall conform to all applicable Federal Motor Vehicle Safety Standards established pursuant to @ 103 of Title 1 of the National Traffic and Motor Vehicle Safety Act of 1966, approved September 9, 1966 (80 Stat. 719; 15 U.S.C. @ 1392).

40-1205.

Application of chapter

This chapter shall apply to any person operating a motor vehicle in the District of Columbia.

40-1206.

Penalty; waiver of fine

(a) Any individual who violates any provision of this chapter shall be subject to a fine of $ 55, and the violation shall be processed and adjudicated under the provisions applicable to parking, standing, stopping, and pedestrian infractions which are set forth in subchapter III of Chapter 6 of this title.

(b) The fine for the first violation of @ 40-1203 (a) by any operator shall be waived upon presentation of proof by the operator that an approved child restraint seat has been acquired subsequent to the violation, either by purchase, gift or through an officially designated child restraint seat loan program, by the operator or by the parent or legal guardian of the child who was transported without being properly restrained.

(c) The Director of the Department of Transportation shall assign 2 points under the provisions of 18 DCMR to the driver record of any person convicted of a violation of this chapter.

40-1207.

Evidentiary effect; basis for civil liability

Neither a violation of this chapter nor compliance herewith shall constitute any evidence of negligence or contributory negligence, nor shall either a violation or compliance provide any basis for a civil action for damages.

40-1208 (1992)

Rules; public information program

Within 180 days from March 7, 1992, the Mayor shall issue rules to implement this chapter and, through public or private programs, shall maintain a childrestraint seat loan program for residents of the District of Columbia, and make available to the public information about this chapter.

FLORIDA

Fla. Stat. 316.613 (1991)

Child restraint requirements

(1)(a) Every operator of a motor vehicle as defined herein, while transporting a child in a motor vehicle operated on the roadways, streets, or highways of this state, shall, if the child is 5 years of age or younger, provide for protection of the child by properly using a crash-tested, federally approved child restraint device. For children aged through 3 years, such restraint device must be a separate carrier. For children aged 4 through 5 years, a separate carrier or a seat belt may be used.

(b) The Division of Motor Vehicles shall provide notice of the requirement for child restraint devices, which notice shall accompany the delivery of each motor vehicle license tag.

(2) As used in this section, the term "motor vehicle" means a motor vehicle as defined in s. 316.003 that is operated on the roadways, streets, and highways of the state. The term does not include:

(a) A school bus.

(b) A bus used for the transportation of persons for compensation.

(c) A farm tractor or implement of husbandry.

(d) A truck of net weight of more than 5,000 pounds.

(e) A motorcycle, moped, or bicycle.

(3) The failure to provide and use a child passenger restraint shall not be considered comparative negligence, nor shall such failure be admissible as evidence in the trial of any civil action with regard to negligence.

(4) It is the legislative intent that all state, county, and local law enforcement agencies, and safety councils, in recognition of the problems with child death and injury from unrestrained occupancy in motor vehicles, conduct a continuing safety and

public awareness campaign as to the magnitude of the problem.

(5) Any person who violates the provisions of this section commits a nonmoving traffic infraction punishable as provided for in s. 318.18(12) and shall have 3 points assessed against his driver's license as set forth in s. 322.27.

316.614

Safety belt usage

(1) This section may be cited as the "Florida Safety Belt Law."

(2) It is the policy of this state that enactment of this section is intended to be compatible with the continued support by the state for federal safety standards requiring automatic crash protection, and the enactment of this section should not be used in any manner to rescind or delay the implementation of the federal automatic crash protection system requirements of Federal Motor Safety Standard 208 as set forth in S4.1.2.1 thereof, as entered on July 17, 1984, for new cars.

(3) As used in this section:

(a) "Motor vehicle" means a motor vehicle as defined in s. 316.003 that is operated on the roadways, streets, and highways of this state. The term does not include:

1. A school bus.

2. A bus used for the transportation of persons for compensation.

3. A farm tractor or implement of husbandry.

4. A truck of a net weight of more than 5,000 pounds.

5. A motorcycle, moped, or bicycle.

(b) "Safety belt" means a seat belt assembly that meets the requirements established under Federal Motor Vehicle Safety Standard No. 208, 49 C.F.R. s. 571.208.

(c) "Restrained by a safety belt" means being restricted by an appropriately adjusted safety belt which is properly fastened at all times when a motor vehicle is in motion.

(4) It is unlawful for any person:

(a) To operate a motor vehicle in this state unless each front seat passenger of the vehicle under the age of 16 years is restrained by a safety belt or by a child restraint device pursuant to s. 316.613, if applicable; or

(b) To operate a motor vehicle in this state unless the person is restrained by a safety belt.

(5) It is unlawful for any person 16 years of age or older to be a passenger in the front seat of a motor vehicle unless such person is restrained by a safety belt when the vehicle is in motion.

(6)(a) Neither a person who is certified by a physician as having a medical condition that causes the use of a safety belt to be inappropriate or dangerous nor an employee of a newspaper home delivery service while in the course of his employment delivering newspapers on home delivery routes is required to be restrained by a safety belt.

(b) The number of front seat passengers of a pickup truck required to wear a safety belt pursuant to this section shall not exceed the number of safety belts which were installed in the front seat of such pickup truck by the manufacturer.

(7)(a) After January 1, 1987, any person who violates subsection (4) or subsection (5) shall be fined $ 20, including court costs, for each separate offense.

(b) For the purposes of informing and educating persons who are affected by the provisions of this act, any officer as defined in s. 318.13(5) may, during the period of July 1, 1986, through December 31, 1986, temporarily stop and detain motor vehicles for the purpose of issuing verbal warnings to persons who may be in violation of this section.

(8) It is the intent of the Legislature that all state, county, and local law enforcement agencies, safety councils, and public school systems, in recognition of the fatalities and injuries attributed to unrestrained occupancy of motor vehicles, shall conduct a continuing safety and public awareness campaign as to the magnitude of the problem and adopt programs designed to

encourage compliance with the safety belt usage requirements of this section.

(9) Enforcement of this section by state or local law enforcement agencies shall be accomplished only as a secondary action when a driver of a motor vehicle has been detained for a suspected violation of another section of this chapter, chapter 320, or chapter 322.

n1 (10) A violation of the provisions of this section shall not constitute negligence per se, nor shall such violation be used as prima facie evidence of negligence or be considered in mitigation of damages, but such violation may be considered as evidence of comparative negligence, in any civil action.

GEORGIA

40-8-76 (1992)

Safety belts; safety restraints for children under four years of age

(a)(1) No new private passenger automobile manufactured after January 1, 1964, shall be sold to the general public in this state unless such automobile shall be equipped with two sets of safety belts for the front seat thereof. The safety belts may be installed by the manufacturer prior to delivery to the dealer, or they may be installed by the dealer.

(2) Any person violating paragraph (1) of this subsection shall be guilty of a misdemeanor.

(b)(1) On and after July 1, 1984, every driver who transports a child four years of age or younger in a passenger automobile, van, or pickup truck, other than one operated for hire, which is registered in this state shall, while such motor vehicle is in motion and operated on a public road, street, or highway of this state, provide for the protection of such child in a child passenger restraining system approved by the United States Department of Transportation under Federal Motor Vehicle Safety Standard 213 in effect on January 1, 1983. A driver shall not be deemed to be complying with the provisions of this subsection unless the child passenger restraining system is installed and being used in accordance with the manufacturer's directions for such system. However, if the child is three or four years of age, a seat belt shall be sufficient to meet the requirements of this subsection. The provisions of this subsection shall not apply when the child's personal needs are being attended to.

(2)(A) Upon conviction of an offense under this subsection, the defendant shall be punished by a fine of not more than $25.00.

(B) The provisions of this subsection shall not apply to the driver of a car pool carrying children four years of age or younger to a church or public or private school, unless said church or public or private school is licensed as a day-care center by the Georgia Department of Human Resources and unless such children are being transported to said church or public or private school in a van operated by the church or public or private school.

(c) It shall be the duty of the Governor's Office of Highway Safety to implement and coordinate a program to inform parents and other citizens of Georgia of the reasons for the enactment of subsection (b) of this Code section. Such program shall be carried out prior to January 1, 1989. The Governor's Office of Highway Safety shall solicit the cooperation and assistance of the Georgia State Patrol, the Georgia Sheriffs Association, the Georgia Association of Chiefs of Police, Incorporated, the Peace Officers' Association of Georgia, the Medical College of Georgia, the Georgia Hospital Association, the Georgia Association of Educators, the Georgia Parent-Teacher Association, and other appropriate organizations in educating the citizens of the state and in implementing, coordinating, and carrying out the program provided for herein.

(d) Violation of this Code section shall not constitute negligence per se nor contributory negligence per se.

HAWAII

291-11.5 (1992)

Child passenger restraints

(a) Except as otherwise provided in this section, no person operating a motor vehicle on a public highway in the State shall transport a child under four years of age except under the following circumstances:

(1) If the child is under three years of age, the person operating the motor vehicle shall ensure that the child is properly restrained in a child passenger restraint system approved by the United States Department of Transportation at the time of its manufacture; or

(2) If the child is three years of age or older but less than four years of age, the person operating the motor vehicle must either ensure that the child is properly restrained in a child passenger restraint system approved by the United States Department of Transportation at the time of its manufacture or ensure that the child is restrained by a seat belt assembly.

(b) Operators of the following motor vehicles shall be exempt from the requirements of this section: emergency, commercial, and mass transit vehicles. Further exemptions from this section may be established by the department of transportation pursuant to rules adopted under chapter 91.

(c) This section shall not apply if the number of persons in a vehicle exceeds the greater of the following:

(1) The number of seat belt assemblies available in the vehicle; or

(2) The number of seat belt assemblies originally installed in the vehicle; provided that all available seat belt assemblies are being used to restrain a passenger, and those children not restrained by an approved child passenger restraint system or a seat belt assembly are in the back seat of the motorvehicle.

(d) In no event shall failure of a child under the age of four years to be restrained or failure to restrain such a child in a child passenger restraint system or a seat belt assembly be considered as contributory negligence, comparative negligence, or negligence per se.

(e) Any person violating this section shall be guilty of a violation and subject to the penalties of section 291C-161(b).

(f) As used in this section, "emergency vehicle", "mass transit vehicle", and "seat belt assembly" shall have the same meaning as provided in section 291-11.6.

As used in this section, "commercial vehicle" shall be defined as any motor vehicle that is being used for the transportation of persons for hire, compensation, or profit.

437D-13 (1992)

Notice and posting required concerning seat belt, child passenger restraint, and drunk driving laws

(a) Every lessor shall display at all times in a conspicuous place in each rental motor vehicle offered to the public, a decal, written in plain language and in no less than ten-point type, that informs the lessee of:

(1) Hawaii's seat belt and child passenger restraint laws and the prohibition against driving while under the influence of intoxicating liquor; and

(2) The existence and location of additional information concerning the laws relating to seat belts, child passenger restraints, and driving while under the influence of intoxicating liquor. The requirements and penalties of Hawaii's seat belt laws and child passenger restraint laws, as provided in sections 291-11.5 and 291-11.6, and the prohibition against and penalties for driving while under the influence of intoxicating liquor, as provided in section 291-4, shall be printed on a card which shall be placed in the glove compartment of every rental motor vehicle offered to the public.

(b) Except as provided in section 437D-16, a sign or signs written in plain language calling attention to the laws referred to in subsection (a) shall be prominently posted in the main rental area of all rental locations in a place and manner conspicuous to the public.

(c) The notices and signs required by this section shall include symbolic representations which are of common understanding and clearly recognizable to the public as conveying the required use of seat belts and child passenger restraint systems in the operation of a motor vehicle and the prohibition against driving while under the influence of intoxicating liquor.

(d) The director shall prescribe the form of the notices and the signs required by this section.

IDAHO

49-672 (1992)

Passenger safety for children

(1) No resident noncommercial motor vehicle operator who is a parent or guardian shall transport his child under the age of four (4) years or who weighs less than forty (40) pounds in a motor vehicle manufactured with seat belts after January 1, 1966, unless the child is properly restrained in a car safety seat that meets the requirements of Federal Motor Vehicle Safety Standard 213. The provisions of this section shall not apply:

(a) If all of the motor vehicle's seat belts are in use, but in such an event any unrestrained child to which this section applies shall be placed in the rear seat of the motor vehicle, if it is so equipped; or

(b) When the child is removed from the car safety seat and held by the attendant for the purpose of nursing the child or attending the child's other immediate physiological needs.

(2) A violation of the provisions of this section may be dismissed by a court upon proof of possession of a required safety seat.

(3) The failure to use a child safety seat shall not be considered under any circumstances as evidence of contributory negligence, nor shall such failure be admissible as evidence in any civil action with regard to negligence.

ILLINOIS

625 ILCS 25/2 (1993)

Legislative Finding — Purpose

Sec. 2. Legislative Finding — Purpose. The General Assembly finds that a substantial number of passengers under the age of 6 years riding in motor vehicles, which are most frequently operated by a parent, annually die or sustain serious physical injury as a direct result of not being placed in a child passenger restraint system. The General Assembly further finds that the safety of the motoring public is seriously threatened as indicated by the significant number of traffic accidents annually caused, directly or indirectly, by driver distraction or other impairment of driving ability induced by the movement or actions of unrestrained passengers under the age of 6 years.

It is the purpose of this Act to further protect the health, safety and welfare of motor vehicle passengers under the age of 6 years and the motoring public through the proper utilization of approved child restraint systems.

625 ILCS 25/3 (1993)

Definitions

Sec. 3. Definitions. The terms "highway", "motor vehicle", "owner", "police officer", "recreational vehicle", "roadway" and "street" as used in this Act, unless the context otherwise requires, have the meaning ascribed to them in The Illinois Vehicle Code, as now or hereafter amended [625 ILCS 5/1-100 et seq.]. For the purpose of this Act, "motor vehicle" does not include motorcycles.

625 ILCS 25/4 (1993)

Sec. 4. When any person is transporting a resident child of this State under the age of 4 years in a non-commercial motor vehicle of the first division, a motor vehicle of the second division with a gross vehicle weight rating of 9,000 pounds or less, or a recreational vehicle on the roadways, streets or highways of this State, such person shall be responsible for providing for the protection of such child by properly securing him or her in a child restraint system, except in cases of medical emergency. The parent or legal guardian of a child under the age of 4 years shall provide a child restraint system to any person who transports his or her child. Any person who transports the child of another shall not be in violation of this Section unless a child restraint system was provided by the parent or legal guardian but not used to transport the child.

For purposes of this Section and Section 4a [625 ILCS 25/4a], "child restraint system" means any device which meets the standards of the United States Department of Transportation designed to restrain, seat or position children.

625 ILCS 25/4a (1993)

Sec. 4a. Every person, when transporting a child 4 years of age or older but under the age of 6, as provided in Section 4 of this Act [625 ILCS 25/4], shall be responsible for securing that child in either a child restraint system or seat belts, except in cases of medical emergency.

625 ILCS 25/5 (1993)

Sec. 5. In no event shall a person's failure to secure a child under 6 years of age in an approved child restraint system or properly secure such child, if age 4 or 5, in a seat belt constitute contributory negligence or be admissible as evidence in the trial of any civil action.

625 ILCS 25/6 (1993)

Sec. 6. A violation of this Act is a petty offense punishable by a fine of not more than $25 waived upon proof of possession of an approved child restraint system as defined under this Act.

A subsequent violation of this Act is a petty offense punishable by a fine of not more than $50.

625 ILCS 25/7 (1993)

Sec. 7. Arrests — Prosecutions. The State Police shall patrol the public highways and make arrests for a violation of this Act. Police officers shall make arrests for violations of this Act occurring upon the highway within the limits of a county, city, village, or unincorporated town or park district.

The State's Attorney of the county in which the violation of this Act occurs shall prosecute all violations except when the violation occurs within the corporate limits of a municipality, the municipal attorney may prosecute if written permission to do so is obtained from the State's Attorney.

The provisions of this Act shall not apply to a child passenger with a physical handicap of such a nature as to prevent appropriate restraint in such seat, provided that such handicap is duly certified by a physician who shall state the nature of the handicap, as well as the reason the restraint is inappropriate. No physician shall be liable, and no cause of action may be brought for personal injuries resulting from the exercise of good faith judgment in making certifications under this provision.

625 ILCS 25/8 (1993)

Sec. 8. The " Child Passenger Restraint Act", enacted by the 82nd General Assembly, is repealed.

625 ILCS 25/9 (1993)

Sec. 9. This Act takes effect July 1, 1983.

INDIANA

9-13-2-23 (1992)

Child passenger restraint system

" Child passenger restraint system" means a device that:

(1) Is manufactured for the purpose of protecting children from injury during a motor vehicle accident; and

(2) Meets the standards prescribed in 49 CFR 571.213.

IOWA

321.445 (1991)

321.445 Safety belts and safety harnesses — use required

1. Except for motorcycles or motorized bicycles, 1966 model year or newer motor vehicles subject to registration in Iowa shall be equipped with safety belts and safety harnesses of a type and installed in a manner approved by rules adopted by the department pursuant to chapter 17A. The department shall adopt rules regarding the types of safety belts and safety harnesses required to be installed in motor vehicles and the manner in which they are installed. The rules shall conform with Federal Motor Vehicle Safety Standard numbers 209 and 210 as published in 49 C.F.R. @ 571.209-571.210 and with prior Federal Motor Vehicle Safety Standards for seat belt assemblies and seat belt assembly anchorages applicable for the motor vehicle's model year. The department may adopt rules which comply with changes in the applicable Federal Motor Vehicle Safety Standards with regard to the type of safety belts and safety harnesses and their manner of installation.

2. The driver and front seat occupants of a type of motor vehicle which is subject to registration in Iowa, except a motorcycle or a motorized bicycle, shall each wear a properly adjusted and fastened safety belt or safety harness any time the vehicle is in forward motion on a street or highway in this state except

that a child under six years of age shall be secured as required under section 321.446.

This subsection does not apply to:

a. The driver or front seat occupants of a motor vehicle which is not required to be equipped with safety belts or safety harnesses under rules adopted by the department.

b. The driver and front seat occupants of a motor vehicle who are actively engaged in work which requires them to alight from and reenter the vehicle at frequent intervals, providing the vehicle does not exceed twenty-five miles per hour between stops.

c. The driver of a motor vehicle while performing duties as a rural letter carrier for the United States postal service. This exemption applies only between the first delivery point after leaving the post office and the last delivery point before returning to the post office.

d. Passengers on a bus.

e. A person possessing a written certification from a physician on a form provided by the department that the person is unable to wear a safety belt or safety harness due to physical or medical reasons. The certification shall specify the time period for which the exemption applies. The time period shall not exceed twelve months, at which time a new certification may be issued.

f. Front seat occupants of an authorized emergency vehicle while they are being transported in an emergency. However, this exemption does not apply to the driver of the authorized emergency vehicle.

During the six-month period from July 1, 1986 through December 31, 1986, peace officers shall issue only warning citations for violations of this subsection, except this does not apply to drivers subject to the federal motor carrier safety regulation 49 C.F.R. @ 392.16.

The department, in cooperation with the department of public safety and the department of education, shall establish educational programs to foster compliance with the safety belt and safety harness usage requirements of this subsection.

3. The driver and front seat passengers may be each charged separately for improperly used or nonused equipment under subsection 2. The owner of the motor vehicle may be charged for equipment violations under subsection 1.

4. a. The nonuse of a safety belt or safety harness by a person is not admissible or material as evidence in a civil action brought for damages in a cause of action arising prior to July 1, 1986.

   b. In a cause of action arising on or after July 1, 1986, brought to recover damages arising out of the ownership or operation of a motor vehicle, the failure to wear a safety belt or safety harness in violation of this section shall not be considered evidence of comparative fault under section 668.3, subsection 1. However, except as provided in section 321.446, subsection 6, the failure to wear a safety belt or safety harness in violation of this section may be admitted to mitigate damages, but only under the following circumstances:

      (1) Parties seeking to introduce evidence of the failure to wear a safety belt or safety harness in violation of this section must first introduce substantial evidence that the failure to wear a safety belt or safety harness contributed to the injury or injuries claimed by the plaintiff.

      (2) If the evidence supports such a finding, the trier of fact may find that the plaintiff's failure to wear a safety belt or safety harness in violation of this section contributed to the plaintiff's claimed injury or injuries, and may reduce the amount of plaintiff's recovery by an amount not to exceed five percent of the damages awarded after any reductions for comparative fault.

5. The department shall adopt rules pursuant to chapter 17A providing exceptions from application of subsections 1 and 2 for front seats and front seat passengers of motor vehicles owned, leased, rented, or primarily used by physically handicapped persons who use collapsible wheelchairs.

KANSAS

8-1344 (1991)

STATUS: CONSULT SLIP LAWS CITED BELOW FOR RECENT CHANGES TO THIS DOCUMENTLEXSEE 1992 Kan. HB 2766 — See sections 2 and 7.

8-1344. Child passenger safety; restraining systems for children under the age of four; use of seat belts by children between the ages of five and fourteen; rules and regulations.

Every driver as define in K.S.A. 8-1416, and amendments thereto, who transports a child under the age of 14 years in a passenger car as defined in K.S.A. 8-1445, and amendments, thereto, on a highway as defined in K.S.A. 8-1424, and amendments thereto, shall provide for the protection of such child by properly using:

(a) For a child under the age of four years a child passenger safety restraining system of a type approved under this act; or

(b) for a child four years of age but under the age of 14, a safety belt manufactured in compliance with Federal Motor Vehicle Safety Standard 208, except that if the number of children subject to this requirement exceeds the number of passenger securing locations available for use by children affected by this requirement, and all of those securing locations are in use by children, then there is not a violation of this section. The secretary of transportation shall adopt rules and regulations for the performance, design and installation of child passenger safety restraining systems for use in passenger cars for children under the age of four years, in accordance with Federal Motor Vehicle Safety Standards and shall approve those systems which meet such standards.

KENTUCKY

KRS 189.125

Seat belt anchors required in new passenger vehicles; child restraint systems required; exceptions

(1) No person shall sell any new passenger vehicle in this state nor shall any person make application for registering a new passenger vehicle in this state unless the front or forward seat or seats have adequate anchors or attachments secured to the floor and/or sides to the rear of the seat or seats to which seat belts may be secured.

(2) Any resident parent or legal guardian of a child, forty inches (40") in height or less, when transporting his child in a motor vehicle owned by that parent or guardian operated on the roadways, streets and highways of this state, shall have such child properly secured in a child restraint system of a type meeting Federal Motor Vehicle Safety Standards.

(3) As used in this section, "child restraint system" means any device manufactured to transport children in a motor vehicle which conforms to all applicable Federal Motor Vehicle Safety Standards.

(4) The term "motor vehicle" as used in subsection (2) of this section shall not apply to recreational vehicles or trucks having a tonnage rating of more than one (1) ton.

(5) Failure to wear a child passenger restraint shall not be considered as contributory negligence, nor shall such failure to wear said passenger restraint system be admissible as evidence in the trial of any civil action.

(6) The terms of subsection (2) of this section shall not apply if all seat positions in the pickup truck are occupied by persons other than a child of forty (40) inches in height or less.

LOUISIANA

32:295 (1992)

Child Passenger Restraint System

A. Every resident of this state who transports a child or children under the age of five years in a motor vehicle which is equipped with safety belts at the time of manufacture or assembly, or is currently equipped with safety belts, shall have the child properly secured in accordance with the manufacturer's instructions in a child passenger restraint system which meets the applicable Federal Motor Vehicle Safety Standards in effect on the effective date of this Section, except as provided in R.S. 32:295(C), (D), and (E).

B. The term "motor vehicle" as used in this Section, shall not mean the following: bicycle; farm tractor; motorcycle or motor-driven cycle; truck of manufacturer's rating carrying capacity of over 2000 pounds; ambulance or other emergency vehicle; school bus as defined in R.S. 32:1(62)(a) and (b); church bus, private bus, or recreational vehicle which has a passenger capacity of over ten persons; or commercial truck, van, or taxi.

C. If such child is three to five years of age, securing the child in a lap belt or safety belt in a rear seat shall be sufficient to meet the requirements of this Section. If there are no rear seats, a child passenger restraint system shall be used.

D. When the number of children under the age of five in the motor vehicle exceeds the number of child passenger restraint systems and seat belts available in the motor vehicle, the unrestrained children shall be seated in a rear seat.

E. The provisions of this Section shall not apply when one of the following conditions exists:

(1) The motor vehicle is being used as an ambulance or other emergency vehicle.

(2) An emergency exists which threatens the life of any person operating a motor vehicle to whom this Section otherwise

would apply or the life of any child who otherwise would be required to be restrained under this Section.

(3) Any child who would otherwise be required to be restrained under this Section who is physically unable because of medical reasons to use a child passenger safety system or safety belt.

F. In no event shall failure to wear a child passenger safety seat system be considered as comparative negligence, nor shall such failure be admissible as evidence in the trial of any civil action with regard to negligence, nor shall such failure be considered a moving violation.

G. Any operator of a motor vehicle stopped for a violation of this Section and against whom enforcement action has been taken shall not be guilty of a subsequent violation of this Section until after twenty-four hours have elapsed from the date and time of the violation as indicated on the traffic ticket.

H. Any resident driver who violates this Section prior to January 1, 1985 shall be given a warning ticket only. Subsequent to December 31, 1984, any person who violates this Section shall upon conviction be fined not less than twenty-five nor more than fifty dollars. The fine shall be waived and charges dismissed upon satisfactory proof being presented to the court that the defendant has acquired an approved child passenger restraint system.

MAINE

1368-B. Use of approved child safety seats

1. TRANSPORTATION IN VEHICLE OF PARENT OR GUARDIAN. When any child who is less than 4 years of age is being transported in a motor vehicle in this State and that motor vehicle is owned or operated by the child's parent or legal guardian, and the motor vehicle is required by the United States Department of Transportation to be equipped with seat belts at the time of manufacture or assembly, the operator of the motor vehicle shall have the child properly secured, in accordance with the manufacturer's instructions, in a child

safety seat that meets the standards described in Federal Motor Vehicle Safety Standards, 49 Code of Federal Regulations, Part 571, in effect on January 1, 1981. The parent or legal guardian of the child is responsible for providing and installing the child safety seat.

2. TRANSPORTATION IN VEHICLE NOT OWNED BY PARENT OR GUARDIAN. If the child is being transported in a motor vehicle in this State, and that motor vehicle is neither owned nor operated by the child's parent or legal guardian, and the motor vehicle is required by the United States Department of Transportation to be equipped with seat belts at the time of manufacture or assembly, the operator of the motor vehicle shall have the child properly secured, in accordance with the manufacturer's instructions, in a child safety seat that meets the standards described in Federal Motor Vehicle Safety Standards, 49 Code of Federal Regulations, Part 571, in effect on January 1, 1981. When such a child safety seat is not available, the operator shall have the child properly secured in a seat belt, except when all seating positions equipped with seat belts are occupied. No exception may apply if the child is less than one year of age.

3. EXCEPTION AND LIMITATION. The requirements of subsections 1 and 2 shall not apply to any person over one year of age when the number of passengers exceeds the seating capacity of the vehicle.

4. WARNING. Any person stopped for a violation of this section during the initial 6 months after this section takes effect shall be issued a warning that a violation of this section has occurred.

5. VIOLATION LIMITATION. Any parent, guardian, owner or operator stopped for a violation of this section and against whom enforcement action has been taken shall not be guilty of a subsequent violation of this section until after 24 hours have elapsed from the date and time of the violation, as indicated on the traffic ticket.

6. PENALTY. Following the initial 6-month warning period, violation of this section is a civil violation for which a

forfeiture of $25 for the first violation and $50 for each subsequent violation may be adjudged. The court shall waive any civil fine or cost against a parent or legal guardian who receives a civil violation citation for a first violation of this section if the parent or legal guardian supplies the court with satisfactory evidence that the parent or guardian has acquired or purchased a child safety seat for continuous use by the child of the parent or guardian. This child safety seat shall comply with the standards described in Federal Motor Vehicle Safety Standards, 49 Code of Federal Regulations, Part 571, in effect January 1, 1981, within 30 days of the issuance of the civil violation citation.

7. FAILURE TO SECURE A CHILD; USE AS EVIDENCE. Failure to secure a child in a child safety seat or seat belt shall not be considered negligence imputable to the child, nor shall that failure be admissible as evidence in the trial of any civil or criminal action, except for a violation of this section.

MARYLAND

22-412.2 (1992)

Child safety seats

(a) Definitions. —(1) In this section, " child safety seat" means a device that is manufactured in accordance with the 1981 Federal Motor Vehicle Safety Standards and is used to restrain, seat, or position a child who is transported in a motor vehicle.

(2) " Child safety seat" does not mean a seat belt or combination seat belt-shoulder harness.

(b) Accordance with directions of manufacturer required. —A child safety seat meets the requirements of this section only if it is installed and used in accordance with the directions of the manufacturer.

(c) Application to vehicles. —This section applies to the transportation of a child in a vehicle registered, or of a type capable of being registered, in this State as a:

(1) Class A (passenger) vehicle;

(2) Class E (truck) with a manufacturer's rated capacity of 3/4 ton or less, the gross vehicle weight of which does not exceed 7,000 pounds; or

(3) Class M (multipurpose) vehicle.

(d)Child under age of 4 or weighing 40 pounds or less. —Any person transporting a child under the age of 4 or weighing 40 pounds or less shall position and secure the child in a child safety seat.

(e)Child weighing more than 40 pounds and less than age of 10. —Subject to the provisions of subsection (d) of this section, any person transporting a child weighing more than 40 pounds and who is less than 10 years of age shall:

(1) Position and secure the child in a child safety seat; or

(2) Seat and secure the child in a properly fastened seat belt or combination seat belt-shoulder harness.

(f) Medical exception. —If a physician, who is licensed to practice medicine in the State in which the vehicle transporting the child is registered, certifies in writing that use of a child safety seat by a particular child would be impractical due to the child's weight, physical unfitness, or other medical reason, there is not a violation of this section.

(g) Individual use. —A child safety seat, seat belt or combination seat belt-shoulder harness may not be used to restrain, seat, or position more than 1 individual at a time.

(h) Securing locations. —If the number of children subject to the provisions of this section exceeds the number of passenger securing locations available for use by children affected by this section, and all of those securing locations are in use by children, there is not a violation of this section.

(i) Effect of violation. —A violation of this section is not contributory negligence and may not be admitted as evidence in the trial of any civil action.

(j) Moving violation. —A violation of this section is not considered a moving violation for purposes of @ 16-402 of this article.

(k) Separate violations. —The failure to provide a child safety seat, seat belt, or combination seat belt-shoulder harness for more than 1 child in the same vehicle at the same time, as required by this section, shall be treated as a single violation.

(l) Fine; waiver. —(1) Any person convicted of a violation of this section is subject to a fine of $ 25.

(2) A judge may waive the fine if the person charged with violation of this section:

(i) Did not possess a child safety seat at the time of the violation;

(ii) Acquires a child safety seat prior to the hearing date; and

(iii) Provides proof of acquisition to the court.

(m) Implementation; compliance. —The Department of Transportation and the Department of Health and Mental Hygiene shall jointly implement the Child Safety Seat Program and foster compliance with this section through educational and promotional efforts.

22-412.3.

Mandatory seat belt use

(a) Definitions. —(1) In this section, the following words have the meanings indicated.

(2) (i) "Motor vehicle" means a vehicle that is:

1. Registered or capable of being registered in this State as a Class A (passenger), Class E (truck), Class F (tractor), Class M (multipurpose) vehicle, or Class P (passenger bus); and

2. Required to be equipped with seat belts under Federal Motor Vehicle Safety Standards contained in the Code of Federal Regulations.

(ii) "Motor vehicle" does not include a Class L (historic) vehicle.

(3) "Outboard front seat" means a front seat position that is adjacent to a door of a motor vehicle.

(4) (i) "Seat belt" means a restraining device described under @ 22-412 of this article.

(ii) "Seat belt" includes a combination seat belt-shoulder harness.

(b) Seat belts required. —A person may not operate a motor vehicle unless the person and each outboard front seat occupant under 16 years old are restrained by a seat belt or a child safety seat as provided in @ 22-412.2 of this article.

(c) Passengers. —(1) The provisions of this subsection apply to a person who is at least 16 years old.

(2) Unless a person is restrained by a seat belt, the person may not be a passenger in an outboard front seat of a motor vehicle.

(3) A person who violates the provisions of this subsection shall be subject to the penalties under Title 27 of this article.

(d) Physically disabled persons. —If a physician licensed to practice medicine in this State determines and certifies in writing that use of a seat belt by a person would prevent appropriate restraint due to a person's physical disability or other medical reason, the provisions of this section do not apply to the person.

(e) Certification of disability. —A certification under subsection (d) of this section shall state:

(1) The nature of the physical disability; and

(2) The reason that restraint by a seat belt is inappropriate.

(f) U.S. Postal Service and contract carriers. —The provisions of this section do not apply to U.S. Postal Service and contract carriers while delivering mail to local box routes.

(g) Violations not moving violation. —A violation of this section is not considered a moving violation for purposes of @ 16-402 of this article.

(h) Failure to use seat belt. —(1) Failure of an individual to use a seat belt in violation of this section may not:

(i) Be considered evidence of negligence;

(ii) Be considered evidence of contributory negligence;

(iii) Limit liability of a party or an insurer; or

(iv) Diminish recovery for damages arising out of the ownership, maintenance, or operation of a motor vehicle.

(2) Subject to the provisions of paragraph (3) of this subsection, a party, witness, or counsel may not make reference to a seat belt during a trial of a civil action that involves property damage, personal injury, or death if the damage, injury, or death is not related to the design, manufacture, installation, supplying, or repair of a seat belt.

(3) (i) Nothing contained in this subsection may be construed to prohibit the right of a person to institute a civil action for damages against a dealer, manufacturer, distributor, factory branch, or other appropriate entity arising out of an incident that involves a defectively installed or defectively operating seat belt.

(ii) In a civil action in which 2 or more parties are named as joint tort-feasors, interpleaded as defendants, or impleaded as defendants, and 1 of the joint tort-feasors or defendants is not involved in the design, manufacture, installation, supplying, or repair of a seat belt, a court shall order separate trials to accomplish the ends of justice on a motion of any party.

(i) Prevention and education programs. —The Administration and the Maryland State Police shall establish prevention and education programs to encourage compliance with the provisions of this section.

(j) Annual evaluation report on State's highway safety plan. —The Administration shall include information on this State's experience with the provisions of this section in the annual evaluation report on the State's highway safety plan that this State submits to the National Highway Traffic Safety Administration and the Federal Highway Administration under 23 U.S.C. @ 402.

(k) Enforcement of provisions by police officers; construction. —(1) A police officer may enforce the provisions of this section only as a secondary action when the police officer detains a driver of a motor vehicle for a suspected violation of another provision of the Code.

(2) Nothing contained in paragraph (1) of this subsection may be construed to limit the enforcement of a violation under @ 22-412.2 of this subtitle.

MASSACHUSETTS

Mass. Ann. Laws ch. 90, @ 7AA (1993)

Use of Child Passenger Restraints Required in Certain Motor Vehicles; Penalties.

No child five years old or less shall ride as a passenger in a motor vehicle on any way unless said child is wearing a safety belt which is properly adjusted and fastened or unless such child is properly fastened and secured by a child passenger restraint as defined in section one.

No child who is older than five years of age but not older than twelve years of age shall ride as a passenger in a motor vehicle on any way unless said child is wearing a safety belt which is properly adjusted and fastened.

The provisions of this section shall not apply to any such child who is: (1) riding as a passenger in a motor vehicle in which all seating positions equipped with safety belts or child passenger restraints are occupied by other passengers who are using said restraints; (2) riding as a passenger in a motor vehicle used to transport passengers for hire; (3) riding as a passenger in a motor vehicle not equipped with safety belts; (4) physically unable to use safety belts or child passenger restraints. Any operator of a motor vehicle who violates the provisions of this section shall be subject to a fine of not more than twenty-five dollars; provided, however, that such fine may be waived if the court is satisfied that the defendant has purchased a child passenger restraint as defined in section one.

A violation of this section shall not be used as evidence of contributory negligence in any civil action.

MINNESOTA

Minn. Stat. 169.685 (1992)

Seat belts and passenger restraint systems for children

Subdivision 1. Requirement; exemptions. After January 1, 1964, all new motor vehicles, not exempt from Minnesota license fees, other than a bus, school bus, motorcycle, motorized bicycle, farm tractor, road tractor, and truck, sold or offered for sale or registered in Minnesota shall be equipped to permit the installation of seat belts in the front seat thereof.

Subd. 2. Required after registration. Within 30 days after the registration of such motor vehicle, it shall be equipped with seat belts installed for use in the left front and right front seats thereof.

Subd. 3. Standards. The specifications and requirements for seat belts or seat belt assemblies shall conform with the minimum standards for seat belts or seat belt assemblies heretofore adopted by the society of automotive engineers and in effect on January 1, 1963.

Subd. 4. Admissibility into evidence. Proof of the use or failure to use seat belts or a child passenger restraint system as described in subdivision 5, or proof of the installation or failure of installation of seat belts or a child passenger restraint system as described in subdivision 5 shall not be admissible in evidence in any litigation involving personal injuries or property damage resulting from the use or operation of any motor vehicle.

Subd. 5. Violation; penalty. (a) Every motor vehicle operator, when transporting a child under the age of four on the streets and highways of this state in a motor vehicle equipped with factory-installed seat belts, shall equip and install for use in the motor vehicle, according to the manufacturer's instructions, a child passenger restraint system meeting Federal Motor Vehicle Safety Standards.

(b) No motor vehicle operator who is operating a motor vehicle on the streets and highways of this state may transport a child under the age of four in a seat of a motor vehicle equipped with a factory-installed seat belt, unless the child is properly fastened in the child passenger restraint system. Any motor vehicle operator who violates this subdivision is guilty of a petty misdemeanor and may be sentenced to pay a fine of not more than $ 25.

Subd. 6. Exceptions; rental vehicles. (a) This section does not apply to:

(1) a person transporting a child in an emergency medical vehicle while in the performance of official duties and when the physical or medical needs of the child make the use of a child passenger restraint system unreasonable or when a child passenger restraint system is not available;

(2) a peace officer transporting a child while in the performance of official duties and when a child passenger restraint system is not available, provided that a seat belt must be substituted; and

(3) a person while operating a motor vehicle for hire, including a taxi, airport limousine, and bus, but excluding a rented, leased, or borrowed motor vehicle.

(b) A child passenger restraint system is not required for a child who cannot, in the judgment of a licensed physician, be safely transported in a child passenger restraint system because of a medical condition, body size, or physical disability. A motor vehicle operator claiming exemption for a child under this paragraph must possess a typewritten statement from the physician stating that the child cannot be safely transported in a child passenger restraint system. The statement must give the name and birth date of the child, be dated within the previous six months, and be made on the physician's letterhead or contain the physician's name, address, and telephone number. A person charged with violating subdivision 5 may not be convicted if the person produces the physician's statement in court or in the office of the arresting officer.

(c) A person offering a motor vehicle for rent or lease shall provide a child passenger restraint device to a customer renting or leasing the motor vehicle who requests the device. A reasonable rent or fee may be charged for use of the child passenger restraint device.

MICHIGAN

257.710d (1991)

Child restraint system required; exceptions; violation as civil infraction; points; abstract; exemption by rules; alternate means of protection.

Sec. 710d. (1) Except as provided in this section, or as otherwise provided by law, a rule promulgated pursuant to the administrative procedures act of 1969, Act No. 306 of the Public Acts of 1969, as amended, being sections 24.201 to 24.328 of the Michigan Compiled Laws, or federal regulation, each driver transporting a child in a motor vehicle shall properly secure each child in a child restraint system as follows:

(a) Any child less than 1 year of age in a child restraint system which meets the standards prescribed in 49 C.F.R. 571.213, except as provided in subsection (6).

(b) Any child 1 year of age or more but less than 4 years of age, when transported in the front seat, in a child restraint system which meets the standards prescribed in 49 C.F.R. 571.213, except as provided in subsection (6).

(c) Any child 1 year of age or more but less than 4 years of age, when transported in the rear seat, in a child restraint system which meets the standards prescribed in 49 C.F.R. 571.213, unless the child is secured by a safety belt provided in the motor vehicle, except as provided in subsection (6).

(2) This section does not apply to any child being nursed.

(3) This section does not apply if the motor vehicle being driven is a bus, school bus, taxicab, moped, motorcycle, or other motor vehicle not required to be equipped with safety belts under federal law or regulations.

(4) A person who violates this section is responsible for a civil infraction.

(5) Points shall not be assessed under section 320a for a violation of this section. An abstract required under section 732 shall not be submitted to the secretary of state regarding a violation of this section.

(6) The secretary of state may exempt by rules promulgated pursuant to Act No. 306 of the Public Acts of 1969, as amended, a class of children from the requirements of this section, if the secretary of state determines that the use of the child restraint system required under subsection (1) is impractical because of physical unfitness, a medical problem, or body size. The secretary of state may specify alternate means of protection for children exempted under this subsection. HISTORY: Add. 1981, Act 117, Eff. Mar. 31, 1982;—Am. 1990, Act 90, Eff. Mar. 28, 1991.

257.710e (1991)

Safety belt required; driver or passenger to which section inapplicable; transporting child 4 years of age but less than 16 years of age; enforcement of section; violation as evidence of negligence; reduction of recovery for damages; violation as civil infraction; assessment of points prohibited.

Sec. 710e. (1) This section shall not apply to a driver or passenger of:

(a) A motor vehicle manufactured before January 1, 1965.

(b) A bus.

(c) A motorcycle.

(d) A moped.

(e) A motor vehicle if the driver or passenger possesses a written verification from a physician that the driver or passenger is unable to wear a safety belt for physical or medical reasons.

(f) A motor vehicle which is not required to be equipped with safety belts under federal law.

(g) A commercial or United States postal service vehicle which makes frequent stops for the purpose of pickup or delivery of goods or services.

(h) A motor vehicle operated by a rural carrier of the United States postal service while serving his or her rural postal route.

(2) This section shall not apply to a passenger of a school bus.

(3) Each driver and front seat passenger of a motor vehicle operated on a street or highway in this state shall wear a properly adjusted and fastened safety belt, except that a child less than 4 years of age shall be protected as required in section 710d.

(4) Each driver of a motor vehicle transporting a child 4 years of age or more but less than 16 years of age in a motor vehicle shall secure the child in a properly adjusted and fastened safety belt. If the motor vehicle is transporting more children than there are safety belts available for use, all safety belts available in the motor vehicle are being utilized in compliance with this section, and the driver and all front seat passengers comply with subsection (3), then the driver of a motor vehicle transporting a child 4 years of age or more but less than 16 years of age for which there is not an available safety belt is in compliance with this subsection, if that child is seated in other than the front seat of the motor vehicle. However, if thatmotor vehicle is a pickup truck without an extended cab or jump seats, and all safety belts in the front seat are being used, the driver may transport such a child in the front seat without a safety belt.

(5) Enforcement of this section by state or local law enforcement agencies shall be accomplished only as a secondary action when a driver of a motor vehicle has been detained for a suspected violation of another section of this act.

(6) Failure to wear a safety belt in violation of this section may be considered evidence of negligence and may reduce the recovery for damages arising out of the ownership, maintenance, or operation of a motor vehicle. However, such negligence shall not reduce the recovery for damages by more than 5%.

(7) A person who violates this section is responsible for a civil infraction.

(8) Points shall not be assessed under section 320a for a violation of this section.

MISSISSIPPI

63-7-301 (1991)

Child passenger restraint devices required; failure not considered negligence.

Every person transporting a child under the age of two (2) years in a motor vehicle required to be registered as a private carrier of passengers in this state pursuant to Article 1, Chapter 19, Title 27, Mississippi Code of 1972, and operated on the roadways, streets or highways of this state shall provide for the protection of the child by properly using a child passenger restraint device or system meeting applicable Federal Motor Vehicle Safety Standards.

Failure to provide and use a child passenger restraint device or system shall not be considered contributory or comparative negligence.

63-7-303 (1991)

Rights or liabilities between parent and child.

No provision of sections 63-7-301 through 63-7-313 shall be construed as creating any duty, standard of care, right or liability between parent and child that is not recognized under the laws of the state of Mississippi as they exist on July 1, 1983, or as they may at any time in the future be constituted by statute or court decision.

63-7-305 (1991)

Enforcement.

The provisions of section 63-7-301 may be enforced by any duly sworn law enforcement officer of this state, or of any county or political subdivision thereof.

63-7-307 (1991)

First time offenders; dismissal of action.

No person charged with violating section 63-7-301 for the first time shall be convicted if, prior to or at the time of his court or hearing appearance, he produces in court or submits to the clerk of the court in which the charge is pending, proof of acquisition of the required child restraint device or system. The clerk of the court is authorized to dismiss such cases at any time if proof of such acquisition is produced prior to the defendant's scheduled court or hearing appearance.

63-7-309 (1991)

Penalties.

Any person convicted of violating the provisions of Section 63-7-301 shall be fined not more than Twenty-five Dollars ($ 25.00) for each offense.

63-7-311 (1991)

Notice of requirement for child restraint devices.

The state tax commission shall provide notice of the requirement for child restraint devices or systems, which notice shall accompany the delivery of a motor vehicle license tag.

63-7-313 (1991)

[Repealed]

MISSOURI

210.104 R.S.Mo. (1991)

Passenger restraint system required for children under four years of age—exceptions—violation, fine

1. After January 1, 1984, every person transporting a child under the age of four years residing in this state shall be responsible, when transporting such child in a motor vehicle operated by that person on the streets or highways of this state, for providing for the protection of such child. When traveling in the front seat of a motor vehicle the child shall be protected by a child passenger restraint system approved by the department of public safety. When traveling in the rear seat of a motor vehicle the child shall be protected by either a child passenger restraint system approved by the department of public safety or the vehicle's seat belt. When the number of child passengers exceeds the number of available passenger positions, and all passenger positions are in use, remaining children shall be transported in the rear seat of the motor vehicle. The provisions of sections 210.104 to 210.107 shall not apply to motor vehicles registered in another state, or to a temporary substitute vehicle.

2. Any person who violates this section is guilty of an infraction and, upon conviction, may be punished by a fine of not more than twenty-five dollars and court costs.

3.The provisions of sections 210.104 to 210.107 shall not apply to any public carrier for hire.

210.106 R.S.Mo. (1991)

210.106. Failure to use passenger restraint system not to be basis for civil or criminal actions and evidence inadmissible

In no event shall failure to employ a child passenger restraint system required by section 210.104 provide the basis for a claim of criminal or civil liability or negligence or contributory negligence of any person in any action for damages by reason of injury sustained by a child; nor shall such failure to employ such child passenger restraint system be admissible as evidence in the trial of any civil or criminal action.

MONTANA

61-9-420 (1992)

Child safety restraint systems — standards — exemptions

(1) No resident of Montana who is the parent or legal guardian of a child under the age of 2 may transport the child in a motor vehicle owned by the resident or his spouse unless the child is properly restrained.

(2) No resident of Montana who is the parent or legal guardian of a child between 2 and 4 years old or weighing less than 40 pounds may transport the child in a motor vehicle owned by the resident or his spouse unless the child is properly restrained or is restrained in a safety belt of the type specified in 61-9-410.

(3) The department shall by rule establish standards in compliance with 61-9-419 through 61-9-423 and applicable federal standards for approved types of child safety restraint systems purchased after January 1, 1984.

(4) No resident or his spouse is required to have more than three child safety restraint systems in a vehicle.

(5) The department may by rule exempt from the requirements of subsection (1) any child who because of a physical or medical condition or body size cannot be placed in a child safety restraint system or safety belt.

NEBRASKA

39-6,103.01 (1992)

Child passenger; use restraint system or occupant protection system; when; information and education program

(1) Any person, who resides in Nebraska and drives any motor vehicle which has or is required to have an occupant protection system, shall ensure that (a) all children under the age of four or weighing less than forty pounds being transported in such vehicle use a child passenger restraint system of a type which meets Federal Motor Vehicle Safety Standard 213 as developed by the National Highway Traffic Safety Administration as of July 10, 1990, and which is correctly installed in such vehicle and (b) all children weighing forty or more pounds or at least four years of age and younger than five years of age being transported in such vehicle use an occupant protection system.

This subsection shall apply to every motor vehicle which is equipped with an occupant protection system or is required to be equipped with restraint systems pursuant to Federal Motor Vehicle Safety Standard 208 except taxicabs, mopeds, motorcycles, and any motor vehicle designated by the manufacturer as a 1963 year model or earlier which is not equipped with an occupant protection system.

(2) Whenever any physician licensed to practice medicine in Nebraska determines, through accepted medical procedures, that use of a child passenger restraint system by a particular child would be harmful by reason of the child's weight, physical condition, or other medical reason, the provisions of subsection (1) of this section shall be waived. The driver of any vehicle transporting such a child shall carry on his or her person or in the vehicle a signed written statement of the physician identifying the child and stating the grounds for such waiver.

(3) The drivers of authorized emergency vehicles as defined in section 39-602 shall not be subject to the requirements of

subsection (1) of this section when operating such authorized emergency vehicles pursuant to their employment.

(4) The Department of Motor Vehicles shall develop and implement an ongoing public information and education program regarding the use of child passenger restraint systems and occupant protection systems.

484.641 (1991)

FIRST OF TWO VERSIONS OF THIS SECTION

484.641. Safety belts and shoulder harness assembly; requirements for child and other passenger; penalty; exemptions.

1. It is unlawful to drive a passenger car manufactured after:

(a) January 1, 1968, on a highway unless it is equipped with at least two lap-type safety belt assemblies for use in the front seating positions.

(b) January 1, 1970, on a highway, unless it is equipped with a lap-type safety belt assembly for each permanent seating position for passengers. This requirement does not apply to the rear seats of vehicles operated by a police department or sheriff's office.

(c) January 1, 1970, unless it is equipped with at least two shoulder-harness-type safety belt assemblies for use in the front seating positions.

2. Any person driving and any passenger 5 years of age or older who rides in the front or back seat of any vehicle described in subsection 1, having an unladen weight of less than 6,000 pounds, on any highway, road or street in this state shall wear a safety belt if one is available for his seating position.

3. A citation must be issued to any driver or to any adult passenger who fails to wear a safety belt as required by subsection 2. If the passenger is a child 5 years of age or older but under 18 years, a citation must be issued to the driver for his failure to require that child to wear the safety belt, but if both the driver and that child are not wearing safety belts, only one citation may be issued to the driver for both violations. A citation may

be issued pursuant to this subsection only if the violation is discovered when the vehicle is halted or its driver arrested for another alleged violation or offense. Any person who violates the provisions of subsection 2 shall be punished by a fine of not more than $25 or by a sentence to perform a certain number of hours of work for the community.

4. A violation of subsection 2:

   (a) Is not a moving traffic violation under NRS 483.473.

   (b) May not be considered as negligence or as causation in any civil action or as negligent or reckless driving under NRS 484.377.

   (c) May not be considered as misuse or abuse of a product or as causation in any action brought to recover damages for injury to a person or property resulting from the manufacture, distribution, sale or use of a product.

5. The department shall exempt those types of motor vehicles or seating positions from the requirements of subsection 1 when compliance would be impractical.

6. The provisions of subsections 2 and 3 do not apply:

   (a) To a driver or passenger who possesses a written statement by a physician certifying that he is unable to wear a safety belt for medical or physical reasons;

   (b) If the vehicle is not required by federal law to be equipped with safety belts;

   (c) To an employee of the United States Postal Service while delivering mail in the rural areas of this state;

   (d) If the vehicle is stopping frequently, the speed of that vehicle does not exceed 15 miles per hour between stops and the driver or passenger is frequently leaving the vehicle or delivering property from the vehicle; or

   (e) To a passenger riding in a means of public transportation, including a taxi, school bus or emergency vehicle.

7. It is unlawful for any person to distribute, have for sale, offer for sale or sell any safety belt or shoulder harness assembly

for use in a motor vehicle unless it meets current minimum standards and specifications of the United States Department of Transportation.

SECOND OF TWO VERSIONS OF THIS SECTION

484.641. Safety belts and shoulder harness assembly.

1. It is unlawful to drive a passenger car manufactured after January 1, 1968, on a highway unless it is equipped with at least two lap-type safety belt assemblies for use in the front seat positions.
2. It is unlawful to drive a passenger car manufactured after January 1, 1970, on a highway, unless it is equipped with a lap-type safety belt assembly for each permanent passenger-seating position. This requirement does not apply to the rear seats of vehicles operated by a police department or sheriff's office.
3. It is unlawful to drive a passenger car manufactured after January 1, 1970, unless it is equipped with at least two shoulder-harness-type safety belt assemblies for use in the front seating positions.
4. The department shall exempt those types of motor vehicles or seating positions from the requirements of this section when compliance would be impractical.
5. It is unlawful for any person to distribute, have for sale, offer for sale or sell any safety belt or shoulder harness assembly for use in a motor vehicle unless it meets current minimum standards and specifications of the United States Department of Transportation.

NEVADA

484.474 (1991)

Child riding in motor vehicle: Device to restrain child under 5 years of age required; penalty; exceptions

1. Except as otherwise provided in subsection 5, any person who is transporting a child who is under 5 years of age and who weighs less than 40 pounds in a motor vehicle registered in this state which is equipped to carry passengers shall secure him in a device for restraining a child which has been approved by the United States Department of Transportation.
2. Any person who violates the provisions of subsection 1 shall be punished by a fine of not less than $35 nor more than $100 unless, within 14 days after the issuance of the citation for such a violation, the person presents to the court specified in the citation proof of his purchase or rental of such a restraining device. Upon presentation of such proof, the court shall void the citation.
3. For the purposes of NRS 483.473, a violation of this section is not a moving traffic violation.
4. A violation of this section may not be considered:
   (a) Negligence in any civil action; or
   (b) Negligence or reckless driving for the purposes of NRS 484.377.
5. This section does not apply:
   (a) To a person who is transporting a child in a means of public transportation, including a taxi, school bus or emergency vehicle.
   (b) When a physician determines that the use of such a restraining device for the particular child would be impractical or dangerous because of such factors as the child's weight, physical unfitness or medical condition. In this case, the person transporting the child shall carry in the vehicle the signed statement of the physician to that effect.

NEW HAMPSHIRE

265:107-a (1991)

Child Passenger Restraints Required

I. No person shall drive a motor vehicle on any way while carrying as a passenger a child less than 12 years of age unless such child is wearing a seat or safety belt which is properly adjusted and fastened or unless such child is properly fastened and secured by a child passenger restraint which is in accordance with the safety standards approved by the United States Department of Transportation in 49 C.F.R. section 571.213. No person shall drive a motor vehicle on any way while carrying as a passenger a child less than 12 years of age unless the motor vehicle was designed for and equipped with the child passenger restraints specified above.

II. A person shall not be guilty of a violation of this section if:

(a) The motor vehicle he is driving is regularly used to transport passengers for hire, is a school bus as defined in RSA 259:96, or is an antique motor car or motorcycle as defined in RSA 259:4; or

(b) The child under 12 years of age whom he is carrying as a passenger has a physical condition which prevents the use of seat or safety belts or child passenger restraints.

III. Any driver who violates the provisions of this section shall be guilty of a violation.

IV. A violation of this section shall not be used as evidence of contributory negligence in any civil action.

NEW MEXICO

66-7-369 (1992)

Child passenger restraint; enforcement

A. No person shall operate a passenger car, van or pickup truck in this state and not an authorized emergency vehicle, public transportation or a school bus unless each passenger under eleven years of age is properly secured in a child passenger restraint device or by a safety belt, unless all seating positions equipped with safety belts are occupied, as follows:

(1) children less than one year of age shall be properly secured in a child passenger restraint device which meets the standards prescribed in 49 CFR 571.213;

(2) children one year of age and older but less than five years of age shall be properly secured in a child passenger restraint device which meets the standards prescribed in 49 CFR 571.213 or in the rear seat by a safety belt provided in the motor vehicle; and

(3) children five years of age and older but less than eleven years of age shall be secured by a safety belt provided in the motor vehicle in either the front or rear seat.

B. Failure to be secured by a child passenger restraint device or by a safety belt as required by this section shall not in any instance constitute fault or negligence and shall not limit or apportion damages.

NEW JERSEY

N.J. Stat. @ 39:3-76.2a (1992)

Child passenger restraint system; use; failure to use not contributory negligence; inadmissibility in evidence

Every person operating a motor vehicle equipped with safety belts who is transporting a child under the age of 5 years on roadways, streets or highways of this State, shall be responsible for the protection of the child by properly using a child passenger restraint system that complies with the Federal Motor Vehicle Safety Standard applicable when it was manufactured, or where the child is 18 months of age or more but under 5 years of age by securing the child with a safety belt in a rear seat. If there are no rear seats, a child restraint system must be used. In no event shall failure to wear a child passenger restraint system be considered as contributory negligence, nor shall the failure to wear the child passenger restraint system be admissible as evidence in the trial of any civil action.

39:3-76.2d.

Fines; suspension of fine

Any person guilty of violating any of the provisions of this act shall be fined not less than $ 10.00 and not more than $ 25.00. The court shall suspend any fine imposed for failure to use a child restraint system if the defendant demonstrates that he possesses a child restraint system that complies with the federal standard applicable when it was manufactured and is using it according to the manufacturer's instructions.

45:21-1.

Definitions

As used in this chapter:

"Person" means any individual, partnership, association, corporation or joint stock company, their trustees or receivers appointed by any court.

"Highway" means any street, avenue, park, parkway, road or other public place.

"Owner" means any and every person engaged in the business of renting or leasing motor vehicles, without a driver, to be operated by the lessee or bailee, his agent or servant, for purposes other than the transportation of passengers for hire.

"Child restraint" means a child passenger restraint system that conforms to the Federal Motor Vehicle Safety Standard applicable when it was manufactured.

N.J. Stat. 45:21-14 (1992)

Child restraints; information and availability to renters; deposit and fees

Every owner who rents a motor vehicle to any person shall inform the person of the requirements of P.L. 1983, c. 128 (C. 39:3-76.2a et seq.) with respect to the use of a child restraint and shall provide, at the request of the renter, an appropriate child restraint. The owner shall also supply the person with simple instructions for its use. The owner may charge a reasonable fee and deposit for the use of the child restraint.

45:21-15. Child restraints; violations

An owner who violates this amendatory and supplementary act shall be fined not less than $ 50.00 nor more than $ 250.00 for each offense, if the owner received at least 24 hours' advance notice from the customer or his agent that a child restraint system was required.

P.L.1992, CHAPTER 92

1992 SENATE NO. 291

SYNOPSIS: AN ACT requiring certain equipment for school buses and supplementing chapter 3B of Title 39 of the Revised Statutes.

BE IT ENACTED by the Senate and General Assembly of the State of New Jersey:

1. In addition to the requirements in Federal Motor Vehicle Safety Standard No. 222 (49 CFR Section 571.222) concerning school bus passenger seating and crash protection, each school bus as defined in R.S.39:1-1 shall be equipped with seats of a minimum seat back height of 28 inches, or 24 inches as measured from the seating reference point, and seat belts of the lap belt type for each seating position on the bus [OR OTHER CHILD RESTRAINT SYSTEMS THAT ARE IN CONFORMITY WITH APPLICABLE FEDERAL STANDARDS] . The design and installation of seat belts [OR OTHER CHILD RESTRAINT SYSTEMS THAT ARE IN CONFORMITY WITH APPLICABLE FEDERAL STANDARDS] shall conform to the regulations promulgated by the State Board of Education, in consultation with the Director of the Division of Motor Vehicles in the Department of Law and Public Safety. The State board shall promulgate regulations, pursuant to the "Administrative Procedure Act," P.L.1968, c.410 (C.52:14B-1 et seq.), for the design and installation of seat belts [OR OTHER CHILD RESTRAINT SYSTEMS

THAT ARE IN CONFORMITY WITH APPLICABLE FEDERAL STANDARDS] .

As used in this section, "seating reference point" shall be defined as the term is defined in 49 CFR Section 571.3.

2. Beginning on September 1 of the second year next following the year of enactment of P.L. , c. (C.) (now pending before the Legislature as this bill), each passenger on a school bus which is equipped with seat belts shall wear a properly adjusted and fastened seat belt [OR OTHER CHILDRESTRAINT SYSTEM THAT IS IN CONFORMITY WITH APPLICABLE FEDERAL STANDARDS] at all times while the bus is in operation. Nothing in this section shall make the owner or operator of a school bus liable for failure to properly adjust and fasten a seat belt [OR OTHER CHILD RESTRAINT SYSTEM THAT IS IN CONFORMITY WITH APPLICABLE FEDERAL STANDARDS] for a passenger who sustains injury as a direct result of the passenger's failure to comply with the requirement established by this section. 1992 N.J. Ch. 92

3. This act shall take effect immediately, but section 1 shall apply only to school buses and equipment for which, on or after the effective date of this act, a bid is submitted or an order for purchase placed.

NEW YORK

516-b (1993)

Reciprocal agreements concerning reporting of traffic offenses and administrative action thereon

(a) The commissioner may execute a reciprocal compact or agreement not inconsistent with the provisions of this chapter with the motor vehicle administrator or other authorized official of another state concerning the reporting of convictions for traffic offenses occurring in each state by a person licensed in, or a resident of, the other state to such licensing or residence state and the treating of any such reported conviction in the same manner as if the conviction occurred in the licensing or residence state for the purpose of administrative action. Any such compact or agreement shall specify the offenses subject to the compact or agreement, and shall include a determination of comparable offenses in each state if any such offenses are of a substantially similar nature but are not denominated or described in precisely the same words in each party state.

(b) The word "state" when used in this section shall mean any state, territory, a possession of the United States, District of Columbia or any province of Canada.

(c) Traffic offenses which may be subject to a reciprocal compact or agreement entered into pursuant to this section shall be limited to the following types of offenses in this state and equivalent offenses in each party state:

(1) Manslaughter, criminally negligent homicide and assault arising from the operation of a motor vehicle;

(2) Operating a motor vehicle while under the influence of alcohol or a drug;

(3) Any felony in the commission of which a motor vehicle is used;

(4) Leaving the scene of a personal injury or fatal incident without reporting;

(5) Any speeding offense;

(6) Any offense consisting of disobeying any traffic control device;

(7) Any offense involving failure to yield the right-of-way;

(8) Any offense involving direction of traffic, overtaking or passing;

(9) Any offense involving failure to use a safety belt or child restraint device;

(10) Reckless driving; and

(11) Passing a stopped school bus.

(d) Nothing in this section shall be construed to prohibit the reporting or recording of convictions other than those included in a reciprocal compact or agreement executed pursuant to this section when the laws of either state require or permit action to be taken or sanctions to be imposed on the basis of such convictions.

NORTH CAROLINA

N.C. Gen. Stat. 20-137.1 (1992)

Child restraint systems required

(a) Every driver who is transporting a child of less than six years of age shall have the child properly secured in a child passenger restraint system (car safety seat) which met applicable federal standards at the time of its manufacture. The requirements of this section may be met when the child is three years of age or older by securing the child in a seat safety belt.

(b) The provisions of this section shall not apply: (i) to vehicles registered in another state or jurisdiction; (ii) to ambulances or other emergency vehicles; (iii) when the child's personal needs are being attended to; (iv) if all seating positions equipped with child passenger restraint systems or seat belts are occupied; or (v) to vehicles which are not required by federal law or regulation to be equipped with seat belts.

(c) Any person convicted of violating this section may be punished by a fine not to exceed twenty-five dollars ($25.00). No driver charged under this section for failure to have a child under three years of age properly secured in a restraint system shall be convicted if he produces at the time of his trial proof satisfactory to the court that he has subsequently acquired an approved child passenger restraint system.

(d) No driver license points or insurance points shall be assessed for a violation of this section; nor shall a violation constitute negligence per se or contributory negligence per se nor shall it be evidence of negligence or contributory negligence.

NORTH DAKOTA

39-21-41.2 (1991)

Child restraint devices — Penalty — Evidence.

1. If a child, under three years of age, is present in any motor vehicle, that motor vehicle must be equipped with at least one child restraint system for each such child. The child restraint system must meet the standards adopted by the United States department of transportation for those systems [49 CFR 571.213]. While the motor vehicle is in motion, each such child must be properly secured in the child restraint system in accordance with the manufacturer's instructions. While the motor vehicle is moving, each child of three through ten years of age who is in the motor vehicle must be in an approved child restraint system or buckled in a seatbelt. Use of child restraint systems and seatbelts is not required in motor vehicles that were not equipped with seatbelts when manufactured. If all of the seatbelts are used by other family members in the vehicle or if a child is being transported in an emergency situation, thissection does not apply. 2. Violation of this section is punishable by a fine not to exceed twenty dollars. 3. Violation of this section is not, in itself, evidence of negligence.

   The fact of a violation of this section is not admissible in any proceeding other than one charging the violation.

OHIO

4511.81

Certain children to be secured in child restraint system; exceptions

(A) When any child who is less than four years of age or weighs less than forty pounds is being transported in a motor vehicle, other than a taxicab, that is owned by his parent or legal guardian and is registered in this state, and the motor vehicle is required by the United States department of transportation to be equipped with seat belts at the time of manufacture or assembly, the operator of the motor vehicle shall have the child properly secured in accordance with the manufacturer's instructions in a child restraint system that meets Federal Motor Vehicle Safety Standards.

(B) When any child who is less than one year of age is being transported in a motor vehicle, other than a taxicab or public safety vehicle as defined in section 4511.01 of the Revised Code, that is registered in this state but is not owned by his parent or legal guardian, and the motor vehicle is required by the United States department of transportation to be equipped with seat belts at the time of manufacture or assembly, the operator of the motor vehicle shall have the child properly secured in accordance with the manufacturer's instructions in a child restraint system that meets Federal Motor Vehicle Safety Standards.

(C) When any child who is one year of age or older but is less than four years of age or weighs less than forty pounds is being transported in a motor vehicle, other than a taxicab, that is registered in this state but is not owned by his parent or legal guardian, and the motor vehicle is required by the United States department of transportation to be equipped with seat belts at the time of manufacture or assembly, the operator of the motor vehicle shall have the child properly secured in accordance with the manufacturer's instructions in a child restraint system that meets Federal Motor Vehicle Safety Standards, if such a system is available. If such a child restraint system is not available, the operator of the motor vehicle shall have the child properly secured in a lap belt, or if a lap belt is not available, in a seat belt.

(D) When any child who is less than four years of age or weighs less than forty pounds is being transported in a motor vehicle, other than a taxicab, that is registered in this state and is owned, leased, or otherwise under the control of a nursery school, kindergarten, or day-care center, the operator of the motor vehicle shall have the child properly secured in accordance with the manufacturer's instructions in a child restraint system that meets Federal Motor Vehicle Safety Standards.

(E) The director of public safety shall adopt such rules as are necessary to carry out this section, and may adopt rules establishing exemptions additional to those established in division (G) of this section if the director determines that use of a child restraint system, lap belt, or seat belt would be impractical because of a physical handicap of a child and if the additional exemptions are directly related to that impracticality.

(F) The failure of an operator of a motor vehicle to secure a child in a child restraint system, lap belt, or seat belt as required by this section is not negligence imputable to the child, is not admissible as evidence in any civil action involving the rights of the child against any other person allegedly liable for injuries to the child, is not to be used as a basis for a criminal prosecution of the operator of the motorvehicle other than a prosecution for a violation of this section, and is not admissible as evidence in any criminal action involving the operator of the motor vehicle other than a prosecution for a violation of this section.

(G) This section does not apply when an emergency exists that threatens the life of any person operating a motor vehicle to whom this section otherwise would apply or the life of any child who otherwise would be required to be restrained under this section.

(H) The court shall dismiss a charge brought against a person who is a resident of this state and is charged with a first violation of division (A), (B), (C), or (D) of this section, and may waive the costs, if the person proves to the court, by a preponderance of the evidence, that he, prior to the scheduled court appearance indicated on the citation issued to him, purchased, borrowed, or rented for the period of time that the child involved in the alleged violation was or will be in the person's care or custody, a child restraint system that meets federal motorvehicle safety standards. The court shall not dismiss a charge brought against the person and shall impose the applicable fine levied by division (H) of section 4511.99 of the Revised Code if the person fails to prove to the court, by a preponderance of the evidence, that he has properly purchased, borrowed, or rented a child restraint system in accordance with this division and is convicted of the offense.

(I) If a person who is a resident of this state is charged with a second violation of division (A), (B) (C), or (D) of this section and is convicted but proves to the court by a preponderance of the evidence that he, prior to the scheduled court appearance indicated on the citation issued to him, purchased, borrowed, or rented for the period of time that the child involved in the violation was or will be in the person's care or custody, a child restraint system that meets Federal Motor Vehicle Safety Standards, the court shall impose the applicable fine levied by division (H) of section 4511.99 of the Revised Code. If the person fails to prove to the court, by a preponderance of the evidence, that he has properly purchased, borrowed, or rented a child restraint system in accordance with this division, the court shall impose the applicable fine levied by division (H) of section 4511.99 of the Revised Code.

(J) If a person who is not a resident of this state is charged with a violation of division (A), (B), (C), or (D) of this section and does not prove to the court, by a preponderance of the evidence, that his use or nonuse of a child restraint system was in accordance with the law of the state of which he is a resident, the court shall impose the fine levied by division (I) of section 4511.99 of the Revised Code.

OKLAHOMA

47 Okl. St. 11-1112 (1991)

Child passenger restraint system required for certain vehicles—Exemptions

A. Every driver when transporting a child under four (4) years of age in a motor vehicle operated on the roadways, streets, or highways of this state shall provide for the protection of said child by properly using a child passenger restraint system, or a properly secured seat belt in the rear seat of the motor vehicle. For purposes of Sections 11-1112 and 11-1113 of this title, " child passenger restraint system" means an infant or child passenger restraint system that meets the federal standards for crash-tested restraint systems as set by the United States Department of Transportation.

B. Children four (4) or five (5) years of age shall be protected by use of a child passenger restraint system or a seat belt.

C. The provisions of this section shall not apply to:

1. A nonresident driver transporting a child in this state; and

2. The driver of a school bus, taxicab, moped, motorcycle, or other motor vehicle not required to be equipped with safety belts pursuant to state or federal laws; and

3. The driver of an ambulance or emergency vehicle; and

4. A driver of a vehicle if all of the seat belts in the vehicle are in use; and

5. The transportation of children who for medical reasons are unable to be placed in such devices.

D. A law enforcement officer is hereby authorized to stop a vehicle if it appears that the driver of the vehicle has violated the provisions of this section and to give an oral warning to said driver. The warning shall advise the driver of the possible danger to children resulting from the failure to install or use a child passenger restraint system or seat belts in the motor vehicle.

E. A violation of the provisions of this section shall not be admissible as evidence in any civil action or proceeding for damages.

F. In any action brought by or on behalf of an infant for personal injuries or wrongful death sustained in a motor vehicle collision, the failure of any person to have the infant properly restrained in accordance with the provisions of this section shall not be used in aggravation or mitigation of damages.

G. Any person convicted of violating subsection A or B of this section shall be punished by a fine of Ten Dollars ($ 10.00) and shall pay a maximum of Fifteen Dollars ($ 15.00) court costs thereof. This fine shall be suspended in the case of the first offense upon proof of purchase or acquisition by loan of a child passenger restraint system. Provided, the Department of Public Safety shall not assess points to the driving record of any licensed or unlicensed person convicted of a violation of this section. 11-1113.

Child passenger restraint system education program

The Oklahoma Highway Safety Office shall develop a program of public education to promote the use of child passenger restraint systems.

OREGON

ORS 807.280 (1991)

Instruction driver permit.

The division shall provide for the issuance of instruction driver permits in a manner consistent with this section. A person who is issued an instruction driver permit may exercise the same driving privileges as those under the class of license or indorsement for which the permit is issued except as provided in this section or under the permit. Except as otherwise provided in this section, an instruction driver permit is subject to the fees, provisions, conditions, prohibitions and penalties applicable to a license or indorsement granting the same driving privileges. The following apply to an instruction driver permit:

(1) An instruction driver permit is subject to the same classifications and indorsements as a license. The division may issue an instruction driver permit to grant the same driving privileges as a Class A commercial, Class B commercial, Class C commercial or Class C driver license or as a motorcycle indorsement, but the permit will also be subject to the provisions of this section.

(2) The division may issue an instruction driver permit to a person who is qualified to obtain the same driving privileges under the corresponding class of license or type of indorsement except for the person's age or lack of experience in the operation of motor vehicles subject to the following:

(a) An applicant must be 15 years of age or older to receive the same driving privileges as are granted under a Class C license.

(b) An applicant must be 16 years of age or older and have a commercial driver license or a Class C license to receive the same driving privileges as are granted under a motorcycle indorsement.

(c) An applicant must be 18 years of age or older to receive the same driving privileges as are granted under any class of license not otherwise provided for under this subsection.

(3) The only fee required for issuance of an instruction driver permit is the instruction driver permit issuance fee under ORS 807.370.

(4) A Class C instruction driver permit shall be valid for 18 months from the date of issuance. All other instruction driver permits issued under this section shall be valid for one year from the date of issuance. A permit issued under this section may not be renewed.

(5) The holder of the permit may not operate a motor vehicle unless the holder has the permit in the holder's immediate possession and is accompanied by a person with a class of license granting the same driving privileges or a license with an indorsement granting the same driving privileges who is not less than 21 years of age. The accompanying person must be occupying a seat beside the holder of the permit unless the permit is for motorcycle driving privileges. For a permit granting motorcycle driving privileges, the holder of the permit must be in the company and under the supervision and visual observation of the accompanying person and the accompanying person must be operating a separate motorcycle. If the permit authorizes its holder to operate a commercial motor vehicle, the accompanying person must have a commercial driver license and the proper indorsements for the vehicle being operated by the holder of the permit.

(6) The holder of a permit granting motorcycle driving privileges is subject to the following in addition to any other requirements under this section:

(a) The holder may only operate a motorcycle during daylight hours.

(b) The holder may not carry any passengers on the motorcycle.

(c) The holder of the permit must wear an approved helmet while operating a motorcycle.

(7) The fee for issuance of a duplicate or replacement permit because of loss, destruction or mutilation of the permit is the permit replacement fee under ORS 807.370.

PENNSYLVANIA

75 Pa.C.S. 4581 (1992)

Restraint systems

(A) OCCUPANT PROTECTION.—

(1) Any person who is operating a passenger car, Class I truck, Class II truck, classic motor vehicle, antique motor vehicle or motor home registered in Pennsylvania and who transports a child under four years of age anywhere in the motor vehicle, including the cargo area, shall fasten such child securely in a child passenger restraint system, as defined in subsection (d). This subsection shall apply to all persons while they are operators of motor vehicles where a seating position is available which is equipped with a seat safety belt or other means to secure the systems or where the seating position was originally equipped with seat safety belts.

(2) Except for children under four years of age and except as provided in paragraph (1), each driver and front seat occupant of a passenger car, Class I truck, Class II truck or motor home operated in this Commonwealth shall wear a properly adjusted and fastened safety seat belt system. A conviction under this paragraph by State or local law enforcement agencies shall occur only as a secondary action when a driver of a motor vehicle has been convicted of any other provision of this title. The driver of a passenger automobile shall secure or cause to be secured in a properly adjusted and fastened safety seat belt system any occupant in the front seat who is four years of age or older

and less than 18 years of age. This paragraph shall not apply to:

(i) A driver or front seat occupant of any vehicle manufactured before July 1, 1966.

(ii) A driver or front seat occupant who possesses a written verification from a physician that he is unable to wear a safety seat belt system for physical or medical reasons, or from a psychiatrist or other specialist qualified to make an informed judgment that he is unable to wear a safety seat belt system for psychological reasons.

(iii) A rural letter carrier while operating any motor vehicle during the performance of his duties as a United States postal service rural letter carrier only between the first and last delivery points.

(iv) A driver who makes frequent stops and is traveling less than 15 miles per hour for the purpose of delivering goods or services while in the performance of his duties and only between the first and last delivery points.

A violation of this paragraph shall not be subject to the assessment of any points under section 1535 (relating to schedule of convictions and points).

(B) OFFENSE.— Anyone who fails to comply with the provisions of subsection (a)(1) shall be guilty of a summary offense with a maximum fine of $ 25. The court imposing and collecting any such fines shall transfer the fines thus collected to the State Treasurer for deposit in the Child Passenger Restraint Fund, pursuant to section 4582 (relating to Child Passenger Restraint Fund). Anyone who violates subsection (a)(2) commits a summary offense and shall, upon conviction, be sentenced to pay a fine of $ 10. No persons shall be convicted of a violation of subsection (a)(2) unless the person is also convicted of another violation of this title which occurred at the same time. No costs as described in 42 Pa.C.S. @ 1725.1 (relating to costs) shall be imposed for summary conviction of subsection (a)(2). Conviction under this subsection shall not constitute a moving violation.

(C) WAIVER OF FINE.— If a person receives a citation issued by the proper authority for violation of subsection (a)(1), a district justice, magistrate or judge shall dismiss the charges if the person prior to or at his hearing displays evidence of acquisition of a child passenger restraint system to such district justice, magistrate or judge. Sufficient evidence shall include a receipt mailed to the appropriate court officer which evidences purchase, rental, transferal from another child seat owner (evidenced by notarized letter) or bailment from a bona fide loaner program of a child passenger restraint system.

(D) STANDARDS.— A child passenger restraint system shall be used as designated by the manufacturer of the system in motor vehicles equipped with seat safety belts and shall meet the Federal Motor Vehicle Safety Standard (49 C.F.R. @ 571.213).

(E) CIVIL ACTIONS.— In no event shall a violation or alleged violation of this subchapter be used as evidence in a trial of any civil action; nor shall any jury in a civil action be instructed that any conduct did constitute or could be interpreted by them to constitute a violation of this subchapter; nor shall failure to use a child passenger restraint system or safety seat belt system be considered as contributory negligence nor shall failure to use such a system be admissible as evidence in the trial of any civil action; nor shall this subchapter impose any legal obligation upon or impute any civil liability whatsoever to an owner, employer, manufacturer, dealer or person engaged in the business of renting or leasing vehicles to the public to equip a vehicle with a child passenger restraint system or to have such child passenger restraint system available whenever their vehicle may be used to transport a child.

(F) CRIMINAL PROCEEDINGS.— The requirements of this subchapter or evidence of a violation of this subchapter are not admissible as evidence in a criminal proceeding except in a proceeding for a violation of this subchapter. No criminal proceeding for the crime of homicide by vehicle shall be brought on the basis of noncompliance with this subchapter.

(G) EXEMPTIONS.— For any child between the ages of one to four years, a seat safety belt in the rear seat of the motor vehicle may be used in lieu of a child passenger restraint system. Further exemptions will be allowed if it is determined, according to the rules and regulations of the department, that the use of a child passenger restraint system would be impractical for physical reasons including, but not limited to, medical reasons or size of the child.

(H) INSURANCE.— An insurer may not charge an insured who has been convicted of a violation of this section a higher premium for a policy of insurance in whole or in part by reason of that conviction.

75 Pa.C.S. 4582 (1992)

Child Passenger Restraint Fund

A Child Passenger Restraint Fund is established in the General Fund as a special restricted receipts account hereby earmarked for and appropriated to the department. This fund shall consist of all fines deposited pursuant to section 4581(b) (relating to restraint systems), all Federal funds granted for said use and any moneys donated into the fund. All such funds shall be used solely for the purpose of purchasing Federally approved child restraint seats and making such seats available to qualified loaner programs within the Commonwealth. A qualified loaner program shall be one determined by the department to loan Federally approved child restraint seats to parents or legal guardians of children under four years of age who, due to financial or economic hardship, are unable to comply with the provisions of this subchapter. The department shall adopt such regulations as are necessary to effectuate the purpose of this section.

75 Pa.C.S. 4583 (1992)

Hospital information program

(A) AVAILABILITY OF RESTRAINT DEVICES. —The hospital, in conjunction with the attending physician, shall provide the parents of any newborn child with any information regarding the availability of loaner or rental programs for child restraint devices that may be available in the community where the child is born.

(B) INSTRUCTION AND EDUCATION PROGRAMS. —The department shall provide instructional and educational program material through all current public information channels and to all relevant State and Federally funded, community-based programs for maximum distribution of information about this child passenger protection law.

75 Pa.C.S. 4584 (1992)

Oral hazard warning

An oral hazard warning shall be given by the State Police or local law enforcement officer to operators of motor vehicles in which children under four years of age are passengers and are not restrained by the use of seat restraints. The officer may advise and urge utilization of seat safety belts that are available in the vehicle and may note that, for children under four years of age, greater protection could be provided by acquiring and utilizing a separate Federally approved child restraint seat. The officer shall notify the parent or legal guardian who is in violation of section 4581 (relating to restraint systems) that, after January 1, 1985, a fine shall be imposed for such violation.

75 Pa.C.S. 4586 (1992)

Civil immunity for lenders of child passenger restraint systems

No person or organization who or which lends to another person or organization a child passenger restraint system, as described in section 4581 (relating to restraint systems), shall be liable for any civil damages resulting from any acts or omission, except any act or omission intentionally designed to harm, or any grossly negligent act or omission resulting in harm to another.

RHODE ISLAND

31-22-22 (1992)

Child passenger restraint

(A) Any person transporting a child three (3) years of age or under in the front or back seat of a motor vehicle operated on the roadways, streets or highways of this state, will provide for the protection of the child and properly use a child passenger restraint system approved by the United States department of transportation under federal standard 213.

(B) Any person transporting a child over the age of three (3) years of age and through the age of twelve (12) years of age in the front or back seat of a passenger motor vehicle operated on the roadways, streets or highways of this state, will ensure that any said child be in a child passenger restraint system as described above or be wearing a regular seat belt or shoulder harness.

Provided that in no event shall failure to wear a child passenger restraint system or regular seat belt be considered as contributory or comparative negligence, nor such failure to wear said child passenger restraint system, regular seat belt or shoulder harness be admissible as evidence in the trial of any civil action.

Any person deemed in violation of subsection (A) herein shall be issued a citation. If said cited person presents proof of purchase of a federally approved child restraint system under standard 213 to the issuing police department within seven (7) days of issuance, said department shall void the violation. If said individual fails to present proof of purchase, he or she shall be required to appear for a hearing before the division for administrative adjudication. Any person who violates the provisions of this section shall be fined thirty dollars ($ 30.00) for the first offense, sixty dollars ($ 60.00) for the second offense, and one hundred dollars ($ 100) for every subsequent violation, and it shall not be recorded on said person's driving record within the rules and regulations governing chapter 43 of this title.

Any person deemed to be in violation of subsection (B) herein shall be fined thirty dollars ($ 30.00) for the first offense, sixty dollars ($ 60.00) for the second offense, and one hundred dollars ($ 100) for every subsequent offense and it shall not be recorded on said person's driving record within the rules and regulations governing chapter 43 of this title.

All fines collected for violations of this section shall be payable to the state of Rhode Island. Provided, that fifty percent (50%) of the proceeds will be shared with the municipality whose law enforcement department issued the citation for the violations.

(C) Any operator of a motor vehicle transporting a person over the age of twelve (12) years in the front or back seat of a motor vehicle operated on the roadways, streets or highways of this state shall provide for the protection of said person a safety belt system as defined by Federal Motor Vehicle Safety Standard 209. The provisions of this subsection shall apply only to those motor vehicles required by federal law to have safety belts.

(D) Any person who is an operator of or passenger in a motor vehicle shall wear a safety belt as defined by Federal Motor Vehicle Safety Standard 209 while said vehicle is in operation on any of the roadways, streets or highways of this state. The provisions of this subsection shall apply only to those motorvehicles required by federal law to have safety belts.

In no event shall failure to wear a child passenger restraint system or safety belt be considered as negligence, nor such failure to wear said child passenger restraint system or safety belt be admissible as evidence in the trial of any civil action.

The provisions of subsection (C) and (D) shall not apply to a driver or passenger of:

(1) A passenger motor vehicle manufactured before July 1, 1966;

(2) A passenger motor vehicle in which the driver or passenger possesses a written verification from a licensed physician

that the driver or passenger is unable to wear a safety seat belt system for physical or medical reasons;

(3) A passenger motor vehicle which is not required to be equipped with a safety seat belt system under federal laws; or

(4) A passenger motor vehicle operated by a letter carrier of the United States postal service while performing the duties of a letter carrier.

A program of public information and education designed to educate the motoring public to the benefits of wearing safety belt systems, shall be developed by the Rhode Island department of transportation's governor's office on highway safety. The Rhode Island department of transportation's office on highway safety in cooperation with the Rhode Island department of health shall study the effectiveness of the implementation of this section and shall submit to the general assembly a report containing its findings by July 1, 1991.

(E) Violations of subsections (C) and (D) shall be considered secondary offenses and no motor vehicle may be stopped by any state or municipal law enforcement agency for failure of an operator or passenger to wear a safety belt system or for any violation of subsections (C) and (D); provided, however, that a motor vehicle may be stopped for failure to comply with the child passenger restraint system as described in subsections (A) and (B).

(F) No fine or sanction shall be imposed for a violation of subsections (C) and (D) other than a verbal warning.

(G) No record of any kind shall be maintained regarding any operator or passenger for violation of subsections (C) and (D), including any records of verbal warnings.

(H) Any verbal warnings issued for violations of subsectons (C) and (D) shall not be recorded regarding any motor vehicle's operator's driving record within the rules and regulations of chapter 43 of this title.

SOUTH CAROLINA

56-5-6410 (1991)

Age as basis for required use of restraining system; standards.

Every driver of a motor vehicle (passenger car, pickup truck, van, or recreational vehicle) registered in this State or primarily operated on the highways and streets of this State when transporting a child under six years of age upon the public streets and highways of the State shall provide an appropriate child passenger restraint system and shall secure the child as follows:

(1) Any child less than one year of age must be properly secured in a child restraint system which meets the standards prescribed by the National Highway Traffic Safety Administration.

(2) Any child under four years of age when transported in the front seat must be properly secured in a child restraint system meeting standards prescribed by the National Highway Traffic Safety Administration.

(3) Any child four until six years of age when transported in the front seat must be secured by a safety belt provided in the motor vehicle.

(4) Any child one year of age or more and under six years of age when transported in a rear seat must be properly secured in a child restraint system which meets the standards prescribed by the National Highway Traffic Safety Administration unless the child is secured by a safety belt provided in the motor vehicle.

Any child restraint system of a type sufficient to meet the physical standards prescribed by the National Highway Traffic Safety Administration at the time of its manufacture is sufficient to meet the requirements of this article.

56-5-6420 (1991)

Transportation of children with insufficient number of restraint devices.

If all the seating positions with restraint devices are occupied by children under the age of six years, a child may be transported and the driver of the motor vehicle is not in violation of the provisions of this article, but priority must be given to children under the age of six years, according to their ages.

56-5-6430 (1991)

Use of restraint device not required under certain circumstances.

The provisions of this article do not apply if a child being transported is being fed, has a physical impairment, or a medical problem or any distress which makes it impractical to use a child restraint system. Alternate restraint protection, such as safety belts, must be utilized if possible.

56-5-6440 (1991)

Persons and vehicles excepted from article.

The provisions of this article do not apply to:

(1) Taxi drivers.

(2) Drivers of emergency vehicles when operating in an emergency situation.

(3) Church, day care and school bus drivers.

(4) Public transportation operators.

(5) Commercial vehicles.

56-5-6445 (1991)

Applicability of chapter.

The provisions of this article apply to all motor vehicles equipped with safety belts.

56-5-6450 (1991)

Custodial arrest not authorized; penalties for violation of article; waiver.

No person shall be subjected to a custodial arrest for violation of the provisions of this article. Any person violating the provisions of this article shall upon conviction be fined not more than twenty-five dollars. The court shall waive any fine against any person who, before, or upon the appearance date on the summons, supplies the court with evidence of acquisition, purchase or rental of a child restraint system meeting the requirements of this article.

56-5-6460 (1991)

Violation of article not to constitute negligence.

A violation of this article shall not constitute negligence, per se, contributory negligence nor be admissible as evidence in any trial of any civil action.

56-5-6470 (1991)

Enforcement after June 30, 1984.

After June 30, 1984, any person violating the provisions of Article 47 of Chapter 5 of Title 56 may be, when apprehended, issued a summons, to appear in court for the violation, but no person shall at any time be placed under arrest or taken into custody for such a violation, other than upon a warrant issued for failure to appear in court in accordance with the summons or upon failure to pay a fine duly imposed by a court upon conviction.

SOUTH DAKOTA

32-37-1 (1992)

Use of system required — Violation as petty offense

Any operator of any passenger vehicle transporting a child under five years of age on the streets and highways of this state shall properly secure the child in a child passenger restraint system according to its manufacturer's instructions. The child passenger restraint system shall meet department of transportation motor vehicle safety standard 213 as in effect January 1, 1984. The requirements of this section are met if the child is at least two and under five years of age by securing the child in a seat belt. An operator who violates this section commits a petty offense.

TENNESSEE

Tenn. Code Ann. 55-9-602 (1992)

Child passenger restraint systems

(a) Any person transporting a child under the age of four (4) years in a motor vehicle upon a road, street or highway of Tennessee is responsible for providing for the protection of the child and properly using a child passenger restraint system meeting Federal Motor Vehicle Safety Standards. Nothing in this subsection restricts a mother from removing the child from the restraint system and holding the child when the mother is nursing the child, or attending to its other physiological needs.

(b) All passenger vehicle rental agencies doing business in the state of Tennessee shall make available at a reasonable rate to those renting such vehicles an approved restraint as described in subsection (a).

(c) [Deleted by 1989 amendment.]

(d)(1) A violation of this section is a Class C misdemeanor.

(2) In addition to or in lieu of the penalty imposed under subsection (d)(1), persons found guilty of a first offense of violating this section may be required to attend a court approved offenders' class designed to educate offenders on the hazards of not properly transporting children in motor vehicles. A fee may be charged for such classes sufficient to defray all costs of providing such classes.

(e) Any incorporated municipality may by ordinance adopt by reference any of the provisions of this section, it being the legislative intent to promote the protection of children wherever and whenever possible.

(f) Prior to the initial discharge of any newborn child from a health care institution offering obstetrical services, such institution shall inform the parent that use of a child passenger restraint system is required by law. Further, the health care institution shall distribute to the parent related information provided by the department of safety.

(g)(1) There is established within the general fund a revolving special account to be known as the "child safety fund," hereinafter referred to as the "fund."

(2) All fines imposed by this section shall be sent by the clerk of the court to the state treasurer for deposit in the fund.

(3) Any unencumbered funds and any unexpended balance of this fund remaining at the end of any fiscal year shall not revert to the general fund, but shall be carried forward until expended in accordance with the provisions of this section and @ 55-9-611.

(4) Interest accruing on investments and deposits of the fund shall be returned to the fund and remain a part of the fund.

(5) Disbursements from, investments of and deposits to the fund shall be administered and invested pursuant to the provisions of title 9, chapter 4, part 5.

(6) The state treasurer may deduct reasonable service charges from the fund pursuant to procedures established by the treasurer and the commissioner of finance and administration.

(7) Moneys in the fund shall be distributed quarterly to those health care institutions providing obstetric services that have not notified the treasurer of their desire to be excluded from such distribution. Such funds shall be distributed in the following manner, based on statistics to be supplied by the department of health:

(A) Each institution shall first receive that fraction of the funds to be distributed that corresponds to the fraction of Tennessee medicaid births occurring in that institution, up to a maximum of thirty dollars ($30.00) per medicaid birth; and

(B) Any excess funds remaining in the fund after distribution pursuant to subdivision (g)(7)(A) shall be distributed based on that fraction of the additional funds that corresponds to the fraction of Tennessee non-medicaid births occurring in that institution up to a maximum of thirty dollars ($30.00) per non-medicaid birth.

Such funds so distributed shall be used solely for the purchase of child passenger safety systems to be loaned or given to the parent or guardian of newborns in accordance with the provisions of Acts 1989, ch. 564.

UTAH

41-6-148.20 (1992)

Child restraint device required — Violation as infraction — Dismissal of charge — Failure not admissible as to negligence

(1) As used in this section:

(a) "Motor vehicle" means a vehicle defined in Section 41-1a-102; except authorized emergency vehicles defined in Sections 41-6-1 and 41-6-1.5, mopeds, campers, sleepers, motorcycles, motor homes, school buses, taxicabs, vehicles owned, operated, or leased by a public transit district, commercial vehicles owned or operated by persons holding a certificate of convenience and necessity issued by the Public Service Commission, or vehicles that weigh over 10,000 pounds gross weight and are not equipped with seat belts by the manufacturer.

(b) "Seating position" means any area within the passenger compartment of a motor vehicle in which the manufacturer has installed seat belts.

(2) A driver transporting a child in a motor vehicle shall:

(a) provide for the protection of a child younger than two years of age by using a child restraint device approved by the commissioner of public safety to restrain the child in the manner prescribed by the manufacturer of the device; and

(b) provide for the protection of a child two years of age up to eight years of age by using an appropriate child restraint device or a safety belt approved by the commissioner of public safety to restrain the child in the manner prescribed by the manufacturer of the device.

(3) Subsection (2) does not apply if all seating positions are occupied by other passengers.

(4)(a) A driver convicted of a violation of this section is guilty of an infraction and shall be fined not more than $20 per offense.

(b) The court in which a charge is pending for a first violation of this section shall dismiss the action against a driver who, during or before any court appearance on the matter, submits proof of acquisition, rental, or purchase of a child restraint device or safety belt as required by Subsection (2).

(5) Failure to provide and use a child restraint device or safety belt to restrain a child as required under this section may not be considered comparative negligence, nor is the failure to provide and use the restraint device or safety belt admissible as evidence in the trial of a civil action with regard to negligence.

VERMONT

23 V.S.A. 1281 (1991)

Additional equipment

In addition to other equipment required by this title, any school bus as described in section 4 of this title shall be equipped as follows:

(1) A door in the rear and a door on the right side for entrace or exit purposes.

(2) At least one fire extinguisher of a type approved by the commissioner at all times in good and usable condition and easily accessible to the driver.

(3) A standard first-aid kit of a type approved by the commissioner at all times filled with necessary articles.

(4) A hot water heater at all times capable of keeping the interior at a comfortable temperature or other type of heater approved by the commissioner of motor vehicles.

(5) Adequate ventilation facilities.

(6) At least two windows of safety glass on each side to provide interior light and so secured as to afford protection against wind and rain.

(7) Seats securely fastened to the floor or sides of the interior and providing at least thirteen inches of seat space for each child to be transported.

(8) In addition to the foregoing, all motor vehicles in which the original seating equipment has been modified or added to must comply with the following:

(A) All seats must be readily accessible by use of an aisle or door without interference from any other seat or seats.

(B) Minimum of 36 inches headroom for sitting position above top of undepressed cushion line of all seats shall be provided.

(C) Minimum of 12 inches shall be provided from the top of the undepressed cushion line to the floor.

(D) Seats shall be covered with fire-resistant material.

(E) Jump seats or portable seats shall not be used.

(F) Seat beside driver, if regular equipment or installed by vehicle manufacturer, may be used for pupil seating. It shall be securely fastened to body and shall be so constructed as not to interfere with pupils entering or leaving vehicle.

(G) All seats shall be at least 12 inches overall depth.

(H) If forward-facing seats are used, they shall be so placed that distance from center to center measured at top center of backs shall be not less than 26 inches.

(I) If longitudinal seats are used, only two shall be installed against sides of vehicle and distance between front edges of seat cushions shall be at least 24 inches.

23 V.S.A. 4 (1991)

Definitions

Except as may be otherwise provided herein, and unless the context otherwise requires in statutes relating to motor vehicles and enforcement of the law regulating vehicles, as provided in this title and part 5 of Title 20, the following definitions shall apply:

(1) "Authorized emergency vehicle" means vehicle of a fire department, police vehicle, public and private ambulance and a vehicle to which a permit has been issued pursuant to section 1252(a)(1) or section 1252(a)(2) of this title;

(2) "Button" is a traffic control marking consisting of an object, either permanently attached to the pavement or temporarily placed, and projecting above the surface;

(3) "Carrying capacity of a motor truck" shall be deemed to be the heaviest net load to be carried;

(4) "Commissioner" shall mean in this title only the commissioner of motor vehicles;

(5) "Construction area" shall mean and include all of that portion of a highway while under construction, by order of the state or a municipality thereof, located within properly posted warning signs maintained at each end thereof showing such area to have been designated as a "Construction Area";

(6) "Contractor's trailer" means any trailer or semi-trailer towed by a motor truck or truck tractor both of which have been owned or leased and registered for a period of thirty days or more by the using contract highway builder and used solely for the purpose of transporting road-making appliances or motorized highway building equipment from job to job in connection with his business of building, repair or maintenance of highways;

(7) "Crosswalks"

(A) That part of a roadway at an intersection included within the connections of the lateral lines of the sidewalks on opposite sides of the highway measured from the curbs or, in the absence of curbs, from the edges of the traversable roadway;

(B) Any portion of a roadway at an intersection or elsewhere distinctly indicated for pedestrian crossing by lines or other markings on the surface;

(8) "Dealer" includes "new car dealer," "used car dealer," "finance car dealer" as well as other types of motor vehicle dealers;

(A) "New car dealer" or "used car dealer" means a person whose primary activity is in the business of buying, selling or exchanging new or used motor vehicles and who may, as part of or incidental to such business, repair such vehicles, sell motor vehicle parts and accessories or lease or rent motor vehicles and who:

(i) Has had no previous record of willful violations of dealer laws or regulations in this or any other jurisdiction;

(ii) Has no unsatisfied judgments against him or her arising out of violations of consumer protection laws in this or any other jurisdiction;

(iii) Presents proof of compliance with the provisions of 23 V.S.A. 800 at the time application for registration is made;

(iv) Is open for business at least 104 days during the calendar year. When the application for registration as a new car dealer or used car dealer is made, the applicant shall provide the commissioner with the hours of operation of the business which the person shall maintain during the registration period.

(v) Owns real estate (as defined in section 132 of Title 1) as his or her place of business or has a lease with an expiration date not earlier than the last day of the registration year for which registration is sought under the provisions of subchapter 4 of chapter 7 of this title which has an appraised value (as defined in section 3481 of Title 32) of not less than ten thousand dollars and includes a building which has suitable and adequate facilities for the repair of motor vehicles, and has inside storage facilities for at least five standard sized pleasure cars. The building shall have adequate facilities for the maintenance of the records required by law to be kept including, but not limited to, those required by section 466 of this title and for the transfer of motor vehicles.

(B) "New car dealer" shall mean a person who, in addition to satisfying all of the requirements set forth in subdivision (8)(A) of this section, has a valid sales and service agreement, franchise or contract with a manufacturer, assembler, importer or distributor of new motor vehicles for the retail sale of new motor vehicles.

(C) "Finance dealer" means a person who is authorized to do business in this state and is actively engaged in and devoting a principal portion of his or her time to the wholesale and retail financing of motor vehicle sales by and through direct wholesale loans to those who are registered motor vehicle dealers under subdivisions (A) or (B) above or the purchase of retail conditional sales contracts from the dealers. A person entitled to dealer registration under this subdivision shall be deemed a dealer only to the extent of moving or operating under dealer registration a motor vehicle which he or she is repossessing in the regular course of his or her business. A person entitled to dealer registration under this subdivision shall also be entitled to demonstrate repossessed motorvehicles.

(D) "Auction dealer" means a person who is authorized to do business in this state and is engaged in the sale of motor vehicles at public auction subject to the provisions of sections 458, 459, 463, 466, 467 and 468 of this title. A motor vehicle owned by the auction dealer and to be sold at public auction by the auction dealer may be transported to the place of auction for a period of up to 30 days prior to the date of auction on auction dealer plates and then only by the dealer or his or her employee. A motor vehicle sold by an auction dealer may only be operated on auction dealer plates on the date of sale and then only by the dealer or his or her employee or by the purchaser when accompanied by the dealer or employee within ten miles of the place of auction.

(E) A person shall not be considered to have as his or her primary activity the business of buying, selling or exchanging new or used motor vehicles so as to qualify him or her for new or used car dealer registration under the provisions of 23 V.S.A. @ 451 unless, during the immediately preceding registration year, he or she has sold not less than 12 pleasure cars or trucks not owned and registered by him or her, or has sold not less than 12 pleasure cars or trucks owned or registered, or both, by him or her which have been used in lease or rental service. Any vehicle sold by a leasing or rental company to a registered new or used car dealer shall not count toward the 12 vehicles required for registration as a dealer. The requirements of this subdivision shall not prevent the registration of a person who has not previously been registered as a new car dealer or used car dealer in this state but who is otherwise qualified for registration provided, however, the requirements of this subdivision shall be applicable to that person in all years subsequent to the initial year of registration.

(F) As used in this subdivision, "person" shall include any individual or, in the case of partnerships, corporations or other entities, the directors, shareholders, officers or partners in these entities.

(9) "Edge of the roadway" is the extreme right-hand limit of any improved area within the right of way of the highway;

(10) "Eight-light system" shall mean four alternately flashing red signal lamps, two at the front and two at the rear to operate automatically when a school bus is stopped; and four alternately flashing amber signal lamps, two at the front and two at the rear, to be operated by the driver at an appropriate distance before stopping the bus;

(11) "Enforcement officers" shall include sheriffs, deputy sheriffs, constables, police officers, state's attorneys, motor vehicle inspectors, state game wardens and state police and, for en-

forcement of offenses relating to parking of motor vehicles, meter checkers and other duly authorized employees of a municipality employed to assist in the enforcement of parking regulations;

(12) "Fresh pursuit" as used in this chapter includes fresh pursuit as defined by the common law, and also the pursuit of a suspected violator of the criminal laws or other laws of this state, for which he is, or might be, subject to arrest, by an enforcement officer. Fresh pursuit as used in this chapter is not necessarily instant pursuit, but pursuit without unreasonable delay;

(13) "Highway," "road," "public highway" or "public road" shall include all parts of any bridge, culvert, roadway, street, square, fairground or other place open temporarily or permanently to public or general circulation of vehicles, and shall include a way laid out under authority of law;

(14) "Intersecting highway" shall mean any highway which joins another at an angle, whether or not it crosses the other; but a driveway leading to or from private grounds shall not be interpreted to be a highway;

(15) "Jitney" shall include any motor vehicle, not designated for the carrying of merchandise or freight, advertised or regularly used for carrying passengers for hire, but not operating over a fixed route, including motor vehicles operated for hire in connection with a livery business, but shall not include any such vehicle which the owner thereof uses in an emergency for such purpose, nor one which an employer uses to transport his employees to and from their work, nor one which is used solely in the transportation of school children or under authority granted to a school board under section 562 of Title 16 to transport other than school children, nor one which is used in the transfer of United States mail on a star route, so-called, nor one which is used to transport elderly and handicapped persons for whom special transportation programs are designed and funded by state and federal authority through public and private, nonprofit social service agencies; nor shall it apply to cooperative use transportation;

(16) "Junior operator" shall include only such persons as are sixteen and seventeen years of age;

(17) "Motor bus" shall include any motor vehicle with a seating capacity of more than seven persons, other than a street car, operated upon the public streets and highways along a regular route, and in such operation receiving, discharging and transporting passengers for hire; provided, that nothing herein contained shall be construed to apply to transportation service the route and destination of which are under the direction and subject to the control of the passengers so transported; nor shall it apply to cooperative use transportation;

(18) "Motorcycle" shall mean any motor driven vehicle having a seat or saddle for the use of the rider and designed to travel on not more than three wheels in contact with the ground, but excluding mo-peds, golf carts, track driven vehicles, tractors and vehicles on which the operator and passengers ride within an enclosed cab;

(19) "Motorized highway building equipment" shall include all bulldozers, rollers, scrapers, graders, spreaders, pavers, bituminous mixers, compressors, power shovels, excavators, dumptors, concrete mixers, bucket loaders, snow loaders, rooters and scarifiers, except road oilers and bituminous distributors, which contain as an integral part thereof and within the same unit facilities for generating motor power for propelling the same and while being used exclusively for the building, repair or maintenance of highways, or being transported or moved from job to job in connection with the building, repair or maintenance of highways; tractors used exclusively as a power unit in drawing road making appliances or in the transportation of same or of such tractor from job to job in connection with the building, repair or maintenance of highways;

(20) "Motor truck" means any motor vehicle designed primarily for the transportation of property and shall be construed to include truck tractor-semitrailer and truck tractor-semitrailer-trailer combinations;

(21) "Motor vehicle" shall include all vehicles propelled or drawn by power other than muscular power, except tractors used entirely for work on the farm, vehicles running only upon stationary rails or tracks, motorized highway building equipment, road making appliances or snowmobiles, or implements of husbandry;

(22) "Non-gasoline driven motor vehicle" shall include all motor vehicles, the power for which is generated otherwise than by gasoline, except steam road rollers, tractors used entirely for work on the farm and vehicles running only upon rails or tracks;

(23) "Nonresident" shall include any person who does not come under the definition of a resident;

(24) "Operate," "operating" or "operated" as applied to motor vehicles shall include "drive," "driving" and "driven" and shall also include an attempt to operate, and shall be construed to cover all matters and things connected with the presence and use of motor vehicles on the highway, whether they be in motion or at rest;

(25) "Operator" shall include all persons eighteen years of age or over, properly licensed to operate motor vehicles;

(26) "Owner" shall include any person, corporation, copartnership or association, holding legal title to a motor vehicle, or having exclusive right to the use or control thereof for a period of thirty days or more;

(27) "Person" as used in this title, shall include a corporation, association, co-partnership, company, firm or other aggregation of individuals;

(28) "Pleasure car" shall include all motor vehicles not otherwise defined in this title;

(29) [Repealed.]

(30) "Resident" shall include all legal residents of this state and in addition thereto, any person except a person who is domiciled in another state and who returns to the state on a regular basis of no less than weekly who accepts employment or engages in a trade, profession or occupation in this state for a

period of at least six months. Also in addition thereto, any foreign partnership, firm, association or corporation having a place of business in this state shall be deemed to be a resident as to all vehicles owned or leased and which are garaged or maintained in this state;

(31) "Road making appliances" shall mean all bulldozers, rollers, scrapers, graders, spreaders, pavers, retreading machines, compressors, power shovels, excavators, rock crushers, concrete mixers, snow loaders, bucket loaders, rooters, portable electric generators, pavement heaters, sweepers, steam boilers, traffic control boards, screening plants, asphalt reclaimers and scarifiers, designed to be and while being drawn by a separate motorized power unit and while being used exclusively for building, repair or maintenance of roads or highways or while being transported from job to job in connection with the building, repair or maintenance of roads or highways, except contractor's trailers;

(32) "Roadway" is that portion of a highway improved, designed or ordinarily used for vehicular traffic, exclusive of the shoulder;

(33) "Safety glass" shall mean any product composed of safety glazing materials so manufactured, fabricated or treated as substantially to prevent shattering and flying when struck or broken;

(34) "Type I school bus" means any motor vehicle with motor power, except a trailer, used to carry pupils for school purposes and is designed to carry more than 15 passengers including the operator. This definition includes vehicles that are at any time used to carry school children and school personnel exclusively, and does not include vehicles that only carry school children along with other passengers as part of the operations of a common carrier.

"Type II school bus" means any motor vehicle used to carry pupils for school purposes and is designed to carry 15 passengers or less including the operator, except a private motor vehicle used to carry members of the owner's household. However, a private motor vehicle

(A) used to carry pupils without compensation shall not be considered a Type II school bus. For the purpose of this subdivision, compensation shall mean payment in any form except that it shall not include reimbursement for mileage or the normal salary or compensation paid to a person otherwise employed by the school.

(B) carrying from seven to 15 pupils inclusive for compensation, including a private motor vehicle leased or otherwise provided to a school on a single trip basis to provide transportation to or from an athletic event or special field trip, shall be subject to all Type I school bus safety and equipment standards, except:

(1) Those requirements prescribed in subdivisions (a)(2) and (a)(3) of section 1283 of this title,

(2) The aisle or door requirement prescribed in subdivision (8)(A) of section 1281 of this title, and

(3) The rear door requirement prescribed in subdivision (1) of section 1281 of this title; provided, that if no rear door is present, there shall be one additional door, operable from inside the vehicle, located to the rear of the operator.

(35) "Sidewalk" that portion of a street between the curb lines or the lateral lines of a roadway, and the adjacent property lines, intended for use by pedestrians;

(36) "Single axle load" is the total load transmitted to the highway by all wheels whose centers may be included within two parallel transverse vertical planes less than forty-eight inches apart, extending across the full width of the vehicle;

(37) "Standard equipment" and "properly equipped" as applied to a motor vehicle shall include adequate tires, head lamps, tail lamps, lenses, reflectors, brakes, muffler, rear view mirror, windshield wiper, horns, windshield, number plate brackets, and only such motor fuel tank or tanks as are regularly installed by the manufacturer. "Standard equipment" and "properly equipped," as applied to motor vehicles designated by the manufacturer as 1964 or later models, shall also include safety

seat belts or harnesses installed in the left and right front seats of pleasure cars and windshield defroster on pleasure cars, motor trucks and motor buses, both to be of a type approved by the commissioner of motor vehicles;

(38) "Tandem axle load" is the total load transmitted to the highway by all wheels whose centers may be included between two parallel transverse vertical planes not less than forty-eight inches apart and not more than eight feet apart, extending across the full width of the vehicle. A trunnion axle, with eight wheels in line, shall be considered to be a tandem axle, except that when operated on portions of the highways which are designated as the national system of interstate and defense highways it shall be considered a single axle;

(39) "Tractor" shall include a motor vehicle designed or used primarily as a traveling power plant or for drawing other vehicles, and not so constructed as to carry any load other than a part of the weight of the vehicles and load so drawn, excepting, however, motorized highway building equipment;

(40) "Trailer" is a vehicle without motive power designed to be drawn by a motor vehicle, and so constructed that no part of its weight rests upon the towing vehicle, excepting however, implements of husbandry, road making appliances and transportation dollies, and "semi-trailer" is a vehicle without motive power, designed to be drawn by a motor vehicle, and so constructed that some part of its weight and that of its load rests upon or is carried by the towing vehicle, excepting however, poledinkeys, implements of husbandry, transportation dollies and road making appliances;

(41) "Trailer coach" shall mean any trailer or semi-trailer designed to be towed by a motor vehicle and designed, equipped or used for sleeping, eating or living quarters;

(42) "Transporter" shall mean every person engaged in the business of delivering vehicles of a type required to be registered hereunder from a manufacturing, assembling, or distributing plant to dealers or sales agents of a manufacturer, and includes persons regularly engaged in the business of towing trailer coaches, owned by them or temporarily in their custody, on

their own wheels over public highways, persons towing office trailers owned by them or temporarily in their custody, on their own wheels over public highways, and persons regularly engaged in the business of moving modular homes over public highways and shall also include dealers and automobile repair shop owners when engaged in the transportation of motor vehicles to and from their place of business for repair purposes. "Transporter" shall include other persons, firms or corporations, provided the transportation and delivery of motor vehicles is a common and usual incident to the repossession of motor vehicles in connection with their business;

(43) "Truck crane" shall mean a motor truck equipped with a permanently mounted hoisting apparatus, winch or derrick, designed and used for the moving of motor vehicles or other objects, with no provision for carrying a load on the body of such truck crane except an inoperable motor vehicle, parts and equipment used for the operation and for the repair of motor vehicles, and equipment used for the operation of a hoisting apparatus, winch or derrick;

(44) "Moving violation" shall mean any violation of any provision of this title, while the motor vehicle is being operated on a public highway, over which operation the operator has discretion as to commission of the act, with the exception of offenses pertaining to a parked vehicle, equipment, size, weight, inspection or registration of the vehicle and child restraint systems or seat belts as required in section 1258 of this title;

(45) "Mo-ped" means a motor driven cycle equipped with two or three wheels, foot pedals to permit muscular propulsion, a power source providing up to a maximum of two brake horsepower and having a maximum piston or rotor displacement of 50 cubic centimeters if a combustion engine is used, which will propel the vehicle, unassisted, at a speed not to exceed 30 miles per hour on a level road surface and is equipped with a power drive system that functions directly or automatically only, not requiring clutching or shifting by the operator after the drive system is engaged. As motor vehicles, mo-peds shall be subject to the purchase and use tax imposed under chapter 219 of Title 32 rather than to a general sales tax;

(46) "Implement of husbandry" means every vehicle designed and adapted exclusively for agricultural, horticultural or livestock raising operations or for lifting or carrying an implement of husbandry and in either case not subject to registration if used upon the highway;

(47) "Cooperative use transportation" is defined as the collective nonprofit use by two or more people of privately-owned vehicles when the providing of transportation is not the primary business of the owner and/or driver of the vehicle, but is incidental to their livelihood. Cooperative use shall include, but not be limited to, shared driving, and shared expense; employer-owned or leased vehicles, including buses, which are operated for employee commuting purposes, commuter services organized and arranged by employee cooperatives, labor unions, credit unions, and neighborhood groups which are operated for the convenience of their members;

(48) "License to operate a motor vehicle."

Any operator's license or any other license or permit to operate a motor vehicle issued under, or granted by, the laws of this state including:

(1) Any temporary license or learner's permit;

(2) The privilege of any person to operate a motor vehicle whether or not such person holds a valid license;

(3) Any nonresident's operating privilege.

(49) "Revocation of license" means the termination by formal action of the commissioner of a person's license or privilege to operate a motor vehicle onthe public highways whereby the license or privilege shall not be subject to renewal or restoration except upon an application for a new license presented to and acted upon by the commissioner after the expiration of the applicable period of time prescribed in this title. The term also includes the refusal of the right of an unlicensed person to apply for a license.

(50) "Suspension of license" means the withdrawal by formal action of the commissioner, for a specific period of time and until reinstatement by the commissioner, of a person's license

or privilege to operate a motor vehicle on the public highways. The term also includes the refusal of the right of an unlicensed person to apply for a license.

(51) "Single-axle tow dolly" is a vehicle towed by a self-propelled motor vehicle and designed and used exclusively to transport another self-propelled motor vehicle and upon which the front or rear wheels of the towed self-propelled motor vehicle are mounted, while the wheels of the towed self-propelled motor vehicle remain in contact with the ground. These vehicles shall not be subject to registration or titling nor shall they be treated as a separate vehicle when used in combination with another vehicle. They shall be subject to equipment safety requirements.

(52) "Alcohol assessment screening" means an assessment of an individual's use of alcohol which includes consideration of the results of any available tests relating to the individual's blood alcohol content, the individual's motor vehicle record, responses to an alcohol screening questionnaire approved by the secretary of human services, personal interviews, and any other relevant information which is identified in any subsequent report.

(53) "Truck tractor" shall include a motor vehicle designed and used primarily for drawing other vehicles but so constructed as to carry a load other than a part of the weight of the vehicle and load so drawn.

(54) "Transportation dolly" means a vehicle towed by a motor vehicle and designed and used exclusively in the transport of buildings which are not normally transported over the highway and whose dimensions and/or weight would require a permit subject to engineering inspection, which consists of sets of single or double axles with wheels set in such configurations underneath the building to be moved so as to distribute the weight of the load. This vehicle shall not be subject to registration and shall be exempt from titling and so treated whether used singly or in conjunction as one separate vehicle when used in combination with another vehicle. However, all moves shall be governed by the commissioner's rules and regulations for oversize and overdimension moves.

(55) "Unprocessed milk products" means raw milk transported in bulk when transported in a milk tank truck, semi-trailer, trailer or combination thereof.

(56) "Full or semi-flotation applicator vehicle" means a vehicle used for the application of lime, fertilizer, or agricultural chemicals.

(57) "Month" means 30 days and "year" means 365 days.

(58) "Privilege to operate" includes the privilege of a nonresident to operate a motor vehicle within the state and includes the privilege of a resident to obtain a license.

(59) "Disqualification" means a withdrawal of the privilege to drive a commercial motor vehicle.

23 V.S.A. 1258 (1991)

Child restraint system

(a) No person shall operate a motor vehicle in this state upon a public highway while transporting a child under the age of five years unless the child is properly restrained as follows:

(1) in a federally approved child passenger restraining system if the child being transported is under the age of one year;

(2) in a federally approved child passenger restraining system if the child being transported is in the front seat of the vehicle;

(3) in a federally approved child passenger restraining system or seat belt if the child being transported is between the ages of one and five and is in a seat other than the front seat of the vehicle.

(b) No person shall operate a motor vehicle, other than a school bus, in this state upon a public highway while transporting a child aged 5 through 12 unless the child is properly secured in a federally approved safety belt.

(c) A person shall not be guilty of a violation of this section if:

(1) the motor vehicle is regularly used to transport passengers for hire except a motor vehicle owned or operated by a day care facility; or

(2) the motor vehicle is not equipped with seat belts and was manufactured without seat belts; or

(3) the child being transported has a physical condition which prevents the use of the child passenger restraining system or seat belts where otherwise applicable; or

(4) the total number of persons being transported exceeds the number of seat belts, so long as:

(A) all children under the age of one year are restrained in a federally approved child passenger restraining system; and

(B) all seat belts are being utilized.

(d) A person violating this section shall be fined $ 25.00, except such fine shall be waived for a first violation upon proof of acquisition of a federally approved child passenger restraining system or seat belts.

VIRGINIA

46.2-1095 (1992)

Child restraint devices required

Any person who drives on the highways of Virginia any motor vehicle manufactured after January 1, 1968, shall ensure that any child under the age of four (i) of which he is the parent or legal guardian or (ii) which he regularly transports therein is provided with and properly secured in a child restraint device of a type which meets the standards adopted by the United States Department of Transportation.

WASHINGTON

46.61.688 (1991)

Safety belts, use required——Penalties——Exemptions

(1) For the purposes of this section, the term "motor vehicle" includes:

(a) "Buses," meaning motor vehicles with motive power, except trailers, designed to carry more than ten passengers;

(b) "Multipurpose passenger vehicles," meaning motor vehicles with motive power, except trailers, designed to carry ten persons or less that are constructed either on a truck chassis or with special features for occasional off-road operation;

(c) "Passenger cars, " meaning motor vehicles with motive power, except multipurpose passenger vehicles, motorcycles, or trailers, designed for carrying ten passengers or less; and

(d) "Trucks," meaning motor vehicles with motive power, except trailers, designed primarily for the transportation of property.

(2) This section only applies to motor vehicles that meet the manual seat belt safety standards as set forth in Federal Motor Vehicle Safety Standard 208. This section does not apply to a vehicle occupant for whom no safety belt is available when all designated seating positions as required by Federal Motor Vehicle Safety Standard 208 are occupied.

(3) Every person sixteen years of age or older operating or riding in a motor vehicle shall wear the safety belt assembly in a properly adjusted and securely fastened manner.

(4) No person may operate a motor vehicle unless all passengers under the age of sixteen years are either wearing a safety belt assembly or are securely fastened into an approved child restraint device.

(5) A person violating this section shall be issued a notice of traffic infraction under chapter 46.63 RCW. A finding that a person has committed a traffic infraction under this section shall be contained in the driver's abstract but shall not be available to insurance companies or employers.

(6) Failure to comply with the requirements of this section does not constitute negligence, nor may failure to wear a safety belt assembly be admissible as evidence of negligence in any civil action.

(7) Enforcement of this section by law enforcement officers may be accomplished only as a secondary action when a driver of a motor vehicle has been detained for a suspected violation of Title 46 RCW or an equivalent local ordinance or some other offense.

(8) This section does not apply to an operator or passenger who possesses written verification from a licensed physician that the operator or passenger is unable to wear a safety belt for physical or medical reasons.

(9) The state patrol may adopt rules exempting operators or occupants of farm vehicles, construction equipment, and vehicles that are required to make frequent stops from the requirement of wearing safety belts.

RCW 48.19.500 (1991)

Motor vehicle insurance——Seat belts, etc

Due consideration in making rates for motor vehicle insurance shall be given to any anticipated change in losses that may be attributable to the use of seat belts, child restraints, and other lifesaving devices. An exhibit detailing these changes and any credits or discounts resulting from any such changes shall be included in each filing pertaining to private passenger automobile (or motor vehicle) insurance.

WEST VIRGINIA

W. Va. Code 16-2-6 (1992)

Local boards of health authorized to make available child safety car seats; requirements for renting and loaning such seats; immunity from liability

(a) Any county, municipal or combined board of health, whether created and maintained pursuant to the provisions of this article or article two-A [@ 16-2A-1 et seq.] of this chapter, shall be authorized to:

(1) Retain and make available child safety car seats;

(2) Collect such reasonable rental and security deposit fees to cover the expenses of retaining and making available child safety car seats;

(3) Conduct public information and education activities designed to convey the need for and potential benefit of the use of child safety car seats and prevent misuse of child safety car seats.

(b) Any county, municipal or combined board of health offering a child safety car seat program pursuant to this section shall:

(1) Thoroughly examine each seat before it is rented or loaned out and document, in writing, such examination;

(2) Provide written and verbal instructions for proper use of the seat to each borrower prior to renting or loaning out a seat to such borrower;

(3) Require each borrower to demonstrate correct use of child safety car seat prior to renting or loaning the seat to such borrower;

(4) Require each borrower to sign a statement indicating that he or she understands how to use the child safety car seat correctly and has so demonstrated; and

(5) Comply with any other requirements which the state board of health may, by regulation, prescribe.

(c) A county, municipal or combined board of health offering a child safety car seat program shall not make available for loan or rental any child safety car seat which the board knows or has reason to believe was in use in a vehicle which was involved in a moderate or severe crash.

(d) This section is not intended to relieve any driver of a motor vehicle of his or her legal duty as prescribed by chapter seventeen-C, article fifteen, section forty-six [@ 17C-15-46] of this Code, to provide for the protection of a child by properly placing, maintaining and securing such child in a child passenger restraining system meeting applicable Federal Motor Vehicle Safety Standards.

(e) Any county, municipal or combined board of health or employee or agent thereof which offers a child safety car seat program pursuant to this section shall be immune from civil or criminal liability in any action resulting from the improper use or malfunctioning or inadequate maintenance of a child safety car seat or from the improper placement, maintenance or securing of a child in a child safety car seat.

HISTORY: 1984, c. 85.

USER NOTE: For more generally applicable notes, see notes under the first section of this part, article, or chapter.

W. Va. Code 17C-15-46 (1992)

Child passenger safety device required

Every driver who transports a child under the age of nine years in a passenger automobile, van or pickup truck other than one operated for hire, shall, while such motor vehicle is in motion and operated on a street or highway of this state, provide for the protection of such child by properly placing, maintaining and securing such child in a child passenger safety device system meeting applicable Federal Motor Vehicle Safety Standards: Provided, That if such child is between the age of three and eight, both inclusive, a vehicle seat belt shall be sufficient to meet the requirements of this section.

Any person who violates any provision of this section is guilty of a misdemeanor, and, upon conviction thereof, shall be fined not less than ten dollars nor more than twenty dollars.

A violation of this section shall not be deemed by virtue of such violation to constitute evidence of negligence or contributory negligence or comparative negligence in any civil action or proceeding for damages.

If any provision of this section or the application thereof to any person or circumstance is held invalid, such invalidity shall not affect other provisions or applications of this section, and to this end the subsections of this section are declared to be severable.

If all seat belts in a vehicle are being used at the time of examination by a law officer and the vehicle contains more passengers than the total number of seat belts or other safety devices as installed in compliance with Federal Motor Vehicle Safety Standards, the driver shall not be considered as violating this section.

WISCONSIN

347.48

Safety belts and child safety restraint systems

(1) SAFETY BELTS REQUIRED. (a) No person may buy, sell, lease, trade or transfer a motor vehicle other than an automobile at retail from or to Wisconsin residents unless the vehicle is equipped with safety belts installed for use as required under 49 CFR 571, and no such vehicle may be operated in this state unless such belts remain installed.

(b) No person may buy, sell, lease, trade or transfer an automobile that is required under 49 CFR 571 to be equipped with safety belts from or to a resident of this state unless the front designated seating positions of the automobile are equipped with safety belts installed for use as required under 49 CFR 571 and unless each rear outboard designated seating position of the automobile is equipped with a safety belt consisting of a combination of a pelvic and upper torso restraint that conforms to standards for a Type 2 seat belt assembly under

49 CFR 571.209, and no automobile may be operated in this state unless such belts remain installed. Nothing in this section applies to antique reproductions.

(2) TYPE AND MANNER OF INSTALLING. All such safety belts must be of a type and must be installed in a manner approved by the department. The department shall establish specifications and requirements for approved types of safety belts and attachments thereto. The department will accept, as approved, all seat belt installations and the belt and anchor meeting the society of automotive engineers' specifications.

(2m) REQUIRED USE. (a) In this subsection, "properly restrained" means wearing a safety belt approved by the department under sub. (2) and fastened in a manner prescribed by the manufacturer of the safety belt which permits the safety belt to act as a body restraint.

(b) If a motor vehicle is required to be equipped with safety belts in this state, no person may operate that motor vehicle unless the person is properly restrained in a safety belt.

(c) If a motor vehicle is required to be equipped with safety belts in this state, no person may operate that motor vehicle unless he or she reasonably believes that each passenger who is at least 4 years old and not more than 15 years old and who is seated at a designated seating position in the front seat required under 49 CFR 571 to have a safety belt installed or at a designated seating position in the seats, other than the front seats, for which a shoulder harness has been installed is properly restrained.

(d) If a motor vehicle is required to be equipped with safety belts in this state, no person who is at least 4 years old and who is seated at a designated seating position in the front seat required under 49 CFR 571 to have a safety belt installed or at a designated seating position in the seats, other than the front seats, for which a shoulder harness has been installed may be a passenger in that motor vehicle unless the person is properly restrained.

(dm) Paragraphs (b), (c) and (d) do not apply to the operation of an authorized emergency vehicle by a law enforcement officer or other authorized operator under circumstances in which compliance could endanger the safety of the operator or another.

(dr) Paragraph (b) does not apply to the operator of a vehicle while on a route which requires the operator to make more than 10 stops per mile involving an exit from the vehicle in the scope of his or her employment. Paragraphs (c) and (d) do not apply to a passenger while on a route which requires the passenger to make more than 10 stops per mile involving an exit from the vehicle in the scope of his or her employment.

(e) The department shall, by rule, exempt from the requirements under pars. (b) to (d) persons who, because of a physical or medical condition, cannot be properly restrained in a safety belt.

(f) 1. This subsection does not apply if the motor vehicle is a taxicab or is not required to be equipped with safety belts under sub. (1) or 49 CFR 571.

2. This subsection does not apply to a privately owned motor vehicle while being operated by a rural letter carrier for the delivery of mail or while being operated by a delivery person for the delivery of newspapers or periodicals.

3. This subsection does not apply to a motor vehicle while being operated by a land surveying crew while conducting a land survey along or upon the highway.

7. This subsection does not apply to a farm truck or dual purpose farm truck while being used in conjunction with the planting or harvesting of crops and not being operated upon the highway.

(g) Evidence of compliance or failure to comply with par. (b), (c) or (d) is admissible in any civil action for personal injuries or property damage resulting from the use or operation of a motor vehicle. Notwithstanding s. 895.045, with respect to injuries or damages determined to have been caused by a failure to comply with par. (b), (c) or (d), such a failure shall not reduce the recovery for those injuries or damages by more than 15%. This paragraph does not affect the determination of causal negligence in the action.

(gm) Notwithstanding s. 349.02, a law enforcement officer may not stop or inspect a vehicle solely to determine compliance with this subsection or sub. (1) or (2). This paragraph does not limit the authority of a law enforcement officer to issue a citation for a violation of this subsection or sub. (1) or (2) observed in the course of a stop or inspection made for other purposes, except that a law enforcement officer may not take a person into physical custody solely for a violation of this subsection or sub. (1) or (2).

(h) This subsection does not apply after June 30, 1991.

(3) MANDATORY USE BY RULE; PROHIBITED. Except as provided under sub. (4) (a) 2, the department may not, by rule, require directly or indirectly the wearing of safety belts or shoulder harnesses. This subsection applies after June 30, 1991.

(3m) SAFETY BELT INFORMATION PROGRAM. The department shall develop and administer a public information program to promote safety belt awareness and use.

(4) CHILD SAFETY RESTRAINT SYSTEMS REQUIRED; STANDARDS; EXEMPTIONS. (a) 1. No resident, who is the parent or legal guardian of a child under the age of 2, may transport the child in a motor vehicle unless the child is properly restrained in a child safety restraint system approved by the department or, when present in the vehicle, permit the child to be transported in a motor vehicle unless he or she has provided for the proper restraint of the child. If a resident who is not the parent or legal guardian of the child transports the child in a motor vehicle when the parent or legal guardian of the child is not present, the resident shall properly restrain the child. In this subdivision, "properly restrained" means fastened in a manner prescribed by the manufacturer of the system which permits the system to act as a body restraint but

does not include a system in which the only body restraint is a safety belt of the type required under sub. (1). The department shall, by rule, establish standards in compliance with applicable federal standards for approved types of child safety restraint systems for those child restraint systems purchased after November 1, 1982. No resident is required to have more than 3 child safety restraint systems in a vehicle.

2. No resident, who is the parent or legal guardian of a child who is at least 2 years old but less than 4 years old, may transport the child in a motor vehicle unless the child is by the department under subd. 1 or in a safety belt approved by the department under sub. (2) or, when present in the vehicle, permit the child to be transported in a motor vehicle unless he or she has provided for the proper restraint of the child. If a resident who is not the parent or legal guardian of the child transports the child in a motor vehicle when the parent or legal guardian of the child is not present, the resident shall properly restrain the child. In this subdivision, "properly restrained" means fastened in a manner prescribed by the manufacturer of the system which permits the system to act as a body restraint.

3. Notwithstanding subds. 1 and 2, a person other than the operator of a motor vehicle transporting a child required to be properly restrained under subd. 1 or 2 may temporarily remove a child from a safety restraint system to attend to the personal needs of the child under all of the following conditions:

   a. When the child safety restraint system is attached to a back passenger seat.

   b. When the person attending to the child's personal needs is seated in a back passenger seat.

   c. When the person physically restrains the child while attending to the child's personal needs.

(b) The department may, by rule, exempt from the requirements under par. (a) any child who because of a physical or medical condition or body size cannot be placed in a child safety restraint system or safety belt.

(c) 1. This subsection does not apply if the motor vehicle is a motor bus, school bus, taxicab, moped, motorcycle or is not required to be equipped with safety belts under sub. (1) or 49 CFR 571.

2. This subsection does not apply to a vehicle with a seating capacity, as designated by the manufacturer, of 2 persons if there are 2 persons 4 years of age or older in the vehicle.

(d) Evidence of compliance or failure to comply with par. (a) is admissible in any civil action for personal injuries or property damage resulting from the use or operation of a motor vehicle but failure to comply with par. (a) does not by itself constitute negligence.

WYOMING

31-5-1303 (1992)

Child safety restraint system; required use; exception

(a) Except as otherwise provided in subsection (b) of this section, no person shall operate a passenger car in this state unless each child who is a passenger in that car and who is two (2) years of age or under, and who weighs forty (40) pounds or less, and who is forty (40) inches tall or less, is properly secured in a child safety restraint system.

(b) Any child who is within the age, weight and height requirements specified in subsection (a) of this section need not be properly secured in a child safety restraint system if:

(i) A licensed physician has determined that the weight or physical or medical condition of the child requires that the child not be secured in such a system. The person operating a passenger car transporting such a child shall carry in the car the physician's signed statement certifying that the child should not be secured in a child restraint system;

(ii) The child is at least one (1) year old and there is no available space in the passenger car for a child restraint system, in which case the child shall be secured in the seat by a safety belt provided in the passenger car;

(iii) The passenger car in which the child is riding was not equipped with safety belts at the time of manufacture;

(iv) The passenger car in which the child is riding does not provide sufficient space or sufficient safety belts; or

(v) The passenger car in which the child is riding is owned or operated by persons other than the child's parent or guardian.

Chapter 5

Trends In Legislation

The legislatures of many states have realized that the many exemptions and loopholes that exist under current laws deter from the general purpose of the legislation which is to insure safety. As a result, there are many bills currently pending in state houses to close the loopholes and repeal the exemptions that exist under current law.

On January 13 of 1993, Arizona was the first state to introduce a bill to repeal the various exemptions from the law that required drivers to put children in safety seats. The bill was referred from the house to the committee on transportation and the committee decided to pass the legislation.

In March of this year, Connecticut considered legislation that would include child car seats that violate federal standards under a list of hazardous substances. This type of legislation is very important because of the hundreds, if not thousands, of child restraints that are sold all across the country at garage sales and flea markets to unsuspecting consumers. As noted in the recall section, these child car seats do not meet the minimal requirements of the federal standard and are hazardous substance which can be deadly to a child. In February, Connecticut also introduced legislation that requires car seat manufacturers located at state or doing business in that state to offer consumers a choice of repairing, replacement, or refunds in situations where the child restraint is found to be defective. The latest action in this bill was a favorable report from the joint select committee on children. The bill has been referred to the joint committee on general law.

Florida, a state that has dealt harshly with violations of child restraint laws in the past, is considering the bill that provides that a person charged for a first offense for violating the law dealing with child restraint devices may elect to attend a child restraint offender class instead of receiving a fine and having three points added to their license record. The legislation withholds adjudication of the case until successful completion of the class. The maximum fee that can be charged for the class is $40.00 and the legislation provides for time tables for the election and completion of the class.

The authors believe that legislation such as this proposed bill are in the spirit of addressing all of the components to successful child restraint program. In addition to legislation, and adequate enforcement, the education component must also be satisfied to prove use of child restraint devices.

Florida is also considering a new piece of legislation entitled The Highway Safety and Motor Vehicles Operations and Efficiency Act of 1993. In addition to fiscal and economic concerns, the bill revises the uniform traffic code in Florida to require daycare vans to provide child safety seat restraints. The legislation would, in effect, close one of the exemptions for mandatory child restraint legislation.

Hawaii is another state that has recently introduced legislation that would give the option to violators of the child restraint laws the opportunity to attend a child passenger restraint safety course for certain traffic violations.

Idaho is also attempting to close up the loopholes in arbitrary exemptions from coverage of the child restraint laws by introducing Idaho house bill 361. The bill requires that a child under four years of age or who weighs less than 40 pounds be restrained in a car safety seat by **any** motor vehicle operator transporting the child. In addition, the Idaho bill deletes language requiring that violation of the section may not be cited without a violation of another traffic law.

Illinois has followed a similar trend in their 1993 senate bill 180. The Illinois bill provides that any person transporting a child shall comply with child restraint laws. As written, the Illinois law applies only to resident children. The senate bill also removes the medical emergency exception to the act.

Indiana has introduced a bill on an issue that has been hotly debated amongst legislature, consumer groups, or federal agencies. House bill 1993 HB 1378 requires that for school buses that are purchased after June 30th, 1998 and which exceed 40 miles per hour when transporting school children, that they have safety belts or other child restraint system for each school child who is transported by the bus. As noted in the chapter on current state laws, emergency vehicles and public transportation offered by schools are two prime examples of vehicles that are exempted from child restraint requirements.

In its current session, the main legislature has sponsored house bill 383, which increases the first violation penalty for failure to secure a child under the age of four in a federally approved child safety seat. This proposed law would repeal an obsolete provision which gave the violator an initial six month warning period. The new law would also allow for a waiver of the first violation fine if the court is satisfied that a child safety seat has been purchased by the offender.

In its current set of bills, the Massachusetts legislature is considering a bill that would mandate safety restraint in shopping carts. In many states, most grocery and other type of large discount stores provide child restraint devices in their shopping carts for the convenience and safety of their customers. However, these child restraints remain largely untested and in many cases suffer from serious defects in design. The major flaws with these type of shopping carts lie in the way the buckles are designed or manufactured and in the way that the straps are secured to the child restraint.

In Minnesota the legislature is considering Minnesota house bill 477, which would in effect double the fine for child passenger restraint violations to $50.00. But like in many other states, the fine could be waived upon showing proof of purchase of a federally approved child restraint system within 14 days after the violation. Another Minnesota house bill takes a harsher approach to violations of child restraint laws by making them a primary offense and a misdemeanor punishable by a $100.00 fine for failing to use a child passenger restraint system.

The Mississippi legislature is currently considering house bill 201 which would, in effect, increase the age of children who use child restraint devices in motor vehicles.

New Hampshire is considering New Hampshire house bill 101 which will require child restraint protection for all children under four years of age according to federal standards. The bill would also require children from age 4 to 12 to be either in a child restraint seat or to wear safety belts. This bill was introduced on January 6 of 1993 and it was sent to the committee on transportation. It passed both the house and the senate and was signed into law by the governor of New Hampshire on March 29, 1993.

In an interesting piece of legislation the New Jersey senate is considering New Jersey senate bill 528. This bill provides liability protection to organizations which lend child restraint systems to be used by children. The authors believe that such legislation can be helpful in protecting those organizations which seek to help needy parents and guardians by providing them with a means of safely transporting children in motor vehicles. However, such legislation needs to be worded carefully so that tortfeasors who unknowingly provide unsafe child restraints do not go unpunished.

New Mexico voiced its concern with the compensation of auto accident victims in the form of senate bill 171 which provides that failure to be secured by a safety device shall not constitute fault or negligence and shall not limit damages. Many states apply the comparative negligence principle to motor vehicle accidents by reducing the amount of damages recoverable by a set percentage if the person suffering injuries is found to have some degree of fault or negligence in those injuries.

Oklahoma is considering the use of rear seatbelts as an alternative to child passenger restraint systems required for children under four years of age. This legislation is in the form of Oklahoma house bill 1046 which would also require that children aged four to fifteen years of age be protected by the use of passenger restraint systems or seatbelts. This legislation will also delete the exemption for non-resident drivers who would transport children in Oklahoma. Again, it is important to note that more and more states are considering closing the loophole created by current laws that exempt non-residents. In the future it may be necessary to consult a current map and check the existing state laws before making a trip to determine what the laws of each state are.

Oregon is considering senate bill 779 which requires the use of a child safety seat system in a motor vehicle if a child is under four years of age and weighs 40 pounds or less.

The Pennsylvania legislature is considering two bills this session: House Bill 461 and House Bill 1165. House bill 461 has decided to regulate child passenger restraint systems to achieve some degree of uniformity on the child restraint systems that are currently used in that state. House bill 1165, on the other hand, would delete the alternative to using seat belts in place of child restraint systems in rear seats. Pennsylvania has also considered senate bill 160, which amends the Pennsylvania vehicle code and provides for restraint systems for vehicles which are registered out of state.

Tennessee, the first state to enact a mandatory child restraint law, has considered Tennessee house bill 612 which would permit a judge to impose a fine of up to $250.00 for a violation of the child passenger restraint system law. If this bill passes and becomes Tennessee's law, it will contain one of the harshest penalties in the country equal only to that of New Hampshire.

Texas is considering a law that relates to the distribution of child passenger safety seat systems by the department of health.

Vermont senate bill 81 is intended to amend a child passenger restraining law by requiring that all children under the age of three must be restrained in a child passenger restraint system. The bill would require that all children between the ages of three and five be restrained in a child passenger restraint system or a seatbelt if transported in a seat other than the front seat. The new legislature would also repeal the fine waiver provision.

Virginia is also considering a bill that would make a violation of the motor vehicle ordinance such as the seatbelt violation a primary offense. The legislation would also allow the adoption of local ordinances that parallel the state safety belt statute.

Virgina house bill 803 would increase a civil penalty applicable for failing to secure a child in an approved child restraint device from $25.00 to $50.00, but would allow the court to dismiss any case where the person purchases or obtains a child restraint device after being cited.

Washington, through Washington senate bill 5879 proposes to conform state law on child passenger restraint systems to the uniform vehicle code.

Chapter 6

Recalls & Defects

Child restraint devices are designed to prevent injury by restraining the child in place and preventing or minimizing injury to the child in a crash or stop. Most car seats are designed to distribute the impact forces over a greater portion of a child's body and thereby reducing injury to the child. The impact forces are distributed in a child restraint system by the use of straps, harnesses or shields.

Child safety restraint devices are among the most recalled products in the market. In the past two years, more child restraint devices have been recalled than in all of the combined history of child restraint devices. In 1992 a record 8 1/2 million seats were recalled due to several problems.

The majority of the problems are cosmetic in nature. By cosmetic we mean minor. But often serious defects are the cause of recalls. The defects range from faulty buckles, broken shields, or faulty harness straps. Usually the problem can be corrected by repairing the defective part or by upgrading the defective part. When a product is subject to recall, the manufacturer supplies the needed parts or makes needed repairs as necessary free of charge.

Most consumers never do find out about recalls. Recall information is disseminated in very few publications and consumer attention to recalls announced through the media is minimal at best.

Manufacturers of consumer products usually place a registration card with their product. This registration card is supposed to be used as a means to contact the client in the event of a recall or as a means of contacting the client in case updated information becomes available. However, more often than not, registration cards are tossed in the garbage and never returned to the manufacturer. Those cards that are returned are mainly used by the manufacturers to compile mailing lists which they can sell to other manufacturers or which they can use to promote their own products.

For many years, child restraint manufacturers were not required to provide registration cards with their child restraining devices. As of 1992, NHTSA requires that all manufacturers provide a registration card with each car seat that is sold. Prior to the NHTSA ruling, only two companies, Fisher-Price and Century, provided registration cards on a regular and consistent basis.

In 1988, thousands of restraints manufactured by Cosco, Inc. were recalled because of a tendency of the shell to break away from the seat belt during a crash. In 1991, over three million child safety seats manufactured by Evenflo Juvenile Furniture between 1985 and 1990 were recalled for failure to meet Federal Motor Vehicle Safety Standard 213. The defect prompting the recall consisted of defective buckles that failed to latch properly, resulting in release during an accident or sudden stop, leaving the child unrestrained.

Problems with child restraint latches are very common. A case involving a defective child restraint latch in a Century 400XL car seat resulted in a $1.75 million dollar verdict (the judgment was $2.25 million with interest). The facts of this case show that plaintiff's car skidded out of control on a patch of ice. The vehicle crashed against a tree at an estimated 30 mph. The child restraint latch failed, and as a result the child struck her head against the interior of the car compartment. The child suffered a head injury and brain hemorrhage that requires an intraventricular shunt to drain the excess fluid for the rest of her life. Between the period of time of manufacture and the time that plaintiff's purchased the child restraint, Century received over 100 complaints of the defective buckle. As a result Century modified their design and added a warning. In 1987, the Century 400XL, which had a unique spring latching mechanism, was discontinued due to the number of problems with the latch mechanism.

More recently, the Century Corporation has recalled several models of its car seats, manufactured from 1989 to 1992. Again, the recall focused on the seat latch, which was discovered to stick during crash tests, thus locking the child in the safety seat.

Defects in booster seats have also had serious consequences. In 1988, a child suffered severe abdominal injuries after a collision with another vehicle. The injuries were the cause of her death. The child was properly restrained in a Century Commander Booster Seat, Model 4813. The plaintiff's contended that the defective design of the shield on the booster concentrated the crash forces on her abdomen and ultimately caused her death. Century denied that the booster was negligently designed.

Recalls are not unknown to the industry, but only a very small percentage of consumers find out about recalls. In general, few customers take the time to fill out and return registration cards on the products that they buy. Those consumers that do find out about any recall through personal notification or the media may not take action to correct the problem. Of all the child restraint devices recalled in 1990 and 1991 only about 11% have been removed from use or repaired. Worse yet, families that are unable to afford a new child restraint may buy defective car seats at a flea market or garage sales.

Although a used child restraint may be an attractive economical option for many, the safety of such restraints is highly questionable. Child restraints bought at a garage sale often do not have the necessary instructions, parts and attachments. Often, used child restraints are missing critical components like the harness, shield or tether strap. Also, the buyer of a used restraint has no guarantee that the used restraint has not been in a crash - which would compromise the overall safety of the restraint. A recall does not remove the car seat from the market or ensure that corrections of the defects will take place, and occasionally defective restraints are not recalled because the manufacturer has gone out of business. 352,000 defective restraints manufactured by the Strolee company in 1987 and 1988 were not recalled because the company went out of business. One of the models was found to be defective when used in the rearward position. Another model was prone to cracks.

Another very serious defect associated with child restraints is the lack of adequate instructions and warnings to parents on how to properly use the restraint. Although manufacturers are aware of many common misuses of restraints, they are unlikely to take action unless the government intervenes and forces their hand. Labeling used in warnings is such an example of the callous disregard by the industry. FMVSS does not address the permanence of labels that are placed on a restraint. Section 4.1 of FMVSS 213 deals with the labeling requirements. Though the standard requires a "permanent" label no provision is made on how to best ensure permanence. Labels on child restraints are known to wear and peel off. Yet, it is foreseeable that warnings on a used restraint may peel off or become illegible.

Defenses to child restraint cases vary from blaming the parents, to blaming the death of the child on Acts of God or Sudden Infant Death Syndrome. In 1987, a three-week-old infant died during a car trip to California. The plaintiff's alleged that the child's fatal injuries were the result of a defective child restraint design, given that a red band around the child's neck indicated that he had been strangled by the straps. Plaintiffs contended that a more reclined restraint could have prevented the injuries and the unnecessary death. The defense convinced the jury that the child died by Sudden Infant Death Syndrome, and that the red band around the child's neck was caused by blood pooled in the neck as a result of *livor mortis*. Child restraint manufacturers often raise the parents' disregard for automobile safety as a defense to show misuse. If the parents are not in the habit of wearing seat belts, the manufacturer may be able to prove that the child's injuries, even though properly restrained, were caused by another unrestrained adult rather than a defective seat.

In general, if the child restraint is defective, one of the best ways for the plaintiff' to prove the defect is through the passengers' injuries. The ideal case is were the child sustains severe injuries while properly secured in the child restraint, and all the other passengers receive minor or no injuries. In such a scenario the work for the plaintiff's attorney and experts is greatly decreased because the causation factors are drastically reduced.

Defense attorneys for the child restraint manufacturers often use protective orders and confidential settlements as a tactic against litigants and prospective litigants. In 1988, the family of a five-year-old child rendered quadriplegic settled their lawsuit for $4.25 million dollars. As part of the settlement plaintiff's signed a confidentiality order. The order included a provision that prohibits the disclosure of the defendant manufacturer to third parties. However, the case docket number was not part of the confidential information and journalists were able to discover the defendant in the case. Kolcraft, the defendant, denied liability and stated that the settlement was a business decision. Attorney Michael Pope of Pope & John of Chicago stated that the decision to settle by their client avoided unnecessary "massive exposure" and a possible sympathy verdict in the $20 million range.

Nevertheless, the plaintiffs had a film of a sled test that showed that the booster seat ejected a small dummy even when used properly. The factual scenario was a virtual recreation of a laboratory test. The collision was a head-on collision with a "delta V" of 30 miles per hour. The child at the time of the accident was 16 months and weighed 22 pounds. Kolcraft marketed and advertised its product for use by children as small as 20 pounds. NHTSA only recommends boosters for use by children that weight over 40 pounds.

Confidential agreements and protective orders used by the defense in this type of cases may hide more than potential lawsuits, the documents in those cases may also contain information vital to consumer safety. Although Kolcraft discontinued manufacture of the QuickStep booster seat, it is unknown how many of those boosters are being used by unsuspecting parents. The same holds true for all other child restrained devices that are recalled.

A more constructive approach and concerted effort is needed to improve the standards that govern child restraints, the laws that enforce use and the designs that the manufacturers apply. The safety of our country's future must be a priority item and based on more than "business decisions".

The section that follows is a compilation of all child restraints that have been recalled. Attorneys handling a defective child restraint case must ascertain if the restraint in question has ever been recalled, the nature of the defect and how the manufacturer notified consumers.

Recalls

MODEL(S): 326
MANUFACTURER: Alkot
PHONE NUMBER: N/A
MANUFACTURE DATES: March 1984 - November 1984
PROBLEM AREA: Shell
ACTION: Refund
RESULT:

MODEL(S): 8982200-147
MANUFACTURER: American Motors Corporation
PHONE NUMBER: N/A
MANUFACTURE DATES: March 1984 - November 1984
PROBLEM AREA: Shell
ACTION: Refund
RESULT:

MODEL(S): 500
MANUFACTURER: Babyhood Ind.
PHONE NUMBER:
MANUFACTURE DATES: N/A
PROBLEM AREA: Test failure
ACTION: Out of business
RESULT: Repairs unavailable

MODEL(S): 501
MANUFACTURER: Babyhood Ind.
PHONE NUMBER:
MANUFACTURE DATES: N/A
PROBLEM AREA: Test failure
ACTION: Out of business
RESULT: Repairs unavailable

MODEL(S): 501B
MANUFACTURER: Babyhood Ind.
PHONE NUMBER:
MANUFACTURE DATES: N/A
PROBLEM AREA: Test failure
ACTION: Out of business
RESULT: Repairs unavailable

MODEL(S): All
MANUFACTURER: Babyhood Ind.
PHONE NUMBER:
MANUFACTURE DATES: January 1982 - December 1982
PROBLEM AREA: Buckle
ACTION: Out of business
RESULT: Repairs available

MODEL(S): Saddle #820
MANUFACTURER: Babyhood Manufacturing, Inc.
PHONE NUMBER: 508-845-4231
MANUFACTURE DATES: N/A
PROBLEM AREA: Test failure
ACTION: Replace cushions
RESULT:

MODEL(S): All
MANUFACTURER: Bolform
PHONE NUMBER: N/A
MANUFACTURE DATES: N/A
PROBLEM AREA: Buckle
ACTION: Out of business
RESULT: Repairs unavailable

MODEL(S): 1280, 1290
MANUFACTURER: Buckeye Plastics Co.
PHONE NUMBER: N/A
MANUFACTURE DATES: N/A
PROBLEM AREA: Test failure
ACTION: Out of business
RESULT: Repairs unavailable

MODEL(S): 810
MANUFACTURE DATES: NA
SEAT DESCRIPTION: Wonda-Chair 810
MANUFACTURED BY: Babyhood Ind.
PROBLEM: Provides inadequate protection in crash
SOLUTION: Contact manufacturer for instructions
NOTES: Manufacturer no longer in child safety seat business.

MODEL(S): 100
MANUFACTURE DATES: Apr. 1985 - Feb. 1986
SEAT DESCRIPTION: 200
MANUFACTURED BY: Century Products Inc.
PROBLEM: Shell can crack in rear-facing position
SOLUTION: Obtain insert kit from Century and install on seat
NOTES: None

MODEL(S): 200
MANUFACTURE DATES: Apr. 1985 - Feb. 1986
SEAT DESCRIPTION: 200
MANUFACTURED BY: Century Products, Inc.
PROBLEM: Shell can crack in rear-facing position
SOLUTION: Obtain insert kit from Century and install on seat
NOTES: None

MODEL(S): 200
MANUFACTURE DATES: Jan. 1981 - Jan. 1983
SEAT DESCRIPTION: 200
MANUFACTURED BY: Century Products, Inc.
PROBLEM: 4SE of lubricants can cause buckle jamming, breakage
SOLUTION: Obtain replacement buckle and crotch strap from Century. Do not lubricate with oil.
NOTES: None.

MODEL(S): 300
MANUFACTURE DATES: Apr. 1985 - Feb. 1986
SEAT DESCRIPTION: 300
MANUFACTURED BY: Century Products, Inc.
PROBLEM: Shell can crack in rear-facing position
SOLUTION: Obtain insert kit from Century and install on seat
NOTES: None

MODEL(S): 400 XL
MANUFACTURE DATES: Nov. 1984 - Apr. 1986
SEAT DESCRIPTION: 400 XL
MANUFACTURED BY: Century Products, Inc.
PROBLEM: Shield pops open when not fully latched
SOLUTION: Obtain red sticker from Century which warns if lock not engaged
NOTES: None.

MODEL(S): 400 XL
MANUFACTURE DATES: Apr. 1985 - Feb. 1986
SEAT DESCRIPTION: 400 XL
MANUFACTURED BY: Century Products, Inc.
PROBLEM: Shell can crack in rear-facing position
SOLUTION: Obtain insert kit from Century and install on seat
NOTES: None.

MODEL(S): 4100
MANUFACTURE DATES: Jan. 1981 - Apr. 1981
SEAT DESCRIPTION: 4100
MANUFACTURED BY: Century Products, Inc.
PROBLEM: Child can remove plastic upholstery button and place in mouth.
SOLUTION: Contact manufacturer from button replacement
NOTES: None.

MODEL(S): 4153
MANUFACTURER: Century Products, Inc.
PHONE NUMBER: 800-837-4044
MANUFACTURE DATES: December 1990 - October 1991
PROBLEM AREA: Label
ACTION: Replace label
RESULT:

MODEL(S): 4163
MANUFACTURER: Century Products, Inc.
PHONE NUMBER: 800-837-4044
MANUFACTURE DATES: December 1990 - October 1991
PROBLEM AREA: Label
ACTION: Replace label
RESULT:

MODEL(S): 4200
MANUFACTURE DATES: Jan. 1981 - Apr. 1981
SEAT DESCRIPTION: 4100
MANUFACTURED BY: Century Products, Inc.
PROBLEM: Child can remove plastic upholstery button and place in mouth.
SOLUTION: Contact manufacturer for button replacement
NOTES: None

MODEL(S): 4253
MANUFACTURE DATES: Apr. 1986 - Jun. 1989
SEAT DESCRIPTION: 2000 STE
MANUFACTURED BY: Century Products, Inc.
PROBLEM: Shoulder strap glued rather than sewn.
SOLUTION: Contact manufacturer for replacement straps
NOTES: None.

MODEL(S): 4261
MANUFACTURER: Century Products, Inc.
PHONE NUMBER: 800-837-4044
MANUFACTURE DATES: December 1990 - October 1991
PROBLEM AREA: Label
ACTION: Replace label
RESULT:

MODEL(S): 4263
MANUFACTURE DATES: Apr. 1986 - Jun. 1989
SEAT DESCRIPTION: 2000 STE
MANUFACTURED BY: Century Products, Inc.
PROBLEM: Shoulder strap glued rather than sewn
SOLUTION: Contact manufacturer for replacement straps
NOTES: None

MODEL(S): 4263
MANUFACTURER: Century Products, Inc.
PHONE NUMBER: 800-837-4044
MANUFACTURE DATES: December 1990 - October 1991
PROBLEM AREA: Label
ACTION: Replace label
RESULT:

MODEL(S): 4265
MANUFACTURE DATES: Apr. 1986 - Jun. 1989
SEAT DESCRIPTION: 2000 STE
MANUFACTURED BY: Century Products, Inc.
PROBLEM: Shoulder strap glued rather than sewn.
SOLUTION: Contact manufacturer for replacement straps
NOTES: None

MODEL(S): 4265
MANUFACTURER: Century Products, Inc.
PHONE NUMBER: 800-837-4044
MANUFACTURE DATES: December 1990 - October 1991
PROBLEM AREA: Label
ACTION: Replace label
RESULT:

MODEL(S): 4266
MANUFACTURER: Century Products, Inc.
PHONE NUMBER: 800-837-4044
MANUFACTURE DATES: December 1990 - October 1991
PROBLEM AREA: Label
ACTION: Replace label
RESULT:

MODEL(S): 4353
MANUFACTURE DATES: Mar. 1987 - Dec. 1990
SEAT DESCRIPTION: 3000STE Child Safety Seat
MANUFACTURED BY: Century Products, Inc.
PROBLEM: The buckle release force may exceed 16 pounds when not used in appropriate forward latch position for a child weighing 30 pounds or more
SOLUTION: Change instructions and seat labeling to indicate that the rear latch position is not to be used with children weighing 30 pounds or more.
NOTES: None

MODEL(S): 4365
MANUFACTURER: Century Products, Inc.
PHONE NUMBER: 800-837-4044
MANUFACTURE DATES: December 1990 - October 1991
PROBLEM AREA: Label
ACTION: Replace label
RESULT:

MODEL(S): 4365
MANUFACTURE DATES: Mar. 1987 - Dec. 1990
SEAT DESCRIPTION: 3000 STE Child Safety Seat
MANUFACTURED BY: Century Products, Inc.
PROBLEM: The buckle release force may exceed 16 pounds when not used in appropriate forward latch position for a child weighing 30 pounds or more
SOLUTION: Change instructions and seat labeling to indicate that the rear latch position is not to be used with children weighing 30 pounds or more
NOTES: None.

MODEL(S): 4365 DT
MANUFACTURE DATES: May 1990 - Jun. 1990
SEAT DESCRIPTION: 3000 STE Infant Car Seat
MANUFACTURED BY: Century Products, Inc.
PROBLEM: Latch tongues broke during impact testing
SOLUTION: Century will replace latch tongue or return seat for refund of purchase price.
NOTES: None

MODEL(S): 4365 DT
MANUFACTURE DATES: Mar. 1989 - Oct. 1989
SEAT DESCRIPTION: 3000 STE
MANUFACTURED BY: Century Products, Inc.
PROBLEM: Child can remove foam from pad and place in mouth or nose.
SOLUTION: Contact manufacturer for replacement pad.
NOTES: None.

MODEL(S): 4365 MC
MANUFACTURE DATES: May 1990 - Jun. 1990
SEAT DESCRIPTION: 3000 STE Infant Car Seat
MANUFACTURED BY: Century Products, Inc.
PROBLEM: Latch tongues broke during impact testing.
SOLUTION: Century will replace latch tongue or return seat for refund of purchase price.
NOTES: None.

MODEL(S): 4366
MANUFACTURER: Century Products, Inc.
PHONE NUMBER: 800-837-4044
MANUFACTURE DATES: December 1990 - October 1991
PROBLEM AREA: Label
ACTION: Replace label
RESULT:

MODEL(S): 4366
MANUFACTURE DATES: Mar. 1987 - Dec. 1990
SEAT DESCRIPTION: 3000 STE Child Safety Seat
MANUFACTURED BY: Century Products, Inc.
PROBLEM: The buckle release force may exceed 16 pounds when not used in appropriate forward latch position for a child weighing 30 pounds or more.
SOLUTION: Change instructions and seat
NOTES:

MODEL(S): 4366
MANUFACTURE DATES: March 1989 - October 1989
SEAT DESCRIPTION: 3000 STE
MANUFACTURED BY: Century Products, Inc.
PROBLEM: Child can remove foam from pad and place in mouth or nose.
SOLUTION: Contact manufacturer for replacement pad.
NOTES: None.

MODEL(S): 4366BH
MANUFACTURE DATES: May 1990 - June 1990
SEAT DESCRIPTION: 3000 STE Infant Car Seat
MANUFACTURED BY: Century Products, Inc.
PROBLEM: Latch tongues broke during impact testing.
SOLUTION: Century will replace latch tongue or return seat for refund of purchase price.
NOTES: None.

MODEL(S): 4367
MANUFACTURER: Century Products, Inc.
PHONE NUMBER: 800-231-2755
MANUFACTURE DATES: September 1989 - April 1992
PROBLEM AREA: Harness
ACTION: Repair kit
RESULT:

MODEL(S): 4367
MANUFACTURER: Century Products, Inc.
PHONE NUMBER: 800-837-4044
MANUFACTURE DATES: December 1990 - October 1991
PROBLEM AREA: Label
ACTION: Replace label
RESULT:

MODEL(S): 4368
MANUFACTURER: Century Products, Inc.
PHONE NUMBER: 800-837-4044
MANUFACTURE DATES: December 1990 - October 1991
PROBLEM AREA: Label
ACTION: Replace label
RESULT:

MODEL(S): 4368
MANUFACTURE DATES: March 1987 - December 1990
SEAT DESCRIPTION: 3000 STE Child Safety Seat
MANUFACTURED BY: Century Products, Inc.
PROBLEM: The buckle release force may exceed 16 pounds when not used in appropriate forward latch position for a child weighing 30 pounds or more.
SOLUTION: Change instructions and seat labeling to indicate that the rear latch position is not to be used with children weighing 30 pounds or more.
NOTES: None.

MODEL(S): 4368BH
MANUFACTURER: Century Products, Inc.
PHONE NUMBER: 800-837-4044
MANUFACTURE DATES: May 1990 - June 1990
PROBLEM AREA: Test failure
ACTION: Replace latch
RESULT:

MODEL(S): 4369
MANUFACTURER: Century Products, Inc.
PHONE NUMBER: 800-231-2755
MANUFACTURE DATES: September 1989 - April 1992
PROBLEM AREA: Harness
ACTION: Repair kit
RESULT:

MODEL(S): 4380
MANUFACTURER: Century Products, Inc.
PHONE NUMBER: 800-231-2755
MANUFACTURE DATES: September 1989 - April 1992
PROBLEM AREA: Harness
ACTION: Repair kit
RESULT:

MODEL(S): 4380
MANUFACTURER: Century Products, Inc.
PHONE NUMBER: 800-837-4044
MANUFACTURE DATES: December 1990 - October 1991
PROBLEM AREA: Label
ACTION: Replace label
RESULT:

MODEL(S): 4381
MANUFACTURER: Century Products, Inc.
PHONE NUMBER: 800-837-4044
MANUFACTURE DATES: December 1990 - October 1991
PROBLEM AREA: Label
ACTION: Replace label
RESULT:

MODEL(S): 4450
MANUFACTURER: Century Products, Inc.
PHONE NUMBER: 800-231-2755
MANUFACTURE DATES: September 1989 - April 1992
PROBLEM AREA: Harness
ACTION: Repair kit
RESULT:

MODEL(S): 4450
MANUFACTURE DATES: March 1987 - December 1990
SEAT DESCRIPTION: 5000 STE Child Safety Seat
MANUFACTURED BY: Century Products, Inc.
PROBLEM: The buckle release force may exceed 16 pounds when not used in appropriate forward latch position for a child weighing 30 pounds or more.
SOLUTION: Change instructions and seat labeling to indicate that the rear latch position is not to be used with children weighing 30 pounds or more.
NOTES: None.

MODEL(S): 4450 GD
MANUFACTURE DATES: December 1988 - November 1989
SEAT DESCRIPTION: 5000 STE
MANUFACTURED BY: Century Products, Inc.
PROBLEM: Possible buckle release problem.
SOLUTION: Contact Century for new harness assembly and instructions.
NOTES: None.

MODEL(S): 4450 GD
MANUFACTURE DATES: May 1990 - June 1990
SEAT DESCRIPTION: 5000 STE Infant Car Seat
MANUFACTURED BY: Century Products, Inc.
PROBLEM: Latch tongues broke during impact testing.
SOLUTION: Century will replace latch tongue or return seat for refund of purchase price.
NOTES: None.

MODEL(S): 4460
MANUFACTURER: Century Products, Inc.
PHONE NUMBER: 800-231-2755
MANUFACTURE DATES: September 1989 - April 1992
PROBLEM AREA: Harness
ACTION: Repair kit
RESULT:

MODEL(S): 4460
MANUFACTURER: Century Products, Inc.
PHONE NUMBER: 800-837-4044
MANUFACTURE DATES: March 1987 - December 1990
PROBLEM AREA: Buckle
ACTION: Contact manufacturer
RESULT:

MODEL(S): 4460
MANUFACTURER: Century Products, Inc.
PHONE NUMBER: 800-837-4044
MANUFACTURE DATES: December 1990 - October 1991
PROBLEM AREA: Label
ACTION: Replace label
RESULT:

MODEL(S): 4460
MANUFACTURE DATES: March 1987 - December 1990
SEAT DESCRIPTION: 5000 STE Child Safety Seat
MANUFACTURED BY: Century Products, Inc.
PROBLEM: The buckle release force may exceed 16 pounds when not used in appropriate forward latch position for a child weighing 30 pounds or more.
SOLUTION: Change instructions and seat labeling to indicate that the rear latch position is not to be used with children weighing 30 pounds or more.
NOTES: None.

MODEL(S): 4460 FE
MANUFACTURE DATES: December 1988 - November 1989
SEAT DESCRIPTION: 5000 STE
MANUFACTURED BY: Century Products, Inc.
PROBLEM: Possible buckle release problem.
SOLUTION: Contact Century for new harness assembly and instructions.
NOTES: None.

MODEL(S): 4460 DT
MANUFACTURE DATES: May 1990 - June 1990
SEAT DESCRIPTION: 5000 STE Infant Car Seat
MANUFACTURED BY: Century Products, Inc.
PROBLEM: Latch tongues broke during impact testing.
SOLUTION: Century will replace latch tongue or return seat for refund or purchase price.
NOTES: None.

MODEL(S): 4460 FE
MANUFACTURE DATES: May 1990 - June 1990
SEAT DESCRIPTION: 5000 STE Infant Car Seat
MANUFACTURED BY: Century Products, Inc.
PROBLEM: Latch tongues broke during impact testing.
SOLUTION: Century will replace latch tongue or return seat for refund of purchase price.
NOTES: None.

MODEL(S): 4470
MANUFACTURE DATES: March 1987 - December 1990
SEAT DESCRIPTION: 5000 STE Child Safety Seat
MANUFACTURED BY: Century Products, Inc.
PROBLEM: The buckle release force may exceed 16 pounds when not used in appropriate forward latch position for a child weighing 30 pounds or more.
SOLUTION: Change instructions and seat labeling to indicate that the rear latch position is not to be used with children weighing 30 pounds or more.
NOTES: None.

MODEL(S): 4470 MC
MANUFACTURE DATES: May 1990 - June 1990
SEAT DESCRIPTION: 5000 STE Infant Car Seat
MANUFACTURED BY: Century Products, Inc.
PROBLEM: Latch tongues broke during testing.
SOLUTION: Century will replace latch tongue or return seat for refund of purchase price.
NOTES: None.

MODEL(S): 4475
MANUFACTURE DATES: March 1987 - December 1990
SEAT DESCRIPTION: 5000 STE Child Safety Seat
MANUFACTURED BY: Century Products, Inc.
PROBLEM: The buckle release force may exceed 16 pounds when not used in appropriate forward latch position for a child weighing 30 pounds or more.
SOLUTION: Change instructions and seat labeling to indicate that the rear latch position is not to be used with children weighing 30 pounds or more.
NOTES: None.

MODEL(S): 4475 GA
MANUFACTURE DATES: December 1988 - November 1989
SEAT DESCRIPTION: 5000 STE
MANUFACTURED BY: Century Products, Inc.
PROBLEM: Possible buckle release problem.
SOLUTION: Contact Century for new harness assembly and instructions.
NOTES: None.

MODEL(S): 4475 GU
MANUFACTURE DATES: May 1990 - June 1990
SEAT DESCRIPTION: 5000 STE Infant Car Seat
MANUFACTURED BY: Century Products, Inc.
PROBLEM: Latch tongues broke during impact testing.
SOLUTION: Century will replace latch tongue or return seat for refund of purchase price.
NOTES: None.

MODEL(S): 4476
MANUFACTURER: Century Products, Inc.
PHONE NUMBER: 800-231-2755
MANUFACTURE DATES: September 1989 - April 1992
PROBLEM AREA: Harness
ACTION: Repair kit
RESULT:

MODEL(S): 4476
MANUFACTURER: Century Products, Inc.
PHONE NUMBER: 800-837-4044
MANUFACTURE DATES: December 1990 - October 1991
PROBLEM AREA: Label
ACTION: Replace label
RESULT:

MODEL(S): 4480
MANUFACTURER: Century Products, Inc.
PHONE NUMBER: 800-231-2755
MANUFACTURE DATES: September 1989 - April 1992
PROBLEM AREA: Harness
ACTION: Repair kit
RESULT:

MODEL(S): 4480
MANUFACTURER: Century Products, Inc.
PHONE NUMBER: 800-837-4044
MANUFACTURE DATES: December 1990 - October 1991
PROBLEM AREA: Label
ACTION: Replace label
RESULT:

MODEL(S): 4490
MANUFACTURER: Century Products, Inc.
PHONE NUMBER: 800-231-2755
MANUFACTURE DATES: September 1989 - April 1992
PROBLEM AREA: Harness
ACTION: Repair kit
RESULT:

MODEL(S): 4490
MANUFACTURER: Century Products, Inc.
PHONE NUMBER: 800-837-4044
MANUFACTURE DATES: December 1990 - October 1991
PROBLEM AREA: Label
ACTION: Replace label
RESULT:

MODEL(S): 4580
MANUFACTURE DATES: July 1986 - December 1989
SEAT DESCRIPTION: Century 580 Infant Seat/Carrier
MANUFACTURED BY: Century Products, Inc.
PROBLEM: Instructions for threading shoulder straps through the metal retention slides may be unclear. Misthreaded shoulder straps will not restrain child.
SOLUTION: Call the 800 number for "rethreading" label. Rethread shoulder straps according to new instructions.
NOTES: None.

MODEL(S): 4581
MANUFACTURE DATES: July 1986 - December 1989
SEAT DESCRIPTION: Century 580 Infant Seat/Carrier
MANUFACTURED BY: Century Products, Inc.
PROBLEM: Instructions for threading shoulder straps through the metal retention slides may be unclear. Misthreaded shoulder straps will not restrain child.
SOLUTION: Call the 800 number for "rethreading" label. Rethread shoulder straps according to new instructions.
NOTES: None.

MODEL(S): 4581
MANUFACTURE DATES: November 1986 - October 1989
SEAT DESCRIPTION: 580, Infant Car Seat
MANUFACTURED BY: Century Products, Inc.
PROBLEM: Retaining screws on handle may loosen and allow handle to separate from seat.
SOLUTION: Contact Century.
NOTES: None.

MODEL(S): 4583
MANUFACTURE DATES: July 1986 - December 1989
SEAT DESCRIPTION:
MANUFACTURED BY:
PROBLEM: Instructions for threading shoulder straps through the metal retention slides may be unclear. Misthreaded shoulder straps will not restrain child.
SOLUTION: Call the 800 number for "rethreading" label. Rethread shoulder straps according to new instructions.
NOTES: None.

MODEL(S): 4585
MANUFACTURER: Century Products, Inc.
PHONE NUMBER: 800-837-4044
MANUFACTURE DATES: July 1986 - December 1989
PROBLEM AREA: Harness
ACTION: Contact manufacturer
RESULT:

MODEL(S): 4585
MANUFACTURE DATES: February 1988 - October 1989
SEAT DESCRIPTION: 580, Infant Car Seat
MANUFACTURED BY: Century Products, Inc.
PROBLEM: Retaining screws on handle may loosen and allow handle to separate from seat.
SOLUTION: Contact Century.
NOTES: None.

MODEL(S): 4600
MANUFACTURE DATES: March 1984 - November 1984
SEAT DESCRIPTION: Child Love Seat, Lot #4477C4.
MANUFACTURED BY: T.R.W.
PROBLEM: Plastic shell may crack exposing sharp edges, and shoulder harness may loosen.
SOLUTION: Refund, exchange program expired. No action can be taken.
NOTES: None.

MODEL(S): Safe-T-Rider
MANUFACTURE DATES: May 1980 - August 1980
SEAT DESCRIPTION: Safe-T-Rider
MANUFACTURED BY: Century Products, Inc.
PROBLEM: Auxiliary harness defect.
SOLUTION: Obtain replacement auxiliary harness from manufacturer.
NOTES: Child safety seats manufactured before 1-1-81 are not required to meet the applicable FMVSS 213.

MODEL(S): 3867649
MANUFACTURE DATES: Child Love Seat, Lot #4477C4
MANUFACTURED BY: T.R.W.
PROBLEM: Plastic shell may crack exposing sharp edges, and shoulder harness may loosen.
SOLUTION: Refund, exchange program expired. No action can currently be taken.
NOTES: Manufacturer no longer in safety seat business. No forwarding information available.

MODEL(S): All
MANUFACTURE DATES: December 1984 - April 1985
SEAT DESCRIPTION: Safe and Sound II
MANUFACTURED BY: Collier
PROBLEM: Buckle failure.
SOLUTION: Contact manufacturer for assistance.
NOTES: Manufacturer no longer in child safety seat business.

MODEL(S): 02-081A
MANUFACTURE DATES: October 1980 - June 1983
SEAT DESCRIPTION: Safe-T-Shield
MANUFACTURED BY: Cosco, Inc.
PROBLEM: Metal pin in shield may jam, trapping child.
SOLUTION: Contact Cosco for replacement seat.
NOTES: In Indiana call (812) 372-0141. Child safety seats manufactured before 1-1-81 are not required to meet the applicable FMVSS 213.

MODEL(S): 02-081B
MANUFACTURE DATES: October 1980 - June 1983
SEAT DESCRIPTION: Safe-T-Shield
MANUFACTURED BY: Cosco, Inc.
PROBLEM: Metal pin in shield may jam, trapping child.
SOLUTION: Contact Cosco for replacement seat.
NOTES: In Indiana call (812) 372-0141. Child safety seats manufactured before 1-1-81 are not required to meet the applicable FMVSS 213.

MODEL(S): 02-090
MANUFACTURE DATES: October 1989 - June 1990
SEAT DESCRIPTION: Cosco Soft Shield Safety Seat
MANUFACTURED BY: Cosco, Inc.
PROBLEM: Tests reveal that the child occupant's head could exceed 32 inches of excursion from the childseat in a sudden stop or accident.
SOLUTION: Repair the seat with a harness retainer to maintain child with safe area.
NOTES: None.

MODEL(S): 02-181A
MANUFACTURE DATES: October 1980 - June 1983
SEAT DESCRIPTION: Safe-T-Shield
MANUFACTURED BY: Cosco, Inc.
PROBLEM: Metal pin in shield may jam, trapping child.
SOLUTION: Contact Cosco for replacement seat.
NOTES: In Indiana call (812) 372-0141. Child safety seats manufactured before 1-1-81 are not required to meet the applicable FMVSS 213.

MODEL(S): 02-086
MANUFACTURER: Cosco, Inc.
PHONE NUMBER: 800-544-1108
MANUFACTURE DATES: October 1987 - February 1988
PROBLEM AREA: Pad
ACTION: Replace pad
RESULT:

MODEL(S): 02-190
MANUFACTURE DATES: October 1989 - June 1990
SEAT DESCRIPTION: Cosco Soft Shield Child Safety Seat
MANUFACTURED BY: Cosco, Inc.
PROBLEM: Tests reveal that the child occupant's head could exceed 32 inches of excursion from the childseat in a sudden stop or accident.
SOLUTION: Repair the seat with a harness retainer to maintain child with safe area.
NOTES: None.

MODEL(S): 02-290
MANUFACTURE DATES: October 1989 - June 1990
SEAT DESCRIPTION: Cosco Auto Trac Child Safety Seat
MANUFACTURED BY: October 1989 - June 1990
PROBLEM: Tests reveal that the child occupant's head could exceed 32 inches of excursion from the childseat in a sudden stop or accident.
SOLUTION: Repair the seat with a harness retainer to maintain child with safe area.
NOTES: None.

MODEL(S): 02-790
MANUFACTURE DATES: October 1989 - June 1990
SEAT DESCRIPTION: Cosco Auto Trac Child Safety Seat
MANUFACTURED BY: Cosco, Inc.
PROBLEM: Tests reveal that the child occupant's head could exceed 32 inches of excursion from the childseat in a sudden stop or accident.
SOLUTION: Repair the seat with a harness retainer to maintain child with safe area.
NOTES: None.

MODEL(S): 02-890
MANUFACTURE DATES: October 1989 - June 1990
SEAT DESCRIPTION: Cosco Auto Trac Child Safety Seat
MANUFACTURED BY: Cosco, Inc.
PROBLEM: Tests reveal that the child occupant's head could exceed 32 inches of excursion from the childseat in a sudden stop or accident.
SOLUTION: Repair the seat with a harness retainer to maintain child with safe area.
NOTES: None.

MODEL(S): 13-168
MANUFACTURE DATES: April 1971 - October 1971
SEAT DESCRIPTION: 13-168
MANUFACTURED BY: Cosco, Inc.
PROBLEM: Vehicle seats with soft foam may allow restrained child to move in forward crashes.
SOLUTION: Return program expired. No action can be taken.
NOTES: In Indiana call (812) 372-0141. Child safety seats manufactured before 1-1-81 are not required to meet the applicable FMVSS 213.

MODEL(S): 13-169
MANUFACTURE DATES: April 1971 - October 1971
SEAT DESCRIPTION: 13-169
MANUFACTURED BY: Cosco, Inc.
PROBLEM: Vehicle seats with soft foam may allow restrained child to move in forward crashes.
SOLUTION: Return program expired. No action can be taken.
NOTES: In Indiana call (812) 372-0141. Child safety seats manufactured before 1-1-81 are not required to meet the applicable FMVSS 213.

MODEL(S): 313
MANUFACTURE DATES: January 1984 - June 1985
SEAT DESCRIPTION: Safe and Easy
MANUFACTURED BY: Cosco, Inc.
PROBLEM: Plastic shell can crack.
SOLUTION: Obtain brace assembly modification kit from Cosco.
NOTES: In Indiana call (812) 372-0141.

MODEL(S): 323
MANUFACTURE DATES: January 1984 - June 1985
SEAT DESCRIPTION: Safe and Snug
MANUFACTURED BY: Cosco, Inc.
PROBLEM: Plastic shell can crack.
SOLUTION: Obtain brace assembly modification kit from Cosco.
NOTES: In Indiana call (812) 372-0141.

MODEL(S): 423
MANUFACTURE DATES: January 1984 - June 1985
SEAT DESCRIPTION: Safe and Snug
MANUFACTURED BY: Cosco, Inc.
PROBLEM: Plastic shell can crack.
SOLUTION: Obtain brace assembly modification kit from Cosco.
NOTES: In Indiana call (812) 372-0141.

MODEL(S): 201
MANUFACTURE DATES: April 1985 - December 1985
SEAT DESCRIPTION: Dyn-O-Mite/Evenflo with black buckle housing and red push button release.
MANUFACTURED BY: Evenflo
PROBLEM: False latching, could come open and eject the child in an accident or sudden stop, substantially reducing the protection provided to the child.
SOLUTION: Install replacement buckle assembly available from manufacturer.
NOTES: None.

MODEL(S): 201
MANUFACTURE DATES: January 1986 - April 1990
SEAT DESCRIPTION: Dyn-O-Mite/Evenflo with black buckle housing and red push button release.
MANUFACTURED BY: Evenflo
PROBLEM: False latching, could come open and eject the child in an accident or sudden stop, substantially reducing the protection provided to the child.
SOLUTION: Install replacement buckle assembly available from manufacturer.
NOTES: None.

MODEL(S): 202
MANUFACTURE DATES: April 1985 - December 1985
SEAT DESCRIPTION: Evenflo
PROBLEM: False latching, could come open and eject the child in an accident or sudden stop, substantially reducing the protection provided to the child.
SOLUTION: Install replacement buckle assembly available from manufacturer.
NOTES: None.

MODEL(S): 202
MANUFACTURE DATES: January 1986 - April 1990
SEAT DESCRIPTION: False latching, could come open and eject the child in an accident or sudden stop, substantially reducing the protection provided to the child.
SOLUTION: Install replacement buckle available from manufacturer.
NOTES: None.

MODEL(S): 221
MANUFACTURE DATES: April 1985 - December 1985
SEAT DESCRIPTION: One Step with black buckle housing and red push button release.
MANUFACTURED BY: Evenflo
PROBLEM: False latching, could come open and eject the child in an accident or sudden stop, substantially reducing the protection provided to the child.
SOLUTION: Install replacement buckle assembly available from manufacturer.
NOTES: None.

MODEL(S): 221
MANUFACTURE DATES: January 1986 - April 1990
SEAT DESCRIPTION: False latching, could come open and eject the child in an accident or sudden stop, substantially reducing the protection provided to the child.
SOLUTION: Install replacement buckle assembly available from manufacturer.
NOTES: None.

MODEL(S): 222
MANUFACTURE DATES: April 1985 - December 1985
SEAT DESCRIPTION: False latching, could come open and eject the child in an accident or sudden stop, substantially reducing the protection provided to the child.
SOLUTION: Install replacement buckle assembly available from manufacturer.
NOTES: None.

MODEL(S): 222
MANUFACTURE DATES: January 1986 - April 1990
SEAT DESCRIPTION: False latching, could come open and eject the child in an accident or sudden stop, substantially reducing the protection provided to the child.
SOLUTION: Install replacement buckle assembly available from manufacturer.
NOTES: None.

MODEL(S): 223
MANUFACTURE DATES: April 1985 - December 1985
SEAT DESCRIPTION: False latching, could come open and eject the child in an accident or sudden stop, substantially reducing the protection provided to the child.
SOLUTION: Install replacement buckle assembly available from manufacturer.
NOTES: None.

MODEL(S): 223
MANUFACTURE DATES: January 1986 - April 1990
SEAT DESCRIPTION: False latching, could come open and eject the child in an accident or sudden stop, substantially reducing the protection provided to the child.
SOLUTION: Install replacement buckle assembly available from manufacturer.
NOTES: None.

MODEL(S): 227
MANUFACTURE DATES: January 1990 - June 1990
SEAT DESCRIPTION: Ultara II; Evenflo Child Safety Seat
MANUFACTURED BY: Evenflo
PROBLEM: Seat failed the head and knee excursion test of FMVSS 213. In case of a sudden stop or accident, the child would be subject to greater risk of injury.
SOLUTION: Replace the Utlara II shell with the Evenflo champion shell provided by Evenflo. Keep and use the Ultara II T-shield with the champion shell.
NOTES: The Evenflo champion shell has been tested, and has passed the FMVSS standards.

MODEL(S): 228
MANUFACTURE DATES: April 1985 - December 1985
SEAT DESCRIPTION: Seven Year Car Seat with black buckle housing and red push button release.3
MANUFACTURED BY: Evenflo
PROBLEM: False latching, could come open and eject the child in an accident or sudden stop, substantially reducing the protection provided to the child.
SOLUTION: Install replacement buckle assembly available from manufacturer.
NOTES: None.

MODEL(S): 228
MANUFACTURE DATES: January 1986 - April 1990
SEAT DESCRIPTION: Seven Year Car Seat with black buckle housing and red push button release.
MANUFACTURED BY: Evenflo
PROBLEM: False latching, could come open and eject the child in an accident or sudden stop, substantially reducing the protection provided to the child.
SOLUTION: Install replacement buckle assembly available from manufacturer.
NOTES: None.

MODEL(S): 242
MANUFACTURE DATES: January 1986 - April 1990
SEAT DESCRIPTION: Evenflo booster with black buckle housing and red push button release.
MANUFACTURED BY: Evenflo
PROBLEM: False latching, could come open and eject the child in an accident or sudden stop, substantially reducing the protection provided to the child.
SOLUTION: Install replacement buckle assembly available from manufacturer.
NOTES: None.

MODEL(S): 242
MANUFACTURE DATES: January 1986 - April 1990
SEAT DESCRIPTION: Evenflo booster with black buckle housing and red push button release.
MANUFACTURED BY: Evenflo
PROBLEM: False latching, could come open and eject the child in an accident or sudden stop, substantially reducing the protection provided to the child.
SOLUTION: Install replacement buckle available from manufacturer.
NOTES: None.

MODEL(S): 401
MANUFACTURE DATES: April 1985 - December 1985
SEAT DESCRIPTION: One Step with black buckle housing and red push button release.
MANUFACTURED BY: Evenflo
PROBLEM: False latching, could come open and eject the child in an accident or sudden stop, substantially reducing the protection provided to the child.
SOLUTION: Install replacement buckle available from manufacturer.
NOTES: None.

MODEL(S): 401
MANUFACTURE DATES: January 1986 - April 1990
SEAT DESCRIPTION: One Step with black buckle housing and red push button release.
MANUFACTURED BY: Evenflo
PROBLEM: False latching, could come open and eject the child in an accident or sudden stop, substantially reducing the protection provided to the child.
SOLUTION: Install replacement buckle available from manufacturer.
NOTES: None.

MODEL(S): 402
MANUFACTURE DATES: April 1985 - December 1985
SEAT DESCRIPTION: One Step with black buckle housing and red push button release.
MANUFACTURED BY: Evenflo
PROBLEM: False latching, could come open and eject the child in an accident or sudden stop, substantially reducing the protection provided to the child.
SOLUTION: Install replacement buckle assembly available from manufacturer.
NOTES: None.

MODEL(S): 402
MANUFACTURE DATES: January 1986 - April 1990
SEAT DESCRIPTION: One Step with black buckle housing and red push button release.
MANUFACTURED BY: Evenflo
PROBLEM: False latching, could come open and eject the child in an accident or sudden stop, substantially reducing the protection provided to the child.
SOLUTION: Install replacement buckle available from manufacturer.
NOTES: None.

MODEL(S): 403
MANUFACTURE DATES: April 1985 - December 1985
SEAT DESCRIPTION: One Step with black buckle housing and red push button release.
MANUFACTURED BY: Evenflo
PROBLEM: False latching, could come open and eject the child in an accident or sudden stop, substantially reducing the protection provided to the child.
SOLUTION: Install replacement buckle assembly available from manufacturer.
NOTES: None.

MODEL(S): 403
MANUFACTURE DATES: January 1986 - April 1990
SEAT DESCRIPTION: One Step with black buckle housing and red push button release.
MANUFACTURED BY: Evenflo
PROBLEM: False latching, could come open and eject the child in an accident or sudden stop, substantially reducing the protection provided to the child.
SOLUTION: Install replacement buckle available from manufacturer.
NOTES: None.

MODEL(S): 404
MANUFACTURE DATES: April 1985 - December 1985
SEAT DESCRIPTION: One Step with black buckle housing and red button release.
MANUFACTURED BY: Evenflo
PROBLEM: False latching, could come open and eject the child in an accident or sudden stop, substantially reducing the protection provided to the child.
SOLUTION: Install replacement buckle assembly available from manufacturer.
NOTES: None.

MODEL(S): 404
MANUFACTURE DATES: January 1986 - April 1990
SEAT DESCRIPTION: One Step with black buckle housing and red button release.
MANUFACTURED BY: Evenflo
PROBLEM: False latching, could come open and eject the child in an accident or sudden stop, substantially reducing the protection provided to the child.
SOLUTION: Install replacement buckle available from manufacturer.
NOTES: None.

MODEL(S): 405
MANUFACTURE DATES: April 1985 - December 1985
SEAT DESCRIPTION: One Step with black buckle housing and red button release.
MANUFACTURED BY: Evenflo
PROBLEM: False latching, could come open and eject the child in an accident or sudden stop, substantially reducing the protection provided to the child.
SOLUTION: Install replacement buckle assembly available from manufacturer.
NOTES: None.

MODEL(S): 405
MANUFACTURE DATES: January 1986 - April 1990
SEAT DESCRIPTION: One Step with black buckle housing and red button release.
MANUFACTURED BY: Evenflo
PROBLEM: False latching, could come open and eject the child in an accident or sudden stop, substantially reducing the protection provided to the child.
SOLUTION: Install replacement buckle available from manufacturer.
NOTES: None.

MODEL(S): 406
MANUFACTURE DATES: April 1985 - December 1985
SEAT DESCRIPTION: One Step with black buckle housing and red button release.
MANUFACTURED BY: Evenflo
PROBLEM: False latching, could come open and eject the child in an accident or sudden stop, substantially reducing the protection provided to the child.
SOLUTION: Install replacement buckle assembly available from manufacturer.
NOTES: None.

MODEL(S): 406
MANUFACTURE DATES: January 1986 - April 1990
SEAT DESCRIPTION: One Step with black buckle housing and red button release.
MANUFACTURED BY: Evenflo
PROBLEM: False latching, could come open and eject the child in an accident or sudden stop, substantially reducing the protection provided to the child.
SOLUTION: Install replacement buckle available from manufacturer.
NOTES: None.

MODEL(S): 407
MANUFACTURE DATES: April 1985 - December 1985
SEAT DESCRIPTION: One Step with black buckle housing and red button release.
MANUFACTURED BY: Evenflo
PROBLEM: False latching, could come open and eject the child in an accident or sudden stop, substantially reducing the protection provided to the child.
SOLUTION: Install replacement buckle assembly available from manufacturer.
NOTES: None.

MODEL(S): 407
MANUFACTURE DATES: January 1986 - April 1990
SEAT DESCRIPTION: One Step with black buckle housing and red button release.
MANUFACTURED BY: Evenflo
PROBLEM: False latching, could come open and eject the child in an accident or sudden stop, substantially reducing the protection provided to the child.
SOLUTION: Install replacement buckle available from manufacturer.
NOTES: None.

MODEL(S): 408
MANUFACTURE DATES: April 1985 - December 1985
SEAT DESCRIPTION: One Step with black buckle housing and red button release.
MANUFACTURED BY: Evenflo
PROBLEM: False latching, could come open and eject the child in an accident or sudden stop, substantially reducing the protection provided to the child.
SOLUTION: Install replacement buckle assembly available from manufacturer.
NOTES: None.

MODEL(S): 408
MANUFACTURE DATES: January 1986 - April 1990
SEAT DESCRIPTION: One Step with black buckle housing and red button release.
MANUFACTURED BY: Evenflo
PROBLEM: False latching, could come open and eject the child in an accident or sudden stop, substantially reducing the protection provided to the child.
SOLUTION: Install replacement buckle available from manufacturer.
NOTES: None.

MODEL(S): 409
MANUFACTURE DATES: April 1985 - December 1985
SEAT DESCRIPTION: One Step with black buckle housing and red button release.
MANUFACTURED BY: Evenflo
PROBLEM: False latching, could come open and eject the child in an accident or sudden stop, substantially reducing the protection provided to the child.
SOLUTION: Install replacement buckle assembly available from manufacturer.
NOTES: None.

MODEL(S): 409
MANUFACTURE DATES: January 1986 - April 1990
SEAT DESCRIPTION: One Step with black buckle housing and red button release.
MANUFACTURED BY: Evenflo
PROBLEM: False latching, could come open and eject the child in an accident or sudden stop, substantially reducing the protection provided to the child.
SOLUTION: Install replacement buckle available from manufacturer.
NOTES: None.

MODEL(S): 410
MANUFACTURE DATES: June 1988 - April 1989
SEAT DESCRIPTION: 410
MANUFACTURED BY: Evenflo
PROBLEM: Slide adjusters on harness may slip.
SOLUTION: Obtain replacement harness from Evenflo.
NOTES: In Ohio call (800) 233-5920.

MODEL(S): 411
MANUFACTURE DATES: April 1985 - December 1985
SEAT DESCRIPTION: Bobby-Mack with black buckle housing and red push button release.
MANUFACTURED BY: Evenflo
PROBLEM: False latching, could come open and eject the child in an accident or sudden stop, substantially reducing the protection provided to the child.*
SOLUTION: Install replacement buckle available from manufacturer.
NOTES: None.

MODEL(S): 411
MANUFACTURE DATES: January 1986 - April 1990
SEAT DESCRIPTION: Bobby-Mack with black buckle housing and red push button release.
MANUFACTURED BY: Evenflo
PROBLEM: False latching, could come open and eject the child in an accident or sudden stop, substantially reducing the protection provided to the child.
SOLUTION: Install replacement buckle available from manufacturer.
NOTES: None.

MODEL(S): 412
MANUFACTURE DATES: April 1985 - December 1985
SEAT DESCRIPTION: Bobby-Mack with black buckle housing and red push button release.
MANUFACTURED BY: Evenflo
PROBLEM: False latching, could come open and eject the child in an accident or sudden stop, substantially reducing the protection provided to the child.
SOLUTION: Install replacement buckle available from manufacturer.
NOTES: None.

MODEL(S): 412
MANUFACTURE DATES: January 1986 - April 1990
SEAT DESCRIPTION: Bobby-Mack with black buckle housing and red push button release.
MANUFACTURED BY: Evenflo
PROBLEM: False latching, could come open and eject the child in an accident or sudden stop, substantially reducing the protection provided to the child.
SOLUTION: Install replacement buckle assembly available from manufacturer.
NOTES: None.

MODEL(S): 414
MANUFACTURE DATES: April 1985 - December 1985
SEAT DESCRIPTION: Bobby-Mack with black buckle housing and red push button release.
MANUFACTURED BY: Evenflo
PROBLEM: False latching, could come open and eject the child in an accident or sudden stop, substantially reducing the protection provided to the child.
SOLUTION: Install replacement buckle assembly available from manufacturer.
NOTES: None.

MODEL(S): 414
MANUFACTURE DATES: January 1986 - April 1990
SEAT DESCRIPTION: Bobby-Mack with black buckle housing and red push button release.
MANUFACTURED BY: Evenflo
PROBLEM: False latching, could come open and eject the child in an accident or sudden stop, substantially reducing the protection provided to the child.
SOLUTION: Install replacement buckle available from manufacturer.
NOTES: None.

MODEL(S): 415
MANUFACTURE DATES: April 1985 - December 1985
SEAT DESCRIPTION: Bobby-Mack with black buckle housing and red push button release.
MANUFACTURED BY: Evenflo
PROBLEM: False latching, could come open and eject the child in an accident or sudden stop, substantially reducing the protection provided to the child.
SOLUTION: Install replacement buckle assembly available from manufacturer.
NOTES: None.

MODEL(S): 415
MANUFACTURE DATES: January 1986 - April 1990
SEAT DESCRIPTION: Bobby-Mack with black buckle housing and red push button release.
MANUFACTURED BY: Evenflo
PROBLEM: False latching, could come open and eject the child in an accident or sudden stop, substantially reducing the protection provided to the child.
SOLUTION: Install replacement buckle available from manufacturer.
NOTES: None.

MODEL(S): 416
MANUFACTURE DATES: April 1985 - December 1985
SEAT DESCRIPTION: Bobby-Mack with black buckle housing and red push button release.
MANUFACTURED BY: Evenflo
PROBLEM: False latching, could come open and eject the child in an accident or sudden stop, substantially reducing the protection provided to the child.
SOLUTION: Install replacement buckle assembly available from manufacturer.
NOTES: None.

MODEL(S): 416
MANUFACTURE DATES: January 1986 - April 1990
SEAT DESCRIPTION: Bobby-Mack with black buckle housing and red push button release.
MANUFACTURED BY: Evenflo
PROBLEM: False latching, could come open and eject the child in an accident or sudden stop, substantially reducing the protection provided to the child.
SOLUTION: Install replacement buckle available from manufacturer.
NOTES: None.

MODEL(S): 417
MANUFACTURE DATES: April 1985 - December 1985
SEAT DESCRIPTION: One Step deluxe with black buckle housing and red push button release.
MANUFACTURED BY: Evenflo
PROBLEM: False latching, could come open and eject the child in an accident or sudden stop, substantially reducing the protection provided to the child.
SOLUTION: Install replacement buckle available from manufacturer.
NOTES: None.

MODEL(S): 417
MANUFACTURE DATES: January 1986 - April 1990
SEAT DESCRIPTION: One Step deluxe with black buckle housing and red push button release.
MANUFACTURED BY: Evenflo
PROBLEM: False latching, could come open and eject the child in an accident or sudden stop, substantially reducing the protection provided to the child.
SOLUTION: Install replacement buckle available from manufacturer.
NOTES: None.

MODEL(S): 420
MANUFACTURE DATES: September 1988 - July 1989
SEAT DESCRIPTION: Ultara I
MANUFACTURED BY: Evenflo
PROBLEM: Buckle release may be difficult.
SOLUTION: Obtain new harness from Evenflo.
NOTES: In Ohio call (800) 233-5920.

MODEL(S): 441
MANUFACTURE DATES: April 1985 - December 1985
SEAT DESCRIPTION: Dyn-O-Mite/Evenflo with black buckle housing and red push button release.
MANUFACTURED BY: Evenflo
PROBLEM: False latching, could come open and eject the child in an accident or sudden stop, substantially reducing the protection provided to the child.
SOLUTION: Install replacement buckle available from manufacturer.
NOTES: None.

MODEL(S): 441
MANUFACTURE DATES: January 1986 - April 1990
SEAT DESCRIPTION: Dyn-O-Mite/Evenflo with black buckle housing and red push button release.
MANUFACTURED BY: Evenflo
PROBLEM: False latching, could come open and eject the child in an accident or sudden stop, substantially reducing the protection provided to the child.
SOLUTION: Install replacement buckle available from manufacturer.
NOTES: None.

MODEL(S): 441-6
MANUFACTURE DATES: January 1985 - January 1989
SEAT DESCRIPTION: Dyn-O-Mite
MANUFACTURED BY: Evenflo
PROBLEM: Extreme reclined (4th position) of both models failed maximum back support angle requirements.
SOLUTION: Don't use in extreme reclined position except with shoulder belt around back; obtain warning label from Evenflo.
NOTES: In Ohio call (800) 233-5920.

MODEL(S): 442
MANUFACTURE DATES: April 1985 - December 1985
SEAT DESCRIPTION: Dyn-O-Mite/Evenflo with black buckle housing and red push button release.
MANUFACTURED BY: Evenflo
PROBLEM: False latching, could come open and eject the child in an accident or sudden stop, substantially reducing the protection provided to the child.
SOLUTION: Install replacement buckle assembly available from manufacturer.
NOTES: None.

MODEL(S): 442
MANUFACTURE DATES: January 1986 - April 1990
SEAT DESCRIPTION: Dyn-O-Mite/Evenflo with black buckle housing and red push button release.
MANUFACTURED BY: Evenflo
PROBLEM: False latching, could come open and eject the child in an accident or sudden stop, substantially reducing the protection provided to the child.
SOLUTION: Install replacement buckle available from manufacturer.
NOTES: None.

MODEL(S): 443
MANUFACTURE DATES: April 1985 - December 1985
SEAT DESCRIPTION: Dyn-O-Mite/Evenflo with black buckle housing and red push button release.
MANUFACTURED BY: Evenflo
PROBLEM: False latching, could come open and eject the child in an accident or sudden stop, substantially reducing the protection provided to the child.
SOLUTION: Install replacement buckle available from manufacturer.
NOTES: None.

MODEL(S): 443
MANUFACTURE DATES: January 1986 - April 1990
SEAT DESCRIPTION: Dyn-O-Mite/Evenflo with black buckle housing and red push button release.
MANUFACTURED BY: Evenflo
PROBLEM: False latching, could come open and eject the child in an accident or sudden stop, substantially reducing the protection provided to the child.
SOLUTION: Install replacement buckle available from manufacturer.
NOTES: None.

MODEL(S): 444
MANUFACTURE DATES: April 1985 - December 1985
SEAT DESCRIPTION: Dyn-O-Mite/Evenflo with black buckle housing and red push button release.
MANUFACTURED BY: Evenflo
PROBLEM: False latching, could come open and eject the child in an accident or sudden stop, substantially reducing the protection provided to the child.
SOLUTION: Install replacement buckle available from manufacturer.
NOTES: None.

MODEL(S): 444
MANUFACTURE DATES: January 1986 - April 1990
SEAT DESCRIPTION: Dyn-O-Mite/Evenflo with black buckle housing and red push button release.
MANUFACTURED BY: Evenflo
PROBLEM: False latching, could come open and eject the child in an accident or sudden stop, substantially reducing the protection provided to the child.
SOLUTION: Install replacement buckle available from manufacturer.
NOTES: None.

MODEL(S): 445
MANUFACTURE DATES: April 1985 - December 1985
SEAT DESCRIPTION: Dyn-O-Mite/Evenflo with black buckle housing and red push button release.
MANUFACTURED BY: Evenflo
PROBLEM: False latching, could come open and eject the child in an accident or sudden stop, substantially reducing the protection provided to the child.
SOLUTION: Install replacement buckle available from manufacturer.
NOTES: None.

MODEL(S): 445
MANUFACTURE DATES: January 1986 - April 1990
SEAT DESCRIPTION: Dyn-O-Mite/Evenflo with black buckle housing and red push button release.
MANUFACTURED BY: Evenflo
PROBLEM: False latching, could come open and eject the child in an accident or sudden stop, substantially reducing the protection provided to the child.
SOLUTION: Install replacement buckle available from manufacturer.
NOTES: None.

MODEL(S): 446
MANUFACTURE DATES: April 1985 - December 1985
SEAT DESCRIPTION: Dyn-O-Mite/Evenflo with black buckle housing and red push button release.
MANUFACTURED BY: Evenflo
PROBLEM: False latching, could come open and eject the child in an accident or sudden stop, substantially reducing the protection provided to the child.
SOLUTION: Install replacement buckle assembly available from manufacturer.
NOTES: None.

MODEL(S): 446
MANUFACTURE DATES: January 1986 - April 1990
SEAT DESCRIPTION: Dyn-O-Mite/Evenflo with black buckle housing and red push button release.
MANUFACTURED BY: Evenflo
PROBLEM: False latching, could come open and eject the child in an accident or sudden stop, substantially reducing the protection provided to the child.
SOLUTION: Install replacement buckle assembly available from manufacturer.
NOTES: None.

MODEL(S): 448
MANUFACTURE DATES: April 1985 - December 1985
SEAT DESCRIPTION: Dyn-O-Mite/Evenflo with black buckle housing and red push button release.
MANUFACTURED BY: Evenflo
PROBLEM: False latching, could come open and eject the child in an accident or sudden stop, substantially reducing the protection provided to the child.
SOLUTION: Install replacement buckle assembly available from manufacturer.
NOTES: None.

MODEL(S): 448
MANUFACTURE DATES: January 1986 - April 1990
SEAT DESCRIPTION: Dyn-O-Mite/Evenflo with black buckle housing and red push button release.
MANUFACTURED BY: Evenflo
PROBLEM: False latching, could come open and eject the child in an accident or sudden stop, substantially reducing the protection provided to the child.
SOLUTION: Install replacement buckle available from manufacturer.
NOTES: None.

MODEL(S): 448
MANUFACTURE DATES: January 1985 - January 1989
SEAT DESCRIPTION: Infant Car Seat
MANUFACTURED BY: Evenflo
PROBLEM: Extreme reclined (4th position) of both models failed maximum back support angle requirements.
SOLUTION: Don't use in extreme reclined position except with shoulder belt around back; obtain warning label from Evenflo.
NOTES: In Ohio call (800) 233-5920.

MODEL(S): 453
MANUFACTURE DATES: February 1987 - August 1988
SEAT DESCRIPTION: Seven Year Car Seat
MANUFACTURED BY: Evenflo
PROBLEM: The black plastic push pins used to attach fabric or vinyl to the seat structure can be removed by a child; loose pins could pose a choking hazard.
SOLUTION: Replacement push pins of a new design and appropriate instructions will be sent to seat owners to replace the defective push pins.
NOTES: None.

MODEL(S): 453
MANUFACTURE DATES: April 1985 - December 1985
SEAT DESCRIPTION: Seven Year Car Seat with black buckle housing and red push button release.
MANUFACTURED BY: Evenflo
PROBLEM: False latching, could come open and eject the child in an accident or sudden stop, substantially reducing the protection provided to the child.
SOLUTION: Install replacement buckle assembly available from manufacturer.
NOTES: None.

MODEL(S): 453
MANUFACTURE DATES: January 1986 - April 1990
SEAT DESCRIPTION: Seven Year Car Seat with black buckle housing and red push button release.
MANUFACTURED BY: Evenflo
PROBLEM: False latching, could come open and eject the child in an accident or sudden stop, substantially reducing the protection provided to the child.
SOLUTION: Install replacement buckle assembly available from manufacturer.
NOTES: None.

MODEL(S): 454
MANUFACTURE DATES: February 1987 - August 1988
SEAT DESCRIPTION: Seven Year Car Seat
MANUFACTURED BY: Evenflo
PROBLEM: The black plastic push pins used to attach fabric or vinyl to the seat structure can be removed by a child; loose pins could pose a choking hazard.
SOLUTION: Replacement push pins of a new design and appropriate instructions will be sent to seat owners to replace the defective push pins.
NOTES: None.

MODEL(S): 454
MANUFACTURE DATES: April 1985 - December 1985
SEAT DESCRIPTION: Seven Year Car Seat with black buckle housing and red push button release.
MANUFACTURED BY: Evenflo
PROBLEM: False latching, could come open and eject the child in an accident or sudden stop, substantially reducing the protection provided to the child.
SOLUTION: Install replacement buckle assembly available from the manufacturer.
NOTES: None.

MODEL(S): 454
MANUFACTURE DATES: January 1986 - April 1990
SEAT DESCRIPTION: Seven Year Car Seat with black buckle housing and red push button release.
MANUFACTURED BY: Evenflo
PROBLEM: False latching, could come open and eject the child in an accident or sudden stop, substantially reducing the protection provided to the child.
SOLUTION: Install replacement buckle assembly available from the manufacturer.
NOTES: None.

MODEL(S): 456
MANUFACTURE DATES: April 1985 - December 1985
SEAT DESCRIPTION: Dyn-O-Mite/Evenflo with black buckle housing and red push button release.
MANUFACTURED BY: Evenflo
PROBLEM: False latching, could come open and eject the child in an accident or sudden stop, substantially reducing the protection provided to the child.
SOLUTION: Install replacement buckle available from manufacturer.
NOTES: None.

MODEL(S): 456
MANUFACTURE DATES: January 1986 - April 1990
SEAT DESCRIPTION: Dyn-O-Mite/Evenflo with black buckle housing and red push button release.
MANUFACTURED BY: Evenflo
PROBLEM: False latching, could come open and eject the child in an accident or sudden stop, substantially reducing the protection provided to the child.
SOLUTION: Install replacement buckle available from manufacturer.
NOTES: None.

MODEL(S): 456
MANUFACTURE DATES: January 1985 - January 1989
SEAT DESCRIPTION: Infant Car Seat
MANUFACTURED BY: Evenflo
PROBLEM: Extreme reclined (4th position) of both models failed maximum back support angle requirements.
SOLUTION: Don't use in extreme reclined position except with shoulder belt around back; obtain warning label from Evenflo.
NOTES: In Ohio call (800) 233-5920.

MODEL(S): 458
MANUFACTURE DATES: April 1985 - December 1985
SEAT DESCRIPTION: Dyn-O-Mite/Evenflo with black buckle housing and red push button release.
MANUFACTURED BY: Evenflo
PROBLEM: False latching, could come open and eject the child in an accident or sudden stop, substantially reducing the protection provided to the child.
SOLUTION: Install replacement buckle assembly available from manufacturer.
NOTES: None.

MODEL(S): 458
MANUFACTURE DATES: January 1986 - April 1990
SEAT DESCRIPTION: Dyn-O-Mite/Evenflo with black buckle housing and red push button release.
MANUFACTURED BY: Evenflo
PROBLEM: False latching, could come open and eject the child in an accident or sudden stop, substantially reducing the protection provided to the child.
SOLUTION: Install replacement buckle assembly available from manufacturer.
NOTES: None.

MODEL(S): 458
MANUFACTURE DATES: January 1985 - January 1989
SEAT DESCRIPTION: Infant Car Seat
MANUFACTURED BY: Evenflo
PROBLEM: Extreme reclined (4th position) of both models failed maximum back support angle requirements.
SOLUTION: Don't use in extreme reclined position except with shoulder belt around back; obtain warning label from Evenflo.
NOTES: In Ohio call (800) 233-5920.

MODEL(S): 470
MANUFACTURE DATES: February 1987 - August 1988
SEAT DESCRIPTION: Booster Seat
MANUFACTURED BY: Evenflo
PROBLEM: The black plastic push pins used to attach fabric or vinyl to the seat structure can be removed by a child; loose pins could pose a choking hazard.
SOLUTION: Replacement push pins of a new design and appropriate instructions will be sent to seat owners to replace the defective push pins.
NOTES: None.

MODEL(S): 470
MANUFACTURE DATES: April 1985 - December 1985
SEAT DESCRIPTION: Evenflo Booster with black buckle housing and red push button release.
MANUFACTURED BY: Evenflo
PROBLEM: False latching, could come open and eject the child in an accident or sudden stop, substantially reducing the protection provided to the child.
SOLUTION: Install replacement buckle available from manufacturer.
NOTES: None.

MODEL(S): 470
MANUFACTURE DATES: January 1986 - April 1990
SEAT DESCRIPTION: Evenflo Booster with black buckle housing and red push button release.
MANUFACTURED BY: Evenflo
PROBLEM: False latching, could come open and eject the child in an accident or sudden stop, substantially reducing the protection provided to the child.
SOLUTION: Install replacement buckle available from manufacturer.
NOTES: None.

MODEL(S): 471
MANUFACTURE DATES: February 1987 - August 1988
SEAT DESCRIPTION: Booster Seat
MANUFACTURED BY: Evenflo
PROBLEM: The black plastic push pins used to attach fabric or vinyl to the seat structure can be removed by a child; loose pins could pose a choking hazard.
SOLUTION: Replacement push pins of a new design and appropriate instructions will be sent to seat owners to replace the defective push pins.
NOTES: None.

MODEL(S): 471
MANUFACTURE DATES: April 1985 - December 1985
SEAT DESCRIPTION: Evenflo Booster with black buckle housing and red push button release.
MANUFACTURED BY: Evenflo
PROBLEM: False latching, could come open and eject the child in an accident or sudden stop, substantially reducing the protection provided to the child.
SOLUTION: Install replacement buckle assembly available from manufacturer.
NOTES: None.

MODEL(S): 471
MANUFACTURE DATES: January 1986 - April 1990
SEAT DESCRIPTION: Evenflo Booster with black buckle housing and red push button release.
MANUFACTURED BY: Evenflo
PROBLEM: False latching, could come open and eject the child in an accident or sudden stop, substantially reducing the protection provided to the child.
SOLUTION: Install replacement buckle available from manufacturer.
NOTES: None.

MODEL(S): GT 1000
MANUFACTURE DATES: August 1988 - October 1988
SEAT DESCRIPTION: Renolux
MANUFACTURED BY: FBS, Inc.
PROBLEM: Belt buckle release failed minimum requirements - could release easier than expected.
SOLUTION: Contact manufacturer for replacement harness.
NOTES: None.

MODEL(S): GT 2000
MANUFACTURE DATES: August 1988 - October 1988
SEAT DESCRIPTION: Renolux
MANUFACTURED BY: FBS, Inc.
PROBLEM: Belt buckle release failed minimum requirements - could release easier than expected.
SOLUTION: Contact manufacturer for replacement harness.
NOTES: None.

MODEL(S): GT 5000
MANUFACTURE DATES: February 1990 - April 1991
SEAT DESCRIPTION: Turn-A-Tot Childseat with striped seat covers.
MANUFACTURED BY: FBS, Inc.
PROBLEM: The striped seat covers of the childseat failed to meet the flammability requirements of FMVSS 213. This could increase the risk of injury in case of fire.
SOLUTION: Replace the seat cover with a new, less flammable seat cover supplied by the manufacturer.
NOTES: None.

MODEL(S): GT 5000
MANUFACTURE DATES: February 1990 - April 1991
SEAT DESCRIPTION: Turn-A-Tot Childseat.
MANUFACTURED BY: FBS, Inc.
PROBLEM: The childseat failed to meet the head excursion requirements of FMVSS 213 during sudden stop testing.
SOLUTION: Replace the faulty base section of the childseat with a new base and a repair kit from the manufacturer.
NOTES: None.

MODEL(S): 9100
MANUFACTURE DATES: July 1986 - October 1990
SEAT DESCRIPTION: 9100
MANUFACTURED BY: Fisher-Price, Inc.
PROBLEM: Button on shield strap can become loose and be removed by a child. Children could put pieces of button in their mouths and choke.
SOLUTION: Remove the button and install replacement that will be sent by manufacturer to involved seat owners who call the toll free telephone number 1-800-527-1034.
NOTES: None.

MODEL(S): 9100
MANUFACTURE DATES: May 1987 - January 1989
SEAT DESCRIPTION: 9100
MANUFACTURED BY: Fisher-Price, Inc.
PROBLEM: Plastic part inside the buckle breaks making it difficult to fasten; if buckle is not fastened the child would not be restrained.
SOLUTION: Install new shield that will be sent by fisher Price to involved seat owners calling the toll free number 1-800-527-1034
NOTES: None.

MODEL(S): 9100
MANUFACTURE DATES: Apr. 1985 - Aug. 1985
SEAT DESCRIPTION: 9100
MANUFACTURED BY: Fisher Price, Inc.
PROBLEM: Stress on shield could lead to breakage and separation of the shield from the buckle and thus not properly restrain the child in a sudden stop or accident.
SOLUTION: Install new shield that will be sent by Fisher Price to involved seat owners who call toll free number 1-800-527-1034.
NOTES: None.

MODEL(S): 9100
MANUFACTURE DATES: 1900 Sop - Jul. 1989
SEAT DESCRIPTION: 9100
MANUFACTURED BY: Fisher Price, Inc.
PROBLEM: Label can be removed or peeled off and child may place in mouth.
SOLUTION: If label is loose, peel it off and discard
NOTES: None.

MODEL(S): 9100
MANUFACTURE DATES: Apr. 1985 - Jan. 1989
SEAT DESCRIPTION: 9100
MANUFACTURED BY: Fisher Price, Inc.
PROBLEM: Pad fails flammability
SOLUTION: Obtain free replacement pad from manufacturer
NOTES: None.

MODEL(S): 9100
MANUFACTURE DATES: Apr. 1985 - Jul. 1986
SEAT DESCRIPTION: 9100
MANUFACTURED BY: Fisher Price, Inc.
PROBLEM: Difficult to remove child if shoulder belt retracts too far.
SOLUTION: Obtain button which limits shoulder belt retraction from manufacturer.
NOTES: None.

MODEL(S): 9101
MANUFACTURE DATES: Jul. 1986 - Oct. 1990
SEAT DESCRIPTION: 9101
MANUFACTURED BY: Fisher Price, Inc.
PROBLEM: Button on shield strap can become loose and be removed by a child. Children could put pieces of button in their mouths and choke.
SOLUTION: Remove the button and install replacement that will be sent by manufacturer to involved seat owners who call the toll free telephone number 1-800-527-1034.
NOTES: None.

MODEL(S): 9101
MANUFACTURE DATES: May 1987 - Jan. 1989
SEAT DESCRIPTION: 9101
MANUFACTURED BY: Fisher Price, Inc.
PROBLEM: Plastic part inside the buckle breaks making it difficult to fasten, if buckle is not fastened the child would not be restrained.
SOLUTION: Install new shield that will be sent by Fisher Price to involved seat owners calling the toll free number 1-800-527-1034.
NOTES: None.

MODEL(S): 9101
MANUFACTURE DATES: 1900 Sop - Jul. 1989
SEAT DESCRIPTION: 9101
MANUFACTURED BY: Fisher Price Inc.
PROBLEM: Label can be removed or peeled off and child may place in mouth.
SOLUTION: If label is loose, peel it off and discard
NOTES: None.

MODEL(S): 9101
MANUFACTURE DATES: Feb. 1990 - Mar. 1990
SEAT DESCRIPTION: 9101
MANUFACTURED BY: Fisher Price Inc.
PROBLEM: Harness assembly metal tongue may break
SOLUTION: Have seat available and contact manufacturer for free modification kit.
NOTES: None.

MODEL(S): 9101
MANUFACTURE DATES: Apr. 1985 - Jan. 1989
SEAT DESCRIPTION: 9101
MANUFACTURED BY: Fisher Price Inc.
PROBLEM: Pad fails flammability
SOLUTION: Obtain free replacement pad from manufacturer
NOTES: None.

MODEL(S): 9104
MANUFACTURER: Fisher-Price, Inc.
PHONE NUMBER: 800-432-5437
MANUFACTURE DATES: June 1992 - September 1992
PROBLEM AREA: Buckle
ACTION: Refund
RESULT:

MODEL(S): 9149
MANUFACTURE DATES: Jan. 1991 - Feb. 1991
SEAT DESCRIPTION: Infant car seats with blue canopies for very young infants.
MANUFACTURED BY: Fisher Price Inc.
PROBLEM: The breast shield could separate from the tongue of the restraint assembly in crash conditions because of a faulty buckle frame.
SOLUTION: Replace the breast shield assembly.
NOTES: Fisher Price is recalling these child seats sold in the United States and Canada.

MODEL(S): Five filer Bros
MANUFACTURE DATES: Apr. 1971 - Feb. 1972
SEAT DESCRIPTION: Five Filer Bros.
MANUFACTURED BY: Five Filer Bros.
PROBLEM: Harness webbing failed crash strength testing.
SOLUTION: Program expired. No action can currently be taken.
NOTES: Manufacturer no longer in child safety seat business. Child safety seats manufactured before 1-1-81 are not required to meet the applicable FMVSS 213.

MODEL(S): 786
MANUFACTURE DATES: NA
SEAT DESCRIPTION: 786
MANUFACTURED BY: Frank F. Taylor
PROBLEM: Vehicle seats of soft material may allow restrained child to strike interior.
SOLUTION: Replacement program expired. No action can currently be taken.
NOTES: Manufacturer no longer in child safety seat business. Child safety seats manufactured before 1-1-81 are not required to meet the applicable FMVSS 213.

MODEL(S): 787
MANUFACTURE DATES: NA
SEAT DESCRIPTION: 787
MANUFACTURED BY: Frank F. Taylor
PROBLEM: Vehicle seats of soft material may allow restrained child to strike interior.
SOLUTION: Replacement program expired. No action can currently be taken.
NOTES: Manufacturer no longer in child safety seat business. Child safety seats manufactured before 1-1-81 are not required to meet the applicable FMVSS 213.

MODEL(S): Gerry Guardian
MANUFACTURER: Gerry Guardian
PHONE NUMBER: 800-845-8813
MANUFACTURE DATES: January 1990 - May 1990
PROBLEM AREA: Buckle
ACTION: Repair kit
RESULT:

MODEL(S): GT 1000
MANUFACTURE DATES: Jan. 1985 - Jan. 1986
SEAT DESCRIPTION: GT 1000
MANUFACTURED BY: Graco
PROBLEM: Recline adjustment lever may not latch in infant position.
SOLUTION: Obtain corrective action from Graco
NOTES: Manufacturer no longer in child safety seat business.

MODEL(S): 9100
MANUFACTURER: International
PHONE NUMBER: N/A
MANUFACTURE DATES: December 1980 - August 1981
PROBLEM AREA: Harness
ACTION: Replace harness
RESULT:

MODEL(S): 131-100
MANUFACTURER: Kolcraft Enterprises, Inc.
PHONE NUMBER: 800-453-7673
MANUFACTURE DATES: SOP* 1900 - August 1989
PROBLEM AREA: Pad
ACTION: Replace clips
RESULT:

MODEL(S): 131-101
MANUFACTURER: Kolcraft Enterprises, Inc.
PHONE NUMBER: 800-453-7673
MANUFACTURE DATES: SOP* 1900 - August 1989
PROBLEM AREA: Pad
ACTION: Replace clips
RESULT:

MODEL(S): 140-155
MANUFACTURER: Kolcraft Enterprises, Inc.
PHONE NUMBER: 800-453-7673
MANUFACTURE DATES: SOP* 1900 - August 1989
PROBLEM AREA: Pad
ACTION: Replace clips
RESULT:

*SOP = Start of Production

MODEL(S): 180-150
MANUFACTURER: Kolcraft Enterprises, Inc.
PHONE NUMBER: 800-453-7673
MANUFACTURE DATES: March 1989 - October 1990
PROBLEM AREA: Pad
ACTION: Replace clips
RESULT:

MODEL(S): 180-150
MANUFACTURER: Kolcraft Enterprises, Inc.
PHONE NUMBER: 800-453-7673
MANUFACTURE DATES: March 1989 - October 1990
PROBLEM AREA: Test failure
ACTION: Repair kit
RESULT:

MODEL(S): 180 - 200
MANUFACTURE DATES: SOP* 1900 - Aug. 1990
SEAT DESCRIPTION: Dial-a-Fit
MANUFACTURED BY: Kolcraft Enterprises Inc.
PROBLEM: Upholstery clip fasteners may break, loosen and a child may place in mouth.
SOLUTION: Inspect seat clips for looseness, breakage discard old clips and contact Kolcraft for replacement clips.
NOTES: All seats manufactured prior to August, 1989

MODEL(S): 180 - 200
MANUFACTURE DATES: Oct. 1988 - Aug. 1989
SEAT DESCRIPTION: Dial-a-fit
MANUFACTURED BY: Kolcraft Enterprises, Inc.
PROBLEM: Head movement exceeded standard limits during crash tests.
SOLUTION: Contact Kolcraft for replacement abdominal shield and harness straps.
NOTES: None.

*SOP = Start of Production

MODEL(S): 180 - 300
MANUFACTURE DATES: SOP* 1900 - Aug. 1989
SEAT DESCRIPTION: Dial-a-Fit
MANUFACTURED BY: Kolcraft Enterprises Inc.
PROBLEM: Upholstery clip fasteners may break, loosen and a child may place in mouth.
SOLUTION: Inspect seat clips for looseness, breakage discard old clips and contact Kolcraft for replacement clips.
NOTES: All seats manufactured prior to August, 1989

MODEL(S): 180 - 300
MANUFACTURE DATES: Apr. 1988 - Jun. 1989
SEAT DESCRIPTION: Dial-a-Fit
MANUFACTURED BY: Kolcraft Enterprises, Inc.
PROBLEM: Head movement exceeded standard limits during crash tests.
SOLUTION: Contact Kolcraft for replacement abdominal shield and harness straps.
NOTES: None.

MODEL(S): 180 - 400
MANUFACTURE DATES: Dec. 1989 - Aug. 1990
SEAT DESCRIPTION: Playskool child safety seat
MANUFACTURED BY: Kolcraft Enterprises, Inc.
PROBLEM: The foam seat cushion burns at a rate faster than permitted by Federal Standard. Seat occupants would face an increased risk of injury in the event of a fire.
SOLUTION: Replace the foam seat cushion with a new seat cushion provided by Kolcraft.
NOTES: None.

MODEL(S): 180 - 600
MANUFACTURE DATES: Nov. 1990 - Aug. 1991
SEAT DESCRIPTION: Dial-a-Fitt II Child safety seats
MANUFACTURED BY: Kolcraft Enterprises, Inc.
PROBLEM: The seats did not comply with the structural integrity standards of FMVSS 213. Stresses from dynamic impact testing cracked the seat shell.
SOLUTION: Replace the seat shell with a newly manufactured shell of an equivalent Kolcraft child safety seat.
NOTES: None.

*SOP = Start of Production

MODEL(S): 13123
MANUFACTURER: Kolcraft Enterprises, Inc.
PHONE NUMBER: 800-453-7673
MANUFACTURE DATES: February 1985 - June 1985
PROBLEM AREA: Shell
ACTION: Contact manufacturer
RESULT:

MODEL(S): 19127
MANUFACTURE DATES: Jan. 1985 - Mar. 1987
SEAT DESCRIPTION: Flip-n-go
MANUFACTURED BY: Kolcraft Enterprises, Inc.
PROBLEM: Defect in shape of shield
SOLUTION: Obtain free kit from Kolcraft
NOTES: None.

MODEL(S): 19130
MANUFACTURE DATES: Jan. 1985 - Mar. 1987
SEAT DESCRIPTION: Flip-n-go
MANUFACTURED BY: Kolcraft Enterprises, Inc.
PROBLEM: Defect in shape of shield
SOLUTION: Obtain free kit from Kolcraft
NOTES: None.

MODEL(S): Traveler 700
MANUFACTURE DATES: Jan. 1991 - Aug. 1991
SEAT DESCRIPTION: Traveler 700 Child safety seat
MANUFACTURED BY: Kolcraft Enterprises, Inc.
PROBLEM: The armrests crack at the points the seats are attached to the plastic seat shell because of excessive tension between the armrest spring and the shell
SOLUTION: Replace the seat shell with a new seat shell that eliminates the spring and strengthens the plastic of the armrest.
NOTES: None.

MODEL(S): ALL
MANUFACTURE DATES: Jan. 1987 - Jul. 1989
SEAT DESCRIPTION: Lin Lih, all models
MANUFACTURED BY: MCP Enterprises, Inc.
PROBLEM: May offer no crash protection
SOLUTION: Contact manufacturer for refund.
NOTES: Manufacturer no longer in child safety seat business.

MODEL(S): 875 - 879
MANUFACTURE DATES: Apr. 1971 - Nov. 1971
SEAT DESCRIPTION: Guardian
MANUFACTURED BY: Pride Trimble
PROBLEM: Fails forward movement restriction
SOLUTION: Seat replacement program expired. No action can currently be taken.
NOTES: No longer in safety seat business - no forwarding information available. Safety seats manufactured before 1-1-81 are not required to meet applicable FMVSS 213.

MODEL(S): ALL
MANUFACTURE DATES: May 1969 - Mar. 1973
SEAT DESCRIPTION: Kantwet
MANUFACTURED BY: Pride Trimble
PROBLEM: Fails forward movement restriction
SOLUTION: Seat replacement program expired. No action can currently be taken.
NOTES: No longer in safety seat business, no forwarding information available. Safety seats manufactured before 1-1-81 are not required to meet applicable FMVSS 213.

MODEL(S): 71
MANUFACTURE DATES: 1900 Sop - Aug. 1973
SEAT DESCRIPTION: Chairs manufactured through August 1973
MANUFACTURED BY: Rex-stroll-o-stroll-chair
PROBLEM: Seat adapter may fail and cause ejection or contact with vehicle interior.
SOLUTION: Dealer provided new adapter frame. No action can currently be taken.
NOTES: No longer in child safety seat business. No forwarding information available. Child safety seats manufactured before 1-1-81 not required to meet FMVSS 213.

MODEL(S): 599
MANUFACTURE DATES: Dec. 1980 - May 1981
SEAT DESCRIPTION: Wee Care
MANUFACTURED BY: Strolee
PROBLEM: Plastic upholstery clips may loosen and be swallowed
SOLUTION: Out of business as of May 1989. No action can be taken.
NOTES: No longer in safety seat business. No forwarding information available. Child safety seats manufactured before 1-1-81 are not required to meet FMVSS 213.

MODEL(S): 605
MANUFACTURE DATES: Apr. 1985 - Apr. 1985
SEAT DESCRIPTION: Booster seat
MANUFACTURED BY: Strolee
PROBLEM: Shield may crack during an accident and allow contact with interior areas.
SOLUTION: Out of business as of May, 1989. No action can be taken.
NOTES: Manufacturer no longer in safety seat business - no forwarding information available.

MODEL(S): 326
MANUFACTURE DATES: March 1984 - Nov. 1984RCHILD LOVE SEAT
MANUFACTURED BY: T.R.W.
PROBLEM: Plastic shell may crack exposing sharp edges, and the harness may loosen.
SOLUTION: Refund/Exchange program expired. No action can be taken.
NOTES: Manufacturer no longer in child safety seat business.

MODEL(S): 8982200-147
MANUFACTURE DATES: Mar. 1984 - Nov. 1984
SEAT DESCRIPTION: Child Love Seat
MANUFACTURED BY: T.R.W.
PROBLEM: Plastic shell may crack exposing sharp edges, and shoulder harness may loosen.
SOLUTION: Refund/Exchange program expired. No action can currently be taken.
NOTES: Manufacturer no longer in safety seat business.

MODEL(S): ALL
MANUFACTURE DATES: Mar. 1984 - Nov. 1984
SEAT DESCRIPTION: Child Love Seat
MANUFACTURED BY: TRW Auto Products
PROBLEM: Plastic shell may crack exposing sharp edges, and shoulder harness may loosen.
SOLUTION: Refund, replacement program expired. No action can currently be taken.
NOTES: Manufacturer no longer in safety seat business. No forwarding information available.

MODEL(S): 832
MANUFACTURE DATES: Jan. 1988 - Apr. 1989
SEAT DESCRIPTION: Pride Trimble
MANUFACTURED BY: Virco
PROBLEM: Seat failed head excursion test when optional shield only used.
SOLUTION: Consumer can remove optional shield and use only harness straps, or return car seat for replacement.
NOTES: Request telephone extension 280 or 351.

MODEL(S): 890
MANUFACTURE DATES: Feb. 1986 - Oct. 1987
SEAT DESCRIPTION: Pride Trimble Booster seat
MANUFACTURED BY: Virco
PROBLEM: Failed head excursion tests.
SOLUTION: Contact manufacturer for seat replacement.
NOTES: None.

MODEL(S): 891
MANUFACTURE DATES: Feb. 1986 - Oct. 1987
SEAT DESCRIPTION: Pride Trimble Booster Seat
MANUFACTURED BY: Virco
PROBLEM: Failed head excursion tests
SOLUTION: Contact manufacturer for seat replacement
NOTES: None.

MODEL(S): 892
MANUFACTURE DATES: Feb. 1986 - Oct. 1987
SEAT DESCRIPTION: Click-n-Go Booster seat
MANUFACTURED BY: Virco
PROBLEM: Failed head excursion tests
SOLUTION: Contact manufacturer for seat replacement
NOTES: None.

MODEL(S): 1394332
MANUFACTURE DATES: 1900 Sop - Dec. 1988
SEAT DESCRIPTION: All manufactured through December 1988.
MANUFACTURED BY: Volvo
PROBLEM: Buckle to easily opened and may allow release of child.
SOLUTION: Contact Volvo for refund of purchase price.
NOTES: Manufacturer no longer in child safety seat business.

MODEL(S): ALL
MANUFACTURE DATES: Jan. 1987 - Jul. 1989
SEAT DESCRIPTION: Lin Lih, All models
MANUFACTURED BY: World Toy Discount
PROBLEM: May offer no crash protection
SOLUTION: Contact World Toys for refund.
NOTES: None.

Chapter 7

Taking on the Child Restraint Case

Initial Interview

The purpose of the initial interview is to determine what the facts of the case are and whether or not a cause of action exists. Some seasoned attorneys claim that they can judge the merit and value of a case from the first meeting with a client. However, most attorneys will have to conduct some investigation into their client's claim before such a determination can be made.

Very rarely will a child restraint defect case land on an attorney's desk in a pre-packaged format. Many attorneys can not recognize the child restraint case even when all the medical and physical evidence points in that direction.

The typical child restraint case comes about after a careful investigation into the facts of a motor vehicle accident. The interview is the time to get the facts, down to the last detail. Tell clients what you want them to do to assist in the litigation, and who from the office will contact them.

Dictate a case capsule, in their presence, detailing essential facts, then summarize the entire discussion with a caveat for them to correct erroneous statements or impressions that you make. That way, the attention of your clients is drawn to their involvement in the case. This further guarantees accuracy of the initial facts gleaned from the meeting.

Our office practice has always been to conduct the first interview and offer the initial consultation with any prospective personal injury client free of charge, no matter how much time is spent at this initial meeting. An advocate who does less can hardly be called a trial lawyer. In accident cases every one who seeks an interview with a lawyer should be heard at no initial cost. That is the strength and burden of our profession.

Psychologists tell us that first impressions are the most lasting. Similarly, what we hear first, we tend to believe, and remember the clearest. Keeping this in mind, and remembering that clients come to see you because they or a loved one have sustained a serious injury or death, take your time and empathize with their situation. Be straight-forward, and as informative as circumstances allow.

This is the time when the injured clients, usually novices to the legal system, are introduced to their champion, the individual who will pursue what they perceive to be a just claim, defend them from the opposition, and most importantly, secure an adequate award to compensate them for their damages.

It is important to make your clients feel at ease, comfortable, and confident that their best interests are of paramount concern to you—as well they should be. The interviewer should remember to request information in detail, and explain issues in simple terms so the clients understand what can/will be done for them. Likewise, clients should understand what they can do to assist in the understanding and preparation of the case. Remember that you have had legal training, and your clients have not; otherwise, they wouldn't need you.

Use terms the client will understand, but never talk down to the client. You must make it easy for the client to confide in you and recount his or her accident/injury honestly and accurately. Treat the client as you would like to be treated. Listen carefully; ask questions.

This is also the time to determine whether the damages appear sufficient to justify further investigation, or pursuing the lawsuit. It is wiser to advise clients of the problems early on, than to try to convince them the case has little merit when a settlement offer is made some time later. Sometimes, we must take egregious conduct cases for small amounts to insure a continued fight against gross misconduct.

Above all, reinforce your clients' basic belief that something happened for which they are blameless. Most parents of child restraint accident victims blame themselves. Had we not believed that a 14 year-old was innocent of his little brother's death, that the machine suddenly shot into the path of the automobile that hit them, Pawlak would never have won. Honda would have walked free, while we would have pursued the innocent automobile driver, into whose path the Honda had flown, resulting in a great tragedy. The same analogy applies to child restraint cases or any product liability case for that matter.

Intake Form

CLIENT INTAKE SHEET

TODAY'S DATE ______________
S/L ______________

NAME: ______________ AGE: ______________
DATE OF BIRTH: ______________ DRIVERS LICENSE #: ______________
SEX: [ ] Male [ ] Female SOCIAL SECURITY #: ______________
MARITAL STATUS: [ ] Single [ ] Married [ ] Divorced [ ] Widowed
ADDRESS: ______________
HOME PHONE #: ______________ WORK PHONE #: ______________
SPOUSE'S NAME: ______________ SPOUSE'S AGE: ______________
DATE OF BIRTH: ______________ SOCIAL SECURITY #: ______________
DATE OF MARRIAGE: ______________ PLACE OF MARRIAGE: ______________

CHILDREN: AGES:

____
____
____
____
____
____

BROTHERS/SISTERS: AGES:

____
____
____
____

DEFENDANT(S): (PERSON(S) RESPONSIBLE)

(Name)	(Name)	(Name)
(Address)	(Address)	(Address)
(City) (State) (Zip)	(City) (State) (Zip)	(City) (State) (Zip)
(Phone)	(Phone)	(Phone)

(1)

ACCIDENT/INJURY INFORMATION

WHAT IS THE PRIMARY REASON FOR YOUR VISIT? ______________
HOW DID THIS PROBLEM FIRST BEGIN? ______________
DATE OF ACCIDENT/INJURY: ___ STATUTE OF LIMITATIONS: ______
LOCATION: ______________
POLICE REPORT NO: ______________
HOW DID THE ACCIDENT/INJURY OCCUR? ______________
WHO WAS INVOLVED OR PRESENT? ______________

____
DID THIS HAPPEN AT WORK? ______________
DID YOU GO TO A HOSPITAL? [ ] yes [ ] no WHEN: ______________
NAME OF HOSPITAL: ______________
HOW DID YOU GET TO HOSPITAL: ______________
NAME OF AMBULANCE SERVICE: ______________
HAVE YOU HAD SIMILAR PROBLEMS: [ ] yes [ ] no WHEN: ________
IF "YES", PLEASE EXPLAIN: ______________
IS THIS THE FIRST ACCIDENT YOU HAVE HAD? ______________
DESCRIBE THE ROAD CONDITIONS: ______________
WHAT TIME OF DAY WAS IT? ______________
WHAT WERE THE TRAFFIC CONDITIONS? ______________
DESCRIBE THE WEATHER: ______________
BRIEF DESCRIPTION OF THE INCIDENT: ______________

____
____
____

WHICH POLICE DEPARTMENT WAS CALLED? ______________

HAVE YOU EVER RECEIVED?

	When?
[ ] Worker's Compensation	______________
[ ] No-Fault Auto Wage Replacement	______________
[ ] Long Term Disability	______________
[ ] Short Term Disability	______________
[ ] Social Security Disability	______________
[ ] Other	______________

(2)

EMPLOYMENT INFORMATION

EMPLOYER: ____________ CITY: ____________________________
JOB TITLE: ______________ CONTACT PERSON: ______________
WAGE: _________________ LENGTH OF EMPLOYMENT: _________
SUPERVISOR'S NAME: _________________ PHONE_____________
ATTENDANCE RECORD: [ ] Excellent [ ] Good [ ] Poor [ ] Fai
ARE YOU CURRENTLY WORKING? [ ] yes [ ] no
YOU ARE WORKING: [ ] full time [ ] part time
IF "NO", IS YOUR REGULAR JOB AVAILABLE ONCE YOU ARE RE-LEASED?
[ ] yes [ ] no [ ] don't know
WHEN DID YOU LAST WORK? ______________________________
WERE YOU WORKING FULL DUTY AT THE TIME? [ ] yes [ ] no
YOUR REGULAR JOB IS: [ ] full time [ ] part time
ABILITY TO WORK REGULAR EMPLOYMENT PRESENTLY: _________
WAS TIME LOST FROM WORK BECAUSE OF INJURY: ___________
DATES AND AMOUNT OF TIME LOST:
Date: ___________________ Employer: _______________ Time Lost:
Date: ___________________ Employer: _______________ Time Lost:
Date: ___________________ Employer: _______________ Time Lost:
HAS A PHYSICIAN PLACED ANY RESTRICTIONS ON YOUR WORK?
[ ] yes [ ] no
IF "YES" PLEASE EXPLAIN: _______________________________
PLEASE LIST ALL CURRENT SOURCES AND AMOUNTS OF INCOME:
____
____
____

FELLOW WORKERS YOU KNOW WELL AND HAVE WORKED CLOSELY WITH:

Name	Address	Phone

PREVIOUS JOBS	DATES	REASON FOR LEAVING	JOB DUTY

PLEASE LIST ALL INSURANCE COVERAGE (HEALTH, HOSPITALIZATION, ACCIDENT, LIFE, ETC.):

Company Amount and Type of Coverage

____

____

____

____

____

____

HAS APPLICATION FOR SOCIAL SECURITY BENEFITS BEEN MADE?
DATE OF APPLICATION FOR SOCIAL SECURITY BENEFITS: ________
AMOUNT OF SOCIAL SECURITY BENEFITS RECEIVED: ___________
HAS APPLICATION FOR WORKMEN'S COMPENSATION BEEN FILED?
DATE OF WORKMEN'S COMPENSATION CLAIM: _______________
AMOUNT OF WORKMEN'S COMPENSATION BENEFITS BEING RECEIVED: ______________
DO YOU HAVE ANY PHOTOS OR WRITTEN STATEMENTS REGARDING THE ACCIDENT?

____

DESCRIBE: ____________________________________

MILITARY INFORMATION

PRIOR MILITARY SERVICE: ______________ DATES: ____________
SERVICE #: ______________ HOW LONG: _________________
BRANCH OF SERVICE AND JOB: ______________________________
ANY VETERAN OR SERVICE CONNECTED DISABILITY: ___________

EDUCATIONAL BACKGROUND

PLEASE CIRCLE THE LAST GRADE COMPLETED:
Less than: 8 9 10 11 12 13 14 15 16+
PLEASE CHECK YOUR PROGRAM: [ ] High School Diploma [ ] Associates
[ ] BA/BS [ ] MA/MS [ ] Doctorate
SPECIALIZED TRAINING IN: _____________________________

(4)

PRIOR INJURIES OR CLAIMS

PRIOR INJURIES OR CLAIMS (INCLUDING COURT, WORKMEN'S COMPENSATION—ALL TYPES INCLUDING SPORTS, ACCIDENTS, CHILDHOOD, ETC.—GIVE NATURE, DATE, DOCTORS, ETC.):

I. Type of Injury: ______________________
Where Injured: ______________________
Treated By: ______________________
Date of Accident: ______________________
Damages Awarded: ______________________
Attorney Who Handled: ______________________

II. Type of Injury: ______________________
Where Injured: ______________________
Treated By: ______________________
Date of Accident: ______________________
Damages Awarded: ______________________
Attorney Who Handled: ______________________

LIST ALL CAR ACCIDENTS YOU HAVE BEEN INVOLVED IN:

Location	Approximate Date	Were you injured

MEDICAL INFORMATION

PLEASE LIST ALL HOSPITALIZATIONS SINCE CHILDHOOD FOR WHATEVER REASON:

Date	Institution	Physician	Purpose

(5)

PLEASE LIST ALL PHYSICIANS SEEN SINCE CHILDHOOD FOR WHATEVER REASON:

Date	Name	Address	Purpose

DESCRIPTION OF PHYSICAL AILMENT: ______________________

____

____

RECITE A GENERAL STATEMENT OF HOW YOU FEEL TODAY: _____

____

____

LIST THINGS USED TO DO BUT NO LONGER CAN DO, OR COULD DO BEFORE ACCIDENT/DIAGNOSIS:

____

____

____

ANY SPECIAL EQUIPMENT (CRUTCHES, BRACES, WHEELCHAIR, ETC.) USED TO ASSIST YOU GETTING AROUND?

____

____

____

OVERALL, DO YOU FEEL YOUR SYMPTOMS ARE:

[ ] getting better [ ] getting worse [ ] not changing

PLEASE LIST <u>ALL</u> MEDICATIONS YOU ARE CURRENTLY TAKING (PRESCRIPTION AND OVER THE COUNTER DRUGS)? FOR ANY REASON.

____

____

____

____

____

(6)

PLEASE INDICATE ON THE DRAWING THE LOCATION, TYPE AND INTENSITY OF YOUR PAIN USING THE KEY BELOW:

Key: 0000 Pins & Needles
XXXX Burning
//// Stabbing
==== Numbness
Aching

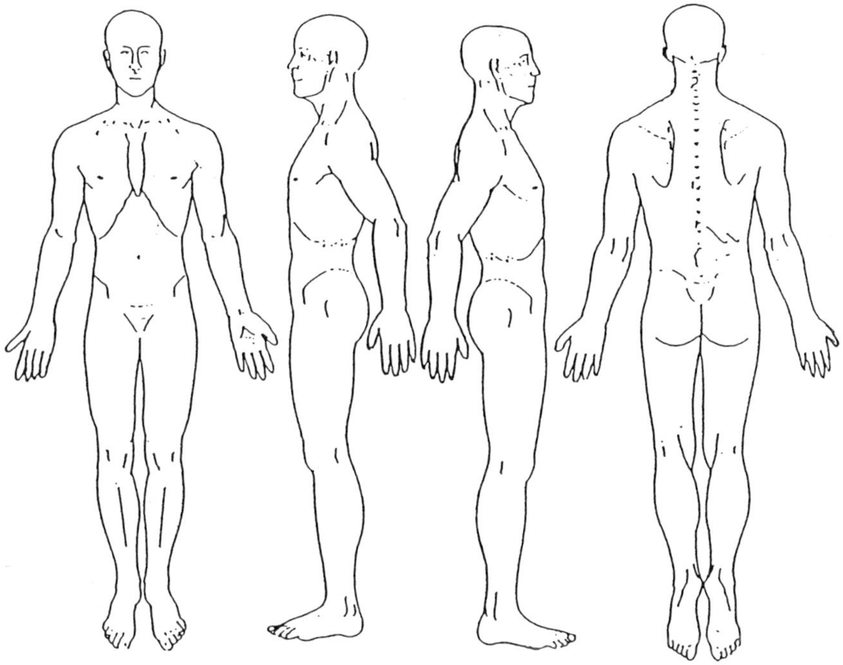

WHAT IS YOUR LEVEL OF PAIN? ______________________

10+__ Maximal
10 __ Very, Very Strong
9 __
8 __
7 __ Very Strong
6 __
5 __ Strong
4 __ Somewhat Strong
3 __ Moderate
2 __ Weak
1 __ Very Weak
0.5 __ Very, Very Weak
0 __ Nothing at All

(7)

WHAT DO YOU DO TO RELIEVE YOUR PAIN?

[ ] Rest/Lie Down	[ ] Increased activity
[ ] Ice	[ ] Heat
[ ] Sit	[ ] Stand
[ ] Medication	[ ] Alcohol
[ ] Decreased Activity	[ ] Other ____________

DOES YOUR PAIN CHANGE WITH THE TIME OF DAY? [ ] yes [ ] no
BEST TIME OF DAY: _______ WORST TIME OF DAY: ____________
WHAT TESTS HAVE YOU HAD FOR YOUR INJURY:

Test When Facility

X-Rays ____
CAT Scan ____
MRI ____
Myelogram ____
EMG ____
Diagnostic Injections ________________________________
Physical Therapy (How Long?) __________________________
Other: ____

HAVE YOU BEEN TREATED FOR ANY OF THE FOLLOWING? (PLEASE CHECK)

[ ] Fainting	[ ] Diabetes	[ ] Ulcers
[ ] High Blood Pressure	[ ] Allergies	[ ] Asthma
[ ] Emphysema	[ ] Stomach Pain	[ ] Cancer
[ ] Bladder	[ ] Thyroid	[ ] Sweats
[ ] Swelling	[ ] Circulation	[ ] Heart
[ ] Dizziness	[ ] Swelling	[ ] Liver
[ ] Chronic Fatigue	[ ] Bowel Problems	[ ] Kidney
[ ] Sexual Dysfunction	[ ] Sleeping Disorder	[ ] Chills
[ ] Nerves/anxiety	[ ] Easy Bruising	[ ] Weight
[ ] Chest Pains	[ ] Stiff or Swollen Joints	

HAS ANYONE IN YOUR IMMEDIATE FAMILY HAD A HISTORY OF SERIOUS ILLNESS OR INJURY? PLEASE EXPLAIN:

____
____
____
____

(8)

LIST ALL THE DOCTORS YOU HAVE SEEN FOR THIS CONDITION.

Physician Name	Specialty	Date Seen

WHO IS YOUR FAMILY DOCTOR? ______________________

WHAT SURGERIES HAVE YOU HAD?

Type of Surgery	Doctor's Name	Facility	Any Complications
			[ ] yes [ ] no
			[ ] yes [ ] no
			[ ] yes [ ] no
			[ ] yes [ ] no
			[ ] yes [ ] no
			[ ] yes [ ] no

WHICH TREATMENTS HAVE YOU HAD FOR THIS CONDITION?

TREATMENT	Somewhat Helpful	Helpful	No Help	Doctor
Back School	[ ]	[ ]	[ ]	________
T.E.N.S.	[ ]	[ ]	[ ]	________
Injections	[ ]	[ ]	[ ]	________
Nerve blocks	[ ]	[ ]	[ ]	________
Pain Program	[ ]	[ ]	[ ]	________
Work Hardening	[ ]	[ ]	[ ]	________
Exercise	[ ]	[ ]	[ ]	________
Surgery (How Many)?	[ ]	[ ]	[ ]	________
Counseling	[ ]	[ ]	[ ]	________
Nutritional Counseling	[ ]	[ ]	[ ]	________
Job Counseling	[ ]	[ ]	[ ]	________

HOW WOULD YOU RATE YOUR AVERAGE ACTIVITY LEVEL SINCE THE TIME OF YOUR INJURY?

[ ] no activity
[ ] most activities
[ ] some activity
[ ] all activities

WHAT IS THE HEAVIEST ITEM YOU HAVE LIFTED SINCE YOUR INJURY?

Item: ______________________ Weight: __________

(9)

WHAT ARE YOUR HOBBIES, LEISURE ACTIVITIES OR RECREATIONAL ACTIVITIES?

Past: ______________________________

Present: ______________________________

Activity	I did this before my injury	I do this now without help	I do this now with help
Put on shoes/socks	[ ]	[ ]	[ ]
Get into/out of bathtub	[ ]	[ ]	[ ]
Laundry	[ ]	[ ]	[ ]
Ironing	[ ]	[ ]	[ ]
Light house cleaning	[ ]	[ ]	[ ]
Meal preparation	[ ]	[ ]	[ ]
grocery shopping	[ ]	[ ]	[ ]
car repairs	[ ]	[ ]	[ ]
car washing	[ ]	[ ]	[ ]
scrub floors	[ ]	[ ]	[ ]
scrub bathtub	[ ]	[ ]	[ ]
take out garbage	[ ]	[ ]	[ ]
Washing dishes	[ ]	[ ]	[ ]
Loading dishwasher	[ ]	[ ]	[ ]
Driving	[ ]	[ ]	[ ]
Washing walls/windows	[ ]	[ ]	[ ]
Shoveling snow	[ ]	[ ]	[ ]
Raking	[ ]	[ ]	[ ]
Gardening	[ ]	[ ]	[ ]
Vacuuming	[ ]	[ ]	[ ]
Dusting	[ ]	[ ]	[ ]
Picking up around house	[ ]	[ ]	[ ]

PLEASE LIST ANYTHING ELSE YOU THINK WE SHOULD KNOW ABOUT YOUR CURRENT SITUATION.

____

____

____

____

____

WHAT IS YOUR GOAL FOR MEDICAL TREATMENT? ______________

____

____

WHAT IS YOUR GOAL FOR EMPLOYMENT? ______________

____

____

(10)

SPOUSE'S EMPLOYMENT INFORMATION

EMPLOYER: ______________ CITY: ______________________________
JOB TITLE: ______________ CONTACT PERSON: ______________
WAGE: __________________ LENGTH OF EMPLOYMENT: ________

PAIN WORDS

INSTRUCTIONS

There are many words that describe pain. some of these are grouped below. Look at each group of words and circle any word which describes the pain you are experiencing <u>right now</u>. Continue until you have finished all 20 word groups. you should choose only one word from every word group, but you do not have to choose a word from every word group. If none of the words in a particular word group describe your pain, go to the next word group.

1. Flicking, Quivering, Pulsing, Throbbing, Beating, Pounding
2. Jumping, Flashing, Shooting
3. Pricking, Boring, Drilling, Stabbing, Lancinating
4. Sharp, Cutting, Lacerating
5. Pinching, Pressing, Gnawing, Cramping, Crushing
6. Tugging, Pulling, Wrenching
7. Hot, Burning, Scalding, Searing
8. Tingling, Itchy, Smarting, Stinging
9. Dull, Sore, Hurting, Aching, Heavy
10. Tender, Taut, Rasping, Splitting
11. Tiring, Exhausting
12. Sickening, Suffocating
13. Fearful, Frightful, Terrifying
14. Punishing, Grueling, Cruel, Vicious, Killing
15. Wretched, Blinding
16. Annoying, Troublesome, Miserable, Intense, Unbearable
17. Spreading, Radiating, Penetrating, Piercing
18. Tight, Numb, Drawing, Squeezing, Tearing
19. Cool, Cold, Freezing
20. Nagging, Nauseating, Agonizing, Dreadful, Torturing

(11)

Once you've reviewed the your initial intake sheet, observed the prospective client, asked questions, listened to his story, and dictated your case capsule, you are at the point of making a judgment call. Do you thank him for the opportunity to have discussed his case and refer him elsewhere, or do you get involved? The latter decision starts the wheels turning at your office, depending on what the issues are and how much you are willing to spend.

In an effort to obtain as much information as possible at the first consultation, you should take notes on all the details of the crash. This book deals exclusively with child restraint injuries, and addresses the areas of the law dealing with product liability, not malpractice action arising from an child restraint accident-induced injury.

PI Cases & Contingency Fees

CAL:	C CPA 1021
NY:	22 NYCR 603.7, 691.20, 806.13, 1022.31
FL:	FSA Code of Prof Resp, Canon 2, DR 2-106
IL:	SHA Ch 110A, Canon 2, Rule 2-106
LA:	LSARS 37:218; Art. 16, Rules of Prof Conduct
MI:	MCR 8.121

RETAINER CONTRACT — CONTINGENCY

I hereby employ the LAW OFFICES OF JOSEPH WILLIAM MOCH, to represent my interest in regard to any claims for damages on account of personal injuries and/or property damage suffered by me.

I agree to pay the Law Offices of JOSEPH WILLIAM MOCH, as compensation for their services 33 1/3% of the net recovery per Michigan Court Rules of 1985, Rule 8.121. This does NOT include probate or appellate work done in regard to my claim.

The fee shall be computed on the net sum recovered after deducting all disbursements properly chargeable to my case. In computing the fee, the costs of taxes and any interest included in or upon the amount of judgment shall be deemed part of the amount recovered.

In the event of no recovery, I shall owe no attorneys fees, but I shall reimburse attorneys for all costs and expenses advanced in their investigation and prosecution of my claim.

Said law firm may, in its sole discretion, make arrangements with other law firms to act as co-counsel in prosecution of this claim.

If a settlement offer is received and same is recommended by the law firm and said settlement offer is rejected by the client and a lesser amount is obtained, said law firm's attorney fee will be based on the percentage of the settlement offer as if the settlement offer had been accepted.

It is understood that this law firm reserves the right to withdraw from this retention anytime at its sole discretion.

This retention agreement gives this law firm 90 days to review the facts and circumstances surrounding the Plaintiff's alleged claim prior to becoming bound to represent the client.

DATED: ________________ ________________________

____

If, however, a client should insist upon your representation under the terms of an hourly agreement,

HOURLY ATTORNEY FEE RETAINER CONTRACT

I hereby retained the Law Offices of Joseph William Moch at $300 - per hour.

This contract is above and beyond the 1/3 contingency fee contract covered by Michigan Court Rules of 1985, Rule 8.121 under which the Law Office of Joseph William Moch is representing me against the party who caused my personal injuries.

This contract is for representation against my own insurance company to collect the benefits I am entitled to under the Michigan No-Fault auto insurance law as well as any other legal work requested by me.

DATED: ______________ ________________________

Signature

Rejecting the Claim

If a thorough review of the facts and laws leads you to conclude there is <u>no</u> cause of action, get the file out of your office immediately. If you believe either the Defendant was not negligent or that

Plaintiff's injuries were not proximately caused by the accident, be frank with your clients, thank them for the chance to review their situation, answer their questions, reject the claim and inform them of the statute of limitations.

Document the rejection of the file with a letter. This may be of significant value if the claim is later pursued and the statute of limitations becomes an issue. This procedure also gives the client an opportunity to determine other legal opinions. A million dollar plus recovery for one of our clients was an induced quadriplegic case resulting from an inground swimming pool diving accident. Eight local attorneys had consulted with the young man and declined the case.

So if you don't see a cause of action, have the common courtesy (and good business sense) to refer it out immediately.

GENERAL AUTHORIZATION

TO:

You are hereby authorized to disclose and deliver to my attorneys, the LAW OFFICES OF JOSEPH WILLIAM MOCH, or their authorized representative, any and all records or documents of any kind including medical reports that pertain to me or my charge.

The LAW OFFICES OF JOSEPH WILLIAM MOCH or its representatives are further authorized to photocopy, microfilm or otherwise reproduce said records.

They are also authorized to photograph or video tape me or anyone in my charge.

A copy of this document shall have the same effect as an original.

This shall serve to release and discharge the holder/releasor of said documents and/or information from any and all liability arising from releasing said documents and/or information.

DATED:

NAME OF SUBJECT	NAME OF PARENT OR GUARDIAN
SOCIAL SECURITY NUMBER	DATE OF INCIDENT

GENERAL AUTHORIZATION

TO:

You are authorized to disclose and deliver to the LAW OFFICES OF JOSEPH WILLIAM MOCH, or their authorized representative, any and all records or documents of any kind including medical reports that pertain to me or my charge.

The LAW OFFICES OF JOSEPH WILLIAM MOCH or its representatives are further authorized to photocopy, microfilm or otherwise reproduce said records.

They are also authorized to photograph or video tape me or anyone in my charge.

A copy of this document shall have the same effect as an original.

This shall serve to release and discharge the holder/releasor of said documents and/or information from any and all liability arising from releasing said documents and/or information.

DATED:

__________________	__________________
NAME OF SUBJECT	NAME OF PARENT OR GUARDIAN
__________________	__________________
SOCIAL SECURITY NUMBER	DATE OF INCIDENT
__________________	__________________
DATE OF BIRTH	SIGNATURE

File Organization

Now that the client has retained your services and executed a contract and a records release you can begin to gather the evidence necessary to secure an adequate award for the client. What follows are suggestions for file organization.

For convenience, we've found it practical to have a secretary type stick-on day-glo orange labels, with the following information, for the front of each file:

1. Client Name/Address/Phone #, Home & Work
2. Defendant's Name/Address/Phone #, Home & Work
3. Defense Counsel's Name/Address/Phone #, Home & Work
4. Reference Source

It's good business to drop a thank you note to reference sources. When it comes to referring attorneys, there is no quicker way to lose a source of cases than to forget them.

Separate the material you collect right from the beginning. Tab and label material so it can be indexed and retrieved from the file with minimal effort; keep the index in the front of each folder. Our office uses the following category files within the master folder:

1. Research—client's name, intake sheet, witness statements, accident reports, investigation reports, insurance policies.
2. Medical—group individually, tagged by doctor/hospital/therapist.
3. Background—employment records, school records, military service, athletic.
4. Master—all pleadings and correspondence in chronological order.
5. Trial—complaint, answers, interrogatories , requests to admit, depositions.
6. Legal—the applicable laws set out in memoranda-of-law.
7. Photo's—in a separate envelope, designating date, photographer, location, etc.
8. Damages—all bills incurred by the client, in chronological order.
9. Expenses—all bills incurred by our office for preparation and investigation of the case.
10. Experts—a separate and distinct file titled with the expert's name. Inside the file is the issue he or she is called upon to

deal with, the curriculum vitae, copies of all materials pertaining to the issue; we use a separate file for Plaintiff and Defendant witnesses.

This, or a similar, system will make it extremely easy to gather all necessary information, file materials, and retrieve it when necessary. Filing can be handled by a support staff person. However, a monthly check through a tickler system by the assigned attorney is important, and can uncover and prevent unpleasant surprises. So check your own file. It beats being embarrassed by the opposition or bench.

Clients, like all of us, are often possessors of that human frailty, short memory. In an effort to counteract this natural phenomenon, we strongly recommend writing the client a follow-up letter. This letter should recount what you discussed during the initial consultation, stressing the do's and don'ts of litigation that we as lawyers may take for granted, but may never cross the mind of our legally naive client.

Investigating the Case - Starting With the Vehicle

Few inventions have changed our lives as much as the American automobile has. The American dream of two American cars in every garage is today a virtual necessity. As more and more cars hit the road, the public has become more aware of safety concerns and it has periodically demanded that manufacturers include passenger safety as a consideration in their designs.

Early automobiles were difficult to steer, had many mechanical problems, and in some, were unreliable, unpredictable, and ineffective. Many components experienced breakdowns quite often. For example, the tires, the brakes, the suspension, and the steering were not only unreliable, but the cause of many accidents in early model cars. Tire blowouts were one of the major causes of accidents in early automobiles. Brakes were often quite unbalanced and ineffective. The driver who tried to make a sudden stop would often find himself doing a spin and going off the road.

Occupant safety in automobiles is often referred to in terms of "crash worthiness". While manufacturers cannot produce a vehicle that is 100% crash proof, the technology exists today to create cars that will protect the occupants in all but the most serious of crashes. Nevertheless, the implementation of the designs usually is based upon a cost benefit analysis. Sometimes, the designs by the automobile manufacturers are motivated by the bottom line rather than passenger safety. A most notable example of this policy is the Ford Pinto, and more recently the problems with the external fuel tanks in GM trucks.

As the evolution of the automobile progressed, cars became faster, more efficient, reliable, and therefore the need for safer cars was just part of the evolution. With newer model cars the risk of injury has increased and thus, the manufacturers duty has increased in direct proportion. The manufacturer must meet its duty of building safe and crash worthy automobiles to the ultimate satisfaction of a fact finding jury.

Physics 101

The terminology used in accidents is often confusing if not misleading and unnecessarily uncomplicated. A jury of lay people may be unable to understand terms like crash worthiness, momentum, kinematics, Delta fee, and the myriad of other terms which describe physical characteristics that take place during the crash. For this reason it is important that the attorney handling the motor vehicle case which involves a child passenger occupant, use the services of a biomechanical expert who can relate to a lay person and describe complicated mechanical and physical events in simple, easy to understand language. That same expert should also be able to speak to opposing counsel at depositions in the parlance of his trade. An ideal expert witness would be one who understands the principles involved in a motor vehicle crash and who also understands the physics and mechanics of child restraints and how they behave during a collision. This same expert may very often help the attorney handling the motor vehicle case find if a defect in a child restraint device was responsible for the injury or death of the child in the accident.

The basic laws of physics tell us that an object in motion tends to remain in motion unless another force acts upon the object. We can safely conclude, therefore, that passengers traveling in an automobile will continue traveling at the vehicle's speed when that vehicle abruptly stops due to a sudden stop or crash. A person traveling in a car at 30 miles per hour that crashes into a solid barrier will continue traveling in a forward direction at 30 miles per hour unless an outside force acts on that person. We have all seen the commercials and advertisements that show the test dummies crashing through the windshield of a car when unrestrained or improperly restrained. The basic kinematics of the crash show that a vehicle slows down on impact while the occupants continue moving in the direction of the vehicle. This movement continues even if the occupants are restrained. However, the restraint serves as a buffer and slows down the passengers motion. The tragedy of failing to use a restraint has been graphically illustrated many times. A vehicle in a 30 mile per hour crash stops in about a tenth of a second. An unrestrained occupant in that car continues to travel at 30 miles per hour in that tenth of a second. That fraction of a second can spell the difference between life and death for the person in the vehicle.

The manufacturers have met part of their burden in designing safer cars by designing cars that distribute the impact load during a crash. Newer model cars are lighter than their counterparts from the 50's, 60's, and 70's but the newer designs are made to maximize protection to the passenger compartment in the event of a crash. In a frontal crash, the front part of the vehicle collapses in stages.

Automobile manufacturers also meet the burden of providing safer vehicles for their consumers by including several occupant protection options in their cars. Most of the options have become standard equipment in all vehicles. This includes lap and shoulder belts for front and rear seat occupants, air bags, anti-lock brakes, and automatic seat belts.

The addition of occupant protection devices has made the manufacturer's duty universal. The state-of-the-art recognizes passive restraint devices as a basic part of motor vehicle designed and standard equipment.

Types of Crashes

During a collision vehicle occupants can experience many injuries as a result of contact with the interior of the vehicle during the crash. Most of those fatalities or injuries can be prevented by using adequate designs on the part of the manufacturer in the use of restraints on the part of the occupant. The attorney taking on a motor vehicle case must realize that there are many complex issues to be resolved in what may first appear to be a simple car crash. The complications grow exponentially when a child restraint defect is involved. Immediate investigation of the vehicle, the child restraint, the police report, and medicals are a must in this area of product liability litigation. An attorney handling a child restraint case may miss a defect that caused the victim's injury. The first two things the attorney should figure out is how the vehicle was moving at the time of the crash, and secondly, how the victim was moving in the inside of the car. If there were several occupants in the car, the interactions of movement among the different passengers must be determined.

All of the answers to the attorney's questions lie in the damaged vehicle. The car provides a physical evidential record of the external forces that were applied to the vehicle during the crash and of interior forces applied to the vehicle by the occupant.

The photographs can also provide the attorney and the expert with valuable information. Photographs that show the location of the vehicle after the crash, skid marks, weather conditions, and other physical evidence are a critical part of the investigation process. The attorney should obtain photographs from the police department or have the vehicle photographed by an independent photographer as soon as possible. Sometimes the attorney may have to take the photograph himself or herself. A photo should be taken of everything on the car and inside the car. Although photographs of the front, rear, sides, top, and bottom are a must. Close-ups of damaged areas should also be taken. The interior compartment must also be photographed.

If there were witnesses at the scene of the accident it is important to find out if they saw any objects inside the car immediately after the collision. For example, if a large box was placed in the rear seat next to the child restraint seat, this evidence would be critical in determining the cause of the injuries to the child. A list should be compiled as soon as possible of all the items that were inside the vehicle at the time of the accident. The attorney or investigator should note all the structural damage that is visible such as intrusions in the compartment, structural separation, and broken windows. Broken windows are critical because they may indicate occupant contact against the glass. Note here that the interior of the doors should also be photographed. The photographic evidence from the doors can show whether the windows were open at the time of the crash.

Interviews with witnesses at the scene of the accident is critical. Not only can they provide firsthand information but also with respect to damage to the vehicle, they can tell the attorney or investigator whether the damage was caused by the forces of the crash or whether rescue crews using jaws-of-life or other equipment caused the damage.

As stated earlier, exterior damage to a vehicle provides reference point as to the direction and velocity of a vehicle before and after the crash. Interior damage provides a similar reference point as to occupant injuries and points of contact during the crash. The following areas of the vehicle should be examined thoroughly for damage: the instrument panel, the roof, the window glass, the pillars supporting the roof, the steering wheel, the shifting lever, and the seats. In a child restraint case, it is also important to determine the ending position of the child restraint in the car. This information may have to be obtained from firsthand witnesses such as rescue teams because often they will be the first ones on the scene and the ones most likely to remove a child from the child restraint.

In gathering and compiling this information, you must also take note of the physical characteristics of all the occupants in the vehicle that were involved in the crash. The size, shape, and weight of the occupants must be noted. Age, sex, medical history, and physical characteristics are also valuable sources of information for an expert involved in reconstructing the accident.

Some reconstruction experts may even use a similarly sized person in order to give the lawyer or opposing counsel and ultimately the jury, a clear perspective of the interactions of the occupants in the vehicle. Using such exemplary evidence can provide insight into the fit of passive protection devices, the position of the occupants at the time of contact, and the contact points during the crash.

Solving the Puzzle

Determining the cause of injuries in an accident involving a child passenger can be likened to solving a good mystery or putting together a puzzle. The available physical evidence includes the vehicle itself, photographs of the vehicle, eyewitness accounts, police and medical reports, expert witness opinions, and the victims themselves.

Sometimes one or more of the pieces of the puzzle will be missing. In some cases, all the pieces will be present but some may contradict each other or distort the picture somewhat. Once a rough picture of the accident is compiled then the decision must be made whether a defect in the automobile or the child restraint device actually caused the fatality or injury to the child. Only once this question is answered can the attorney conclusively decide the merits of his case. The help of a reconstruction or a biomechanical expert can also determine if a change in the design would have prevented the injuries to the child.

Other available designs in the market at the time of the accident can also help the attorney argue his case through mediation or to explain it to a jury during a trial.

Child restraint defect cases involve a lot of time, effort, and expense. The child restraint device manufacturers heavily defend lawsuits and will often seek protective orders to prevent others from using information discovered in earlier cases. This, in essence, forces each plaintiff to reinvent the wheel and start from scratch. Nevertheless, proper preparation, investigation, and the use of knowledgeable experts can help the attorney compensate victims of defective child restraint systems.

Experts that can be used in a child restraint case include medical doctors, emergency and rescue personnel, biomechanical experts, reconstruction experts, and economic analysts.

Before retaining any expert, the attorney should carefully review the expert's experience with similar accidents and the expert's background. If at all possible, expert referrals should be obtained from plaintiff's organizations such as ATLA or AIEG or from other practitioners who have handled similar cases.

In closely contested cases, the expert may require more testing to determine the defect that caused the child's injuries. A sled test conforming to FMVSS 213 may be necessary for this purpose. Sled tests are expensive and involve resources that are not available to many experts or attorneys in this area of litigation. Calspan Corporation in Buffalo, New York does the testing on child restraints for both manufacturers and the government. They also keep a videotape record of all the tests that they perform on child restraints. Therefore, it might be more inexpensive for the attorney to secure a tape that shows the testing of the particular child restraint involved in the crash rather than order a new test at great expense to his clients.

Letter to Defendant

Notice to Defendant

RE:Client's name:
Date of accident:
Location:
Our File:

Dear Defendant:

This letter is sent to put you on notice that our office has been retained to represent the interests of the above-named party in regard to the injuries he/she/they sustained on the date and place above, as a result of your negligence.

If you are insured, present this letter to your insurance carrier immediately, for your own protection. If you should be uninsured, please contact our office directly.

If for any reason we do not hear from your insurance adjuster or yourself within five working days, we will commence suit immediately.

Sincerely,

Joseph William Moch
Teresa M. Hendricks
JWM:sam
TMH:sam

Settlement Demand

RE:Client:
Date of Injury:
Your insured:
Your file #:

Dear :

Enclosed please find in reference to the aforementioned claim: accident report, medical documentation, accident investigation, photographic documentation and economic report. Based on the enclosures, we would be willing to recommend settlement of the aforementioned claim to our client for
$______.

After you have had an opportunity to evaluate the materials, please contact the writer directly so we can discuss your position and set the course of future action.

Sincerely,

Joseph William Moch
JWM:sam

Filing the Complaint

Once you have decided to take on your client's case, you have to determine whom to sue. For your convenience, please refer to the appendix on Manufacturers. We have provided the names, addresses, and phone numbers of the major child restraint manufacturers in the United States. Another determination that will have to be made before you file the complaint will be whether to sue in federal or state court. This decision will be based mainly on tactical considerations, and will vary from jurisdiction to jurisdiction. You should familiarize yourself with the tort laws applicable in your jurisdiction as to defective products.

Susan A. Fox is an Arkansas trial attorney who has successfully mediated and tried automobile cases including those dealing with child restraint defects.

Sample Complaint

IN THE UNITED STATES DISTRICT COURT FOR THE WESTERN DISTRICT OF MICHIGAN

Jane L. Doe, as Personal
Representative of the Estate of
Mary ANN Doe
1-4 Road
City, Michigan 12345

and

Jane L. Doe, individually
1-4 Main Street
City, Michigan 12345

and

John Doe, individually
1-4 Main Street
City, Michigan 12345

and

Jack Doe, a Minor, By and
Through His Mother and Next Friend,
Jane L. Doe
1-4 Main Street
City, Michigan 12345

Plaintiffs

V.

SPAULDING and EVENFLO COMPANIES,
INC., a Foreign Corporation
5750-A North Hoover Boulevard
Tampa, Florida 33636

SERVE: Robert K. Adikes, Esquire
General Counsel Spaulding and Evenflo
Companies, Inc.
5750-A N. Hoover Blvd.
Tampa, FL 33634

Defendant

Law Offices of Joseph W. Moch
The Moch Building
121 Michigan Ave., N.E.
Grand Rapids, MI 49503
(616) 456-1449

By: ____________________

Attorneys for Plaintiffs

COMPLAINT AND DEMAND FOR TRIAL BY JURY

NOW COME the Plaintiffs, Jane L. Doe, personal administrator of the Estate of Mary Ann Doe, deceased; and, Jane L. Doe, individually, and John Doe, individually, and Jack Doe, a minor, by and through his mother and next friend, Jane L. Doe, by their attorneys, The Law Offices of Joseph W. Moch and sue the Defendant, Spaulding and Evenflo Companies, Inc. as follows:

JURISDICTIONAL FACTS COMMON TO ALL COUNTS

1. The Plaintiff, Jane L. Doe, is the duly qualified and acting personal representative of the Estate of Mary Ann Doe, deceased.

2. At all times pertinent, the decedent, Mary Ann Doe, was a citizen of the State of Michigan and her Estate is in probate before the Probate Court for Kent County, Michigan.

3. At all times pertinent, Jane L. Doe is, and was, a citizen of the State of Michigan.

4. At all times pertinent, John Doe is, and was, a citizen of the State of Michigan.

5. At all times pertinent, Jack Doe, a minor, is, and was, a citizen of the State of Michigan.

6. The Defendant, Spaulding and Evenflo Companies, Inc. (hereinafter "Spaulding and Evenflo") is a foreign corporation which,-at all times pertinent, has done business and is doing business in the State of Michigan. Its principal place of business is located in Tampa, Florida.

7. Evenflo Juvenile Furniture Company is presently a division of Spaulding and Evenflo which maintains offices in Piqua, Ohio.

8. Spaulding and Evenflo is the successor to Evenflo Juvenile Furniture Company, Inc. (Hereinafter referred to as "Evenflo or "predecessor")

9. There is complete diversity of the parties and this Court has jurisdiction pursuant to Title 28 U.S.C. Section 1332.

10. This Court has jurisdiction in that the amount in controversy exceeds Fifty Thousand Dollars ($50,000.00), exclusive of interest, cost and attorney's fees.

11. At all times pertinent, the Defendant, Spaulding and Evenflo and its predecessor, Evenflo, were, and are, engaged in the design, testing and manufacturing of child restraints for children.

12. Since approximately 1980, the Defendant and its predecessor company designed, tested and manufactured a child restraint which is commonly known as the Kantwet, One Step, Model 401. (Hereinafter sometimes referred to as the "child restraint")

13. The child restraint was purchased in Lansing, Michigan, by John and Jane Doe in approximately 1983.

14. This action arises out of the wrongful death of Mary Ann Doe which occurred on November 20, 1990, in Lansing, Michigan while the minor was using the child restraint.

COUNT I
(Wrongful Death of Mary Ann Doe)

15. The allegations contained in paragraphs one (1) through fourteen (14) are realleged and incorporated herein by reference as though fully set forth herein.

16. The Defendant, Spaulding and Evenflo, and its predecessor company, owed a duty to consumers generally and to the minor decedent, Mary Ann Doe, to use reasonable care in the design, testing and manufacturing of the Kantwet, one Step, Model 401 child restraint.

17. In designing the child restraint, it became, and was, the duty of the Defendant and its predecessor to use due care and diligence to the public in general and to the minor, Mary Ann Doe, in particular to reasonably assure that the child restraint protected infants and minor children in the event of an automobile accident and to reasonably assure that the said minor children and infants using the child restraint would be properly secured and restrained.

18. It further became, and was, the duty of the Defendant in designing the Kantwet, One Step, Model 401 child restraint that the latch and buckle would be designed in such a fashion so that it would not appear the buckle was engaged when, in fact, it was not fully engaged.

19. If further became, and was, the duty of the Defendant in designing the Kantwet, One Step, Model 401 child restraint to perform reasonable tests of the buckle to determine whether it would falsely latch and to perform reasonable and adequate tests to determine how consumers would know if the buckle was falsely latched.

20. It further became, and was, the duty of the Defendant in manufacturing the buckle to maintain sufficient quality control procedures to eliminate flaws and metal burrs on the buckle and latch plate components which could contribute to causing the false latch condition.

21. The Defendant, Spaulding and Evenflo, and its predecessor, negligently breached its various duties in that it failed to use reasonable and due care in designing, manufacturing and testing the latch and buckle on the Kantwet, One Step, Model 401 child restraint.

22. The Defendant, Spaulding and Evenflo, and its predecessor, negligently breached its duties in that it failed to perform reasonable and adequate tests to determine how consumers would reasonably know and determine if the buckle was falsely latched.

23. At least as early as 1983 when the Defendant's predecessor company revised the instruction sheet for the child restraint, the Defendant and its predecessor knew, or should have known, that the latch and buckle on the Kantwet, One Step, Model 401 could be falsely latched by consumers so that the buckle would appear to be latched when, in fact, the buckle was not fully engaged.

24. The Defendant, Spaulding and Evenflo, and its predecessor knew, or should have known, that the false latch condition was unreasonably dangerous at the time the Kantwet, One Step, Model 401 was manufactured and placed in the stream of commerce.

25. The Defendant, Spaulding and Evenflo, and its predecessor had a further duty to warn consumers that the buckle could be falsely latched.

26. The Defendant, Spaulding and Evenflo, and its predecessor negligently breached its duty in failing to have adequate warnings and instructions on the instruction sheet of the Kantwet, One Step, Model 401 child restraint instruction sheet in that the instructions provided only, "The One Step buckles easily if you squeeze the 'push' button on the crotch strap as you insert the metal tongue. Check that buckle has engaged by pulling up on the shield."

27. The Defendant was further negligent in that it failed to perform reasonable tests to determine whether the instruction that consumers should "check that buckle has engaged by pulling upon the shields" was adequate to reveal the false latch condition.

28. In truth and in fact, the instruction to consumers of "pulling up on the shield" was not adequate since it would not necessarily reveal that the buckle was falsely latched and had not been fully engaged.

29. At least as of March 6, 1990, Spaulding and Evenflo knew that independent testing confirmed that there could be buckle failures on its Kantwet, One Step, Model 401 child restraints and the buckle could be falsely latched.

30. On or about June 12, 1990, the Defendant, Spaulding and Evenflo, did represent to employees of the National Highway Transportation Safety Administration (hereinafter referred to as "NHTSA") that the Kantwet, One Step, Model 401 child restraints manufactured by Evenflo after 1986 would be recalled due to the fact that the buckles did not comply with the federal standards for false latching and that the Kantwet, One Step, Model 401 "seats made prior to 1986 would be taken care of but on an informal basis and not as part of the official safety campaign."

31. Upon information and belief, the Defendant, Spaulding and Evenflo, was negligent in that it, contrary to representations made to NHTSA, Spaulding and Evenflo did not take "care of" the pre-1986 Kantwet, One Step, Model 401 child restraints and did not undertake any measures on an "informal basis" to correct or replace any possible defective buckles on child restraints which were manufactured prior to 1986.

32. At least as of June, 1990, Spaulding and Evenflo were further negligent in failing to recall child restraints which were manufactured prior to 1986 since Spaulding and Evenflo knew that such child restraints had buckles which could be falsely latched.

33. On November 20, 1990, the minor, Mary Ann Doe, was riding in the aforesaid Kantwet, one Step, Model 401 child restraint as the Doe vehicle was proceeding on South Waverly in Lansing, Michigan.

34. At approximately 8:00 a.m., the Doe motor vehicle was involved in an automobile collision with another vehicle being operated by John Smith.

35. Notwithstanding that the minor child, Mary Ann Doe, had been placed in the child restraint in the manner described in the instructions, the buckle was falsely latched and was not fully engaged.

36. Subsequent to the impact, the minor child, Mary Ann Doe, was ejected from the child restraint and was thrown outside of the motor vehicle.

37. Each of the above-mentioned acts of negligence by the Defendant, Spaulding and Evenflo Companies, Inc., was a proximate cause of the death of Mary Ann Doe and the injuries and damages sustained by Mary Ann Doe.

38. The Plaintiff, as the personal representative of the deceased, is entitled to recover herein such damages as shall be deemed fair and reasonable under all the circumstances to those persons who may be entitled to such damages, including the decedent's parents and siblings, when recovered under the Michigan wrongful death statute, and that such damages shall include, but are not limited to: (a) the necessary and reasonable expenses incurred or paid by reason of medical, hospital, funeral and burial expenses; (b) the costs of raising the minor child; (c) the pain and suffering endured by the Plaintiff's decedent during the interim period of time extending between the Defendant's negligence and the Plaintiff's ultimate death; (d) the loss, and future loss, to the family, including the parents and siblings of the decedent, of the decedent's love, companionship, services and comfort; and, (f) the loss of earnings of the estate; (e) all other damages properly recoverable under the aforesaid Michigan Wrongful Death Act.

WHEREFORE, the Plaintiff, Jane L. Doe, as personal representative of the Estate of Mary Ann Doe, deceased, demands judgment against the Defendant, Spaulding and Evenflo Companies, Inc., a foreign corporation, in the amount of Five Million Dollars ($5,000,000.00) in compensatory damages, plus exemplary damages, together with costs, attorney's fees, interest to date of judgment and such other and further relief as may be just and proper.

COUNT II
(Negligent Infliction of Emotional Distress of Jane L. Doe)

39. The allegations contained in paragraphs one (1) through thirty-eight (38) inclusive of Count I of this Complaint are realleged and incorporated herein by reference as though fully set forth herein.

40. The Plaintiff, Jane L. Doe, is the natural mother of the Plaintiff's decedent, Mary Ann Doe.

41. On November 20, 1990, Jane L. Doe was riding in the motor vehicle with her minor daughter.

42. As a result of the various acts of negligence by the Defendant which are more fully set forth in Count I of this Complaint, the Plaintiff, Jane L. Doe, was caused to witness the infliction of tortuous injuries upon her daughter and to experience consequential effects thereof.

43. As a further direct and proximate result, the Plaintiff has suffered severe emotional, nervous and mental distress and disturbance resulting in physical illness and injury, including, but not limited to, headaches, nightmares, depression and post traumatic stress, all or some of which emotional and mental distress is permanent in nature.

WHEREFORE, the premises considered, the Plaintiff, Jane L. Doe, individually, demands judgment against the Defendant, Spaulding and Evenflo Companies, Inc. in the sum of Five Million Dollars ($5,000,000.00) plus costs, interest, attorney's fees and such other and further relief as this Court deems appropriate.

COUNT III
(Negligent Infliction of Emotional Distress of John Doe)

44. The allegations contained in paragraphs one (1) through thirty-eight (38), inclusive, of Count I of this Complaint are realleged and incorporated herein by reference as though fully set forth herein.

45. The Plaintiff, John Doe, is the natural father of the Plaintiff's decedent, Mary Ann Doe.'

46. On November 20, 1990, John Doe was riding in the motor vehicle with his minor daughter.

47. As a direct result of the negligence of the Defendant, Spaulding and Evenflo Companies, Inc., as more fully set forth in Count I on this Complaint, the Plaintiff, John Doe, was caused to witness the infliction of tortuous injuries upon his daughter and to experience the consequential effects thereof.

48. As a further direct and proximate result thereof, the Plaintiff, John Doe, has been caused to suffer severe emotional, nervous and mental disturbance, resulting in physical illness and injury, including, but not limited to, nausea, headaches, nightmares, depression, and post-traumatic stress, all or some of which emotional and mental condition is permanent.

WHEREFORE, the premises considered, the Plaintiff, John Doe, demands judgment against the Defendant, Spaulding and Evenflo Companies, Inc., in the sum of Five Million Dollars ($5,000,000.00) plus reasonable attorney's fees, costs, interest and such other and further relief as the nature of the case may require.

COUNT IV
(Negligent Infliction of Emotion Distress of Jack Doe)

49. The allegations contained in paragraphs one (1) through thirty-eight (38), inclusive, of Count I of this Complaint are realleged and incorporated herein by reference as though fully set forth herein.

50. The Plaintiff, Jack Doe, a minor, by and through his mother and next friend, Jane L. Doe, is the natural brother of the Plaintiff's decedent, Mary Ann Doe.

51. The Plaintiff, Jack Doe, was riding in the motor vehicle with his sister on November 20, 1990 when the motor vehicle was involved in the above-described collision.

52. As a direct result of the negligence of the Defendant, Spaulding and Evenflo Companies, Inc., the Plaintiff, Jack Doe, was caused to witness the infliction of tortuous injuries upon his sister and to experience the consequential effects thereof.

53. As a further direct and proximate result thereof, the Plaintiff, Jack Doe, has been caused to suffer severe emotional, nervous and mental disturbance, resulting in physical illness and injury, including, but not limited to, nausea, headaches, nightmares, depression, and post-traumatic stress, all or some of which mental and emotional condition is permanent.

WHEREFORE, the premises considered, the Plaintiff, Jack Doe, a minor, by and through his mother and next friend, Jane L. Doe, demands judgment against the Defendant, Spaulding and Evenflo Companies, Inc., in the sum of Five Million Dollars ($5,000,000.00) plus attorney's fees, costs, interest and such other and further relief as the nature of the case may require.

JURY DEMAND

Each of the Plaintiffs herein demand trial by jury as to all issues herein.

Representative Cases

Kentrup v. **Century Products, Inc.**
US District Court, E.D. Ky., No 82-117, Apr. 14, 1984
$244,059 settlement for the wrongful death of 2-year-old child who was thrown from a child car seat during a head-on-collision. While the child was strapped into a child car seat in the front seat of a Plymouth Horizon, another vehicle struck the car head-on at approximately 50 mph. The child flew from the seat and struck the interior of the car, resulting in fatal injuries. Plaintiffs brought an action against Century Products, Inc., the manufacturer of the car seat, and Sears, the retailer, alleging that the car seat buckle was inadequate in that it could be easily unfastened by a child or become unsnapped upon minor impact.
Phillips, Kurt A. : Covington, KY

Mannino v. **International Manufacturing Co.**
650 F.2d 846 (6th Cir.1981)
The Sixth Circuit Court of Appeals, reversing a directed verdict for the manufacturer of an infant car seat, finds reversible error in the exclusion of testimony by plaintiff's expert. Plaintiff, a 14-month old girl, was injured when the car she was riding in was involved in a collision and the strap of her infant seat broke, allowing her to be thrown into the dashboard. Plaintiff sought to call a biomechanical engineer who would testify that the infant seat was improperly designed and inadequately tested. The trial judge ruled that the expert was not properly qualified and did not have a proper basis for his opinion. At the end of plaintiff's case, the judge directed a verdict for the defendant. The court of appeals reverses, emphasizing that, while the admissibility of expert testimony is within the discretion of the trial judge, exclusion of testimony based on an erroneous legal standard is reversible. The court points out that under Fed. R. Evid. 702 the sole test for qualifying and expert is whether the witness's specialized knowledge would assist the trier of fact. In this case, the witness was clearly qualified by virtue of his

academic training and experience. Reservations of the trial judge regarding the weight if testimony should have been left to the jury. The court also holds that a proper basis for expert's testimony was shown. The witness stated that his opinion was based on his experience in bio - mechanics, and on information obtained at seminars and in articles in the field.

Fed. R. Evid. 703 permits an expert to base an opinion on facts or data reasonably relied on by experts in the field. The fact that such material may be inadmissible hearsay does not affect the admissibility of the opinion. The court finds that the basis of the proffered testimony met the standard of Rule 703 and that the expert's opinion on defective design of the car seat should have been admitted.
Shafran, Michael: Cleveland, OH

Nicholson v. **Century Products, Inc.**
U.S. District Court, E.D. Pa., No.81-3040, July 27, 1983
Structured settlement with a present value of $468,000 for a 3-year old child who suffered brain damage when her car seat failed to protect her in an accident. Plaintiff was strapped into a child car seat in the right front seat of a 1980 Pontiac Phoenix. Another vehicle, traveling in the opposite direction, crossed the center line and struck the Plaintiff's car head - on causing plaintiff's head to strike the dashboard, fracturing her skull. Plaintiff brought an action against Century Products, manufacturer of the car seat, alleging that it failed to provide adequate restraint for a child's upper torso and head and that the defendant failed to warn against using the seat in a forward facing position in the front of a vehicle.
McCarthy, Justin: West Chester, PA

Kentrup v. **Century Products, Inc.**
U.S. District Court, E.D. Ky., No. 82-117, Apr. 14, 1984
$244,059 settlement for the wrongful death of 2-year-old child who was thrown from a child car seat during a head-on-collision. While deceased was strapped into a child

car seat in the front seat of a Plymouth Horizon, another vehicle struck the car head-on at approximately 50 mph. The child flew from the seat and struck the interior of the car, resulting in fatal injuries. Plaintiffs brought an action against Century Products, Inc., the manufacturer of the car seat, and Sears, the retailer, alleging that the car seat buckle was inadequate in that it could be easily unfastened by a child or become unsnapped upon minor impact.
Phillips, Kurt A. : Covington, KY

Schleininger v. **Questor Corp.**
200 Cal. Rptr. 634 (Cal. App. 1984)
3 month old infant was strapped into a Questor "Infant seat" infant carrier, which was secured in the family car by a lap style seat belt. Plaintiff's mother swerved to avoid a collision by and hit a concrete abutment. Plaintiff was thrown against the dashboard while strapped in the Infant seat. Head injuries resulting in severe retardation. Other passengers, who were wearing seat belts, sustained only minor injuries. Defendant has advertised the Infant seat for use in cars for 20 years and had ceased such advertising 2 years prior to the accident. Plaintiff alleged that only positive warnings of danger would eliminate the promotional effect of the long advertising campaign. Defendants argued that they were not liable because other manufacturers were producing non-crash worthy baby seats and selling them without warnings against use in the cars. Defense jury verdict reversed by appellate court which held that in products liability cases, industry custom is irrelevant to the issue of defect and the state of the art in products liability refers to industry capability, not custom and practice.
Younger, Milton: Bakersfield, CA
Stiles, David: Bakersfield, CA

Chapter 8

Discovery in Defective Child Restraint Cases

Discovery in a defective child restraint case can be expensive and time consuming. Yet the information that can be gleaned from thorough and precise discovery can be very useful in framing your case. The information obtained during discovery allows the attorney to get a feel for the theories and contentions that the other side intends to use at trial and of the evidence that the other side will be present at trial. Sometimes attorneys forget the purpose of discovery and use it as a tool to harass, intimidate, or bring their opponent down to his knees in blatant violation of the court rules.

Interrogatories

For the purpose of this book, discovery has been broken down into two sections: Interrogatories and requests to admit being written, and depositions being oral. Interrogatories and depositions offer the attorney yet very different yet valuable ways of obtaining information. On the one hand, the deposition allows the attorney to question witnesses in a spontaneous, face to face setting. On the other hand, a carefully worded interrogatory can yield information that is not only precise, but which may be detailed and prepared after careful thought. A major disadvantage of using interrogatories is that it also gives opposing counsel the opportunity to object as to interrogatories that his client does not wish to answer. In such instances, a motion to compel may be necessary when timely responses to interrogatories are not forthcoming. If such an action needs to be taken, the plaintiff's attorney is well advised to seek sanctions when filing the motion to compel.

Interrogatories are defined in Black's Law Dictionary as:

> "a discovery device consisting of written questions about the case submitted by one party to the other party

> or witness. The answers to the interrogatories are usually given under oath, i.e., the person answering the questions signs a sworn statement that the answers are true." FR Civ P 33.

We have included a series of interrogatory questions applicable to a generic defective child restraint accident.

With these as a nucleus the reader can supplement with specific questions to obtain all discoverable material pertinent to his specific situation.

A good set of interrogatories should accomplish the following purposes:

1. identify the manufacturer,
2. identification of component manufacturers,
3. identification of dealers of merchandise,
4. identify the design and testing process used by the defendant,
5. identify government standards that are applicable,
6. treatises used,
7. patents used by the manufacturer,
8. available state-of-the-art safety test conducted,
9. marketing of the product to include sale, distribution, warranties, advertising, prior warnings, and instructions provided with the product,
10. foreseeable misuses of the product,
11. subsequent measures taken by the manufacturers that show improvements in the basic design or subsequent safety measures added to the product,
12. anticipated use of the product,
13. anticipated misuse of the product,
14. alterations or modifications of the product,
15. any prior claims and injuries as a result of the product,
16. recalls of the product, and

17. any other legal actions or suits filed or pending against the manufacturer.

We have found that judges will often not give us everything we ask for at first but will narrow discovery requests initially and gradually allow expansion.

Remember under the rules of evidence you are entitled to the information so keep plugging away. Be persistent. Build a record for appeal purposes and be ready, willing and able to take the judge up on an interlocutory appeal whenever necessary. But, make sure to tailor your interrogatories and requests to match the theory of your case, or you be subject to rule 11 type sanctions for propounding too many interrogatories.

State Restrictions on Interrogatories

Below we have prepared a chart that shows restrictions (if any) placed upon the number of interrogatories or on the format of such interrogatories.

STATE	RESTRICTIONS
Alabama	No restrictions.
Alaska	No restrictions.
Arizona	No restrictions.
Arkansas	No restrictions.
California	Must use official form interrogatories. Can include up to 35 additional special interrogatories. There can be no subparts in the special interrogatories. No definitions can be included except those specified by statute.
Colorado	No restrictions.
Connecticut	No restrictions.
Delaware	No restrictions.
Florida	Limit of 25 interrogatories. Subparts are counted as separate interrogatories.
Georgia	Limit of 50 interrogatories. Subparts are counted as separate interrogatories.
Hawaii	No restrictions.
Idaho	Limit of 4 interrogatories. Subparts counted as separate interrogatories.

STATE	RESTRICTIONS
Illinois	No restrictions.
Indiana	No restrictions.
Iowa	No restrictions.
Kansas	No restrictions.
Kentucky	Limit of 3 interrogatories. Subparts counted as separate interrogatories.
Louisiana	No restrictions.
Maine	No restrictions.
Maryland	Limit of 30 interrogatories. Subparts counted as subpart interrogatories.
Massachusetts	Limit of 30 interrogatories. Subparts counted as separate interrogatories.
Michigan	No restrictions.
Minnesota	Limit of 50 interrogatories.
Mississippi	No restrictions.
Missouri	No restrictions.
Montana	No restrictions.
Nebraska	No restrictions.
Nevada	Limit of 40 interrogatories and subparts counted as separate interrogatories.
New Hampshire	No restrictions.
New Jersey	No restrictions.
New Mexico	No restrictions.
New York	No restrictions.
North Carolina	Limit of 50 interrogatories. Subparts counted as separate interrogatories.
North Dakota	No restrictions.
Ohio	No restrictions.
Oklahoma	Limit of 30 interrogatories. Subparts counted as separate interrogatories.
Oregon	No restrictions.
Pennsylvania	No restrictions.
Rhode Island	Limit of 30 interrogatories.
South Carolina	Limit of 50 interrogatories. Subparts counted separately.
South Dakota	No restrictions.

STATE	RESTRICTIONS
Tennessee	No restrictions.
Texas	Requires no more than 30 answers.
Utah	No restrictions.
Vermont	No restrictions.
Virginia	Limit of 30 interrogatories. Subparts count as separate interrogatories.
Washington	No restrictions.
West Virginia	No restrictions.
Wisconsin	No restrictions.
Wyoming	No restrictions.

Sample Interrogatories

DEFINITIONS

These interrogatories all relate to the specific vehicle model known as the (Manufacturer) (Model) child safety seat or booster seat. Unless otherwise indicated, make the following interpretations given to the words and phrases indicated below:

a. "Accident" shall be understood to refer to the particular accident which is the subject matter of this lawsuit.

b. "The Plaintiff's Vehicle" shall be understood to mean the vehicle owned, occupied, or operated by the Plaintiff which was involved in the alleged occurrence.

c. The letters "CSS" shall be understood to mean "child safety seat."

d. The letters "CRD" shall be understood to mean "child restraint device."

e. "Identify," when referring to a person shall include, (1) his or her name, (2) address at the time referred to, (3) present or last known address, (4) employer at the time referred to and employer's address, (5) present employer and employer's address, and (6) position, title and responsibilities at the time referred to and present or most recent position, title and responsibilities.

f. "Document," includes any statement, paper, writing, letter, memorandum, report, log book, note, article, magazine, sketch, book, text book, brochures, laboratory records, audio or video tape, record, recording, photograph, moving picture, negative, computer tape or disk, or any other object containing a written, printed, spoken, electronic, or photographic image, record or sound.

g. "Identify," when referring to a document shall include: (1) the location of the document and its custodian or possessor, (2) the identity of the maker or author of the document, (3) the identity of the person(s) to whom the document was directed, (4) the date on which the document was made or prepared, and (5) if a book, journal or other publication, its name and publisher and the volume, date, issue and pages in which the document appears.

h. "Test" or "Tests" includes any examination, experiment, accident simulation or trial to ascertain or evaluate the characteristics of a part, parts or group of assembled parts.

i. "You" refers to the named defendant, e.g. Century Products Corp., or another; similarly YOUR is to be construed as an extension of the word YOU indicating the sense of "or pertaining to." The words YOU and YOUR shall be taken to include all agents, employees, employee's agents, attorneys, investigators, consultants and anyone else acting on YOUR or their behalf.

l. "Person" includes a natural person, firm, association, organization, partnership, business trust, corporation or public entity.

m. "Custodian" refers to the PERSON having possession, custody, or control.

n. "Describe" or "specify" means:

1. Describe fully and in detail by reference to underlying fact rather than by reference to ultimate facts or conclusions of facts or law; and

2. Where applicable particularize as to (1) time, (2) place, and (3) manner; and

3. Set forth all relevant facts necessary to the complete understanding of the act, process, event or thing in question.

o. Subject of this lawsuit means (Manufacturer) (Model) Child Safety Seat (serial #)

1. Please set forth the name, address, and job title of the person or persons answering these interrogatories on your behalf.

2. If you are a corporation, please set forth:

   a. the date of incorporation;

   b. the state or jurisdiction of incorporation;

   c. the address of your principal place of business at the time of the occurrence herein;

   d. the address of your principal place of business at the present time; and

   e. whether you have been legally qualified to transact business within the state of _______ and if so, the date upon which you qualified to do business in the state of __________.

3. Please state whether, within the last ten years, you have done business under any other name, including a fictitious name, and further state:

   a. each said alternative or fictitious name;

   b. the jurisdiction and/or political subdivision, if any, in which any registration statement or fictitious name statement is filed;

   c. whether you are doing business under such alternative or fictitious name in any jurisdiction at the present time;

   d. identify by name each such jurisdiction.

4. Please state whether you were the manufacturer of the child safety seat and if so, please state:

   a. the date upon which the child safety seat was manufactured;

b. the address of the factory and/or such other place at which child safety seat was manufactured;

c. whether, at the time of the manufacture of the child safety seat, you had a quality control department and/or individual, or a department and/or individual denominated by a different name which was primarily responsible for quality control procedures for the child safety seats; and

d. if you answer to the foregoing subpart was in the affirmative, the identity of the supervisor and/or person primarily responsible for implementing the quality control procedures, if any, respecting the manufacturer of the child safety seat.

e. The retail or wholesale establishment(s) to which the product was shipped, and the approximate date(s) of shipment(s);

f. If the defendant has any record of sale to wholesaler(s) or retailer(s), date, number, serial number, and other identification features of such record(s), and the name, title and address of each person who has custody of any such records;

g The name and address of each person in defendant's employ who made the shipment to retailer(s) or wholesaler(s).

5. Do you perform any auxiliary services in relation to the sale, use, or servicing of the subject child safety seat or similar child safety seats?

6. If the answer to the preceding interrogatory is in the affirmative, please state as to each such service:

a. A description of the service in complete detail;

b. The exact nature of the obligation assumed by you for maintenance of the product;

c. The names and addresses of the persons in your employment or contracted by you who performed maintenance on the subject child safety seat or similar child safety seats;

d. The relationship of the persons performing maintenance of the subject child safety seat or similar child safety seats;

e. All reports of malfunctioning made at the time of maintenance or servicing of the subject child safety seat or similar child safety seats, with an exact description of the malfunction and the action taken to correct it;

f. Describe as accurately as possible any and all tests or inspections made at the time of maintenance to ascertain the subject child safety seat's performance; and

g. Give the name, title, and address of persons having custody of all records relating to each such service.

7. Do you contend that any other person and/or business entity was the manufacturer of the child safety seat?

8. If your answer to the foregoing interrogatory was in the affirmative, please identify by name, business, and residence address, and telephone number any person and/or entity which you contend to be the original manufacturer of the child safety seat, and further set forth:

a. whether you presently have any contractual relationship with the person and/or entity identified and if so, the nature of such ownership interest;

b. whether you have any ownership interest in the person and/or business entity identified in this interrogatory and if so, the nature of such ownership interest;

c. whether you have at any time acquired the assets and/or liabilities of the person and/or entity referred to in your answer to this interrogatory and if so, the means by which such assets or liabilities were acquired; and

d. an identification, with such specificity as you would require in a motion to produce, of each and every document pertaining to your acquisition of the assets and liabilities of any such person and/or entity.

9. Have there been other notices, claims, statements, lawsuits, or complaints of other incidents or similar incidents involving the subject child safety seat or similar child safety seats where it is specifically alleged that the subject child safety seat or similar child safety seat was defectively designed in that the design of the child safety seat permitted the child to suffer injuries? If so, then for each such claim, complaint, lawsuit, notice or statement, state:

   a. The substance of the complaint and the date defendant became aware of it;

   b. The name and address of the person or entity making the complaint;

   c. How the claim was communicated to defendant;

   d. Whether a lawsuit was filed, and if so:

      i. The court where initiated;

      ii. The case number;

      iii. The name of plaintiff's attorney;

      iv. The disposition of the lawsuit.

10. Did the defendant or any agent or employee of the defendant have any knowledge of the existence of any alleged defect or defective condition of the subject child safety seat and/or similar child safety seats prior to the alleged occurrence?

11. If the answer to the preceding interrogatory is in the affirmative, please state:

   a. When the defendant or any agent or employee of the defendant first learned of the existence of each such alleged defective condition, give the date and time;

   b. How the defendant or any agent or employee of the defendant learned of the existence of each such defect or defective condition;

c. What action or actions, if any, the defendant or any agent or employee of the defendant took to remove, repair or correct each such defect or defective condition so as to safeguard the plaintiff.

12. Do you contend that any other person and/or business entity was the manufacturer of the subject child safety seat?

13. If you answer to the preceding interrogatory was yes, please identify the name, business and residence address, and telephone number of any person or entity which you contend to the original manufacturer of the subject child safety seat.

14. As to each person or entity identified in your answer to the foregoing interrogatory, please set forth:

a. whether you presently have any contractual relationship with said person or entity and if so the nature of such contractual relationship;

b. whether you have any ownership interest in said person and/or business entity;

c. whether you have at any time acquired the assets and/or liabilities of said person and/or entity;

d. an identification, with such particularity as you would require in a motion to produce, of each and every document pertaining to your acquisition of said assets and/or liabilities.

15. Please identify, with such particularity as you would require in a motion to produce, any and all production specifications formulated and/or utilized by you in the manufacture of the child safety seat.

16 .As to each such document and/or writing referred to in your answer to the preceding interrogatory, please identify by name, business and residence address, and telephone number the present custodian of any such writing or document.

17. Please set forth the name, business and residence address, telephone number and job title of each person who had a responsibility to oversee or supervise the manufacture of the child safety seat.

18. Please set forth the name, business and residence address, telephone number and job title of each person who had a responsibility to oversee or supervise the design of the child safety seat.

19. As to each such person identified in your answer to either of the foregoing two interrogatories, please set forth:

    a. a description of their education, work experience or other qualifications considered by you before investing such person(s) with such responsibility and/or authority.

20. Please state whether you designed the child safety seat.

21. If your answer to the foregoing interrogatory was in the affirmative, please further set forth:

    a. the date or dates upon which the child safety seat was designed;

    b. the location of the facility, if applicable, where the child safety seat was designed;

    c. the name of the person and/or persons who participated in the design;

    d. an identification, with such specificity as you would require in a motion to produce, of each and every drawing, plan, or document relating to the design of the child safety seat;

    e. the name, business and residence address, and telephone number of the present custodian of each document identified in your answer to the preceding subpart, and

    f. whether any such document, plan or drawing identified in your answer to subpart (d) has been submitted to any governmental entity for approval, registration, or patent, and if so, the day of said submission and entity to which such document was submitted.

22. Please state whether the personal safety of the user of the child safety seat was considered in the process of designing the child safety seat.

23. If your answer to the foregoing interrogatory was in the affirmative, please further set forth:

    a. whether the design you selected embodied actual or potential safety hazard which were actually anticipated and/or considered by you;

    b. if your answer to the foregoing subpart was in affirmative, the nature of each such safety hazard or risk actually considered by you in selecting the design of the child safety seat;

    c. the means by which any actual or potential safety risks inherent in the design of the child safety seat were identified and/or evaluated by you;

    d. the identity of any person or persons, if applicable, who had the ultimate responsibility to identify actual or potential safety risks inherent in the design of the child safety seat; and

    e. whether there existed a person, department, or other entity charged with the responsibility of determining the means by which actual or potential safety risks anticipated by you would be addressed or considered in the ultimate design of the child safety seat.

24. Please state whether in the design of the child safety seat, you considered the anticipated safety expectations of the ordinary consumer of the child safety seat.

25. If you answer to the foregoing interrogatory was in the affirmative, please further set forth:

    a. what safety expectations you anticipated would be held by the ordinary consumer of the child safety seats;

    b. whether you contend that any anticipated safety expectation of the consumer was or is inconsistent or incompatible with the utility or intended use of the child safety seat;

c. the means by which the safety expectations to the ordinary consumer were identified by you;

d. the means by which the safety expectations of the ordinary consumer were incorporated or utilized by you in the design of the child safety seat.

26. Did you determine that there were any actual and/or potential means by which the child safety seat could or would be misused?

27. If your answer to the foregoing interrogatory was in the affirmative, please further set forth:

a. each actual and/or potential misuse of the child safety seat which you anticipated;

b. the means by which each such actual and/or potential misuse of the child safety seat was identified by you;

c. the measures taken by you, if any, in the design of the child safety seat to mitigate the safety hazards posed by such actual and/or potential misuse, and

d. whether you undertook to warn the consumers of the child safety seat of the safety risks posed by each such actual and/or potential misuse, and the means by which you undertook to do so.

28. Please identify any and all statutes, ordinances, or other regulatory directives of any nature of description which pertain or relate to the design of the child safety seat at the time of manufacture.

29. As to each such statute, rule, or other regulatory directive identified in your answer to the foregoing interrogatory, please further set forth:

a. the date upon which such statute, ordinance, or regulation was promulgated, and by whom;

b. whether you contend that the design of the child safety seat comports in all respects with any such statute, ordinance, or other regulatory directive;

c. if your answer to the foregoing subpart to this interrogatory was in the negative, the reason for any such deviation from such statute, ordinance, or regulation;

d. whether you developed any test, protocol, or procedure to insure that the design of the child safety seat comported in all respects with such statutes, ordinances, regulations, and;

e. the name, business and residence address, and telephone number of the current custodian of such test, protocol and procedure.

30. Please identify any text or treatises pertaining to the design (or manufacture) of products similar to the child safety seat of which you were aware at the time of the design (or manufacture) of the child safety seat.

31. Please state whether the child safety seat is the subject of a current patent, or in the alternative, whether application has been made for a patent which has not yet been granted.

32. If you answer to the foregoing interrogatory was in the affirmative, please further set forth:

a. the date that such outstanding application was made and/or granted;

b. an identification, with such particularity as you would require in a motion to produce, of each and every writing relating to such patent or application; and

c. the name, business, and residence address, and telephone number of the present custodian of any writing identified in your answer to the preceding subpart to this interrogatory.

33. Do you contend that, with due regard for the technological environment existing at the date of manufacture of the product, the product was designed (or manufactured) in accordance with the "state of the art" design (or manufac-

turing) techniques existing as of the date of said design (or manufacture)?

34. If your answer to the foregoing interrogatory was in the affirmative, please further set forth:

    a. any technological or scientific limitations upon the design (or manufacture) of the child safety seat which existed as of the date of said design (or manufacture) and which such limitations had been removed or ameliorated as of the date that these interrogatories are answered;

    b. whether you were aware of such technological limitations as of the date of the design (or manufacture) of the child safety seat;

    c. an identification, with such particularity as you would require in a motion to produce, of each and every writing relating to any such technological limitation which you contend existed as of the date of the design (or manufacture) of the child safety seat;

    d. the name, business and residence address, and telephone number of the current custodian of any writing identified in your answer to the foregoing subpart of this interrogatory.

35. Please state whether there existed, as of the date that the product was manufactured, any design or performance standard applicable or potentially applicable to the child safety seat.

36. If your answer to the foregoing interrogatory was in the affirmative, please further set forth:

    a. a description of each such design and/or performance standard;

    b. the person, entity, or other source which promulgated such design and/or performance standard;

c. the document, register, or index, if any, in which such design and/or performance standard is published in written form;

d. whether you considered the requirements of such design and/or performance standard in the design (or manufacture) of the child safety seat;

e. an identification, with such particularity as you would require in a motion to produce, of each and every writing relating to said design and/or performance standard or your consideration thereof; and

f. the name, business and residence address, and telephone number of the present custodian of any writing identified in your answer to the foregoing subpart of this interrogatory.

37. Please state whether you performed any test, of whatever nature or description, for the purpose of determining whether the child safety seat was reasonably safe for its intended uses and/or misuse foreseen by you.

38. If your answer to the foregoing interrogatory is in the affirmative, please further set forth:

a. a description of each such test conducted by you;

b. the date and location where each such test was conducted;

c. whether there existed a written protocol or format pertaining to each such test and, if so, please describe each such written protocol or format with such particularity as you would require in a motion to produce;

d. whether any aspect of any such test was recorded or memorialized in any document or writing, including photographs, films, videotapes, or other visual representations of whatever nature or description;

e. an identification, with such particularity as you would require in a motion to produce, of each such document, writing, or visual representation;

f. the means by which each test protocol or format was evaluated for the purpose of determining whether it constituted a reasonable replication of the intended uses or foreseeable misuses to which the child safety seat would be put;

g. whether the results of any such test or tests were submitted, or referred to in any manner whatsoever, in any document filed with or tendered to any public entity or regulatory agency;

h. the name, business and residence address, and telephone number of the persons(s)charged with the responsibility to evaluate the performance of the child safety seat in each such test referred to in your answers to the preceding subparts of this interrogatory;

i. the name, business and residence address, and telephone number of the present custodian of any document, writing, or visual representations set forth in your answers to any of the subparts of this interrogatory.

39. What items were included as a standard equipment on the subject child safety seat?

40. What items were included as optional equipment on the subject child safety seat?

41. Did the defendant use, assemble, or incorporate into the subject child safety seat, any parts or components manufactured by any person, firm, or corporation other than defendant?

42. If the answer to the preceding interrogatory is in the affirmative, please state for each such component part:

a. Its designation, or name, as determined by common industry usage, of the part;

b. An exact description of the component part, including dimension and specifications, as received by defendant;

c. The function of the part in relation to the child safety seat shell and liner;

d. The exact location of the part in relation to the child safety seat shell;

e. The name and present address of the person, firm, corporation, or partnership that manufactured, assembled, or otherwise produced the part; and

f. The name and address of each person who has control and custody of any records relating to the ordering and use of the component parts.

43. State the name and address of the person(s) who actually designed the subject child safety seat or had the overall responsibility for the design of the components involved.

44. Will you voluntarily make the above person(s) available for deposition?

45. Did you consider or, have you considered, any alternative approach to the design or construction of the subject child safety seat? If so, please state:

a. Describe in detail each and every alternate approach;

b. Describe in detail the objections to or reasons why you did not follow or adopt such alternative approach;

c. Describe any and all predictive analysis, studies, tests, investigations, or examinations which relate to or reflect your consideration or each alternative approach to the design or construction of the subject child safety seat, by stating the name of the author(s), title of the document containing or reflecting both the performance of any the results of any such predictive analysis, study, test, investigation or examination and the date(s) on which the same was or were conducted and completed, and if you will do so without a motion to produce, please attach a copy of same to your answers to these interrogatories.

46. Has defendant in any way changed the design or construction of the subject child safety seat is manufactured or assembled? If so, then:

a. Describe any such change;

b. State what is or was the purpose of any such change;

c. State on what date or dates any such changes were accomplished and/or completed or when you anticipate they will be accomplished;

d. State the name, address and relationship to you of the person who has in his custody copies of any and all documents relating to or reflecting any such change;

e. Describe and identify each and every document that reflects any and all such changes, and if you will do so without a motion to produce, attach a copy of same to your answers to these interrogatories;

f. State what the increase or decrease of the cost to you of any such change is.

47. Has the defendant changed or is it contemplating any change in the design of the subject child safety seat, or any similar child safety seats? Is so, then:

a. Describe any such change;

b. State what is or was the purpose of any such change;

c. State on what date or dates any such changes were accomplished and/or completed or when you anticipate they will be accomplished;

d. State the name, address and relationship to you of the person who has in his custody copies of any and all documents relating to or reflecting any such change;

e. Describe and identify each and every document that reflects any and all such changes, and if you will do so without a motion to produce, attach a copy of same to your answers to these interrogatories;

f. State what the increase or decrease of the cost to you of any such change is.

48. Were any pamphlets, instruction booklets, brochures, manuals, labels, or other printed matter distributed in conjunction with the sale or distribution of:

a. the subject child safety seat;

b. similar child safety seats?

49. If the answer to the preceding interrogatory is in the affirmative, please set forth in complete detail, for each such booklet, manual, pamphlet, brochure or piece of printed matter:

    a. Its purpose;

    b. Its complete and verbatim contents;

    c. Its size, in number of pages, number of lines of print per page, number of diagrams, charts, etc;

    d. The colors used;

    e. The sizes of print used;

    f. The name, address and job title of the person who composed or formulated the writing and the name and address of the person who ordered it distributed with the product, the subject child safety seat and/or similar child safety seats, and

    g. The name and address of each person who has custody of any records relating to the composition and the distribution of it.

50. Describe the method of distribution and delivery of the subject child safety seat.

51. When was the subject child safety seat first put on the market by defendant?

52. If the subject child safety seat was inspected at any place or at any point in its path of distribution, please state:

    a. The occasions on which the subject child safety seat was inspected;

    b. What said inspection consists of;

    c. Date and location of any such inspection of the "product" which was involved in said incident;

    d. Name, address, and relationship to you of the person who conducted any such inspection of the "product" which was involved in said incident;

e. Identify any and all documents relating to or reflecting the conduct and the results of any such inspection of the child safety seat involved in said incident and if you will do so without a motion to produce, attach a copy of all said documents to your answers to these interrogatories.

53. Please list, by name and address, all persons, firms, or corporations who had control or possession and/or ownership of the child safety seat at any time prior to the plaintiff's alleged occurrence and with whom the defendant had any written or oral agreement concerning the product.

54. Please give the name, title and last known address of the person who has custody of the records concerning the delivery of the child safety seat or similar products, model numbers, quantity, prices, etc., to the establishments listed in the answer to the preceding interrogatory at or about and before the time of the alleged occurrence.

56. Describe your quality assurance program i.e., your efforts and activities conducted for the purpose of ascertaining whether the finished product conforms to your design criteria for the subject child safety seat.

57. If the harness was the subject of any test, study, calculation or examination as part of your quality assurance program, then state:

a. Name and job title of person by whom it was conducted;

b. The date on which it was conducted;

c. The place at which said testing was conducted;

d. The results of each test, study, calculation, or examination;

e. The name and address of the person who has in his custody and all reports (including attachments and exhibits thereto) of any such test, study, calculations, or examinations;

f. Will you voluntarily make the person(s) listed in answers 27(a) and 27(e) available for deposition?

58. Describe or identify by appropriate citation or reference each and every (a) corporate standard specification or requirement; (b) industry standard or custom; (c) governmental standard, specification or regulation; (d) trade association or other professional standard, specification, requirement or regulation which applies to the design or performance of the subject child safety seat which the subject child safety seat was designed to comply with or exceed.

59. Describe and identify any document, by whatever name called, which reflects or is related to any standard, specification or regulation identified in response to the preceding interrogatory and defendant's compliance therewith.

60. Describe any and all predictive analysis, studies, tests, investigations or examinations which relate to or reflect the hazard identified in the table of definitions associated with the subject child safety seat or similar child safety seats by name of the author(s), title of the document containing or reflecting both the performance of any the results of each such predictive analysis, study, test, investigations, or examination and the date(s) on which the same was or were conducted and completed, and if you will do so without a motion to produce, attach a copy of same to your answers to these interrogatories.

61. Does the defendant attempt to ascertain the existence of malfunctions or complaints associated with the subject child safety seat or similar child safety seats? If so, then state:

a. If this is done in the usual and ordinary course of business;

b. The name, job title, and relationship to you of the person(s) who perform this function or the name of any agency, division, affiliate, etc., who performs this function for you; and

c. When and how this activity is conducted.

d. Will you voluntarily make the person(s) listed in the answer 61(b) available for deposition?

62. Describe any and all documents which relate to the performance of or the results of any study, test, investigation, or examination conducted by you or on your behalf or known to you, which relates to or reflects malfunctions or complaints associated with any component on the subject child safety seat or similar child safety seats, and the date on which the same was or were conducted and completed, and if you will do so without a motion to produce, attach a copy of same to your answers to these interrogatories.

63. Does the defendant have a safety department or employees whose jobs or functions include availability for consultation or the making of recommendations or some kind of input into the design and manufacturing process of said product with regard to safety? If so, then state:

a. The name address, job titles, and division and/or department of any such person or persons;

b. Which of these persons were consulted during the design and manufacture of the subject child safety seat;

c. Will you make these persons available for deposition?

64. If you will do so without a request to produce, attach copies of any and all documents or writings identified in your response to the preceding interrogatory above to your answers to these interrogatories.

65. Has the defendant conducted, within the past 20 years, any recall campaigns, operations, programs, or activities for similar products, comparable products, the subject child safety seat, or similar child safety seats it has assembled, manufactured or marketed?

66. If the answer to the preceding interrogatory is in the affirmative, please describe in complete detail each such recall campaign, operation, program, or activity, including, but not limiting the answer to such information as:

a. The exact date of the announcement or beginning of the activity;

b. The purpose of the activity, in terms of potential or real defects sought to be corrected or checked;

c. The types or models of child safety seats involved in the campaign or activity;

d. The number of child safety seats of each type or model, referred to in part (c) of the answer to this interrogatory, sought to be examined or corrected;

e. The number of child safety seats of each type actually examined or corrected;

f. Whether the child safety seat was examined or corrected;

g. The date and locations of the examination or correction of the product;

h. The name and address of the person performing the examination or correction of the product;

i. The name, title, and address of each person having custody of any records relating to the activity.

67. Was the use to which the "product" was put, as described in the Plaintiff's pleadings, a use which the defendant anticipated?

68. Did the defendant, at any time prior to the plaintiff's alleged occurrence, take any actions or precautions whatsoever to avert or warn against possible damage or injuries that have resulted from known or potential hazards, dangers, defects or defective conditions in the "product" and similar products?

69. If the answer to the preceding interrogatory is in the affirmative, please describe in complete detail each such action or precaution taken, including such information as:

a. The specific hazard, danger, defect, or defective condition intended to be addressed, averted, or corrected by the precaution;

b. How the action or precaution altered the product or the appearance of the product and similar products;

c. How the users of the product and similar products were made aware of any actions or precautions taken by the defendant;

d. The name, address, and job title of the agent or employee of the defendant who first detected or suspected the hazard, danger defect, or defective condition in similar products;

e. The date on which the action or precaution was taken or initiated;

f. The name, address and job title of the agent or employee of the defendant who ordered or directed that the action or precaution be taken;

g. The name, title and address of each person who has custody of any records relating to the actions and precautions mentioned in the answer to this interrogatory.

70. Is it the contention of the defendant that the alleged occurrence was caused in whole or in part by some person or persons other than the defendant?

71. If the answer to the preceding interrogatory is in the affirmative, please state fully:

a. The full identity of each such person, firm or corporation, including name, occupation, title, address and professional relationship to the defendant if any;

b. How or in what manner each such other person, etc., caused or contributed to cause the alleged occurrence.

72. Does the defendant contend that the alleged occurrence was caused in whole or in part because of some defect or defective condition in a part, component, or processed material supplied to the defendant by some third party?

73. If the answer to the preceding interrogatory is in the affirmative, please state:

a. A complete description of the part, component or processed material involved;

b. A complete description of the alleged defect or defective condition in it;

c. The name, address and occupation of the person or corporation who supplied the part, component, or processed material to the defendant.

74. Give the name, address, place of employment, home and business telephone number, job title, and capacity and last known whereabouts of:

a. Any person known to you, your agents, employees, or your attorneys who witnessed the incident, or were in its vicinity before, at the time of, or just after its occurrence.

b. Any private individual or firm representative known to you, your agents, your employees or your attorneys who possesses or claims to possess knowledge or information of any facts or record relevant to the occurrence or occurrences herein involved.

75. Have you, your agents, investigators, or your attorneys, or anyone acting on your behalf, obtained any kind of written, recorded, stenographically transcribed, oral or any other type of statement from the plaintiff. If so, please state for each such statement:

a. The date on which such statement was taken;

b. The type of each such statement taken, whether written oral, recorded or transcribed;

c. The name, address and employer of the present custodian of each such statement;

d. The name, address and employer of the person taking the statement;

e. Please attach a copy of each such statement to your answers to these interrogatories.

76. State the full name address, occupation and employer of any and all such persons who have investigated this incident for or on behalf of you, your agents, your attorneys, etc.

77. Please set forth the names, addresses and employers of all persons contacted regarding the incident by such investigators, yourself, your attorneys, and/or your agents.

78. As to all persons whose names are set forth in the answers to these preceding interrogatories, have you, your agents, investigators or attorneys, or anyone acting on your behalf obtained statements of any kind, whether written, oral, recorded, stenographically transcribed, or otherwise from any of the persons so named in these answers to interrogatories. If so, for each such person, please state:

   a. The name, occupation and address of each person;

   b. The type of statement which was taken (whether written, oral recorded, or transcribed);

   c. The name and address of the present custodian of each statement so taken;

   d. The date on which the statement was taken;

   e. Please attach a copy of each statement to your answers to these interrogatories.

79. Have you or your attorney or anyone else on your behalf consulted with any person holding himself out to be an expert or consultant in any field with respect to any of the issues in this case (including medical issues, products liability, and accident reconstruction), including any person employed by your attorneys to assist them in the preparation of your case. If so, state:

   a. The name, address and field of expertise of each such person;

   b. The date of the first contact or consultation with each such person and the name of each person contacting him on your behalf;

c. The dates of all subsequent contact or consultations with him and the name of each person contacting him on your behalf;

d. Whether any written and/or oral report was made by such person;

e. The date of each such report, if any,

f. As to each such report, state whether it was written or oral;

g. As to each such report, state whether it was submitted pursuant to the individual's employment in an advisory capacity, a prospective witness capacity, or both;

h. The nature of the inquiry made by each such person and the subject matter investigated by each such person;

i. Whether you intend to call any of the aforementioned individuals as an expert witness at the time of trial;

j. The date on which you anticipate that you will know whether or not you will call any such person as an expert witness at the time of trial.

80. Do you have any maps, charts, or diagrams of the scene of this incident.

81. Do your attorneys have any maps, charts, or diagrams of the scene of this incident.

82. Do your investigators, or anyone acting on your behalf have any maps, charts, or diagrams of the scene of this incident.

83. Do you, your attorneys, investigators, or anyone acting on your behalf, have any photographs taken of any of the physical or mechanical objects or of the persons involved in this incident.

84. If your answer to Interrogatories 80–83 above is in the affirmative, then as to each state:

a. Identify and describe each map, chart, diagram or photograph which was made or taken;

b. State the date on which each map, chart, diagram or photograph was made or taken;

c. State the name, occupation and address of the person who made each map, chart or diagram, or took each photograph;

d. State the general subject matter of each photograph;

e. State the name, address and employer of the present custodian of each map, chart, diagram or photograph;

f. Attach a copy of each map, chart, diagram, or photograph to your answers to these interrogatories or indicate your willingness to allow Plaintiff to inspect and copy or photograph the same, at Plaintiff's expense.

85. Do you have any motion pictures of the plaintiff taken at anytime following the happening of this incident. If so, please state:

a. The dates on which each motion picture was taken;

b. The name, occupation, address and employer of the person, or persons, who took each motion picture;

c. The activities in which plaintiff was engaged at the time of each motion picture was taken;

d. State the name, occupation, address and employer of the present custodian of each motion picture;

e. Specify a time and place when these motion pictures may be viewed by counsel for plaintiff.

86. Do you know of any documents, papers, books, accounts, letters, photographs, motion pictures, drawings, plans objects, measurements, written descriptions or other tangible things containing evidence relating to this action and not previously listed herein. If so, as to each such item please state:

a. The nature and specific subject matter;

b. The date the same was made or taken;

c. The name, address and employer of the person making or taking the same;

d. The name, address, and employer of the person in whose custody the same now is;

e. The name, address and employer or the person at whose request such item was made or taken.

87. Were there any written reports made by anyone who investigated this incident on your behalf.

a. If so, what is the name and address of the person who presently has custody or possession of such report;

b. Please attach a copy of such reports to your answers to these interrogatories.

88. In the regular course of its business, did you or any agent, servant, employee or representative of you or your company, make or furnish to any insurance company or public authority, a report of the incident? If so, please state:

a. The date of each such report,

b. The name and address of the person who made such report;

c. The name and address of the insurance company and the public authority to which such report was made;

d. Please attach a copy of each such report to your answers to these interrogatories.

89. Do you have knowledge of any written report, statement, or record of testimony, whether written or not, and prepared by someone other than you or not, concerning anything other than previously set out in these interrogatories? If so, state:

a. The name and address of such person;

b. The nature of such report.

90. Is the defendant indemnified or covered by any policy of insurance for the occurrence involved in this case? If so, please state:

a. The name of the insurance company, policy number, date of issue of said policy and expiration date;

b. The amount and/or limits of liability of said coverage;

c. Where the policy was issued;

d. The manner in which insured received the policy;

e. The name, address, telephone number and job title or capacity at the time of issuance of the person who issued the policy;

f. The name, address, telephone number and the job title or capacity at the time of issuance of the person who authorized the issuance;

g. The scope of coverage;

h. The name, address, telephone number and job title or capacity at the time of issuance of each person who witnessed the issuance of the policy;

i. The dates of premium payments;

j. The amount of premium due on each date listed in the preceding subdivision;

k. The manner in which past premium payments have been made, (mailing, personal submission, etc.);

l. The media used for past payments of premium (cash, check, etc.);

m. The name, address, telephone number, and occupation of the person to whom the receipts of premium payments have been issued;

n. The name, address, telephone number and occupation of the person who paid the premiums;

o. If the defendant is covered by any policy of excess insurance, reinsurance, an umbrella policy, or any other type of insurance applicable to the incident alleged in this lawsuit, kindly provide answers to subsections a. through n. of this interrogatory with respect to each and every such policy and/or insurance coverage.

91. Has any insurance company disclaimed liability in this matter on an insurance policy which defendant alleges covered him for said loss? If so, set forth the name and address of the company issuing said policy, the date of said policy, the amount of said policy, and annex hereto a copy of said policy and the number of said policy.

92. Set forth the reasons that said company refused coverage under said policy.

93. Please state whether you distributed the child safety seat.

94. If your answer to the foregoing interrogatory was in the affirmative, please set forth:

    a. the date upon which you began to distribute the child safety seat or the product line of which the child safety seat was representative;

    b. the date upon which you stopped distributing the child safety seat or the product line of which the subject product was representative, if applicable;

    c. the date, if known to you, upon which the child safety seat itself was distributed by you (identification of the date of shipment of the lot number of which the child safety seat was a part shall be a sufficient response to this interrogatory);

    d. the name, title, and address of the person and/or entity who is the present custodian of each and every writing pertaining to the distribution of the child safety seat;

    e. whether the child safety seat was distributed from you to any other corporation and/or business entity whose primary business consisted of the distribution of the child safety seat itself, and if so, the name address, telephone number of each such distribution business and/or entity; and

    f. whether, when you distributed the child safety seat, the person and/or entity to whom you distributed the child safety seat acquired title thereof, and if so, whether the same occurred by virtue of a wholesale or retail sale.

95. Please state whether you issued any express warranty or guarantee as to the nature, quality, or fitness of the child safety seat.

96. If your answer to the foregoing interrogatory was in the affirmative, please further set forth:

    a. as nearly as possible, the exact wording of such warranty and/or guarantee;

    b. the date and place that such warranty or guarantee was issued;

    c. the identity of any person or persons known to you who participated in issuing such guarantee or warranty;

    d. whether such express warranty or guarantee was in writing; and

    e. the name, business and residence address, and telephone number of the present custodian of each such writing.

97. Whether or not you issued any express warranty or guarantee as to any aspect of the child safety seat, please set forth in detail the contend of any representation made by any person to the plaintiff herein regarding the nature, quality, fitness or performance of the child safety seat.

98. As to any such representation identified in your answer to the foregoing interrogatory, please set forth the purpose for which such representation wad made.

99. Please state whether the sale of the child safety seat gave rise to any implied warranty, including the implied warranty of fitness for intended use and/or the implied warranty of merchantability.

100. Please state whether you contend that you or any person or entity acting on your behalf disclaimed any other wise applicable implied warranty of merchantability.

101. Please state whether, at the time of the sale of the child safety seat, you or any person or entity acting on your

behalf disclaimed any otherwise applicable implied warranty of fitness for intended use.

102. If your answer to either of the foregoing two interrogatories is in the affirmative, please further set forth:

a. the nature of the implied warranty which you contend was disclaimed;

b. a description of the means by which you contend such implied warranty was disclaimed;

c. the nature of any claims or damages covered or excluded from the terms of such disclaimer;

d. whether any such disclaimer was embodied in a writing; and

e. the name, business and residence address and telephone number of the present custodian of any writing identified in your answers to the foregoing subpart of this interrogatory.

103. If you contend that you or any person acting on your behalf effectively disclaimed any otherwise applicable implied warranty of merchantability or fitness for intended use, please set forth in detail the means by which your disclaimer of such warranty was communicated by you to the plaintiff.

104. Please state whether the product was advertised by you in any written or print media prior to the occurrence which is the subject of the plaintiff's complaint.

105. If your answer to the foregoing interrogatory is in the affirmative, please further set forth:

a. an identification of the written or print media in which such advertisement appeared, including the date thereof;

b. the text of such advertisement (Note: it is sufficient compliance with this interrogatory for you to attach a copy of such text in lieu of setting forth the same verbatim herein;)

c. the name, business and residence address, and telephone number of each person known to you with responsibility for the composition and approval of such advertisement and;

d. the name, business and residence address, and telephone number of the present custodian of each and every such advertisement.

106. Please state whether the child safety seat was advertised by use of the broadcast media (television and/or radio) prior to the time of the occurrence which is the subject matter of plaintiff's complaint.

107. If your answer to the foregoing interrogatory was in the affirmative, please further set forth:

a. an identification of the broadcast media in which such advertisement appeared, including the date thereof;

b. the text of such advertisement (Note: it is sufficient compliance with this interrogatory for you to attach a copy of such text in lieu of setting forth the same verbatim herein);

c. the name, business and residence address, and telephone number of each person known to you with responsibility for the composition and approval of such advertisement; and

d. the name, business and residence address, and telephone number of the present custodian of each and every such advertisement.

108. Please state whether, at any time prior to the occurrence which is the subject of the plaintiff's complaint, you took any action designed to warn against possible safety hazards related to child safety seat.

109. If your answer to the foregoing interrogatory is in the affirmative, please further set forth:

a. the specific safety hazard which was the subject of any such action;

b. the nature of such action taken by you, and the means, if any by which you determined or identified the most effective means by which the existence of the hazard could be communicated to the ultimate user/consumer of the product;

c. if such action took the form of a written warning; the means, if any, by which it was determined how such a written warning should be worded;

d. the name, business and residence address and telephone number of the person(s) who actually drafted the wording of said warning;

e. an identification, with such specificity as you would require in a motion to produce, of each and every writing relating to the action or warning taken or provided by you, and;

f. the name, business and residence address, and telephone number of the present custodian of any writing identified in your answer to the foregoing subpart of this interrogatory.

110. Please state whether you provided any written instructions as to the use of the child safety seat.

111. If your answer to the foregoing interrogatory was in the affirmative, please further set forth:

a. complete verbatim contents of any such instruction(s) (Note: is shall be sufficient compliance with this interrogatory to attach a copy of such written instructions to your answers hereto in lieu of reproducing the contents of said instructions in answer to this interrogatory)

b. the name, business and residence address, and telephone number of the person(s) who drafted the wording of said instructions (Note: if said instructions were drafted as a joint product of a division or entity within your business, it shall be sufficient compliance with this interrogatory to provide the name, business and residence address, and telephone number of the person or persons with supervisory authority over the drafting and/or construction of said instructions at the time that the product was manufactured;

c. an identification, with such particularity as you would require in a motion to produce, of each and every writing relating to the composition of all printed matter distributed with or affixed to the product; and

d. the name business and residence address, and telephone number of the present custodian of any writing identified in your answer to the foregoing subpart of this interrogatory.

113. Did you make or cause to be made any changes in the design of the product following the date that the child safety seat was manufactured?

114. If your answer to the foregoing interrogatory was in the affirmative, please further set forth:

a. the nature of such design alteration or change;

b. the reason that such alteration or change was undertaken;

c. the date that such alteration or change was undertaken;

d. the name, business and residence address, and telephone number of the person(s) who determined the desirability and/or necessity for the design change;

e. the name, business and residence address, and telephone number of each person(s) who undertook to implement the decision to alter or change the design of the child safety seat;

f. an identification, with such specificity would require in a motion to produce, of any drawing, plan design, or other document relating to such design change and/or the decision to implement such design change, and

g. the name, business and residence address, and telephone number of the present custodian of each plan, drawing, design or document identified in your answer to the foregoing subpart of this interrogatory.

115. Do you contend that any person who used the child safety seat, including the ultimate consumer, should have installed any form of guard, device, or other tangible feature for the purpose of preventing or reducing the likelihood of the type of injury which allegedly occurred to the plaintiff?

116. If your answer to the foregoing interrogatory is in the affirmative, please further set forth:

a. a description of such guard, safety device, or other feature which you contend should have been installed or provided;

b. the means by which you notified each person who subsequently handled and/or distributed the child safety seat of the necessity to install or provide such guard, device, or other feature;

c. an identification, with such particularity as you would require in a motion to produce, of each and every writing relating to the determination that such guard, device, other feature should have been installed or provided and/or the necessity of such determination;

d. the name, business and residence address, and telephone number of the present custodian of any writing or document identified in your answer to the previous subpart of this interrogatory; and

e. the name, business and residence address and telephone number of each and every person who you claim has knowledge of any fact which you claim supports your contention set forth in your answer to the previous interrogatory.

117. Please state whether the use to which the child safety seat was put in the instant case was a use which you anticipated in the design and/or manufacture of the child safety seat.

118. Do you contend that, at the time of the occurrence which is the subject matter of plaintiff's complaint, the child safety seat was being used in any manner inconsistent with or differing from the intended uses of the child safety seat?

119. If your answer to the foregoing interrogatory was in the affirmative, please further set forth:

a. the means by which you contend that the use to which the product was put differed from or was inconsistent with the manner in which it was intended that the child safety seat would be used;

b. the means by which you contend that such use contributed to or enhanced plaintiff's injuries;

c. whether there exists a writing setting forth the recommended or intended uses of the child safety seat, whether or not communicated to the plaintiff;

d. the name, business and residence address, and telephone number of the present custodian of any writing identified in your answer to the foregoing subpart of this interrogatory.

120. Please identify each and every action and/or event which you contend contributed to or caused the injuries which are the subject of plaintiff's complaint.

121. As to each such action or event, please further set forth:

a. the precise manner in which you contend that such action or event contributed to plaintiff's injuries;

b. the name, business and residence address, and telephone number of any person known to you who witnessed or claimed to have witnessed any such action or event;

c. whether there exist any writings or documents relating to any such action or event, and;

d. the name, business and residence address, and telephone number of the current custodian of any writing identified in your answer to the foregoing subpart to this interrogatory.

122. Please state whether you contend that the child safety seat was modified or altered in any material respect after it left your custody and/or control.

123. If your answer to the foregoing interrogatory is in the affirmative, please further set forth:

  a. the date or dates upon which you contend such alterations or modifications took place;

  b. the general nature of such alterations or modifications;

  c. whether you contend that the fact of such alterations or modifications contributed in any manner whatsoever to the occurrence or injuries which are the subject matter of the plaintiff's complaint;

  d. whether the fact of such modification is the subject of any document or writing known to you;

  e. the name, business and residence address, and telephone number of the current custodian of any such writing identified in your answer to the foregoing subpart of this interrogatory.

124. Do you contend that the injury and/or occurrence which was the subject of the plaintiff's complaint occurred as a result of the use of the product following the expiration of the product's useful life?

125. If your answer to the foregoing interrogatory is in the affirmative, please further set forth:

  a. the useful life of the product as anticipated by you as of the date of manufacture;

  b. the means by which the useful life of the child safety seat was identified;

  c. the name, business and residence address, and telephone numbers of any person known to you who was responsible for determining the life expectancy of the child safety seat;

  d. the means, if any, utilized by you to communicate any limitations on the useful life of the child safety seat to the ultimate user or consumer of the child safety seat;

  e. an identification, with such particularity as you would require in a motion to produce, of each and every writing relating to any limitation on the useful life of the child safety seat; and

f. the name, business and residence address and telephone number of the present custodian of any writing identified in your answer to the foregoing subpart of this interrogatory.

126. Do you contend that the product which allegedly caused plaintiff's injuries as "unavoidably unsafe" in the sense that the product could not be rendered substantially safe without eliminating or substantially impairing the product's utility?

127. If your answer to the foregoing interrogatory was in the affirmative, please further set forth:

a. what modifications or changes to the child safety seat would be necessary to render the product substantially safe;

b. the reason why such modifications or changes would eliminate or substantially impair the product's utility;

c. whether you undertook to warn the user or consumer of the child safety seat that the child safety seat was unavoidably unsafe and that it could not be rendered substantially safe without eliminating or substantially impairing its utility;

d. if you undertook to so warn consumers, the means by which such warning was communicated to the user or consumer;

e. an identification, with such particularity as you would require in a motion to produce, of each and every writing relating to said warning;

f. the name, business, and residence address, and telephone number of each custodian of any writing identified in your answer to the foregoing subpart of this interrogatory.

128. Do you contend that the plaintiff assumed the risk of the occurrence and/or the injuries which are the subject of the plaintiff's complaint?

129. If your answer to the foregoing interrogatory is in the affirmative, please further set forth:

    a. whether you contend that such assumption of the risk was express or implied from plaintiff's conduct;

    b. each fact upon which you base your contention that plaintiff assumed the risk;

    c. whether you contend that plaintiff had full knowledge of such risk and subjectively determined to assume the same;

    d. each fact upon which you base your answer to the foregoing subpart of this interrogatory;

    e. the name, business and residence address, and telephone number of each such person known to you who has or may have knowledge of any facts set forth in your answer in response to the foregoing subparts of this interrogatory;

130. Please state whether at the time the product was manufactured, you were a member or affiliated with any organization which had as its primary purpose the evaluation and/or advancement of product safety (e.g. National Safety Council, etc.)

131. If your answer to the foregoing interrogatory was in the affirmative, please further set forth:

    a. the identity of each such organization of which you were a member or with which you were affiliated;

    b. the date that such membership or affiliation became effective;

    c. a general description of your participation as a member or affiliate of such organization or entity;

    d. the identity, if any of any person(s) designated by you as your representative to such organization or entity.

132. If your answer to Interrogatory number 130 was negative, please further set forth:

a. the identity of any such organization known to you which existed or conducted operations as of the date of manufacture of the child safety seat;

b. the reason, if any, why you did not become a member of or affiliated with such organization;

c. an identification, with such particularity as you would require in a motion to produce, of each and every writing relating to your determination not to become a member of or affiliated with said organization;

d. the name, business and residence address, telephone number of the present custodian of any writing identified in your answer to the foregoing subpart of this interrogatory.

133. Please state whether, at any time prior to the event which allegedly injured plaintiff herein, you had any knowledge that any person contended the child safety seat was defective in any respect which is reasonably similar to the defect claimed in plaintiff's complaint.

134. If your answer to the foregoing interrogatory is in the affirmative, please further set forth:

a. the date or dates upon which you were first apprised of any such contention;

b. the name, business and residence address, and telephone number known to you of the person or persons who advanced such contention;

c. whether any such contention was advanced in writing and, if so, describe such writing with such particularity as you would require in a motion to produce, and further identify the present custodian thereof;

d. a description of what actions or steps, if any, you took to evaluate or determine whether such contention was well founded;

e. an identification, with such specificity as you would require in a motion to produce, of each and every writing relating to any activity descried in your answer to the foregoing subpart of this interrogatory;

f. the name, business and residence address, and telephone number of the present custodian of each such writing or document identified in your answer to the foregoing subpart of this interrogatory.

135. Please state whether you or anyone acting on our behalf was aware of any claimed defect in the child safety seat prior to the occurrence which is the subject of plaintiff's complaint.

136. If your answer to the foregoing interrogatory was in the affirmative, please set forth:

a. the nature of any such claimed defect as to which you or anyone acting on your behalf had such prior knowledge;

b. the exact means or manner by which said person acquired such prior knowledge;

c. the name, business and residence address, and telephone number of any person who transmitted such prior knowledge to you or anyone acting on your behalf;

d. the date or dates upon which such prior knowledge was communicated to you;

e. as to any communication identified in your answer to the foregoing interrogatory, whether there exists any writing relating to the communication of such prior knowledge;

f. the name, business and residence address, and telephone number of the current custodian of any writing identified in your response to the foregoing interrogatory.

137. Do you contend that, prior to the occurrence which is the subject matter of plaintiff's complaint on file herein, you

had no knowledge of any defect or dangerous condition existing within the child safety seat?

138. Please state whether, prior to the occurrence which is the subject of plaintiff's complaint, you were apprised of any health risk in any manner associated with the use of the child safety seat.

139. If your answer to the foregoing interrogatory was in the affirmative, please further set forth:

    a. the date or dates upon which you were apprised of any such health risk;

    b. the nature of such health risk;

    c. the name,business and residence address, and telephone number of the person or persons who apprised you of said health risk;

    d. an identification, with such particularity as you would require in a motion to produce, of each and every writing relating to such health risk

    e. the name, business and residence address, and telephone number of the present custodian of any writing identified in your answer to the foregoing subpart of this interrogatory.

140. Do you deny that prior to the sale of the child safety seat to plaintiff you were apprised that the use of the child safety seat entailed a substantial risk to children using the subject child safety seat?

141. If your answer to the foregoing interrogatory was in the affirmative, please further set forth:

    a. each and every fact upon which you base said contention;

    b. the name, business and residence address, and telephone number of any person known to you who has knowledge of any such fact;

c. an identification, with such particularity as you would require in a motion to produce, of each and every writing relating to such contention;

d. the name, business and residence address, and telephone number of the present custodian of any writing identified in your answer to the foregoing subpart of this interrogatory.

142. Please state whether, prior to the sale of the child safety seat to plaintiff, you were apprised of any safety risk associated with the use of the child safety seat.

143. If your answer to the foregoing interrogatory was in the affirmative, please further set forth:

a. the date that you were apprised of such safety risk;

b. the nature of said safety risk;

c. the name, business and residence address, and telephone number of the person who so apprised you of such safety risk;

d. an identification, with such particularity as you would require in a motion to produce, of each and every writing evidencing that you were so apprised;

e. the name, business and residence address, and telephone number of any person having knowledge of any fact relating to such notice to you;

f. an identification, with such particularity as you would require in a motion to produce, of each and every writing relating to such notice to you; and

g. the name, business and residence address, and telephone number of the present custodian of any writing identified in your answer to the foregoing subpart of this interrogatory.

144. Do you deny that prior to the sale of the child safety seat to plaintiff you were apprised that the use of the child safety seat involved a substantial risk that (specify risk)

145. If your answer to the foregoing interrogatory is in the affirmative, please further set forth:

a. each and every fact upon which you base said contention;

b. the name, business and residence address, and telephone number of any person known to you who has knowledge of any such fact;

c. an identification, with such particularity as you would require in a motion to produce, of each and every writing relating to such contention;

d. the name, business and residence address, and telephone number of the present custodian of any writing identified in your answer to the foregoing subpart of this interrogatory.

146. Please state whether you have been apprised, by any means whatsoever, of any alleged defect and/or criticism of the design or manufacture of the child safety seat.

147. If your answer to the foregoing interrogatory is in the affirmative, please further set forth:

a. the nature or form of such contention or allegation;

b. the date upon which such contention or allegation was communicated to you;

c. whether such allegation or contention was manifested in a writing; of whatever nature or description;

d. an identification, with such particularity as you would require in a motion to produce, of each writing relating to such allegation or contention, including your response, if any, thereto; and

e. the name, business and residence address, and telephone number of the current custodian of any writing referred to in your answers to any of the subparts of this interrogatory.

148. Please state whether, during the period of time that you manufactured the child safety seat, you were notified of any injuries or occurrences allegedly arising from the

same alleged defect which is the subject of the plaintiff's complaint.

149. If your answer to the foregoing interrogatory is in the affirmative, please further set forth:

a. the date upon which you were apprised or notified of any such contention;

b. whether such contention was embodied in a written form;

c. if your answer to the foregoing subpart was in the affirmative, an identification of each such writing, with such particularity as you would require in a motion to produce;

d. the name, business and residence address and telephone number of any person known to you who advanced such contention;

e. the actions, if any, taken by you in response to any such contention to evaluate the factual basis therefore;

f. the name, business and residence address, and telephone number of the present custodian of any writing identified in your answers to any of the subparts of this interrogatory.

150. Please state whether any person initiated any legal proceeding against you during the period of time in that manufactured the child safety seat, which such proceeding alleged that the plaintiff suffered a personal injury in a manner similar to the occurrence which is alleged in plaintiff's complaint.

151. If your answer to the foregoing interrogatory is in the affirmative, please further set forth:

a. the name, business and residence address and telephone number of any party to any such litigation;

b. the date upon which such proceeding was initiated;

c. the filing number or other filing identification, if any, under such legal proceeding is indexed or registered in the jurisdiction in which it was filed;

d. the jurisdiction in which it was filed;

e. the disposition, if any, of such claim or legal action;

f. the name, business and residence address, and telephone number of counsel of any party advancing the contentions which were the subject of your answer to the foregoing interrogatory;

g. the name, business and residence address, and telephone number of the current custodian of any writings relating to any such legal action.

152. Please state whether you have been made aware of any claim for compensation, within the past ten years, whether formal or informal, which claim alleged in substance that (describe defect)

153. As to each such claim identified in your answer to the foregoing interrogatory which did not result in a legal proceeding, please set forth:

a. the name, business and residence address, and telephone number of the person or entity who advanced such claim;

b. the means by which such claim was advanced;

c. an identification, with such particularity as you would require in a motion to produce, of each and every document or writing relating to such claim;

d. the name, business and residence address, and telephone number of the current custodian of any and all documents identified in your answer to the foregoing subpart to this interrogatory;

e. the disposition of such claim.

154. As to each such claim or contention identified in your answer to interrogatory number 150, that resulted in a formal legal proceeding, please set forth:

a. the name, business and residence address, and telephone number of the person or entity who advanced such claim;

b. the jurisdiction, caption, and any identifying file or action number pertaining to such claim;

c. an identification, with such particularity as you would require in a motion to produce, of each and every document or writing relating to such claim;

d. the name, business and residence address, and telephone number of the current custodian of any writing identified in your answer to the foregoing subpart of this interrogatory,

e. the disposition of such claim or contention.

155. Please state whether you, or any person acting on your behalf, has conducted any examination of the child safety seat.

156. If your answer to the foregoing interrogatory is in the affirmative, please further set forth:

a. the names, business and residence addresses, and telephone numbers of the person or persons who conducted such an examination;

b. the date upon which subject's examination occurred and the location thereof;

c. whether the results of any such examination were reduced to a writing, document, or other visual representation (such as photograph, film, etc.)

d. an identification, with such particularity as you would require in a motion to produce, of any writing, document or other visual representation relating to or resulting from such examination;

e. the name, business and residence address, and telephone number of the present custodian of any writing, document or visual representation identified in your answer to the foregoing subpart of this interrogatory.

157. Please state whether you are aware of any report, publication, or writing of whatever nature or description which purports to describe, analyze, or evaluate the child safety seat.

158. If your answer to the foregoing interrogatory is in the affirmative, please further set forth:

a. the title, publisher, and date of publication of any such writing or document;

b. the date you became aware of the existence of such document;

c. whether you currently possess a copy of such document;

d. if your answer to the foregoing subpart to this interrogatory was in the affirmative, the date upon which you acquired such document.

159. Please state whether you have conducted, in any manner whatsoever, any recall campaign or related activity for the child safety seat.

160. If your answer to the foregoing interrogatory is in the affirmative, please further state:

a. the reason that such recall campaign or related activity was initiated;

b. the date that such recall campaign or related activity was initiated;

c. whether such recall campaign or related activity was initiated and/or mandated by any consumer regulatory agency or other public entity exercising similar functions;

d. if your answer to the foregoing subpart of this interrogatory was in the affirmative, whether you concur with the determination of such consumer protection agency or other regulatory entity that such recall campaign or related activity was/is necessary;

e. the means by which notice of such recall campaign and/or related activity has or is being communicated to users of the child safety seat.

161. If your answer to interrogatory number 159 was in the negative, please further set forth:

a. whether any person or entity known to you has contended that the child safety seat should be a subject of a recall campaign or related activities;

b. the reasons, if any, known by you that such person or entity contended that the child safety seat should be the subject of a recall campaign;

c. whether you considered a set contention or recommendation that the child safety seat should be the subject of a recall campaign or related activity, and if so, are the means by which such contention or recommendation was evaluated by you and any other person(s).

d. the reason(s) you determined not to engage in a recall campaign or related activity as to the child safety seat;

e. an identification, with such specificity as you would require in a motion to produce, of each and every writing or document, of any nature whatsoever, pertaining to such contention, recommendation, and/or consideration;

f. the name, business and residence address, and telephone number of the present custodian of each such writing or document identified in your answer to the preceding subpart of this interrogatory.

162. Do your answers to each of these interrogatories contain and represent the collective knowledge of you, your attorneys, insurance carrier, and all persons acting on your or their behalf?

163. If your answer to the foregoing interrogatory was in the negative, please set forth:

a. the interrogatory number of each;

b. an answer based on all your collective knowledge;

c. any and all reasons why an answer based on this collective knowledge was not given.

164. Please state the name, business and residence address, and telephone number of each person of whom you inquired to assist in answering any part of these interrogatories, and indicate those persons, if any, who stated they had no information to answer any part of said interrogatories.

165. Please set forth the name, business and residence address, and telephone number of each person known to you and not otherwise identified in your answers to these interrogatories who provided any information, of whatever nature or description, relating to any of your answers to these interrogatories.

166. Please state whether each answer to each interrogatory set forth herein accurately sets forth the sum total of all facts known to you or anyone acting on your behalf, which such facts reasonably relate to the subject matter of each such interrogatory.

167. Please state whether, in compiling your answers to these interrogatories, you have made a reasonable and diligent effort to identify and provide not only such facts as are within your personal knowledge, but such facts as are also reasonably available to you and/or any person acting on your behalf.

Depositions
Preparing the Client

The most useful preparatory tool that we have seen for deposition preparation is the Matthew Bender video tape, "Preparing for a Deposition in a Beosinis' Case 0-2252." Although the topic is not personal injury related, the ideas and thoughts are transferable. We have had hundreds of clients view it with great success.

It is good to keep in mind that although we as attorneys may find discovery depositions a mundane exercise, they are a new and frightening experience to clients. Because of this, explain everything in detail to the client before the deposition and the results will speak for themselves.

In an effort to put your client's mind at ease for a deposition, we have found that it is best to give them a copy of the following explanation of what a deposition is.

A discovery deposition is the oral testimony of a witness taken under oath before trial. The questions you will be asked will involve information pertinent to the case or attempt to discover pertinent facts. A discovery deposition is not like the Perry Mason show. It will be done in private in a lawyer's office, either in our office or in the office of the opposing counsel. We will be there with you during the time that the other side is asking you questions, and have an opportunity to go over your testimony with you before you testify. We will most likely be taking the discovery deposition of the other side also. A court reporter will record everything you say, therefore everything said must be accurate and truthful.

You might be asked to draw or sketch something, so be prepared to designate directions on the ground and by compass if possible. Be sure to cover this with your lawyer before the deposition.

Purpose of Depositions

The purpose of the discovery deposition is to "discover" all the facts a witness knows which will assist the lawyer in the preparation and trial of the lawsuit. It also helps to settle the case because the facts are known to both sides. It is normal to take a discovery deposition in a civil jury case.

At the time of the discovery deposition you should remember that this is probably the first opportunity that the opposing counsel has to meet you. You will be judged by opposing counsel on your honesty, frankness and possible jury appeal. It is important that you make a good impression. You should appear at the deposition dressed as you would expect to dress if you were actually going to court.

Appearance at Deposition

A. You should be clean.

B. You should wear clean, neat clothes.

C. Treat everyone in the deposition room with respect.

D. Come prepared to exhibit any and all injuries which you have suffered.

E. Have with you all the facts and figures with respect to your time lost from work, amount of wages lost, doctor bills, and all other damages caused as a result of your injury.

F. Consider this an important and official occasion; avoid "getting chummy" with opposing counsel or his client.

How to be an Effective Witness

A. Be respectful and just tell the truth.

B. Never argue or lose your temper. Leave your temper at home.

C. Speak slowly and carefully. Answer verbally—don't shake your head yes or no. The court reporter must be able to understand.

D. If you don't understand the question, ask that it be explained.

E. Answer all questions directly, giving brief answers to the questions, and stop talking.

F. Never volunteer information. Wait until the question is asked, answer it, and stop. If you can answer "yes" or "no," do so and stop. Explain your answer if necessary, but don't make speeches.

G. The above rule does not apply to your injuries. Volunteer answers on any information helpful to your case, but do not magnify your injuries or losses. Start at the top of your head and go to your toes, so that you will not forget any of your injuries.

H. Be conservative with respect to a description of your injuries. Adopt an unexaggerated attitude.

I. Stick to the facts and testify only to that which you personally know.

J. Testify only to "basic facts," and do not attempt to give opinions or estimates of time and distance unless you have good reason for knowing such matters.

K. Be positive. Don't say "I think" or "I believe," "I guess," "maybe," "possibly," or "perhaps." It is better to say "as I recall" or "in my judgment."

L. Do not say "I can't." Say you "are not able to do something as well as before." "Can't" means physical impossibility—you can't move your hand if you don't have a hand.

M. Tell the truth about the activities that you have performed since the accident, such as sports, work, etc. If these activities cause you discomfort and pain, however, be sure to add that.

N. If you had any injuries before this accident, be sure to tell the truth. Remember every previous accident or injury, including such things as football injuries. Hiding something at this point could mean that your case will be lost.

O. Be sure your estimates of time and distance are reasonable.

P. If you don't know, admit it. Some witnesses think they should have an answer for every question asked. You cannot know all of the facts, and you do yourself a disservice if you attempt to testify to facts with which you are not acquainted. It is important that you be honest and straightforward in your testimony.

Q. Don't try to memorize your story. Justice requires only that a witness tell the story to the best of his ability.

R. Take your time. Give the questions and answers as much thought as necessary

S. Don't guess. If you know, say so, but don't guess.

T. If you have testified previously on this matter, or given a previous statement, your best answer is that "If it's written, then I must have said it." This may not be accurate, however, if the statement is one that you did not actually write yourself or if it's not a court-reported statement. You may always explain what you meant.

U. Don't say "That's all I know." Later, from your notes or from memory, you may remember something else, so it is better to say "That is all I recall at this moment."

V. Start learning now not to mention at any time "insurance," "claims agent" or "adjustor."

W. Don't look to your lawyer for help when you are testifying. You're on your own.

X. If during your testimony you recall giving a wrong answer, interrupt the proceedings immediately to correct yourself.

Chapter 9

Child Restraints In Commercial Aircraft

Introduction

"What Next—Child Safety Seats in Space!?"

That was the comment overheard from one of the participants at a recent seminar on child passenger safety concerning the proposed legislation that would mandate use of child safety seats aboard commercial aircraft. The controversy is not new. Over the past decade, various government agencies, consumer groups, the press and individuals have wrestled with the controversy.

Though at first the issue may appear petty and capricious, there is more at stake than the cost of an extra flight ticket for the seat occupied by a child in a safety seat. At stake are the lives, not only of the children flying in aircraft, but also the lives and safety of the other passengers in the plane. More than 4 million infants fly across the skies on-board U.S. aircraft each year. On any given day 5,000 to 10,000 infants travel in commercial aircraft. Given that many lives the issue of mandatory child safety seats is not trivial.

Many people when they first seriously consider the issue simply conclude that not many airplanes crash in the first place. In fact, that was the position taken by the FAA in 1990 when it rejected a petition by the airlines to require child safety seats. The same line of thought also concludes that due to the severity of the impact of an aircraft involved in a crash, not much could be accomplished by using a safety seat, therefore the mandatory law is unnecessary.

The same argument was made at different times when the federal government and the states first considered mandatory child restraint legislation for automobiles. However, the main reason supporting mandatory child safety seat laws on board aircraft is that most of the injuries to children and passengers occur during take-off and landing.

Most recently, the controversy was fueled when children, traveling on their parents' laps, flew out of their parents arm during a period of turbulence. It is not a new concept that loose objects can cause serious damage when traveling at high speeds. A child traveling on her parent's lap presents a serious risk to other passengers during the taxiing of an aircraft or during periods of brief turbulence.

The FAA Decision

In 1992 the FAA finally decided not require child safety seats in aircraft. The official reason by the FAA was that increases in air fares would result if the new rule were adopted. The FAA has constantly ignored the evidence that in hard landings and crashes small children become lethal human missiles.

Moreover, competitive pricing programs by the airlines could counteract the increase in price to those families using child safety seats. Southwest Airlines was the first airline to provide travelers with competitive discounts for children under 2 traveling in a child safety seat.

Some airlines have even used safety seats as a marketing strategy. In 1992, Virgin Atlantic Airways introduced 30 child safety seats to be used by infants from 6 months to children 3 years old. The seats are provided at no extra charge to parents who book them at the time of making their reservation. The parents must pay the fare for the extra seat. This concept was first proposed by the Aviation Consumer Action Project ten years ago. The group, founded by consumer advocate Ralph Nader, found that a viable solution would be for each plane to carry two to six child safety seats per plane.

The FAA stated that mandating child safety seat use onboard aircraft would result in more deaths. According to the FAA parents unable to purchase additional tickets for their children will be forced to drive their cars. The odds are that a child is more likely to die in a child restraint in an automobile than an unrestrained child in a plane. However, the FAA's reasoning fails to consider that most parents would not be dissuaded from flying, even at an added cost. The average flight is over one thousand miles. Few parents would actually go through the trouble of driving a great distance and incur the added expenses, time, and inconvenience when "getting there" is of the essence.

Although many more people die in motor vehicle accidents than in air crashes, a mandatory child safety seat law aboard aircraft would also help curb highway deaths. If such a law went into effect, parents would bring their child safety devices on trips and would be more likely to use them in rental vehicles at their destinations.

The recent ruling that became effective in October of 1992, allows parents to bring an approved safety seat for their child on board aircraft. An additional ticket must be bought for the additional seat. Prior to the ruling a few airline companies allowed parents to use available open seats for their child safety seat. The FAA estimates that mandatory child safety seat legislation would cost travelers more than $250 million per year.

New Legislation

Since 1981 child safety seats marketed in the United States must comply with Federal Motor Vehicle Safety Standard 213. The standard regulates child safety seat manufacture, labeling and instructions. Part of the standard labeling required by FMVSS 213 states: "This restraint is certified for use in motor vehicles and aircraft." Yet, the FAA refuses to mandate the use of certified seats aboard planes.

The Bush Administration failed to convey its "Family Values" theme to the FAA. While the Bush administration advocated for the rights of the unborn, the same administration denied "equal protection" to children traveling in our skies.

In the wake of the FAA ruling that was opposed by many groups like the National Transportation Safety Board (NTSB), the Association of Flight Attendants, the Air Transport Association and many consumer advocate groups, Representative Jim Lightfoot, a Republican from Iowa, advocates changes in the FAA and has proposed new legislation in this area. Rep. Lightfoot introduced house bill number 1993 H.R. 1533 to amend the Federal aviation Act of 1958 to require the use of child safety restraint systems approved by the Secretary of Transportation on commercial aircraft. The bill was co-sponsored by 17 Democrats and 6 Republicans.

Lightfoot is an experienced pilot who knows the consequences of air travel first hand. The proposed bill is aimed at addressing the exemption of children under 2 from seat belt usage. At issue are Federal Aviation Regulation Sections 91.107, 121.311, 125.211 and 135.128. These regulations provide no protection for infants aboard commercial aircraft. The pending bill was first proposed in 1990 but was not enacted into law.

Representative Lightfoot's bill was inspired by a tragedy in the Congressman's own district—the 1989 crash landing of United Airlines Flight 232 at Sioux City. The crash took the lives of more than 112 people including a 23 month old child. The child was traveling unrestrained in his parent's lap. Three other infants who were in lap belts suffered injuries but survived the crash. Evan, the 23-month-old child, may have survived the crash if he had been in a child safety seat.

Six months after the Sioux City crash another jet crashed in New York. This time an Avianca airliner crashed and one child died while six other children were injured after being yanked out of their parent's arms during the crash.

The FAA's Head Injury Standard

Another argument put forward by skeptics of mandatory child safety seat legislation, is that unrestrained adults can suffer severe injuries during the in-flight portion of a flight. The argument is valid to some extent. However, during mild turbulence an adult is more likely to be able to control his movements than a child. Nevertheless, the FAA has proposed new head injury criteria to protect passengers whose seats are located directly in front of bulkheads, where the risk of head injury is the greatest.

The new FAA rules are designed to maximize protection to passengers who are involved in survivable crashes or subject to sudden deceleration. The new rules apply to all passenger seats, coach and first class. The FAA rules were developed from a head injury standard developed by the National Highway Traffic Safety Administration.

More objective research is needed to determine how to best protect passengers traveling on commercial aircraft. The decisions that the FAA is making need to be based on more than economics and public perception. The FAA is supposed to protect the public, but its decisions on child passenger safety raise many questions.

The FAA continues to permit booster seats on aircraft. Boosters are raised platforms that consist of a hard plastic shell and a cushion with not back or sides. Boosters are designed for toddlers to ensure a snug fit for the lap belt when placed across the child's thighs. Boosters are not designed for children under forty pounds and are dangerous to infants. However, even toddlers using boosters are at risk in an aircraft environment. The FAA's own research has shown that boosters may increase injuries suffered by toddlers. The injuries can occur during take-off and landing procedures from a seat folding over the toddler in a backless booster seat.

New Designs

The controversy over child passenger safety could be greatly resolved by mandatory legislation and by using some of the designs that are currently state of the art in passenger protection. Why can't the airlines introduce a version of the integrated car seat to their air buses? Integrated car seats fold out from the back of the back seats in many American cars.

Manufacturers have come up with many innovative and unusual designs to meet the new FAA rules. The proposed designs range from the addition of padding and removal of seats directly in front of bulkheads to airbags and shoulder harnesses.

However, when it comes to putting the money where their mouth is, the aircraft manufacturers have been reluctant to carry out the proposed plans. The main concern is economic. Removal of seats from aircraft represents a direct loss in revenues that airlines do not want, and that manufacturers refuse to absorb. Installation of airbags and five point shoulder harnesses on all seats would also be costly.

Moreover, if airbags were to be used on bulkheads to protect passengers seated directly in front of the bulkhead, a new generation of airbag would have to be designed. Crash dynamics of automobiles are totally different from crashes and deceleration in aircraft. The deceleration curve in aircraft is much longer and would require an airbag that remains inflated for a longer period of time.

An alternative that manufacturers are looking at involves a new generation of passenger seats that could be placed in front of bulkhead areas. The new seats rotate the passengers legs upward during a sudden deceleration and prevent the passenger from rolling forward. The new FAA rules also require that all passenger seats be able to withstand more than the old 9g standard. Seats that perform at 16g levels are the current standard. Though not required by the FAA, most of the major manufacturers have adopted this standard. The cost for the higher "16g" seats is a few thousand "G's". A two-seat row for first class costs $10,000 and a three-seat row for coach costs $5,000.

Conclusion

It seems that the time has come for the FAA to listen to reason and enact mandatory child safety seat legislation. In an excellent example of absurd bureaucratic red tape, the FAA requires that our luggage be secure during flights, but exempts infants from a basic flight rule. Our military teaches its air crews and pilots that everything must be secure in a plane. The civilian sector trains its crews in the same way. All states have enacted mandatory child restraint legislation for children traveling on our roads and highways at speeds up to 65 mph—isn't it time to protect our children flying at speeds of 500 mph or more?

Exhibit 10-1

Chapter 10

Considering the Automobile Manufacturers

An often neglected party in child restraint litigation is the automobile manufacturer. Everyone agrees that no child safety seat or restraint system can be effective 100% of the time. However, attorneys often overlook the auto manufacturers as possible parties in child restraint cases.

The interaction between child restraint devices and the automobile is unique. Very little testing has been done to learn how the newer car seats perform in late model cars. The current standard is based on a large 60's model, bench-type seat. Today's cars lack the room of the 60's sedan and the results of a crash can be totally different in different cars.

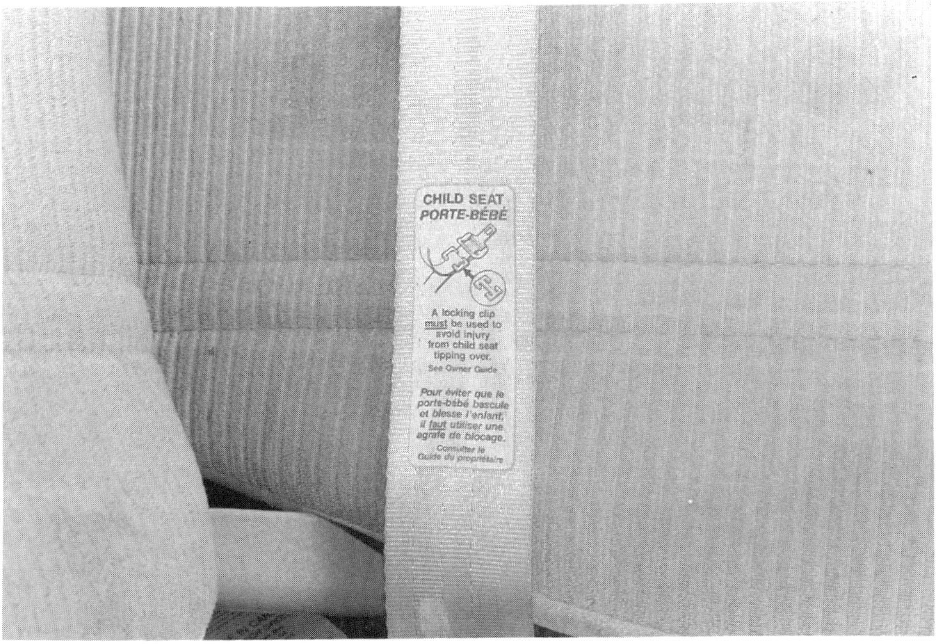

Exhibit 10-2 *Locking clip warning on rear seat belt of the 1990 Ford Taurus.*

Automobile manufacturers realize that they have some responsibility to consumers who use child restraints in their vehicles. Many companies warn against the use of child restraint systems with shoulder belts. In most vehicles a child restraint system can be used if an inexpensive device is used. The device is called a locking clip which prevents seat belts with emergency locking retractors (ELR's) from sliding when pressure is exerted by the child restraint seat. Automobile dealers often provide the clip at no or minimal charge. In other cars, a modification to the seat belt may be necessary and any auto dealer can replace the belt at no charge to the consumer. Other warnings are directed against the use of rear-facing child restraint seats in the front passenger seat that is equipped with an air bag. The companies have the warnings in their owner's manuals and use warning labels on the doors and seat belts to warn consumers. Air bags have been identified as a risk to infants and small children seated near the air bag compartment. Studies estimate that children in rear-facing child restraints can be subjected to forces measure in head injury criteria (HIC) levels as high as 3000 HIC. Serious injury can occur in adults at 1000 HIC. Car design should encourage, not inhibit, child restraint use. Adequate warnings and instruction from the auto manufacturers is essential in decreasing deaths and injuries of children.

The litigator should be aware that what appears to be a child restraint defect case may in fact be an automobile seat belt defect. A seat belt may malfunction due to manufacturing defects and fail to hold the child restraint during a collision. Examples of manufacturing defects in this area include: flawed webbing that breaks in a collision, retractors that fail to lock and buckles that do not hold.

Chapter 11

Technological Innovations

An innovation that has been introduced to the market is the concept of warning devices on child restraints. Shinn & Associates in Lansing, Michigan have developed a warning system that alerts the parent, through audio and visual alarms, if the restraint buckle becomes unfastened or if the child manages to get out of the child restraint. The invention uses a pressure sensitive device energized by a battery pack. The system also sounds an alarm in cases of rapid deceleration. In the confusion of a crash, the high pitched alarm can help rescuers determine the location of the child. Commercial applications include use of the warning system in shopping cart safety seats. The authors are aware of many cases currently pending against grocery stores due to injuries to children who were injured due to defective seats integrated in the shopping cart. Defects cited include use of restraints without belts or defective latches or buckles.

A recent invention marketed by the Westech Group is the Child-Safer™ device. The device is intended for children who have outgrown their child safety seats, or it can be used with booster seats. The Child-Safer™ is best described as a seat belt positioning device. The device consists of a two foot long plastic board that has several slits along its length. The Child-Safer™ restraint device readjusts the shoulder portion of a seat belt to better fit around a child's torso. By doing this the Child-Safer™ removes the seat belt from the uncomfortable and vulnerable neck area. The device is not subject to regulation under FMVSS 208 or FMVSS 213, but has been tested under FMVSS 213 standards. In testing the Child-Safer™ device greatly reduces neck and torso injuries to children restrained in seat belts.

Although today's child restraints hardly resemble the devices marketed three decades ago, more innovations in the area of child restraints are needed to safeguard children traveling in automobiles. Unfortunately, the manufacturing trend in the past has consisted of a "cookie cutter" approach to child restraint designs. The manufacturers will implement designs once they prove marketable.

Exhibit 11-1 *Teresa Hendricks, an attorney with the Law Offices of Joseph W. Moch, demonstrates that child safety can be fun.*

Conclusion

The child passenger protection issue has grown from a small issue of concern by grass roots activists to become a generally accepted issue in our society. Parents, health-care providers, legislators, manufacturers and consumer advocates all play crucial roles in improving the protection provided to children traveling on the road.

In the past two decades a reduction in head injuries can be attributed to safer designs, better laws and stricter enforcement of occupant protection laws. However, changes are needed to eliminate the loopholes and technicalities that exempt children from protection. A revision of the federal standard is needed to ensure that all children are given adequate protection on our roads and highways.

There is growing awareness by manufacturers that restraint systems need to be easier to use. Designs with the user in mind are a welcome change in this industry. More cars are being marketed with passive restraint systems. The introduction of the integrated child restraint is another step in the right direction to ensure access and use of child restraints. New innovations and improved designs contribute to the safety of our most important natural resource: our nation's children.

Exhibit 11-2 *The Century Breverra Booster Seat is the newest booster designed for toddlers who have outgrown regular boosters but who don't quite fit in the automobile's lap and shoulder belts.*

Chapter 12

Probate Issues: Dealing with Minors and Wrongful Death

Considering the nature of automobile accidents, the practitioner may well be asked to pursue the claim of a totally disabled child or deceased individual. For illustration purposes the authors use the law of Michigan in discussing probate issues. Attorneys should look for similar statutes in the jurisdiction in which they file their claim.

The Probate court has jurisdiction over all incompetents, both physical or mental (i.e. the head injured) and legal (i.e. minority), as well as matters relating to the settlement of the estate of a deceased accident victim. In Michigan the applicable statute is MCLA 700.21 et seq. The attorneys handling a motor vehicle accident involving injury or death to a minor in a defective child restraint should check the applicable probate statute(s) in their jurisdiction. Failing to probate a settlement that involves a minor is malpractice.

If your client is a minor, or one rendered incompetent because of his accident, but has no "estate" that presently requires Probate supervision, you have the option of initiating a probate file, and asking that a guardian/conservator be appointed, or asking the Circuit Court hearing the no-fault claim to appoint a "Next Friend."

A next friend has been defined as one who commences an action on behalf of a minor Plaintiff. *Russick v Hicks,* 85 F. Supp 281 (W.D. Mich 1949). The next friend represents the minor's interests under court supervision. Appointment may be secured through a petition such as the one included.

Either the next friend appointed by the Circuit Court, or the guardian/conservator appointed by the Probate Court will represent the interests of the incompetent individual and consent to or contest the court proceedings on their behalf. If the lawsuit results in a recovery in excess of $5,000 in a lump sum or more than $5,000 annually a conservator must be appointed by the Probate Court, MCLA 700,403, MSA 700.450 et seq. Included are the basic forms necessary to initiate a hearing in Probate Court to have a guardian/conservator appointed. For a discussion of the distinction between these two legal roles, see MCLA 700.432. Note however, that both appointments are available and may be appropriate in certain cases.

Payment of money due to minor (powers and duties of guardian):

CA: Cal Prob CA 2350 et seq.

FL: FSA 744.48 et seq.

IL: SHA Ch 37 701-11 et seq.

NY: SCPA 1701 et seq.

If representation of a deceased party is involved, and this is frequently the case in personal injury litigation, an estate must be set up and personal representatives appointed under the jurisdiction of the state's probate court system. In Michigan this procedure is governed by the Wrongful Death Statute's MCLA 600.2922. The procedures to be followed are outlined below.

A. Action brought by and in the name of the Personal Representative of the estate of the decedent (note: Probate Court appointment is necessary before commencing action).

B. Within 30 days after commencing a wrongful death action, a copy of the Complaint and Notice shall be sent to all interested parties. The notice must contain the following:

1. Name and address of Personal Representative and attorney;

2. Notice that within 60 days after receipt of notice, all interested parties shall advise said attorney of any material facts which may evidence reasons why interested party is entitled to damages or else waiver of right is effective;

3. Notice that interested parties will be advised of a settlement hearing;

4. Claim of interested party must be submitted to Personal Representative on or before settlement distribution hearing date. Failure to do so results in a bar to any recovery.

C. New Act limits who is interested party. The following are interested subject to Sec. 251 of Probate Code:

1. Spouse
2. Children of decedent
3. Stepchildren
4. Decedent's parents/grandparents
5. Brother & sisters of decedent
6. Devisees under will
7. Trust beneficiaries

If no survivors then follow interstate succession via Probate Code.

D. Jurisdiction for settling wrongful death claim is Circuit Court where action is pending. The Personal Representative is required to file a motion asking leave of court to settle. The court shall, with or without notice conduct a hearing and approve or reject the proposed settlement.

E. The allowable damages in a wrongful death action are as follows:

1. Economic - hospital, medical, funeral
2. Non-economic - conscious pain and suffering
3. Loss of financial support
4. Loss of society and companionship

F. Settlement proceeds are distributed in the following manner:

1. Personal Representative motions the court for authority to distribute proceeds;
2. Court where action is pending orders a distribution hearing. Notice of said hearing is served on all interested parties. If an interested party is a minor, then a guardian ad litem must be appointed. If an interested party is a legally incapacitated adult then a conservator and/or guardian must be appointed;

3. The court shall first order that all economic expenses for which the estate is responsible shall be paid first. These expenses do not include taxes;

4. The relative damages to persons injured. Any pain and suffering goes to the estate;

5. After amount of damages is calculated per injured person, the adult interested parties can execute a verified stipulation or agreement as to their portion of the proceeds. The Order of the Court then will be in accordance with the stipulation. If no stipulation, evidentiary hearing will be held as to portion of settlement.

G. If no wrongful death action is commenced, then for settlement, one must follow Sections 221-222 of Revised Probate Code.

Similarly, the Probate Court must be involved in any wrongful death claim. wrongful death accident cases are prima-facie compensable no-fault injuries, See MCLA 700.5135. If suit is contemplated or a recovery imminent, a Probate Court appointment of a personal representative for the estate of the deceased accident victim may be sought. Note that when the personal representative files his estate "inventory" with the Probate Court, he may include "wrongful death claim whose value is not yet determined," to notify the Probate Court of the existence of the Circuit Court litigation.

NEXT FRIEND APPOINTMENT PETITION

STATE OF ______________

IN THE CIRCUIT COURT FOR THE COUNTY OF ____________

PLAINTIFF,

vs.

DEFENDANT.

_______________/

PETITION FOR APPOINTMENT

Of Next Friend

The Circuit Court for the County of _________________________
The Petition of ________________ respectfully shows:

1. He is a duly licensed and practicing attorney in the State of ________ with an established place of business at _______________________.

2. ________________ is a minor of the age of ____ years.

3. The minor has a cause of action against ______________, claiming therein a judgment in the sum of __________ dollars on behalf of the minor plaintiff, plus costs and attorneys fees.

4. Petitioner is a suitable and proper person to appear as next friend to to bring suit for him.

WHEREFORE, petitioner prays that he be appointed next friend of _________.

DATED: ____________________, Petitioner
Attorney for Plaintiff

CONSENT

I, ___________________, do hereby consent to act as next friend of the above mentioned ___________________ in the proposed suit mentioned in the foregoing petition.

DATED: ________________________

APPOINTMENT PETITION

STATE OF ________________

IN THE CIRCUIT COURT FOR THE COUNTY OF ______________

PLAINTIFF,

vs.

DEFENDANT.

________________/

PETITION FOR APPOINTMENT OF

Next Friend Nunc Pro Tunc

Plaintiff ______________, by her attorney ________________________, moves that ______________________ be appointed next friend to represent her in the above-entitled action, and that the order appointing such next friend be made nunc pro tunc from the date of commencement of said action.

In support of this motion, plaintiff represents to the Court as follows:

1. She is a minor, _________ years of age.
2. She has a cause of action against defendant __________________, arising out of an automobile accident which occurred on
3. She desires to maintain an action for the purpose of collecting the damages sustained by her in the accident.
4. She has been advised that it is necessary for a next friend to be appointed to represent her in such action.
5. ______________________, whom she desires to be appointed as her next friend, is her father (or as the case may be).

DATED:

____________________________ ____________________________

____________________________ Plaintiff

Attorney for Plaintiff
Business Address:

____

____

Telephone: ________________

Chapter 13

Patents

The careful review of patent information can reveal useful information such as the existing state-of-the-art at the time a particular design was manufactured. It must be noted here that a child restraint system in the form of a child safety seat or a booster may be based on a combination of several patents. Patents owned by a particular manufacturer by assignment from inventors can be found in the files of the United States Patent and Trademark Office.

Sometimes the patents will be identified on the product or on the packaging, but as noted, child restraint designs are based on several patents and that information is usually not found on child restraints. Part of the discovery should include requests of patents granted to the manufacturer. The carefully worded requests should also include patents that are pending or patent applications that have been disallowed or abandoned.

A review of several patents can give the expert or the attorney a broad picture of all the features that have been incorporated into child restraint designs.

Patents have a lifetime of about 17 years and then become available to the public at no cost.

Searching for patents of child restraints can also identify inventors who are experts in the field of child restraint design who may be sources of information and could possibly be used as experts. The patent search may also identify problems in design that have resulted in safety concerns and recalls. Patents often include references to many technical publications which may be of help to an attorney.

Since most of the child restraints on the market today are basic copies of one another, the patent will usually protect a unique feature used in a child restraint system that distinguishes it from all the others. Use of a novel safety feature such as a warning system to alert the driver that the latch on the child restraint system has become disengaged can qualify as such a novel invention.

The patents also offer a lot of drawings and sketches which can give the reader an idea of the structure, use, and operation of the child restraint device.

The beginning place to look at any patent is in the abstract portion. The abstract defines the general subject matter of the patent. Unfortunately, patents are full of stilted language that is of little use to the reader so an expert may be needed to decode the technical language. We have included patents listed alphabetically by the inventor's name, which may be of some help to the attorney researching child restraint patents. Following that list there are some summaries of patents that may be useful to the attorney in identifying different portions of patents.

The backgrounds of patents can also be very useful sources of information. It provides the attorney who is unfamiliar with the technology being patented with an overview of the technology and the use of the technology.

INVENTOR	PATENT	DATE	TITLE
Abe & Fukuda	3992028		Child Restraining Seat
Alexander	4,871,210	10/3/89	Child Holder
Arseneault	5,188,421	2/23/93	Entertainment and feeding device for use by children in automobiles
Aupperlee	5,150,945	9/29/92	Vehicular child seat cover
Barnes	5,026,115	6/25/91	Child car seat cover
Barnes	4,881,780	11/21/89	Securing device and method for holding a child upright on a swing seat
Berlin	3146026		Child's car seat
Blake & Johnson	3767259		Child's Vehicle Safety Seat Assembly
Bloom	3819230		Child's Safety Seat
Bolcerek	4,927,211	5/22/90	Safety harness
Boudreau	4033622		Infant's Car Seat
Bougher	5,039,169	8/13/91	Adjustable lock infant seat
Brittian	5,118,163	6/2/92	Child restraint seat for an aircraft

INVENTOR	PATENT	DATE	TITLE
Bryans, Miller & Single II	4345791		Child Restraint System for a Motor Vehicle
Burke	3094356		Child's Car Seat
Card	3275373		Infant-Holding Attachment for Automobile Seats
Casale	4,902,070	2/20/90	Foldable automobile convertible seat
Castelli	5,060,421	10/29/91	Child and Infant Restraint and Fastener
Converse	4436341		Infant Safety Car Seat
Converse	3563600		Infant Safety Car Seat
Cook	4,867,464	9/19/89	Child restraining safety belt or harness
Coult	4215900		Child's Safety Seat for Vehicles
Crisp	4,900,087	2/13/90	Automobile seat with built-in child seat
Cunningham	4341422		Restraint Device
Dagdagan	5,046,651	9/10/91	Tubular frame support for convertible child carrier
Davis	4,906,043	5/6/90	Child's car seat tray
Delaney	4,936,628	6/26/90	Child car seat
De La Taille, Bernard & Labadie	4046420		Child's Safety Chair
De Vos	3111342		Child's Car Seat
Doughty	4,840,388	6/20/89	Grocery cart
Ettridge	4205877		Children's Reclining Car Seats
Farrell Jr., Cone III & Ellies	4186961		Child Car Seating Apparatus and Method for Assembling the Same
Ferguson	4,883,315	11/28/89	Visor apparatus mounted on protective seat for children
Forlivio	4,913,498	4/3/90	Child restraint seat
Foster Jr.	4,743,063	5/10/88	Convertible Multi-Function Child Restraint System
Gisser	5,002,338	3/26/91	Child restraint
Goor	5,184,844	2/9/93	Integral inflatable occupant restraint system

INVENTOR	PATENT	DATE	TITLE
Griesbaum	4,944,556	7/31/90	Supportive chair, adjustable for growing with a child
Hagerstrom	5,096,260	3/17/92	Child support assembly
Harmon	5,161,855	11/10/92	Vehicle seat with built-in child seat
Haynes	5,154,330	10/13/92	Shopping list holder
Herwig	4,834,460	5/30/89	Baby seat restraint
Holler & Wojciechowski	4486031		Child Restraint for Passive Restraint System
Hudak	3454304		Child's Safety Seat
Huspen	5,074,588	12/24/91	Child safety restraint
Huspen	5,125,863	6/30/92	Toy Safety Restraint
Hyde, Smith, Carmichael & Meader	4429916		Infant Car Seat
Hyde, Vogler, Morelli & Carmichael	3762768		Infant Car Seat
Hyde & Carmichael	3948556		Child's Car Seat
Hyde & Carmichael	3948556		Child's Car Seat
Hyde, Smith, Carmichael & Meader	4429916		Infant Car Seat
Hyde, Vogler, Morelli & Carmichael	3762768		Infant Car Seat
Itkis	5,005,910	4/9/91	Apparatus for restricting relative movement of belt portions
Jakob	3709558		Child Safety Seat
Johnson	5,022,669	6/11/91	Child travel seat
Krambeck	5,119,999	6/9/92	Dual mode seat belt retractor
Leblanc	4,986,600	1/22/91	Collapsible infant seat
Levarek	4,969,658	11/13/90	Child's bicycle seat
Levine	3385883		A-Nor-D-Homosteroids
Levy	3245717		Infant Car Seat
Linden	3305265		Car Seat
Loughney Jr.	3207552		Child's Safety Seat

INVENTOR	PATENT	DATE	TITLE
Mauron	3957303		Safety Seat for a Child
McCracken	5,178,439	1/12/93	Child safety belt sleeve
Meeker	5,181,761	1/26/93	Child restraint system
Meeker	4186962		Car Seat Support and Restraining Stand
Meeker	4231612		Baby Carrier and Car Seat
Meeker	4,826,246	5/2/89	Child Safety Seat
Merelis	3262736		Infant's Car Seat
Merelis	3572827		Child's Car Seat
Morris	3910634		Child Safety Seat
Nania	5,183,312	2/2/93	Child automobile seat with flange revolving upon arched ribs
Neuman	3945678		Harness for Safety Shield Type Children's Car Seat
Nieto-Busby	4,892,357	1/9/90	Child's portable auxiliary seat cushion with upper body support ridge
Norman & Morley	3512830		Safety Belts
Norman & Morley	3633965		Safety Belts
O'Donovan	4,964,551	10/23/90	Bicycle child carrier assembly
Parker	5,061,012	10/29/91	Child car seat with automatic harness adjustment
Perry	5,016,915	5/21/91	Child restraint for use with a seat belt in an automobile
Peterson	3669492		Reclining Car Seat
Plesniarski	4,822,104	4/18/89	Seat Belt Buckle for Child Restraint
P'Simer	3272554		Car Seat for Infants with Seat Anchor
Qureshi	4,989,888	2/5/91	Combination child restraint and stroller
Richardson	5,038,761	8/13/91	Therapeutic apparatus for physically impaired children
Roach	5,083,837	1/28/92	Safety shield for child restraint seat
Roberts & McElhaney	3791694		Child Restraining Seat Assembly
Roberts & McElhaney	3954280		Child Auto Restraint Harness

INVENTOR	PATENT	DATE	TITLE
Robinson	4,973,074	11/7/90	Bicycle frame extension system
Rocker	3166355		Child's Car Seat
Rosen	3388947		Auxiliary Child's Safety Seat for Vehicles
Ruda	4230366		Automotive Seat with Built-In Child Restraint
Sankrithi	4,834,420	5/30/89	Airbag equipped child accommodating device for vehicles
Schmidt	RE 33,679	9/3/91	Combination seat belt retractor mechanism
Selph	5,044,321	9/3/91	Pet carrier and restraint for vehicle use
Severson	4,915,401	4/10/90	Child carrier usable as backpack, stroller and recliner
Sharaf	3737958		Quick Release Locking Mechanism
Single II	4,733,909	3/29/88	Multi-Mode Child Restraint System
Single II	4,729,600	3/8/88	Multi-Mode Child Restraint System
Skold	5,121,965	6/16/92	Child's Car Seat
Smith & Hyde	3338631		Infant's Car Seat
Smith & Hyde	3338631		Infant's Car Seat
Smith, Hyde & Teague	3076628		Baby Seat
Springston	4,938,400	7/3/90	Combination pack and seat
Stark	5,150,728	9/29/92	Umbrella with magnetic fasteners
Steward	4,900,086	2/13/90	Integral folding child restraint system
Switlik	5,143,420	9/1/92	Airplane safety seat for lap children
Tanaka	3912328		Abdominal Restraint and Belt Storage Means for Child Safety Seats for Vehicles
Thary, Bernard, Labadie & De La Taille	4033623		Child's Safety Restraint for Use in a Vehicle
Tomforde	4082350		Shell-Shaped Children's Seat for Vehicles
Tucek	5,188,380	2/23/93	General utility child seat apparatus
Vander Stel	5,100,199	3/31/92	Built-in infant seat

INVENTOR	PATENT	DATE	TITLE
Vander Stel	5,026,118	6/25/91	Built-in infant's seat for vehicles
Von Wimmersperg	4067608		Child Safety Restraint
Von Wimmersperg	4113306		Convertible Child Restraint
Von Wimmersperg	4480870		Infant Restraint for Vehicles
Vorbau	5,063,879	11/12/91	Child restraint method and apparatus for aircraft and other vehicles
Walker	3279848		Child's Car Seat
Weekley	5,004,197	4/2/91	Protective apparatus for a child restraint seat
Whitaker	5,186,520	2/16/93	Force activated tethering device for use with a child safety seat in an automobile
Williams	4502732		Child Car Restraint
Willson	5,000,481	3/19/91	Locking device for vehicle seat belts
Winnale	4256329		Child Restraint for Passive Restraint System
Young	4,762,364	8/9/88	Child Restraint Device

Representative Child Safety Seat Patents:

Patent Number: 5,074,588

Date: Dec. 24, 1991

Title: Child safety restraint

INVENTOR: Huspen, Fred, 2176 Wilderness Dr., Berrien Springs, Michigan 49013

APPL-NO: 608,155

FILED: Nov. 2, 1990

INT-CL: [5] B60R 22#00

US-CL: 280#801; 280#808; 297#465; 297#484

CL: 280;297

SEARCH-FLD: 280#801, 803, 806, 808; 297#250, 253, 254, 384, 385, 389, 465, 484; 128#870, 876

REF-CITED:

U.S. PATENT DOCUMENTS

3,099,486	7/1963	*	Scott et al.	297#389
3,301,594	1/1967	*	Pukish, Jr.	297#389
3,315,671	4/1967	*	Creelman et al	128#134
3,604,750	9/1971	*	Doerling et al.	297#389
3,791,694	2/1974	*	Roberts et al.	297#250
3,889,668	6/1975	*	Ochs et al.	128#134
4,050,737	9/1977	*	Jordan et al.	297#389
4,848,793	7/1989	*	Huspen et al.	280#801

FOREIGN PATENT DOCUMENTS

728849	4/1975	*	United Kingdom

PRIM-EXMR: Rice, Kenneth R.

LEGAL-REP: Welsh & Katz, Ltd.

ABSTRACT: A child safety restraint for a vehicle seat having a safety belt includes a stress plate having at least one safety belt slot for receiving the safety belt to secure the restraint to the seat, at least one harness slot and a harness for releasably securing a wearer's back to the stress plate, the harness including a pair of shoulder straps and a crotch strap secured at one end to the shoulder straps, the shoulder straps being configured to each pass through a respective harness slot in the plate so that the harness is slidably engaged on the plate.

NO-OF-CLAIMS: 20

EXMPL-CLAIM: 1

NO-OF-FIGURES: 5

NO-DRWNG-PP: 2

BACKGROUND OF THE INVENTION

The present invention relates generally to vehicle safety restraints, and more specifically to such restraints used to protect children seated in vehicles from experiencing injury due to vehicular impact or sudden vehicular movement.

The use of "car seats" for infants and young children riding in automobiles has become widespread, largely due to government decree. Such seats usually consist of a hollow seat shell, are often padded, and are designed to be placed on the vehicle seat and secured to the vehicle's existing lap and/or shoulder belt system. In addition, such car seats usually include some sort of internal belt restraint system to prevent the infant from escaping from the seat, or from being thrown from the seat upon a rapid deceleration or impact of the vehicle. Infant car seats of this type are adequate for children up to about three years and about 50 pounds (18.2 kg), but older and larger children often find such a seat too confining and uncomfortable.

For older and/or larger children, larger types of car seats are available which include a metallic tubular frame adapted to be secured to the vehicle seat by the vehicular lap and/or shoulder belt system in similar fashion to the infant car seat described hereinabove. A larger padded seat having a shell type enclosure or housing and a child safety belt restraint is mounted to the frame. Very often, active and/or bored children find such seats unduly restrictive, and sometimes resent the idea of being forced to use a "child's seat", with unruly and disruptive behavior a consequence. Very frequently, these older children are still too small or light weight to properly fit into conventional, "adult size" shoulder and lap belt seat restraints.

In addition, car seats, whether designed for infants or older children, are bulky and difficult to store when not in use. For convenience sake, such seats are often "permanently" mounted in the vehicle even when children are not riding in the car.

In response to the drawbacks of conventional car seats, child restraining vests have been disclosed. Such vests basically consist of a padded plate having a harness for attachment to the child's back, and slots in the plate for accommodating the vehicular lap and/or shoulder belt system. One disadvantage of such vests is that the harness does not include a crotch strap, so that in some cases, a child may "submarine" or slide out from under the harness, either deliberately, or in certain accident conditions. Such a harness structure is also unsuitable for use in aircraft, since the child may easily fall out of the harness if the plane makes fairly rapid loops or rolls.

Another disadvantage of conventional restraining vests is the configuration of the aluminum stress plate, which bends under severe impact. Once bent, the plate may injure the child during the customary post impact rebound or whiplash.

Yet another disadvantage of conventional restraining vests is that the shoulder belts are not properly positioned upon the plate to be pulled evenly upon loading. This disadvantage may cause the plate to shift during impact, providing less than optimum protection to the child.

Thus, there is a need for a child safety restraint including a harness system which prevents "submarining", which enables the stress plate to follow and center upon the wearer's torso, and which includes a stress plate which does not deform under impact.

SUMMARY OF THE INVENTION

Accordingly, the present child safety restraint includes a rigid stress plate and sliding harness system designed to overcome the above-identified disadvantages of conventional vest type vehicle seat restraints. In the present restraint, the plate is more rigid than conventional restraints, and the harness is designed so that the plate centers itself upon the back of the wearer to provide maximum support and to prevent injury.

More specifically, the present restraint includes a stress plate having at least one safety belt slot for receiving the vehicle safety belt to secure the restraint to the seat, at least one harness slot, and a harness for releasably securing a wearer's back to the stress plate. The harness includes a pair of shoulder straps and a crotch strap secured at one end to the shoulder straps, the shoulder straps being configured to each pass through a respective harness slot in the plate so that the harness is slidably engaged on the plate.

DRWDESC: BRIEF DESCRIPTION OF THE DRAWINGS

FIG. 1 is a front elevational view of the present child safety restraint, with portions shown broken away for clarity;

FIG. 2 is a rear elevational view of the safety restraint shown in FIG. 1, with portions shown broken away for clarity;

FIG. 3 is a front perspective elevational view of the restraint of FIG. 1 shown being worn by a child in a vehicle seat;

FIG. 4 is a side elevational view of the child and safety vest as seen in FIG. 3 in the normal riding position; and

FIG. 5 is a side elevational view of the child and safety vest as seen in FIG. 3 showing the effect of the restraint upon a sudden deceleration of the vehicle.

DESCRIPTION OF THE PREFERRED EMBODIMENT

Referring now to FIGS. 1 and 2, the child safety restraint of the invention is indicated generally at 10. The restraint 10 includes a stress plate 12 formed of rigid sheet material such as sheet metal or high-strength molded plastic, and in the preferred embodiment is a single piece of stamped, 6061 TR6 aluminum having a thickness on the order of at least 3/16 inch. It is contemplated that the plate be approximately eight inches wide and eleven inches tall, or with an area of between 85 and 90 square inches. This is a size which will properly fit the upper torsos of children up to about 70 pounds, and will provide sufficient support upon sudden deceleration of the vehicle.

The plate 12 is provided with at least one and preferably two vertical safety belt slots 14, each having a short horizontal slot 16 in communication with the corresponding slot 14 and providing access thereto from a corresponding side edge 18, 20 of the plate 12. The slots 14 are configured to receive a vehicle lap and/or shoulder belt 22 (best seen in FIG. 3) which is used to secure the restraint 10 to a vehicle seat 24 (best seen in FIG. 3). The vehicle seat 24 is designed to be representative of a variety of vehicle seats, including seats installed in automobiles, boats, trains, as well as airplanes.

An upper portion 26 of the plate 12 is provided with at least one upper harness slot 28, two such slots being preferred as seen in FIG. 2. The slot 28 is depicted as being generally horizontal, however it is also contemplated that, in certain applications, both of the slots 28 may be oriented at an angle to the horizontal, with an upper end of each slot pointing toward the center of the upper portion 26. Such orientation is shown at 28a, although it will be appreciated that both slots 28 or 28a will have a similar, i.e., horizontal or angled orientation. A lower portion 30 of the plate 12 is provided with a lower harness slot 32, which in the preferred embodiment is centrally located on the lower portion near a lower edge 34 of the plate 12.

In order to provide comfort to the user, the restraint 10 is provided with a padded covering 36 which in the preferred embodiment includes outer and inner sheets 38, 40 of wear-resistant synthetic material such as vinyl. The sheets 38, 40, are disposed to enclose a layer of resilient filler material 42, such as soft foam made of synthetic material such as polyurethane. If desired, the covering 36 may be made of alternate materials as the dictates of comfort, durability, and cost permit. The covering 36 is made up of a front panel 44, a rear yoke panel 46 secured to an upper edge 48 of the front panel, and a lower rear panel 50 secured to the lower edge of the front panel. The rear yoke panel 46 and the lower rear panel 50 are secured to the front panel 44 such as by stitching, to define a pocket into which the plate 12 is inserted. If desired, the front panel 44 may be provided with slits 51 (best see in FIG. 5) which register with the upper harness slots 28.

Once the plate 12 is inserted behind the front panel 44, and the rear portions 48, 50 of the covering 36 are stitched to the front panel, the plate may not be removed from the covering. This feature promotes the safe use of the restraint 10 by preventing disassembly.

The restraint 10 also includes a harness 52 which secures the covered plate 12 to the back of the user (best seen in FIG. 4). The harness 52 includes a pair of webbed shoulder belts 54 and 56, each of which is fabricated of parachute grade nylon or other material of equivalent strength and flexibility. The shoulder belts 54 and 56 each have respective rear ends 58, 60 which are secured to each other behind a rear side 62 of the plate 12. The belts 54, 56 are also each passed through a respective upper harness slot 28 and a corresponding slit 51 to the front of the restraint 10.

In addition, the belts, 54, 56 are each provided with at least one shoulder pad 64. The shoulder pads 64 are preferably of tubular construction filled with padding material to give them softness and bulk. The pads 64 are configured and disposed upon the belts 54, 56 to provide comfort to the user, as well as to distribute deceleration loads over the user's upper torso. In addition, each of the belts 54, 56 also has a respective front or free end 66, 68 which is passed through an eyelet 70 of one of two tangs 72 of a two-phase quick release buckle 74. In such a buckle 74, the shoulder belts 54, 56 are separately secured within the buckle housing. Each belt 54, 56 may be provided with an additional buckle 76 for purposes of adjusting length.

The harness 52 also includes a crotch strap 78 having a rear end 80 attached such as by stitching to the attached rear ends 58, 60 of the shoulder belts 54, 56. The crotch strap 78 is made of similar material to the shoulder belts 54, 56 and is passed through the lower harness slot 32 in the plate 12, is looped beneath a lower edge 34 of the plate 12, and has a front or free end 82 which is passed through an eyelet 84 in a latch portion 86 of the quick release buckle 74. As was the case with the shoulder belts 54, 56, the crotch strap 78 may be provided with an additional buckle 88 for purposes of adjusting length. Thus, the harness 52 is not secured to the plate 12, but is slidably engaged therein.

Referring now to FIGS. 3 and 4, the restraint 10 of the invention is depicted as worn by a child user 90 seated on the vehicle seat 24 in a normal riding position. It will be seen that the restraint 10 is secured to the seat 24 by the passage of the vehicle seat belt 22 between the front panel 44 of the covering 36 and the front face of the plate 12, and, as described above, through the slots 14.

Once the restraint 10 is secured to the seat 24, the user 90 is secured within the restraint by having the user sit against the front panel 44, disposing a shoulder belt 54, 56 over each of the user's shoulders, and by bringing the crotch strap 78 up between the user's legs. The belts 54, 56 and the strap 78 are fastened together by the buckle assembly including the tangs 72 and the buckle 74. In order to achieve a snug fit of the restraint 10 upon the user 90, adjustment of the respective lengths of the belts 54, 56 and the strap 78 may be made through the use of the buckles 76 and 88.

Referring now to FIG. 5, should the vehicle become subject to rapid deceleration, such as through a sudden stop or an impact, the inertia of the vehicle will act to force the user forward in the direction indicated by the arrow 92. When only conventional lap belts are used by young children, this inertia tends to cause the child's head to contact his knees in an envelope effect. Although the child would be prevented from being thrown around the inside of the vehicle by the lap belt, the bent-over reaction has been known to cause internal and spinal injuries.

In cases where conventional vest type restraints are used, the smaller sized, thinner plates used on such restraints have been known to bend forward through the force of impact loading from the sudden stop. Thus, once the vehicle has stopped, the resulting backward force or whiplash may causes the child to be injured by contacting the hard, forward-facing edge of the plate.

In contrast, the present restraint 10 follows the user 90 forward, remains centrally located on the user's upper torso, and does not bend forward to a noticeable degree upon impact loading. These properties are due in large part to the wider and thicker plate 12 which is resistant to bending and which supports the torso, and to the harness 52 which is slidably engaged with the plate 12. Tests of the present restraint 10 have shown that the force exerted on the plate 12 by the user being thrust forward is centered in the middle of the plate 12. Also, it has been found that the angled orientation of the straps 28a facilitates an even loading of the harness 52.

Further, the addition of the crotch strap 78 facilitates the continued engagement of the user 90 with the restraint 10, and also prevents "submarining" of the user 90 out from under the harness 52. The crotch strap 78 will also more securely restrain the user 90 if the restraint 10 is used in an airplane seat. In this manner, the user's torso will not bend forward, and injury upon the user 90 falling back against the seat 24 is prevented.

When the restraint 10 is not in use, it may be easily unbuckled from the seat and becomes fairly flat for easy storage. Even if the restraint 10 is left buckled to the seat 24, its flat shape will enable the seat to be used for carrying other articles.

While a particular embodiment of the child safety restraint of the invention has been shown and described, it will be appreciated by those skilled in the art that changes and modifications may be made thereto without departing from the invention in its broader aspects and as set forth in the following claims.

CLAIMS: What is claimed is:

1. A child's safety restraint for use in a vehicle having a seat and a safety belt, said restraint comprising:

   a stress plate having a front side and a rear side, at least one safety belt slot for receiving the safety belt to secure the restraint to the seat, and at least one harness slot;

a harness for releasably securing a wearer's upper torso to said stress plate, said harness including a pair of shoulder straps and a crotch strap, said shoulder straps and said crotch strap being configured to each pass through a respective harness slot in said plate so that said harness is slidable as a unit relative to said plate;

said shoulder straps each having a rear end and a free end, said rear ends secured to each other behind said rear side of said plate;

said crotch strap having a rear end and a free end, said rear end attached to said rear ends of said shoulder straps; and

said slidability of said harness relative to said plate being such that, upon rapid deceleration of the vehicle, said restraint follows the user forward and remains centrally located on the user's upper torso.

2. The restraint as defined in claim 1 wherein said stress plate has a pair of shoulder harness slots in an upper portion of said plate, and a crotch strap slot in a lower portion of said plate.

3. The restraint as defined in claim 2 wherein said shoulder harness slots are each slightly angled, with an upper end of said slots pointing toward a center of an upper portion of said plate.

4. The restraint as defined in claim 1 wherein said free end of said crotch strap and said free ends of said shoulder straps are adapted to be releasably secured to each other.

5. The restraint as defined in claim 4 wherein said free ends of said shoulder straps and said crotch strap are releasably secured to each other by a buckle.

6. The restraint as defined in claim 5 wherein said buckle is a two-phase buckle.

7. The restraint as defined in claim 1 further including a cushion fixed to said plate to protect the back of the wearer.

8. The restraint as defined in claim 1 wherein said plate is made of aluminum.

9. The restraint as defined in claim 1 wherein said plate is approximately 8 inches wide and approximately 11 inches tall.

10. The restraint as defined in claim 1 wherein said plate is at least 3/16 inch thick.

11. A child's safety restraint for use in a vehicle having a seat and a safety belt, said restraint comprising:

    a stress plate having a front end and a rear end, at least one safety belt slot for receiving the safety belt to secure the restraint to the seat, and upper and lower harness slots;

    a harness for releasably securing a wearer's upper torso to said stress plate, said harness including a pair of shoulder straps and a crotch strap, said shoulder straps and said crotch strap being configured to each pass through a respective harness slot in said plate so that said harness is slidable as a unit relative to said plate;

    said shoulder straps having a rear end and a free end, said rear ends secured to each other behind said rear portion of said plate;

    said crotch strap having a rear end and a free end, said rear end attached to said rear ends of said shoulder straps;

    said slidability of said harness relative to said plate being such that, upon rapid deceleration of the vehicle, said restraint follows the user forward and remains centrally located on the user's upper torso; and

    said restraint being the only support structure provided to the wearer, and said restraint being utilized independent of any other safety seat structure.

12. The restraint as defined in claim 11 further including a cushion fixed to said plate to protect the back of the wearer.

13. The restraint as defined in claim 11 wherein said plate is made of aluminum.

14. The restraint as defined in claim 11 wherein said plate is approximately 8 inches wide and approximately 11 inches tall to support the back of the wearer.

15. The restraint as defined in claim 11 wherein said plate is at least 3/16 inch thick so as not to deform upon impact loading.

16. A child's safety restraint for use by a child while riding in a vehicle having a seat and a safety belt, said restraint comprising:

    a stress plate configured from a rigid sheet material of at least a 3/16 inch thickness and having a surface area of at least 85 square inches, said plate having a front side and a rear side, said plate having further at least one safety belt slot for receiving the safety belt to secure the restraint to the seat, and upper and lower harness slots;

    a harness for releasably securing a wearer's upper torso to said stress plate, said harness including a pair of shoulder straps and a crotch strap, said shoulder straps and said crotch strap being configured to each pass through a respective harness slot in said plate so that said harness is slidable as a unit relative to said plate;

    said shoulder straps having a rear end and a free end, said rear ends secured to each other behind said rear side of said plate;

    said crotch strap having a rear end and a free end, said rear end attached to said rear ends of said shoulder straps;

    said slidability of said harness relative to said plate being such that, upon rapid deceleration of the vehicle, said restraint follows the user forward and remains centrally located on the user's upper torso; and

    said restraint being the only support structure provided to the wearer, and said restraint being utilized independent of any other safety seat structure.

17. The restraint as defined in claim 16 wherein said shoulder harness slots are each slightly angled, with an upper end of said slots pointing toward a center of an upper portion of said plate.

18. The restraint as defined in claim 16 wherein said shoulder straps each have at least one shoulder pad disposed upon said straps to provide distribution of deceleration loads over the user's upper torso.

19. The restraint as defined in claim 16 wherein said free end of said crotch strap and said free ends of said shoulder straps are adapted to be releasably secured to each other.

20. The restraint as defined in claim 16 further including a cushion fixed to said front side of said plate to protect the back of the wearer.

Patent Number: 5,161,855

Date: Nov. 10, 1992

Title: Vehicle seat with built-in child seat

INVENTOR: Harmon, Michael L., 23897 CR 106, Elkhart, Indiana 46514-9787

APPL-NO: 640,074

FILED: Jan. 11, 1991

INT-CL: [5] B60N 2#30

US-CL: 297#238; 297#391

CL: 297

SEARCH-FLD: 297#238, 484, 467, 391, 464

REF-CITED:

		U.S. PATENT DOCUMENTS		
3,791,694	2/1974	*	Roberts et al.	297#484
4,540,216	9/1985	*	Hassel, Sr.	297#238
4,596,420	6/1986	*	Vaidya	297#238
4,681,367	7/1987	*	Timmers	297#238
4,756,573	7/1988	*	Simin et al.	297#238
4,943,112	7/1990	*	Law	297#238
	FOREIGN PATENT DOCUMENTS			
1243930	11/1988	*	Canada	297#484
2023415	1/1980	*	United Kingdom	97#238

PRIM-EXMR: Brown, Peter R.

LEGAL-REP: Hall; James D.

ABSTRACT: A vehicle seat with built-in child safety seat including a five point restraint system directly anchored to the vehicle seat frame. Foldable headrests are provided which extend outwardly to form lateral headrests for a child carried by the child safety seat. The safety seat and headrests fold into the main vehicle seat back and are concealed when not in use.

NO-OF-CLAIMS: 2

EXMPL-CLAIM: 1

NO-OF-FIGURES: 8

NO-DRWNG-PP: 7

FIELD OF THE INVENTION

This invention relates to a vehicle seat and has specific reference to a vehicle seat with a built-in child seat having a five point restraint system anchored to the vehicle seat frame.

BACKGROUND OF THE INVENTION

Vehicle seats having built-in child seats or provisions for infant or toddler seats are illustrated in U.S. Pat. Nos. 4,533,176; 4,540,216; 4,756,573; and 4,900,087. One problem with the child seats disclosed in the prior art patents is in the manner of attaching the child restraint harnesses and the child seat. The prior art generally connects the harnesses of the restraint system, more commonly referred to as seat belts and shoulder harnesses, to the frame for the child seat. Connection of the restraint system to the child seat frame may create an unsafe condition in a collision. The child seat frame under weight of the child in a collision may break free of the vehicle seat to permit the child and child seat to move freely within the vehicle interior creating a dangerous condition.

Further the prior art patents do not laterally support the child's head. This is especially bothersome when the child carried by the seat is sleeping and the head has a tendency to slump sideways.

SUMMARY OF THE INVENTION

The vehicle seat with built-in child seat of this invention eliminates the problems experienced above by anchoring the seat belts and shoulder harnesses of the child seat five point restraint system directly to the main vehicle seat frame. The five point restraint system when anchored directly to the vehicle seat frame functions independently of the child seat to safely hold the child and child seat in contact with the vehicle seat during a collision. Further, headrests integral with the vehicle seat are positioned on each side of the seat to provide lateral support for the child's head and to provide a support to lean the head against to sleep comfortably. When not in use the child seat and headrests are folded into a recess of the vehicle seat and concealed.

Accordingly, it is an object of the invention to provide for a novel vehicle seat.

Another object of the invention is to provide for a vehicle seat having a built-in child seat wherein the child restraint harnesses are connected directly to the vehicle seat frame.

Another object of the invention is to provide for a vehicle seat with built-in child seat having side head rest supports.

Other objects of the invention will become apparent upon a reading of the following description taken with the accompanying drawings.

DRWDESC: BRIEF DESCRIPTION OF THE DRAWINGS

FIG. 1 is a perspective view of the vehicle seat of the invention with the child seat concealed by a front flap.

FIG. 2 is the perspective view of FIG. 1 with the front flap lowered and the child seat revealed and in a retracted or closed position.

FIG. 3 is the perspective view of FIG. 2 with the child seat in the extended position with the harnesses and head rests in a use position.

FIG. 4 is a fragmented top plan view of FIG. 3.

FIG. 5 is a perspective view of the child seat bottom and back.

FIG. 6 is a side elevational view of the vehicle seat with the child seat attached and in its down or extended position. Portions are shown sectioned and other portions are shown in broken lines for illustrative purposes.

FIG. 7 is the side elevational view of FIG. 6 with the seat in the raised or retracted position.

FIG. 8 is a rear elevational view of the vehicle seat frame and child seat of FIG. 6.

DESCRIPTION OF THE PREFERRED EMBODIMENT

The preferred embodiment herein disclosed is not intended to be exhaustive or to limit the application to the precise form disclosed. Rather, it is chosen and described to enable others skilled in the art to utilize its teachings.

Referring now to the drawings, vehicle seat 10 is illustrated as including a back support 12 and a seat support 14 supported by a pedestal 16. Pedestal 16 is adapted for connection to the floor of a vehicle. Back support 12 includes an inverted U-shaped tubular frame 18 with generally horizontal cross braces 20 connected between the spaced apart frame legs 19. Seat support 14 includes a tubular C-shaped frame 22 having a plurality of seat springs not shown. Seat support frame 22 and back support frame 18 are pivotally interconnected by linkage 24 such that back support 12 may be inclined relative to the seat support 14. A stop 26 is connected to seat support frame 22 to contact linkage 24 and define the fully upright position of back support 12. A known recliner mechanism (not shown) is connected to seat 10 to provide for the controlled recline of the back support 12. An example of a known recliner mechanism may be found by referring to U.S. patent application Ser. No. 390,081 incorporated herein by reference. As thus far described, the construction of seat 10 is known and does not constitute a novel portion of the invention.

A child seat frame 28 (best seen FIG. 5) is provided and includes a seat support 30 and a back support 32 hingedly connected to one another by fasteners 34 as illustrated. Back support 32 includes a back plate 36 with an integral peripheral lip 38. Ear tabs 40 extend outwardly from lip 38. A plurality of openings 42 are formed through back plate 36. Two slots 44 are also formed through back plate 36 in the angled orientation as shown in FIG. 5. Seat support 30 includes a bottom plate 46 integral with a pair of side rails 48. An ear tab 50 extends upwardly from an end of each side rail 48. Ear tabs 50 are adjacent tabs 40 and are connected thereto by fasteners 34 as mentioned for hinged movement of seat support 30 relative to back support 32. A slot 52 is formed through bottom plate 46.

Child seat frame 28 is connected to cross braces 20 of back support 12 by fasteners 54 traversing openings 42 in child seat back plate 36 and extending through openings in the cross braces 20. A nut is turned onto each fastener 54 to secure the child seat frame to back support frame 18.

Back support frame 18 and seat support frame 22 are upholstered for comfort. The upholstery for back support 12 and seat support 14 is shown in broken lines in FIGS. 6-8. Child seat support frame 28 and back support frame is also upholstered for comfort as shown in the figures. A recess 58 is formed in upholstery of back support 12 adjacent the upholstered child seat back support 32 as shown. The seat support 30 of child seat 28 is accommodated by recess 58 when the seat support is in its retracted position as shown in FIGS. 2 and 7. When retracted, seat support 30 fills a substantial portion of recess 58. A decorative outer flap 60 is connected at one end to back support 12. A zipper part 59 along the periphery of flap 60 and a zipper part 62 along the forward peripheral edge of support 12 is provided such that flap 60 may be fully connected to the back support in total concealment of the child seat as shown by reference to FIGS. 1 and 2.

As illustrated seat support 30 of the child seat is pivotal between a retracted or up position as shown in FIGS. 2 and 7 and a down or extended position as shown in FIGS. 3, 5 and 6. In the retracted position the seat support is accommodated within recess 58 such that when flap 60 is zippered or otherwise connected to back support 12 the appearance of the back support and comfort is not disrupted. When flap 60 is unzipped or otherwise substantially disconnected from back support 12 it overlies seat support 14 and forms a protective barrier for the seat support upholstery. Child seat support 30 is pulled downwardly for use and rests on seat support 14 (covered by flap 60). As back support 12 is reclined in a common manner relative to seat support 14, child back support 32 follows back support 12 to recline relative to the child seat support 30.

To safely retain a child within the child seat a five point restraint system including a plurality of straps or harnesses is provided. A shoulder strap 62 terminating in metal tips 63 is connected at one end to linkage 24 by a fastener 65. The strap 62 is threaded through an opening formed in the upholstery of child seat back support 32 and through a slot 44. The other tip 63 of strap 62 is connected by a fastener 54 to a cross brace 20 of the back support frame 18 as shown in FIGS. 6-8. As is further shown in FIG. 8, two L-shaped rods 64 are connected between a cross brace 20 and a leg 19 of tubular frame 18 at an angle substantially corresponding to the angle of slots 44. Strap 62 contacts a rod 64. Rod 64 provides strain relief for strap 62. Similarly a strap 66 includes a metal tip 67 at each end (only one shown). As with strap 62 one end of strap 66 (not shown) is connected in a similar manner to a linkage (not shown) of back support 12 by a fastener on the opposite side of end 63 of strap 62. The strap 66 is threaded through an opening in the upholstery and through the other notch 44 of back plate 36. A tip 67 of strap 66 is connected by a fastener 54 to a cross brace 20 such that strap 66 contacts rod 64 as shown so that the rod provides strain relief for the strap. A male connector 69 is slidably carried on each strap 62, 66. A crotch strap 68 extends through slot 52 in bottom plate 46 and through the upholstery of bottom plate 46. Crotch strap 68 extends along the lower surface of bottom plate 46 and is connected at one to a cross bar 21 by a fastener 70 and a nut 72. The other end of crotch strap 68 terminates in a female connector 74.

In use, a child is positioned on the child seat with crotch strap 68 positioned between the child's legs. The child's neck is substantially between straps 62, 66 as they pass through the child seat back plate. The straps 62, 66 pass over the child's shoulders and male connectors 69 are snap fitted within connector 74 in a known manner such that the lower portion of each strap 62, 66 in combination form a lap belt. Such construction is referred to as a five point harness and may take on many variations within the teachings of this invention. It is important that each of the straps be directly anchored to the vehicle seat frame. Directly anchoring the straps or harnesses to the seat frame provides a safer child confinement over the prior art in the eventuality of a collision.

When the child seat is not in use the straps may be folded between the child seat support and child back support. Flap 60 is then fully connected to the back support 12 as previously described.

To provide lateral head support for the child carried by the seats cushions 78 and 80 are sewn along opposite side edges to back support 12 interior to recess 58. Cushions 78, 80 are positionable in a closed position to span the upper portion of recess 58 above child seat support 30 when retracted. (See FIG. 2). Pillows 78, 80 fill the void above the seat support 30 when the child seat is not in use. As illustrated in FIG. 2 one part 79 of a hook and pile fastener strip commonly referred to as Velcro Registered TM is connected to each side of seat back support 12 adjacent cushions 78, 80. Each pillow carries a mating part 81 of the hook and pile fastener. In use cushions 78, 80 are folded in the manner shown in FIGS. 3 and 4 to form side head rests for a child carried by child seat 28. The cushions are retained in this orientation by the hook and pile fasteners 79, 81 in a well known manner. The width of each cushion 78, 80 is longer than the distance between the edges of recess 58 and the hook and pile fastener strips 79. Therefore, when folded outwardly and the hook and pile fasteners are engaged the cushions bow in the manner illustrated best in FIG. 4 to form side head rests for a child carried by seat 28.

It should be understood that the invention is not limited to the details above but may be modified within the scope of the appended claims.

CLAIMS: I claim:

1. A vehicle seat including a back support frame connected to a seat support frame, said back support frame and said seat support frame being upholstered, a child seat having a back support and a seat support connected to said back support frame, said upholstered back support including a recessed portion adjacent said child seat back support, and headrest means pivotably connected to said upholstered back support shiftable between a retracted position for occupying an upper portion of said recess and an extended position for forming spaced lateral headrests for said child seat, each lateral headrest having fastening means independent of its pivotal connection to said upholstered back support, said fastening means being detachably connected to the upholstered back support when said headrest means is in its said extended position.

2. The vehicle seat of claim 1 wherein each headrest is folded back onto itself in said extended position and is connected to said upholstered back support by said fastening means.

Patent Number: 5,184,844

Date: Feb. 9, 1993

Title: Integral inflatable occupant restraint system

INVENTOR: Goor, Dan, Colorado Springs, Colorado

ASSIGNEE: Goor Associates, Inc., Colorado Springs, Colorado (02)

APPL-NO: 822,272

FILED: Jan. 17, 1992

REL-US-DATA: Continuation-in-part of Ser. No. 618,397, Nov. 27, 1990 now patented 5,100,169

INT-CL: [5] B60R 21#18

US-CL: 280#733; 280#801; 280#808; 297#239

CL: 280;297

SEARCH-FLD: 280#728, 730, 733, 801, 808; 297#293

REF-CITED:

			U.S. PATENT DOCUMENTS	
3,430,979	3/1969	*	Terry et al.	280#733
3,510,150	5/1970	*	Wilfert	280#733
3,706,462	12/1972	*	Lilly	280#733
3,706,463	12/1972	*	Lipkin	280#733
3,844,581	10/1974	*	Fox	280#733
3,866,940	2/1975	*	Lewis	280#733
3,883,053	5/1975	*	Pritchard et al.	224#264
3,905,615	9/1975	*	Schulman	280#733
3,971,569	7/1976	*	Abe et al.	280#733
3,975,037	8/1976	*	Hontschik et al.	280#733
4,348,037	9/1982	*	Law et al.	280#733
4,834,420	5/1989	*	Sankrithi et al.	280#728
4,946,191	8/1990	*	Putsch	280#730
4,971,354	11/1990	*	Kim	280#733
5,062,662	11/1991	*	Cameron	280#733

FOREIGN PATENT DOCUMENTS

2046426	3/1972	*	Federal Republic of Germany	280#733
88/07947	10/1988	*	World Intellectual Property Organization	280#733

PRIM-EXMR: Rice, Kenneth R.

LEGAL-REP: Weingarten, Schurgin, Gagnebin & Hayes

ABSTRACT: An inflatable restraint system for providing protection to an occupant in a moving vehicle including a module disposed adjacent to the chest area of the vehicle occupant, the module having an airbag and an high pressure gas generator for exerting a controlled force against the occupant in a direction opposite the direction of motion of the occupant caused by rapid deceleration of the vehicle while simultaneously inflating the airbag adjacent to the occupant. A second embodiment is disclosed which includes an ancillary module disposed adjacent to the rear base of the occupant's neck, providing an airbag for inflation behind the occupant's head while simultaneously exerting a force opposite the direction of the motion of the occupant's head, as caused by the backlash forces acting against the occupant following initial impact of the occupant with a forward airbag. A third embodiment is disclosed wherein an airbag is in incorporated into a child safety seat providing protection from frontal and lateral impact. A fourth embodiment is disclosed for rear seat passenger protection.

NO-OF-CLAIMS: 29

EXMPL-CLAIM: 1

NO-OF-FIGURES: 17

NO-DRWNG-PP: 8

PARCASE: CROSS REFERENCE TO RELATED APPLICATIONS
This invention is a continuation-in-part of patent application Ser. No. 07/618,397, filed Nov. 27, 1990, entitled "Integral Inflatable Occupant Restraint System," now U.S. Pat. No. 5,100,169.

FIELD OF THE INVENTION

The present invention relates generally to passive vehicle restraint systems and, more specifically, to an integral inflatable occupant restraint system.

BACKGROUND OF THE INVENTION

Various vehicle safety devices and passenger restraint systems are known in the art for protecting the occupants of a vehicle in the event of an accident. Most recently, automobile manufacturers have begun to provide one or more inflatable airbags in the passenger compartment of a vehicle for nearly instantaneous inflation upon rapid deceleration of the vehicle, as caused by a collision. Such airbags provide a cushioned barrier between the occupant and the fixed surroundings of the vehicle passenger compartment for absorbing the forces exerted on the occupant in the collision.

Typically, the airbags of such prior art systems are mounted in various fixed locations in the passenger compartment of the vehicle such as the steering wheel, dashboard or the back panel of a seat (for rear seat passengers). In this configuration, it is necessary for the occupant to be positioned directly in alignment with the position where the airbag is mounted in order to provide effective protection to the occupant This requirement presents a nuisance to the occupant and may actually create a safety risk in cases where the occupant is not positioned directly in front of the airbag when it is inflated.

Other inflatable safety systems have been designed for being disposed adjacent to the vehicle occupant, on a restraining belt, as shown in U.S. Pat. Nos. 3,430,979 and 3,706,462 and in the case of U.S. Pat. No. 4,834,420 a child seat. These systems are designed to provide increased mobility for the occupant while maintaining effective protection thereof by deploying an inflatable cushion adjacent to the occupant in the event of an accident.

Inflatable restraint devices known in the art provide a cushion for absorbing the forces imparted to the occupant in the event of an accident, but do not provide any means for opposing the forces imparted to the occupant at the instant of rapid deceleration of the vehicle. By providing a system for opposing the forces imparted to the occupant, the destructive forces of a collision can be distributed over time and the forces absorbed by the occupant at the point of impact with the airbag can be reduced. Thus, it would be advantageous to provide an occupant restraint system that actually provides a controlled force against the occupant to oppose the motion of the occupant caused by the rapid deceleration of the vehicle while deploying an airbag, thereby reducing the magnitude of the force absorbed by the occupant at the point of impact with the airbag.

SUMMARY OF THE INVENTION

The present invention discloses an inflatable restraint system including a restraint module for being disposed adjacent to the chest area of a vehicle occupant to provide an inflatable shock absorbing cushion adjacent to the occupant while simultaneously exerting a controlled force against the occupant in a direction opposite the direction of motion of the occupant Accordingly, the restraint system of the present invention includes a module housing an inflatable bag and a controlled high pressure gas generator, providing an explosive force upon extremely rapid deceleration or a crash of the vehicle, to deploy the inflatable bag adjacent to the vehicle occupant and to simultaneously generate a reactionary force against the occupant. The reactionary force created by the high pressure gas generator of the invention generates a controlled force against the occupant in a direction opposite the direction of motion of the occupant, thereby increasing the amount of time before the occupant impacts with the inflatable bag and decreasing the magnitude of the force absorbed by the occupant at the moment of impact with the airbag. Embodiments of present invention are disclosed which are useful in protecting against both frontal and lateral impact in either the front or rear seat, as well as an embodiment for a child seat. Yet another embodiment discloses a preinflated cushion within the inflatable bag which accelerates bag inflation and provides back-up cushioning in the event of system failure.

DRWDESC: DESCRIPTION OF THE DRAWINGS

Other features and advantages of the invention will be apparent from the following detailed description of the invention in conjunction with the accompanying drawings, in which:

FIG. 1 is a cross-sectional view of the restraint module of the present invention;

FIG. 2 is a side view showing the occupant restraint system of the present invention in its deployed state;

FIG. 3 is a block diagram of an interdependent sensing and arming system for triggering the present invention;

FIG. 4 is a schematic diagram showing the forces acting on the occupant at the moment that the present invention is deployed;

FIG. 5 is a side view showing an embodiment including a head protection restraint for use in conjunction with the forward airbag of the present invention;

FIG. 6 is a schematic diagram showing the forces acting on the occupant in the embodiment of FIG. 5;

FIG. 7 is a top view viewing showing an embodiment of the present invention utilizing a plurality of restraint modules;

FIG. 8 is a perspective view of a child seat incorporating the restraint module of the present invention in its deployed state;

FIG. 9 is a block diagram of a sensing, arming and indicating system for use in the embodiment of FIG. 8;

FIG. 10 is a top view of the device of FIG. 8 incorporating an adjustable restraint module which affords enhanced lateral protection;

FIG. 11 is a top view of the device of FIG. 8 incorporating multiple restraint modules for enhanced lateral protection;

FIG. 12 is a further embodiment of the device of FIG. 11;

FIG. 13 is a top view of the device of FIGS. 12 and 13 in its fully deployed state;

FIG. 14 is a perspective view of an embodiment of the present invention for protection of rear seat occupants;

FIG. 15 is an overhead view of the embodiment of FIG. 11 in its deployed state;

FIG. 16 is a cross-sectional view of an embodiment of the present invention having a preinflated cushion within the airbag prior to deployment; and

FIG. 17 is a cross-sectional view of the embodiment of FIG. 13 after deployment.

DETAILED DESCRIPTION OF THE INVENTION

Referring now to FIG. 1, the airbag restraint system of the present invention is embodied in a restraint module 10 including an airbag 12, shown in its collapsed state, mounted on a rigid membrane 14 adjacent to a protective cushion 16. A high pressure gas generator 18 is mounted within the module 10, adjacent to the rigid membrane 14 and coupled to an energy source 20 via a motion sensor 22. In addition, or alternatively, the high pressure gas generator 18 is also coupled to a pressure sensor 24 embedded in the protective cushion 16 and/or an impact sensor 26 (shown in FIG. 2) located on the vehicle in which the occupant is seated.

The module 10 is preferably a stand-alone module which can be mounted on a restraining harness in a vehicle, as shown in FIG. 2, or can be disposed on a vest worn by the vehicle occupant. This stand-alone feature allows the flexibility to manufacture and distribute customized airbag restraint systems in accordance with the invention, providing maximum individual comfort and protection for each individual depending on the size and weight of the individual.

Referring now to FIG. 2, there is shown a vehicle 30 with an occupant 32 seated within a shoulder harness 34 in a seat 36. The occupant restraint system of the present invention is shown in its deployed state with airbag 12 inflated to provide an impact absorbing cushion between the occupant 32 and the interior of the vehicle 30. Although the occupant restraint system is shown in conjunction with an automobile, it is contemplated that the present invention can be adapted for use in various passenger vehicles including trains and airplanes.

In operation, the high pressure gas generator 18 is triggered upon very rapid deceleration or crash of the vehicle 30 to generate a transient explosive force. The transient force generated thereby is transmitted throughout the restraint module 10 to create a controlled force against the rigid membrane 14 in a direction opposite the forward motion of the vehicle occupant 32 caused by the rapid deceleration of the vehicle, while simultaneously deploying the airbag 12 from the restraint module 10 into the area immediately adjacent to the occupant 32. The high pressure gas generator 18 may take the form of one of various known systems which may include a self-contained CO2 cartridge or some known chemical discharge mechanism.

High pressure gas generator 18 is triggered by an output signal generated by motion sensor 22, pressure sensor 24, or impact sensor 26, similar to those presently known and in use in the art. A redundant triggering system is contemplated wherein the motion sensor 22, detecting the occupant's rate of movement, the pressure sensor 24, detecting the pressure exerted by the occupant against the module 10, and the vehicle impact sensor 26, detecting vehicle integrity, are each coupled to the high pressure gas generator 18 for providing an output signal thereto.

In the interest of providing a dependable deployment of the airbag 12 while preventing accidental deployment thereof, the sensors 22, 24, 26 can be configured to operate interdependently. For example, sensors 22, 24, 26 can be connected in series or can be coupled to the high pressure gas generator 18 via a microprocessor 19, in a configuration as shown in FIG. 3, wherein the microprocessor can be programmed so that the high pressure gas generator 18 will be triggered only if all three sensors 22, 24, 26 generate an output signal or if a combination of at least any two sensors detects a triggerable condition to generate an output signal. Of course, the restraint system can also be configured to be deployed in response to an output signal from a single sensor 22, 24, or 26.

An interlock arming system including a weight sensor 28 is also provided as a means for preventing accidental deployment of the airbag 12. The arming system is coupled to the high pressure gas generator 18 for detecting a predetermined weight, representing the presence of an occupant in the vehicle seat 36. This weight must be detected in order to "arm" the high pressure gas generator 18 so that it can be triggered by the sensors 22, 24, and/or 26. The interlock arming system may also include a manual switch which may be incorporated into a typical seatbelt buckle. The interlock arming system can also be coupled to the microprocessor 19 triggering system, as shown in FIG. 3.

The advantages of the present invention can be best appreciated by representing the forces acting on the vehicle occupant 32 in schematic form as shown in FIG. 4. Force f2 represents the reactionary force generated against the occupant 32 by the present restraint system. Force f2 is directly opposite the force f1 created by the rapid deceleration of the vehicle 10. The representative forces shown in FIG. 4 can be further reduced to basic physical equations to provide an explanation of the advantages provided by the present invention.

In the following description, it is assumed that the distance d that an occupant 32 travels within the vehicle compartment as the result of rapid deceleration of the vehicle will be constant for a given occupant of mass m. In reality, the present invention may actually reduce the distance that the occupant 32 will travel, resulting in a further reduction of the force f1 acting on the occupant 32. The approach presented herein offers a conservative mathematical analysis for illustrative purposes only.

It is given through the laws of physics that velocity v is equal to distance d divided by time t and that force F is equal to velocity v times mass m as expressed in the following mathematical equations, respectively:

$$v = d/t;\ d = vt \quad (1)$$

$$F = v \times m \quad (2)$$

Thus, the velocity and force generated by an occupant as it is accelerated in a rapidly decelerating vehicle is given by equations (1) and (2).

Applying a force f2 in a direction opposing the acceleration of the occupant 32, as provided by the present invention, the time t that it takes for the occupant's body to travel the distance d from its position at rest to the point of impact with the airbag 16 is increased. Assuming the force exerted on the occupant 32 by the present invention increases the time to impact with the airbag by a factor of two, the velocity of the occupant's body utilizing the restraint system of the present invention becomes:

$$V\ b = d/2t \quad (3)$$

Since the distance d that the occupant travels remains constant, equation (1) can be substituted into equation (3) to show that by using the restraint system of the present invention, the velocity V b of the occupant as it impacts the airbag is:

$$V\ b = vt/2t = v/2 \quad (4)$$

Substituting the value for V b into the force equation:

$$F\ b = V\ b \times m = v/2 \times m = F/2 \quad (5)$$

Thus, it can be seen from this mathematical derivation that the force acting on an occupant 32 in a vehicle 10, during rapid deceleration thereof can be reduced in direct relationship to an increase in the amount of time to impact with the airbag 12. This increase in time is effected by the reactionary force generated by the restraint system of the present invention.

A second embodiment of the present invention is illustrated in FIG. 5 wherein an ancillary restraint module 40 is positioned behind the base of the neck of the occupant 32. As in the embodiment described hereinabove, the ancillary restraint module 10 provides a reactionary force against the acceleration of the occupant's body while simultaneously deploying an airbag 42. In this embodiment, however, a delay mechanism 44 is coupled between the ancillary module 40 and the vehicle sensor 26 so that the ancillary module is triggered at a predetermined time after the triggering of the primary restraint module 10.

As shown in FIG. 6, this second embodiment generates a force f4 to counteract the force f3 acting on the occupant's head generated by the impact of the occupant 32 with the primary airbag 12. It follows, therefore, from the above mathematical derivation, that the reactionary force f4 generated by the ancillary module 40 further reduces the forces exerted against the occupant's neck and thereby reducing whiplash effects on the occupant 32. The dual airbag system shown in FIG. 5 operates to dampen both the forward and rearward movement of the occupant in a severe accident, decreasing the impact forces acting on the occupant 32. The combination of reactionary forces f2 and f4 provided by this dual airbag system can be adapted to the mass and velocity of the occupant being protected that the present invention provides an adaptive restraining system which conforms to the severity of the forces acting on the occupant.

As shown in FIG. 7, the restraint system of the present invention can also be implemented via a plurality of restraint modules 10 disposed across the body of an occupant 32 along a rigid membrane 14, providing multiple independent airbags adjacent to the occupant. This configuration of multiple restraint modules 10 provides additional side protection to the occupant 32 as well as a distribution of the reactionary forces acting against the occupant 32.

A third embodiment of the occupant restraint, suitable for protection of a child, is show in FIG. 8, wherein a child safety seat 50 combines a child sized seat 52 having straps 58 and a pad 60 similar to those in the present art, with the superior impact protection of an airbag 54 deployed from a restraint module 56 which produces reactionary forces. The restraint module 56 may be attached to the seat 52 as an aftermarket add-on, as a vehicle independent seat manufactured with the restraint module 56 or as a seat having a restraint module 56, but vehicle dependent for either acceleration sensing or airbag inflation.

The restraint module 56 when used as an aftermarket add-on to prior art child seats is entirely self contained. The restraint module 56 contains the airbag 54, acceleration sensors 61, the high pressure gas generator 18, and optional microprocessor 19 as described with respect to FIGS. 1-3. It should be understood that the high pressure gas generator 18 may be, but is not necessarily, a gas filled cylinder. It may be a device for releasing highly compressed gas, gas formed from rapidly combining chemicals, or gas produced in a pyrotechnic discharge. The restraint module 56 is attached to the straps 58 and/or pad 60 which serve to restrain the child within the seat 52. Alternatively, the straps 58 and/or pad 60 of the seat 52 may be removed and replaced with an aftermarket system having straps 58 and/or a pad incorporating the restraint module 56. The resulting child safety seat 50, thus configured is triggered in response to a firing signal from an acceleration sensor 61 and/or a pressure sensor 63 mounted on or in the restraint module. Upon activation, the high pressure gas generator 18 generates reactionary forces against the occupant 32 during airbag 54 inflation as described with respect to FIG. 2.

In another embodiment, the child safety seat 50 is designed for manufacture as an integral, vehicle independent seat. In this embodiment the child safety seat 50 may have the high pressure gas generator housed in the body of the seat 52, either under the seat 52 as depicted in FIG. 8, behind it or to one of the sides. When activated, the rapidly expanding gas is conducted to the airbag 54 via an appropriately sized tube 65. Additionally, the child safety seat 50 has an arming switch 64 located in a position inaccessible to the child. The child safety seat 50 may be equipped with pressure or weight sensors (not shown) to prevent arming of an unoccupied seat and indicator flags or lights 66 which signal the activation state of the seat. For example, a red indicator light 66 indicates that the system is turned on, and a second green indicator light 67 then illuminates when the module 56 is secured in place and weight is on the seat.

FIG. 9 illustrates the circuit logic for electrical arming of the child safety seat 50 and is useful in describing the operation and activation of the seat. An electrical power source 70, such as a battery powers both a trigger circuit 72 and an arming status circuit 74. The trigger circuit 72 has several points of interruption on each side of the circuit 72 which act as safety features to prevent inadvertent airbag 54 deployment. To complete one side of the trigger circuit 72, which outputs a signal to activate the high pressure gas generator 18, the manual arming switch 64 must be in the "on" or contact position and the seat pressure switch 76 closed, due to an occupant 32 in the child safety seat 50. The other side of the trigger circuit 72 is completed when the motion/impact switch 78, as described more fully with respect to FIGS. 1 and 2, and the restraint module pressure switch 80 are closed. Thus, when both sides of the trigger circuit 72 are closed, electrical current flows to the trigger 80 which activates the high pressure gas generator 18. A wide variety of switches are compatible with this invention, with solid state switches and piezoelectric pressure sensors having particular applicability.

The arming status circuit 74 provides an indication to the person placing an infant into the child safety seat 50 whether the seat 50 is armed or not. The arming status circuit 74 provides power to the red 66 and green 67 indicator lights when the manual arming switch 64 is on and the seat pressure switch 76 is closed.

Referring now to FIG. 10, a top view of an embodiment of the child safety seat 50 is shown with a modification to enhance protection of the occupant 32 from lateral impacts. In this embodiment, the seat 52 has, in addition to straps 58 and/or a pad 60, a rail or tray 84 extending out from the sides 86 of the seat 52 which passes in front of the occupant's torso. The restraint module 56 being flexibly attached to one end of each telescoping arm 88 and 90 along the back or sides of the restraint module 56 with a mechanical hinge, pivot joint, or elastomeric material, is attached to the rail or tray 84 with the other end of each telescoping arm 88 and 90 with lockable pivot joints 94 which allow the restraint module 56 to be oriented to the right, left or center of the child safety seat 50. Alternatively, the telescoping arms 88 and 90 may be attached directly to the seat 52, thus obviating the need for a supplemental rail or tray 84. Additionally, either an elastomeric pad 92 may be placed between the telescoping arms 88 and 90 on the back of the restraint module 56, or the airbag 54 may be shaped to inflate rearward around and between the arms.

In FIG. 10 the restraint module 56 is positioned to the left to better protect the occupant 32 in the left rear seat from left side impact. When the child safety seat 50 is installed on the right side of a vehicle, in either the front or rear seat, the restraint module 56 is swung to the right side and locked into position. When moving from side to side the telescoping arms 88 and 90 are free to extend and retract as required for movement, but when the restraint module 56 is aligned as desired, an internal mechanism (not shown) is engaged to fix the length of the arms 88 and 90 when the pivot joints 94 are locked. For use in the center of a front or rear seat when lateral impact protection might not be a primary consideration, the arms 88 and 90 are retracted an equal amount to center the restraint module 56 which then operates in the manner described with respect to FIG. 8.

With reference to FIG. 11, another embodiment of the present invention is shown for protection of an occupant 32 from lateral impact. A seat 52, having sides 86 and rail or tray 84, is depicted with three restraint modules 56 affixed to the rail or tray 84. The restraint modules 56 are shown encased in a optional lightweight rail cushion 106 which serves to protect the restraint modules 56 and to provide low cost aesthetic variation. The restraint modules 56 in this figure are completely self contained and incorporate multi-axis acceleration sensors 61 which are responsive to both frontal and lateral impacts, an airbag 54 and a high pressure gas generator 18. As with the child safety seat of FIG. 8, this embodiment using self-contained restraint modules 56 is suitable for sale in the aftermarket.

FIG. 12 depicts a child safety seat 50 with a single high pressure gas generator 18 in communication with three airbags 54 mounted on the rail or tray 84. In this figure, the optional rail cushion 106 is not installed. The child safety seat of FIG. 12 includes sensors 61 and microprocessor 19 (not shown) in addition to the high pressure gas generator 18, as more fully described with respect to FIG. 9. While the drawing depicts a single tube 65 which is has branches going to each airbag 54 from the high pressure gas generator 18, completely individual tubes 65 connected to individual high pressure gas generators 18 may be employed. It is also contemplated that gas output be sequentially directed by the microprocessor 19, as a function of impact direction, through a control valve or valves (not shown) so as to inflate one or more airbags 54 prior to the others. Alternatively, the tubes 65 run from one airbag 54 to the others where, for example, the center airbag 54 upon inflating to its predetermined fill volume, directs the continued influx of gas to the left and right side airbags 54. This order can be altered either through programming of the microprocessor 19 with a simple user control pad (not shown) on the seat designating center, left or right airbag 54 inflation priority. As with the other embodiments, each restraint module 56 generates reactionary forces. Thus, when multiple restraint modules 56 are employed, multiple reactionary forces are generated along the appropriate axis to retard the movement of the occupant 32 into the airbags 54. FIG. 13 depicts the child safety seat 50 with all three airbags 54 inflated to surround the occupant 32. The integral, and therefore portable, child safety seat 50 thus described may be used in any type of conveyance, such as airplanes, buses, trains or trucks, where a frontal or lateral impact protection system is not available or needs to be supplimented. With respect now to FIG. 14 another embodiment of the inflatable occupant restraint is shown for use in a rear seat of a vehicle. This embodiment is primarily intended as a self-contained aftermarket addition to taxis and limousines, but is equally useful for private automobile use as well as in airplanes, helicopters, trains and buses. FIG. 14 depicts the interior of a car with front 96 and rear 98 bench style seats. Behind the front seat 96 an elongated restraint module 56 is incorporated into a restraint rail 100. The restraint rail 100 may be tilted forward towards the front seat 96 to allow passenger ingress, and then tilted back over the passenger's lap or in close proximity to the torso of the passenger. It is envisioned that a work surface 103 can be detachably affixed to the restraint rail 100 as desired. The rail 100 may be articulated at the floor level of the vehicle or at any point along the side tubes 104 of the restraint rail 100 with hinges 102. Furthermore, the high pressure gas generator 18 may be located in one of the side tubes 104 or high pressure gas generators 18 may be placed in each, both of which responsive to the trigger 82 of the trigger circuit 72. Supplemental floor mounted pressure sensors 106 may also be incorporated as shown to inhibit inadvertent system activation.

Inflation of the airbag 54 is triggered, and reactive forces are generated in the same manner as described with respect the preceding embodiments. When inflation of the airbag 54 is triggered, the airbag inflates away from the occupant 32, thus pushing the restraint rail 100 and optional work surface 103 away from the occupant, flush against the front seat back or into a recess designed to receive it.

FIG. 15 is an overhead view of the inflatable occupant restraint described in FIG. 14 with its airbag 54 deployed. In this view the restraint rail 100 containing the restraint module 56 is shown with work surface 103 installed, pushed forward into a recess in the back of the front seat 96. The airbag 54 is shaped so that when inflated, the sides of the airbag 54 inflate between the occupant 32 and the vehicle side for enhanced protection from lateral impact. It is important to note that in this embodiment, as with the others, the restraint module 56 is positioned sufficiently close to the occupant 32 (or occupants) so that the reactive forces serve to attenuate impact forces in addition to providing the cushioning of the airbag 54.

Turning now to FIG. 16, another embodiment of the restraint module 56 of the present invention is shown, wherein the uninflated airbag 54 contains, and is packed inside the restraint module 56 around, a preinflated cushion 105. The preinflated cushion 105 provides a portion of the inflation gas to the airbag 54 as a function of the volume it displaces within the airbag 54. The remainder of the gas is furnished by the high pressure gas generator 18 upon triggering of the system. The preinflated cushion 105 may be connected directly to tube 65 which is the gas conduit from the high pressure gas generator 18. In this arrangement, the sudden influx of gas causes the preinflated cushion 105 to burst, thus releasing both the "old" gas from the preinflated cushion 105 and the "new" gas from the high pressure gas generator into the airbag 54. In a different arrangement, the tube 65 is routed directly into the airbag 54, bypassing the preinflated cushion 105, and results in an inflated airbag 54 with an intact preinflated cushion 105 inside of it as depicted in FIG. 17. In the event of system failure, the preinflated cushion 105 within the restraint module 56 provides partial protection of the occupant 32 subjected to impact forces.

The presently described integral inflatable restraint system is illustrative of a novel apparatus for providing dynamic protection for the occupants of a moving vehicle. It will be appreciated that other modifications, embodiments and departures from the present disclosure are possible without departing from the inventive concept contained herein. Consequently, the invention is to be viewed as embracing each and every novel feature as well as any novel combination of features present in, or possessed by, the inflatable restraint system disclosed herein and is to be limited solely by the scope and spirit of the appended claims.

CLAIMS: What is claimed is:

1. A child safety seat incorporating an inflatable restraint system for protecting an occupant of said child safety seat in a moving vehicle upon rapid deceleration thereof, comprising:

   a child seat, wherein said child seat is adapted for use in said moving vehicle;

   at least one restraint module mounted on said child seat adjustably disposed adjacent to said occupant, said at least one restraint module comprising:

   an inflatable bag for deployment from said at least one restraint module in a direction away from said occupant;

   a high pressure gas generator for inflating said inflatable bag and for exerting a reactionary force against said occupant in a direction opposite the direction of inflation of said inflatable bag;

   at least one sensor means, coupled to said high pressure gas generator for providing an output signal to trigger said inflation upon detection of a predetermined event.

2. The child safety seat of claim 1, further including:

   a cushion being disposed between said module and said occupant for dispersing said reactionary force generated by said high pressure gas generator.

3. The child safety seat of claim 1 wherein said at least one sensor means includes:

   at least one motion sensor coupled to said at least one restraint module for detecting acceleration of said occupant to provide said output signal to said high pressure gas generator upon detection of a predetermined magnitude of acceleration.

4. The child safety seat of claim 1 wherein said at least one sensor means includes:

   at least one impact sensor means coupled to said vehicle for detecting an impact force against said vehicle to provide said output signal to said high pressure gas generator upon detection of a predetermined magnitude of impact force.

5. The child safety seat of claim 1 wherein said at least one sensor means includes:

   at least one pressure sensor coupled to said at least one restraint module for detecting pressure between said at least one restraint module and said occupant to provide said output signal to said high pressure gas generator upon detection of a predetermined magnitude of pressure.

6. The child safety seat of claim 1, further including:

   microprocessor means coupled between said at least one sensor means and said high pressure gas generator, said microprocessor means being programmable to provide a trigger signal to said high pressure gas generator in response to said output signal from any one of said at least one sensing means.

7. The child safety seat of claim 1, further including:

   microprocessor means coupled between said at least one sensor means and said high pressure gas generator, said microprocessor means being programmable to provide a trigger signal to said high pressure gas generator in response to said output signal from a predetermined plurality of at least one sensing means.

8. The child safety seat of claim 1, further including:

   arming means for engaging and disengaging said at least one sensor means to prevent accidental activation thereof.

9. The child safety seat of claim 8, further including:

   microprocessor means coupled between said at least one sensor means, said arming means and said high pressure gas generator;

   said microprocessor means being programmable to provide a trigger signal to said high pressure gas generator in response to an engagement signal from said arming means and said output signal from any one of said at least one sensing means.

10. The child safety seat of claim 8, further including:

    microprocessor means coupled between said at least one sensor means, said arming means and said high pressure gas generator;

    said microprocessor means being programmable to provide a trigger signal to said high pressure gas generator in response to an engagement signal from said arming means and said output signal from a predetermined plurality of said at least one sensing means.

11. The child safety seat of claim 8, wherein said arming means includes manual switch means to engage and disengage said sensor means.

12. The child safety seat of claim 8, wherein said arming means includes a pressure switch means for detecting the presence of said occupant to engage said sensor means in response to the detection of said occupant.

13. The child safety seat of claim 1, further including a shoulder harness disposed over the upper torso of said occupant, said at least one restraint module being disposed thereon.

14. The child safety seat of claim 1, having a restraining pad coupled to a shoulder harness, said at least one restraint module being disposed thereon.

15. The child safety seat of claim 1, wherein said child safety seat is easily removable from said vehicle.

16. The child safety seat of claim 1, wherein said child safety seat is adapted for permanent installation in said vehicle.

17. The child safety seat of claim 1, wherein said child safety seat further comprises:

    a first telescoping arm flexibly attached to said at least one restraint module for pivotally connecting said restraint module to said child seat or an extension thereof;

    a second telescoping arm flexibly attached to said at least one restraint module for pivotally connecting said restraint module to said child seat or an extension thereof; and

    a locking means for stabilizing an axial orientation of said at least one restraint module.

18. The child safety seat of claim 17, wherein said extension is a rail.

19. The child safety seat of claim 1, wherein said high pressure gas generator is pyrotechnic.

20. The child safety seat of claim 1, wherein said high pressure gas generator is highly compressed gas.

21. The child safety seat of claim 1, wherein said high pressure gas generator is a rapid chemical reaction.

22. The child safety seat of claim 1, further including:

    a preinflated cushion disposed inside said inflatable bag, said inflatable bag having an approximate full inflation volume, for reducing an inflation rate of said inflatable bag by releasing

    into said inflatable bag a portion of said full inflation volume of a gas upon triggering said high pressure gas generator, and for further providing a cushion in the event of failure of said inflatable restraint system.

23. A vehicle independent child safety seat comprising:

    a plurality of inflatable bags for deployment in a direction away from an occupant of said vehicle;

    a mounting means for holding said plurality of inflatable bags adjacent said occupant;

    at least one high pressure gas generator for inflating said plurality of inflatable bags and for exerting a reactionary force against said occupant in a direction opposite the direction of inflation of each said plurality of inflatable bags;

a control means responsive to at least one sensor means and a system user for directing high pressure gas from said at least one high pressure gas generator to said plurality of inflatable bags in a predetermined sequence; and

at least one sensor means, coupled to said control means and said high pressure gas generator for providing an output signal to trigger said inflation upon detection of a predetermined event.

24. The vehicle independent child safety seat of claim 23 wherein said predetermined event is a frontal impact upon said vehicle.

25. The vehicle independent child safety seat of claim 23 wherein said predetermined event is a lateral impact upon said vehicle;

26. The vehicle independent child safety seat of claim 23 wherein said predetermined event is a vehicle crash

27. The vehicle independent child safety seat of claim 23, further including:

a preinflated cushion disposed inside each of said plurality of inflatable bags, each of said plurality of inflatable bags having an approximate full inflation volume, for reducing an inflation rate of each of said plurality of inflatable bags by releasing into each of said plurality of inflatable bags a portion of said full inflation volume of a gas upon triggering said at least one high pressure gas generator, and for further providing a cushion in the event of failure of any of said plurality of inflatable bags to deploy.

28. A vehicle independent inflatable passenger restraint system comprising:

at least one inflatable bag for deployment in a direction away from an occupant of said vehicle;

a high pressure gas generator for inflating said at least one inflatable bag and for exerting a reactionary force against said occupant in a direction opposite the direction of inflation of said at least one inflatable bag;

at least one sensor means, coupled to said high pressure gas generator for providing an output signal to trigger said inflation upon detection of a predetermined event;

an articulated structure mounted to a portion of said vehicle, 13 wherein said articulated structure includes said at least one inflatable bag, and is positionable adjacent said occupant.

29. The passenger restraint of claim 23, further including:

a preinflated cushion disposed inside each of said at least one inflatable bag, said at least one inflatable bag having an approximate full inflation volume, for reducing an inflation rate of said at least one inflatable bag by releasing into said at least one inflatable bag a portion of said full inflation volume of a gas upon triggering said high pressure gas generator, and for further providing a cushion in the event of failure of said inflatable restraint system.

Appendix

Glossary of Technical Terms

Airbag—A passive restraint system which automatically inflates a bag in front of the driver and/or the front seat passenger. The airbag provides a cushion against crash forces and is most effective when used with a lap belt.

Armrest—Many child restraint systems have arm rests, but this feature provides no safety function.

Automatic Seat belts—This is a type of passive restraint system that wraps around the passenger without any action on the passenger's part.

Booster Seat—This is a type of child restraint system that consists of a shell and a low cushion without a permanent back. This type of child restraint is designed to raise the child up and overcome problems of lap belt fit. Some booster seats have a shield designed to spread all of the pressure forces evenly over the child's abdomen in the event of a sudden stop or crash.

Child Restraint—Also known as a child safety seat ("CSS"), car seat, baby seat or child restraint device ("CRD"). The device is designed to protect an infant or child passenger from injury in an automobile crash. It is important to note that an infant seat or infant carrier does not refer to a child restraint.

ChildSafer™—This new device, which resembles a long, plastic ruler, with slits at various places along the length of the device, adjusts the shoulder harness or seat belts so that it fits across the chest of a smaller dog or child.

Convertible Child Safety Seat—This is a child restraint device which is capable of serving both a rear facing child restraint for infants up to 17 lb to 20 lb or as a forward facing safety seat for toddlers from 20 lb to 40 lb

Crash Test—The crash test of child restraint systems is a laboratory simulation of the forces that impact a child restraint during a real collision. The crash test is used to certify seats according to the Federal Safety Standard, FMVSS 213. The dynamic test consists of accelerating the dummy strapped in a child restraint on a sled which is then accelerated to 30 miles per hour and brought to an abrupt stop.

Crash worthiness—Crashworthiness is the protection that an occupant of a motor vehicle receives from the design of a vehicle against personal injury or death as a result of a motor vehicle accident.

CRD—Child Restraint Device. See definition for Child Restraint.

CSS—Child Safety Seat. See definition for Child Restraint.

ECE44—This is the European Child Restraint Standard.

Emergency Locking Belt—This type of belt tightens only in an emergency, such as when the occupant is thrown against the belt or when the automobile's speed is suddenly reduced. FMVSS 216 stands for Federal Motor Vehicle Safety Standard 216. This standard regulates the manufacturers of child restraint devices for children up to 50 lb The original standard was enacted in 1971, major revisions were implemented in 1981, and since then various amendments complimented the standard and it continues to regulate both the manufacturer design and instructions that come with child restraint devices.

Five Point Harness or Five Point Restraint—This is a system of straps built into a child restraint system which restrains and anchors a child's body at five points: both shoulders, the crotch and both hips.

Five Point Restraint System—Child restraint devices that have a 5 point restraint system, restrained child in 5 places, both shoulders, the hips, and the crotch area.

FMVSS213—This stands for Federal Motor Vehicle Safety Standard 213. This standard became effective on April 1st, 1971 and has subsequently been modified. Standard 213 regulates to decide manufacture testing and manuals involving child restraint devices. Sled test (see crash test).

Harness—Is a group of straps and belts that are used to secure a child in a child restraint.

Iliac crests—Bony protrusions from the iliac bone that help secure an adult wearing a lap belt. These crests are not as developed in children and for that reason the lap portion of a seat belt is not effective for securing small children (0–5 years).

Integrated Seats—Integrated seats are child restraint devices that are built in right into the rear seat of many automobiles. Volvo was the first to introduce the concept in 1991. American companies such as Chrysler have introduced integrated car seats to their mini-van lines and sedans.

KARS—Kids Are Riding Safe. This is a program that provides information to hospitals and individuals regarding child restraint education. This program is sponsored by the National Easter Seal Society.

Lodgeplate—This is the flat metal plate on a safety belt that fits into the buckle.

Locking Clip—This simple device is manufactured by both car seat manufacturers and auto makers. The device prevents seat belts equipped with emergency lock and retractors, (ELR's) from sliding when pressure is exerted by a child restraint seat. The clip is manufactured in metal and plastic formats. Recently it has been discovered that certain plastic locking clips may not perform as expected.

This device is "H" shaped and is usually made from metal or plastic. The device is used to keep tension on the lap portion of the continuous loop emergency locking belt so that it can be used in conjunction with child restraint systems.

MVA—Motor vehicle accident.

Nineteen City Survey—This survey conducted by NHTSA provides information concerning various forms of restraint use. Distributing current information on helmet use, seat belt, and child restraint use. This study is based on direct observation which takes place in 19 different cities throughout the country. This survey began in 1979.

NHTSA—The National Highway Transportation Safety Administration is an agency within the Department of Transportation responsible for reducing the number of vehicular tragedies by enacting and overseeing federal legislation and studies involving transportation issues.

Preemption—Preemption refers to the concept where federal legislation preempts action by the state courts. An example of preemption is airbag litigation. However, federal law in the form of FMVSS 213 does not preempt state common law claims for child restraints.

Shell—The shell part of a child restraint device is the hard plastic on which all the other parts of a child restraint device are attached: this includes the straps, padding, buckles, shield, and/or harness. The shell plays a crucial role in determining defectiveness of a child restraint device. The shell determines the child's pre-crash position, it determines where the harness and strap anklepoints are located, provides attachment points for attaching the child restraint device to the vehicle and depending on the design, it may determine the side to side excursion of the child's head.

Shield—This is a large padded, somewhat flexible surface which is part of the child restraint system which fits over the child's abdomen. Shields are usually used in place of harnesses.

Tether Strap—A tether strap is a strap attached at the top of certain child restraint systems. The strap prevents the child restraint system from pivoting forward during a head on crash.

Three Point Restraint—This is a strap system with three points of attachment to the vehicle, such as harness/shield combination on a child restraint device, which anchors a child at both shoulders and the crotch, where a lap shoulder belt.

Advocate Groups

American Academy of Pediatrics
141 Northwest Point Boulevard
P.O. Box 927
Elk Grove Village, Illinois 60009
Phone: 1-800-433-9016
or (708) 228-5005
Fax: (708) 228-1281

The National Easter Seal Society
70 East Lake Street
Chicago, Illinois 60601-5907
Phone: (312) 726-6200
TDD: (312) 726-4258
Fax: (312) 726-1494

Harborview Injury Prevention and Research Center
Offices at:
633 Yesler Way, Suite 332
Seattle, Washington 98104
Mailing Address:
325 Ninth Avenue, ZX-10
Seattle, Washington 98104
Phone: (206) 223-8388
Fax: (206) 223-8471

Lifesavers 11
5302 Harbor Court Drive
Alexandria, Virginia 22310
Conference Management Office
Fax: (703) 922-7780

Michigan Substance Abuse & Traffic Safety Information Center
2409 East Michigan
Lansing, Michigan 48912-4019
Phone: (517) 482-9902
Fax: (517) 482-8262
Materials Information:
1-800-626-4636

Minnesota Passenger Protection Program
417 University Avenue
St. Paul, Minnesota 55103-1995
Phone: (612) 224-5121
National WATS Line:
1-800-782-1878
Fax: (612) 224-3407

Office of Occupant Protection
NHTSA, NTS-11
400 Seventh Street SW
Washington, D.C. 20590
Fax: (202) 366-2766

Project Childsafe
1549 University Avenue West
Suite 110
St. Paul, MN 55104

Safe Ride News
American Academy of Pediatrics
P.O. Box 927
Elk Grove Village, IL 60009-0927

SafetyBeltSafe U.S.A.
Box 553
Altadena, California 91003
Phone: (310) 673-2666
1-800-745-SAFE

The USAA Foundation
Phone: 1-800-531-8857
1-800-531-8722

USA-SAFE
P.O. Box 65
Beaverton, Michigan 48612
Phone: 1-800-945-9989

Manufacturers

Century Products
1366 Commerce Drive
Stow, OH 44224
(216) 686-3000

Century Products Company
9600 Valley View Road
Macedonia, Ohio 44056
(216) 468-2000

Chrysler Corporation
P.O. Box 1718
Detroit, MI 48288
(313) 956-5252

Collier/Keyworth Co.
P.O. Box 528
Gardner, MA 01440
(617) 632-0120

Cosco/Peterson
2525 State Street
Columbus, IN 47201
(812) 372-2154

Evenflo Juvenile Furniture Company, Inc.
1801 Commerce Drive
Piqua, OH 45356
(513) 773-3971
(800) 233-5921

E-Z-On Products
500 Commerce Way West
Jupiter, FL 33458
(800) 323-6598

Fisher-Price, Inc.
620 Girard Avenue
East Aurora, NY 14052-1879
(716) 687-3000
(800) 432-5437

Ford Motor Company
Parts and Service
3000 Shaefer Road
Dearborn, MI 48121
(313) 322-3000

Gerico, Inc.
12520 Grant Drive
Denver, CO 80241
(800) 525-2472

Gerry Baby Products
12520 Grant Drive
Denver, CO 80241

Graco
Route 23
Elverson, PA 15920
(215) 286-5981

International Mfg. Co.
2500 Washington Street
Boston, MA 02119
(617) 422-9700

Kolcraft Products
3455 West 31st Place
Chicago, IL 60623
(312) 247-4494

Kolcraft Products of California
1245 South Peerless Way
Montebello, CA 90640
(213) 724-9403

Little Cargo
100 North Broadway #2000
St. Louis, MO 63102
(314) 621-8580

Nissan Motor Corp.in U.S.A.
P.O. Box 191
Gardena, CA 90247
(213) 532-3111

Playschool (See "Kolcraft")

Pride Trimble Corporation
Box 450
Southern Pines, NC 28387
(919) 692-7541

Questor Juvenile Furniture Co.
1801 Commerce Drive
Piqua, OH 45353
(513) 773-3971

Renolux
1071 Batesville Road
Greer, SC 29650
(803) 848-0569

Rupert Industries
851 East Palatine Road
Wheeling, IL 60090
(800) 323-6598

Strolee of California
19067 S. Reyes Avenue
Rancho Dominiquez, CA 90221
(213) 639-9300

Welsh Company
1535 South 18th Street
St. Louis, MO 63104
(314) 231-8822

Westech Group
575 Morgan Boulevard
Baie d'Vrfe, Quebec
Canada H9X 3T6
(514) 457-7330

Westech Group
Airport Road
P.O. Box 629
Franklin County Airport
Swanton, VT 05488
(802) 868-5210

1993 CHILD PASSENGER SAFETY SYMPOSIUM
PARTICIPANT LIST

Ruth Ahrgal
Miami Children's Hospital
6125 SW. 31 Street
Miami, Fl 33155
305/666-6511 x3794

Craig Allred
Utah Highway Safety Office
4501 South 2700 West
Salt Lake City, UT 84119
801/965-4409

Erika Bettale
Denver Dept. Social Services
2200 W. Alameda
Denver, CO 80223
303/727-2932

Ronda Barrett
Children's Rehab. Unit
University of Kansas Med. Cntr
3901 Rainbow Blvd.
Kansas City, KS 66160
913/588-5900

Kristina Beckman
Association for the Advancement of
Automotive Medicine
2340 Des Plaines, Avenue #106
Des Plaines, IL. 60018
708/390-8927

Joan Belmas
Wisconsin Information Network for Safety
1324 CenterPoint Dr.
P.O. Box 634
Stevens Point, WI 54481
715/341-7328 or 344-7130

Christine M. Belser
Automotive Safety for Children
Riley Hospital
702 Barnhill Drive
Indianapolis, IN 46202-5225
317/274-2977

Heather Berschling
Maryland KISS-Kids in Safety Seats
201 West Preston Street
Baltimore, MD 21201
410/225-1376

Sgt. Joel Bolton
Lake Charles Police Department
P.O.Bx 1564
Lake Charles, LA 70602
313/491-1339

Arthur Borja
Law Offices of Joseph William Moch
121 Michigan Street, N.E.
Grand Rapids, MI 49503
616/456-1449

Robert J. Breitenbach
Virginia Commonwealth Univer.
Transp. Safety Training Center
816 W. Franklin Street, Box 2017
Richmond, VA 23284-2017
804/367-6235

Michael B. Brownlee
NHTSA, Dept. of Transportation
Traffic Safety Programs
400 7th Street, SW.
Washington, DC 20590
202/366-1755

Donna Bryan
Safety Council of PBC, Inc.
770 South Military Trail
West Palm Beach, FL 33415
407/689-4733 x 3

Susan Butterfield
Kansas Safety Belt Education Office
235 Seton Hall--KSU
Manhattan, KS 66506
913/532-5780

Bobbie M. Caldwell
NAWHST-TN Representative
530 Riverside Drive
Clinton, TN 37716
615/457-0037

Pamela Chapman
Bronson Hospital
252 E. Lovell
Kalamazoo, MI 49007
616/341-8830

Sharri Chappell
TN Women Hwy Safety Leaders
325 S. Tennessee Blvd.
Murfreesboro, TN 37130
615/890-5309

Beverly Christiansen
University of Illinois
320 Russetway
Palatine, IL 60064

Judy Craig
NHTSA Region VII
PO Box 412515
Kansas City, MO 64141
816/926-5044

Teri Crawley
Chicagoland SAFE KIDS Coalition
Pediatric Surgery, Wyler Children's Hospital
5841 S. Maryland Avenue
Chicago, IL 60637
312/702-6800 x6035

Cpt. Steve Ellis
CA. Highway Patrol
10395 Soquel Drive
Aptos CA 95003
408/662-0116

Joyce Dantzler
Maryland KISS - Kids in Safety Seats
201 West Preston Street
Baltimore, MD 21201
410/225-1362

Sra. Carmen Diaz
Puerto Rico Traffic Safety Commission
P.O. Box 41289-Minillas Station
Santurce, PR 00940
809/723-3590

Kay Diaz
City of Phoenix/Community Traffic Safety Prg.
Street Transportation Dept.
125 E. Washington Street, 3rd Flr.
Phoenix, AZ 85004
602/534-1623

Sra. Lourdes Perez Diaz
Puerto Rico Traffic Safety Commission
P.O. Box 41289 Minillas Station
Santurce, PR 00940
809/723-3590

Patti Dickey
Wisconsin Information Network for Safety
1324 CenterPoint Dr. P.O. Box 634
Stevens Point, WI 54481
715/341-7328 or 344-7130

Carol Dingledy
Cosco, Inc.
2525 State Street
Columbus, IN 47201
812/372-0141 x217

Cpt. Steve Ellis
CA Highway Patrol
10395 Soquel Drive
Aptos, CA 95003
408/662-0116

Felica Espejel
University of Illinois at Chicago, Emergency Medicine
1819 West Polk Street, Rm#618 - CMW, M/C 724
Chicago, IL 60612-7354
312/413-7480

Maria Espejel
University of Illinois at Chicago, Emergency Medicine
1819 West Polk Street, Rm#681 - CMW, M/C 724
Chicago, IL 60612-7354
312/413-7480

Diane Evans
Wisconsin Child Passenger Safety
P.O. Box 792
Chippewa Falls, WI 59729
715/836-9668

Jess Flores
Dept. of Public Safety
Governor's Office of Highway Safety
3010 N. 2nd Street, Suite 105
Phoenix, AZ 85012
602/255-3216

Nancy L. Foster, R.N.
Louisville SAFE KIDS Coalition
3601 Woodside Rd.
Louisville, KY 40222
502/895-9586

Mary Frazer
Monroe-Randolph Bi-County Health Dept.
1227 State St.
Chester, IL 62233
618/826-5007

Carol Gaare
American Academy of Pediatrics
141 Northwest Point Blvd., P.O.Bx 927
Elk Grove Village, IL 60009-0927
708/981-7949

Patti Gaines
No.Kentucky Rural Office of Traffic Safety
P.O. Box 134
109 South Madison Street
Owenton, KY 40359
502/484-5623

Jeanne Givens
N.C. Dept. of Environment, Health and Natural Resources
Injury Control Section, P.O. Box 27687
Raleigh, NC 27611-7687
919/733-3732

Tom Golder
SafeFit
PO Box 4051
Charlotte, NC 28226
704/552-1338

Jan Goldsmith
Iowa Governor's Traffic Safety Bureau
307 East 7th Street
Des Moines, IA 50309
515/281-6583

Carmen Gonzales
University of Illinois at Chicago, Emergency Medicine
1819 West Polk Street, Rm#618 - CMW, M/C 724
Chicago, IL 60612-7354
312/413-7480

Sue Gorcowski
NHTSA, Dept. of Transportation
Office of Occupant Protection
400 7th Street S.W., NTS-11
Washington, DC. 20590
202/366-2712

E. Joanne Grabiel
Arkansas Dept. of Health
4815 W. Markham, Slot 17
Little Rock, AK 72205
501/661-2718

Dennis Griffith
Denver Police Department
1390 Decatur St.
Denver, CO. 80204
303/640-2881

Bill Hall
UNC Highway Safety Research Center
CB# 3430,
Chapel Hill, NC 27599
919/962-2202

Cindy Halstead
KARS/Special KARS
Easter Seal Society Will-Grundy Counties
212 Barney Dr.
Joliet, IL 60435
815/725-2194

Carl Hanson
Jackson Co. Health Dept.
PO. Box 307
Murphysboro, IL 62966
618/684-3143

Leah A. Hayes
F.B.S., Inc./Renolux
1 Freedom Crt.
Greer, SC 29650
803/848-0569

Rhonda Heimericks
MO Division of Highway Safety
P.O. Box 104808
Jefferson City, MO 65110
314/751-5414

Carol Helminski
Century Products, Co.
9600 Valley View Road
Macedonia, OH 44056
216/468-4379

Clark Hepper
South Dakota Department of Health
445 East Capitol
Pierre, SD 57501
605/773-3737

Edward Heussner
8256 Garbor Avenue
Warren, MI 48093
313/756-4548

Julie Hextell
Kolkraft
3455 NW. 31st Place
Chicago, IL 60623
312/247-4494

Bobbet Hines
Denver Police Department
1390 Decatur Street
Denver, CO 80204
303/640-2881

Janet A. Holden
University of Illinois at Chicago,
Emergency Medicine
1819 W. Polk Street, Rm#618 - CMW,
M/C 724
Chicago, IL 60612-7354
312/413-7480

Carol Holzer
North Dakota State Dept. of Health
600 East Boulevard
Bismarck, ND 58505
701/224-4537

Alice Hutter
Wisconsin Child Passenger Safety
707 14th Street
Baraboo, WI 53913
608/356-1523

Chuck Hurley
Insurance Institute for Highway Safety
1005 North Glebe Rd., Suite 800
Arlington, VA 22201
703/247-1500

David V. Jacobsen
Florida Injury Control Program
Dept. of Health and Rehabilitative Services
1317 Winewood Boulevard
Tallahassee, FL 32399-0700
904/487-6747

Judy Johnson
Racine Health Department
730 Washington Avenue
Racine, WI 53403
414/636-3925

Julie Johnson
Ford-Iroquois Public Health Dept.
114 North Third Street, P.O. Box 427
Watseka, IL 60970
815/432-2483

Linda Jones
Elkhart County SAfE KIDS Coalition
205 Hawthorne Dr.
Goshen, IN 46526
219/534-1994

Tim Kennedy
National Safety Council
1121 Spring Lake Drive
Itasca, IL 60143
708/775-2380

Karen C. Kern
State of Virginia
P.O. Box 1172
Richmond, VA 23209
804/786-5993

Beth Kindschi
Wisconsin Child Passenger Safety Association/
Monroe SAFE KIDS
1811 12th Street
Monroe, WI 53566
608/325-4122

Linda S. Kirby
Arizona Dept. of Health Services
1740 W. Adams, Rm#200
Phoenix, AZ 85007
602/542-1880

Elaine Kizewski
Wisconsin Dept. of Transportation
Office of Transportation Safety
PO Box 733
Stevens Point, WI 54481
715/344-7191

Sgt. Linda McKenzie-Krohn
WI State Patrol
Rt. 3 Bx 157
Wautoma, WI 54982
414/787-3320

Kathryn Kruger
Safety Restraint Coalition
917 Kirkland Avenue
Kirkland, WA 98033
206/828-8975

Mary Beth Lewis
Child Magazine
1816 Virnankay Circle
Ann Arbor, MI 48103
313/994-3786

Cathy Lohr
NC. Dept. of Insurance
P.O. Box 26387
Raleigh, NC 27611
919/733-2142

Angelina Loza
University of Illinois at Chicago,
Emergency Medicine
1819 West Polk Street, Rm#618 - CMW,
M/C 724
Chicago, IL 60612-7354
312/413-7480

Katie Lynch
Washington Traffic Safety Commission
1000 S. Cherry Street, MS/PD-11
Olympia, WA 98504
206/586-6489

Lt. Greg Manual
CA Highway Patrol
2555 1st Avenue
Sacramento, CA 95818
Atten: Public Affairs
916/657-8720

Trooper Lori Maples
WI State Patrol
Rt. 3 Box 157
Wautoma, WI 54982
414/787-3320

Jeff Michael
NHTSA, Dept. of Transportation
Office of Occupant Protection
400 7th Street S.W., NTS-11
Washington, DC 20590
202/366-2755

Laura Miller
Kiwanis, Int.
Priority One Program
3636 Woodview Trace
Indianapolis, IN 46268
317/875-8755 x145

Joseph William Moch
Law Offices of Joseph William Moch
121 Michigan Street, NE.
Grand Rapids, MI 49503
616/456-1449

Connie Monahan
Safer New Mexico Now
P.O. Box 9534
Santa Fe, NM 87131
505/984-2898

Cathy Morris
County of Placer, Health & Medical
Services
11484 "B" Avenue
Auburn, CA 95603
916/889-7178

Joel Myers
Iowa City Police Department
410 Washington Street
Iowa City, IA 52240
319/356-5275

Kyaw Naing
Jackson Co. Health Dept.
P.O. Box 307
Murphysboro, IL 62966
618/684-3143

Cheryl Neverman
NHTSA, Dept. of Transportation
Office of Occupant Protection
400 7th Street S. W., NTS-11
Washington, DC. 20590
202/366-2696

James Nichols
NHTSA, Dept. of Transportation
Office of Occupant Protection
400 7th Street S.W., NTS-10
Washington, DC. 20590
202/366-9294

Mel Ott
Chippewa Falls Police Department
210 Island Street
Chippewa Falls, WI
715/723-4424

Isabel Perez
University of Illinois at Chicago,
Emergency Medicine
1819 West Polk Street, Rm#618-CMW,
M/C 724
Chicago,IL 60612-7354
312/413-7480

Sara Perszyk
Childhood Inj. Reduction Prg., Rockford
Mem. Hosp.
Guest and Education Center, Rm# 203
2400 N. Rockton Ave.
Rockford, IL 61103
815/961-6672

Elaine Petrucelli
Assn. for the Advancement of Automotive
Medicine
2340 Des Plaines Ave. #106
Des Plaines, IL 60018
708/390-8927

Ana E. Poma
University of Illinois at Chicago,
Emergency Medicine
1819 W. Polk Street, Rm#618 - CMW,
M/C 724
Chicago, IL 60612-7354
312/413-7480

Julie Prom
Center for Injury Prevention
1549 University Ave. W., Suite 110
St. Paul, MN 55104
612/646-2314

Col. Lucinio Ramirez
Puerto Rico Traffic Commission
P.O. Box 41289-Minillas Station
Santurce, PR 00940
809/723-3590

Susan Rani
IL DOT, Division of Traffic Safety
PO Box 19245
3215 Executive Park Drive
Springfield, IL 62794-9245
217/785-3036

Dianna J. Reed
PA Dept. of Transportation
Rm #204, Transportation & Safety Bldg.
P.O. Box 2047
Harrisburg, PA 17105-2047
717/787-6853

Kleist Rhodes
Governor's Highway Safety Program
215 E. Lane St.
Raleigh, NC 27601
919/733-3083

Ann Ringland
Occupant Safety Education Program
2612-A Lithonia Plaza
Lithonia, GA 30058
404/508-9661

Stephen Rountree
Arkansas State Hwy and Transportation
Dept.
P.O. Box 2261
Little Rock, AR 72203
501/569-2649

Mariluz Sanabria
Puerto Rico Traffic Safety Commission
P.O. Box 41289-Minillas Station
Santurce, PR 00940
809/723-3590

Jean A. Sargent
Dept. of Transportation , Office of Drivers Services
Park Fair Mall, 100 E. Euclid
Des Moines, IA 50306-9204
515/237-3012

P.J. Scott
University of Illinois at Chicago, Emergency Medicine
1819 West Polk Street, Rm#618 - CMW, M/C 724
Chicago, IL 60612-7354
312/413-7480

Bruce Schults
NHTSA Region VI
819 Taylor Street, Room 8A38
Fort Worth, TX 76102-5514
817/334-4423

John H. Shaffer
Center for Injury Prevention
1549 University Ave, W. Suite 110
St. Paul, MN 55104
612/646-2314

Susan Sheets
NHTSA, Region V
18209 Dixie Hwy., Suite A
Homewood, IL 60430
708/206-3311

Annemarie Shelness
Shelness Productions
P.O. Box 326
New Milford, CT 06776
203/355-0323

David Shinn
Shinn & Associates
2853 W. Jolly Road
Okemos, MI 48864
517/332-0211

Mary A. Shinn
Shinn & Associates
2853 W. Jolly Road
Okemos, MI 48864
517/332-0211

Anna Brotherton-Sheheen
Wyoming Transportation Dept. of Highway Safety
5300 Bishop Blvd, P.O. Box 1708
Cheyenne, WY 82003-1708
307/777-4199

DeeDee Singular
Kansas Safety Belt Education Office
235 Seaton Hall, KSU
Manhattan, KS 66506
913/532-5780

Marty Spellicy
Occupant Protection Research Project
U.of So MS Southern Station, Box 10034
Hattiesburg, MS 39406-0034
601/266-5353

Harry Stangel
210 West Mission Street
San Jose, CA 95110

Mark J. Stenson
Office of Transportation Safety
CO DOT
4201 E. Arkansas Avenue
Denver, CO 80222
303/757-9383

Deborah D. Stewart
American Academy of Pediatrics
726 Belmont Place East
Seattle, WA 98102
206/328-1424

Roseann Stiblo
Denver Dept. Social Services
2200 W. Alameda
Denver, CO 80223
303/727-2932

William R. Stout
Governor's Hwy Safety
215 E. Lane St.
Raleigh, NC 27601
919/733-3083

Karen Bruner Stroup
Automotive Safety for Children Program
Rile Hospital
702 Barnhill Drive, Rm#1601
Indianapolis, IN 46202
317/274-2977

Judith Talty
Automotive Safety for Children
Riley Hospital
702 Barnhill Dr. Rm #1601
Indianapolis, IN 46202
317/274-2977

David Thompson
1775 Catalina Blvd.
San Diego, CA 92107

Bill Tolbert
UNC Hwy Safety Research Center
CB# 3430
Chapel Hill, NC 27599
919/962-2202

Stephanie M. Tombrello
SafetyBeltSafe U.S.A.
2938 Santa Rosa
Actadeus, CA 91001
818/798-5197 or 310/673-2666

Randall Townley
University of GA
Occupant Safety Project
P.O. Box 807
Dawsonville, GA 30534
706/265-1593

Jonna Van Dyk
Washington Traffic Safety Commission
1000 S. Cherry Street, MS/PD-11
Olympia, WA 98504
206/753-6197

Patti Van Tiunen
Office of Injury Control
Missouri Department of Health
P.O.Bx 570, 600 Monroe Street
Jefferson City, MO 65102
314/751-6365

Lorrie Walker
PA Traffic Injury Prevention Project
PA Chapter American Academy of
Pediatrics
610 Old Lancaster Rd. #220
Bryn Mawr, PA 19010
215/520-9123

Marilois Walker
Project Safe Ride
Northern Essex Community College
45 Franklin St.
Lawrence, MA 01840
508/688-3181 x 221

Mary Claire Walsh
American Academy of Pediatrics
141 Northwest Point Blvd.
P.O. Box 927
ElkGrove Village, IL 60009-0927
708/981-7933

Philip J. Weiser
NHTSA, Region VIII
555 Zang St.
Lakewood, CO 80228
303/969-6922

Margot Welford
Westech Group
575 Morgan Boulevard
Baie D'Urfe, Quebec, Canada H9x 3T6
514/457-7330

Glenn C. Wilhide
Westech Group
575 Morgan Boulevard
Baie D'Urfe, Quebec, Canada H9X 3T6
514/457-7330

Diane Wolf
Safety and Health Council of Greater
Omaha
8710 F. Street
Omaha, NE 68127
402/592-9004

J. Michele Zotti
Vermont Governor's Highway Safety
Program
133 State Street
Montpelier, VT 05633
802/828-2665

Bibliography

Cases

Dorsey v. Honda Motor Company Ltd., 655 F.2d 650 (1991).

Fox v. Ford Motor Company, 575 F.2d 774 (1978).

Grimshaw v. Ford Motor Company, 174 California Rptr 348 (1981).

Jordan v. Paccar, No. 90-CV-600, 792 F. Supp. 545; 1992 U.S. Dist.; CCH Prod.

Kentrup v. Century Products, Inc., US District Court, E.D. Ky., No 82-117, Apr. 14, 1984

Larsen v. General Motors Corp., 391 F.2d 495 (1968).

Mannino v. International Manufacturing Co., 650 F.2d 846 (6th Cir.1981)

Mitchell v. Volkswagen Werk, A.G., 669 F.2d (1982).

Nevada v. Skinner, 884 F.2d 445; 1989 U.S. App.

Nicholson v. Century Products, Inc.

U.S. District Court, E.D. Pa., No.81-3040, July 27, 1983

Perry v. Mercedes Benz and ABC Insurance Company, 957 F.2d 1257; 1992 U.S. App.; CCH Prod. Liab.

Schleininger v. Questor Corp., 200 Cal. Rptr. 634 (Cal. App. 1984)

Turner v. General Motors Corp., 584 S.W.2d A44 (1979).

Welsh v. Century Products, 754 F. Supp. 313; 1990 U.S. Dist.; CCH Prod.

Welsh v. Gerber Products, Century Products, and Sears Roebuck and Company, 839 F.2d 1035; 1988 U.S. App.

Law Reviews

Barksdale, Bonita C. "Child Safety Restraints: A Controversy Over Safe Infant Air Travel," (Fall 1991), Southern Methodist University School of Law.

Claybrook, Joan and David Bollier, "The Hidden Benefits of Regulation: Disclosing the Auto Safety Payoff," (Fall 1985), Yale Journal on Regulation.

Dedominicis, Gina M. "No Duty at Any Speed?: Determining The Responsibility of the Automobile Manufacturer in Speed-Related Accidents," (Winter 1986), Hofstra Law Review, Vol. 14, p. 403.

Fabian, Rudy. "Federal Preemption: Car-makers' Cushions Against Air Bag Claims?," (Winter 1989), Duquesne University School of Law.

Harvard Law Review. "Negligence — Seat Belt Defense — Failure to Use a Seat Belt Constitutes Evidence of Comparative Negligence, Which May Decrease Recovery for Avoidable Damages—Waterson v. General Motors Corp.," 111 N.J. 238, 544 A.2d 357 (1988), (February 1989), Harvard Law Review, Vol. 102, p. 925.

Van Laningham, John G. "Review of Florida Legislation; Comment: The Making of the 1986 Florida Safety Belt Law: Issues and Insight," (1986), Florida State University Law Review, Vol. 14, p. 685.

Logsdon, Jann B. "Toward a Uniform Child Restraint Law," (1982), J. Fam. L., Vol. 21, Number 2.

Miller, Keith C. "Deflating The Airbag Pre-emption Controversy," (Fall 1988), Emory Law Journal, Vol. 37, p. 897.

Shapiro, M. David. "Torts/Evidence Seat Belt Defense—Whether They Know It or Not, Florida Motorists Must 'Buckle Up' or Risk Loss of Full Recovery— Insurance Co. Of North America V. Pasakarnis, 451 So. 2d 447 (Fla. 1984), Florida State University Law Review, Vol.12, p. 669.

Theroff, Ellen L. "Preemption of Airbag Litigation: Just a Lot of Hot Air?," (April 1990), Virginia Law Review Association.

Government Documents

1. Safety Belt Usage Among Drivers. 2. Use of Child Restraint Devices, Passenger Safety Belts and Position of Passengers in Cars. 3. Motorcycle Helmet Usage, USDOT NHTSA PB 80-205750, May 1980.

A Family Shopping Guide to Infant/Child Automobile Restraints, American Academy of Pediatrics, University of North Carolina Highway Safety Research Center, CTP 187-A Capitol Hill, North Carolina.

A Global Approach to Child Restraint Systems, Turbell and Aldman.

A New Concept for Infant Passenger Protection, Heinrich F. von-Winnersperg, American Association for Automotive Medicine Proceedings, Oct. 7-9, 1980.

A Summary of the National Transportation Safety Board, Child Passenger Safety Study, Goldman, NTSB

An Analytical Model of Children in a Panic-Breaking Environment with Experimental Validation, Cheng and Guenther.

An Experimental Study of the Effects of Child Restraint Improper Installation and Crash Protection for Larger Size Children, Kelleher and Walsh.

Are 1974-1975 Automotive Belt Systems Hazardous to Children? Snyder and O'Neil, American Journal of Diseases of Children Vol. 129 p. 946, Aug. 1975.

Behavior and Parental Expectations of Child Pedestrians, Dunne, Asher, Rivara Pediatrics, Vol. 89, No. 3, March 1992.

Birth to Birthday; Safety Mead Johnson (1987).

Booster Cushions & Adult Seatbelts Evaluation of the Strength of Anchorages Needed for Attachment of Child Restraint Tether Belts, Kenneth N. Naab, U.S. Dept. of Transportation, National Highway Traffic Safety Administration, DOTHS 806639 PB 85-163129

Car Restraint Devices Designed for Children, Burg et al, Modern Medicine, Mar. 8, 1971.

Car Seat Safety—Pass, Present, and Future, Richard E. Hyde,

Characteristics of Child Safety Seat Users, Wagenaar, Molnar, & Margolis, The University of Michigan, Transportation Research Institute and School of Public Health (1987).

Child and Adult Travel Exposure and Fatality Risks, Carspen and Weber, University of Michigan, Highway Safety Research Institute.

Child and Infant Restraints, NHTSA PB 297656, June 1979.

Child Boosters: Test Reveal Questionable Performance, IIHS Status Report, Vol. 23, No. 11, Dec. 3, 1988.

Child Car Restraints, in Car and Driver, Karl S. Thelin, Experts at Law, May-June 1990, p. 23.

Child Passenger Protection Against Death, Disability, and Disfigurement in Motor Vehicle Accidents, National Transportation Safety Board, PB83-917005, NTSB/SS-83/01, September 7, 1983.

Child Passenger Protection: The Tennessee Enforcement Strategy, Tennessee Department of Safety, J. Roberts.

Child Passenger Safety Legislation, Implementation and Enforcement, Lawless and Siani.

Child Passenger Safety Programs for Hospitals, Questor, Shinn and Associates, 1983.

Child Pedestrian Injuries in the United States Current Status of the Problem, Potential Interventions and Future Research Needs, Rivara American Journal of Diseases of Children, Vol. 144, June 1990.

Child Restraint Development, DOT NTSB PB 214046, Sept. 1972.

Child Restraint Evaluation by Experimental and Mathematical Simulation, Weismans and Maltha and Melvin Stalnaker.

Child Restraint Systems, 8th International Technical Conference on Experimental Safety Vehicles, sponsored by the Government of the Federal Republic of Germany, hosted by W. Neil, Oct. 21-24, 1980. USDOT NHTSA

Child Restraint Systems Testing, USDOT NHTSA, PB-283-512 May 1978.

Child Restraints, USDOT NHTSA, DOTHS-803 819, March 1980.

Child Restraints and Legislation in Europe, Bastiaanse and Maltha.

Child Safety in Motor Vehicles, USDOT NHTSA, Public Meeting, Dec. 12, 1979.

Child Safety Seats for Your Automobile, USDOT, NHTSA, DOT HS HO5 1974, Sept. 1982.

Child Seat and Restraint Systems Tests Results, Appendix D, The University of Michigan Highway Safety Research Institute, USDOT NHTSA, PB 197 (1970).

Child Seat Retention Tests, DOT NHTSA PB85-139616, April, 1984.

Children in Crashes, Insurance Institute for Highway Safety, May 1983.

Children in Crashes, Insurance Institute for Highway Safety, June 1981, Editor, Ann Fleming.

Children of Passengers in Automobiles: The Neglected Minority on the Nation's Highways, Shelness and Seymour Charles, Pediatrics, Vol. 56 No. 2, Aug. 1975.

Childrens Car Seat Restraints: When Top Tether Straps are Ignored or Are These Restraints Safe? Quentin H. McDonald.

Comparison Between Child Cadavers and Child Dummy by Using Child Restraint Systems in Simulated Collisions, Kallieris, J. Barz, G. Schmidt, G. Heess and R. Mattern, University of Heidelberg, West Germany.

Compliance Testing to the New Dynamic Standard for Child Restraint Systems, Gilkey, USDOT NHTSA

Consumer Information, US DOT, NATSA, Jan. 1989.

Crash Victim Simulation—First Step in Child Auto Safety, Stalnaker, Dept. of Mechanical Engineering, Ohio State University, Columbus, OH.

Current Activities in Canada Relating to the Protection of Children in Automobile Accidents, Dalmotas et al, World Safety and Motor Vehicle Regulations Directory, Transport Canada.

Defective UK Seat Belt Legislation and Restraint Usage by Children, Lowne and Roberts.

Development of Infant and Child Restraint Regulations and Their Application, Radovich, Office of Vehicle Safety Standards, NHTSA.

Development of Testing and Evaluation of Child Restraint Systems and Child Test Dummys, USDOT, NHTSA, Radovich and Bayer, 1979.

Document Anthropometry for Child Restraints, UHDOT NHTSA, PB 204186 (1971).

Dynamic Performance of Child Seating Systems, Roberts and Mcelhaney, Highway Safety Research Institute, University of Michigan.

Dynamic Testing of Child Occupant Protection Concepts, NHTSA 1982. PB 83-201483.

Dynamic Testing of Innovative Solutions to Child Occupant Protection Problems, Kathleen Weber and John W. Melvin, The University of Michigan Transportation Research Institute, DTNH 22-82-C-07176 (1984).

Early Rider, How to Establish and Operate an Infant and Child Restraint Loan Program, NHTSA in cooperation with Michigan's Motor Vehicle Occupant Protection Program, the Michigan Jaycee auxiliary and Action for Child Transportation Safety.

Early Rider, Medical Community Child Restraint Project, US DOT, NHTSA, (1979).

Elements of an Effective Child Restraint System, Rogers and Silver, Proving Ground, General Motors Corp.

Enactment of Mandatory Seatbelt—Use Legislation—An Analysis of the Political Process in North Carolina, Terence Chorba, M.D., M.P.H., and Frank Vinicor, M.D., NCMJ, November 1990, Volume 51, Number 11.

Epidemiology of Road Accidents in Childhood, American Journal of Public Health, Vol. 77 No. 3, March 1987.

Establishment of the Performance Characteristics of the SA 1031 Six-Month-Old Infant Dummy, NHTSA PB 81-179459, July 1980.

Establishment of the Repeatability of Performance of the SA103C Three-Year-Old Child Size Dummys, NHTSA, PB80-112204, June 1979.

Evaluation of Child Passenger Safety, The Effectiveness and Benefits of Safety Seats Summary, NHTSA PB 86-184710 1986.

Evaluation of the Effectiveness of Child Safety Seats in Actual Use, Kahane and Klossar.

Evaluation of the Effectiveness of Occupant Protection, Federal Motor Vehicle Safety Standard 208, U.S. Department of Transportation, National Highway Traffic Safety Administration, Interim Report, June 1992.

Evaluation of the Response Characteristics of the ACE Six-Year-Old Child Size Dummy, Saverio N. Pugliesa, USDOT, NHTSA, PB 85154714, Dec. 1991.

Exploration of Biomechanical Data Towards a Better Evaluation of Tolerance for Children Involved in Automobile Accidents, Dejeannen et al,

Factors Affecting Consumer Acceptance in Use of Child Restraint Systems, NHTSA PB 82-255605, Jan. 1982.

Factors Affecting Consumer Usage and Acceptance of Child Restraints, NHTSA, Sept. 1983, PB 84240977.

Factors Associated with Child Use of Automobile Restraining Devices, Knowledge, Attitudes and Practice, Neumann et al, American Journal of Diseases of Children, Vol. 128, p. 469, Oct. 1974.

Fatal Motor Vehicle Accidents of Child Passengers from Birth Through Four Years of Age in Washington State, Robert G. Scherz, Pediatrics Vol. 68, No. 4, Oct. 1981.

Final Design and Implementation Plan for Evaluating the Effectiveness of FMVSS 213: Child Seating Systems, NHTSA, PB-283 095 Dec. 1977.

From Three-Years-Old to Adult Size, How to Ensure Child Protection in Automobile Accidents, Tarriere et al

Frontal Crash Evaluation Tests of a Five Point Harness Child Restraint, Richard M. Schreck and Lawrence M. Patrick.

Growth of the Pelvis in Children, Chumlea.

Guidelines for Observing Child Safety Seat Use, DOT NTSB PB 852399____

Highway Safety 1990, A Report on Activities Under the Highway Safety Cut of 1966 or Amended, US DOT, NHTSA. (Jan. 1 - Dec. 31, 1990)

Incidence & Factors Associated with Child Safety Seat Misuse, Michael J. Cunecki, Michael E. Corey, PB85-174415, December 1984, DOTHS-806676

Increasing Child Restraint Use in N.S.W. Australia: The Development of an Effective Mass Media Campaign, Friedman, et al of the Traffic Accident Research Unit _________ Motor Transport, Sydney, Australia.

Increasing Correct Use of Child Safety Seats, USDOT NHTSA, PB 86-187481, April 1986.

Injuries to Children in Automobile Collisions, Seigal et al, School of Medicine, University of California, Los Angeles.

Injury Potential with Misused Child Restraining Systems, K. Weber and J.W. Melvin, Transportation Research Institute, University of Michigan.

Institute Urges Action to Improve Child Restrait Use, Ins. Inst. for Highway Safety, Sept. 17, 1988.

Instructor's Guide and Fact Book for the Safe Passage Program, Questor, Shinn and Associates, 1983.

Investigation of the Performance of Child Restraints in Serious Crashes, Insurance Institute of Highway Safety, Melvin, Weber and Lux, PB 80-200579 May 1980.

Motor Vehicle Occupant Injuries in Non-Crash Events, Phyllis Agran, Pediatrics Vol. 67, No. 6, June 1981.

Motor Vehicle Occupant Injuries to Children in Crash and Non-Crash Events, Agren and Dunkel, Pediatrics Vol. 70, No. 6, Dec. 1982.

NHTSA Child Safety Activities, Stephenson, USDOT NHTSA.

National Safety Belt Usage Program: Progress and Assessment Report, USDOT, NHTSA, (1983).

Net, Sack, Harness or No Infant Restraint?, Herbert et al, American Association for Automotive Medicine Proceedings, Oct. 1-3, 1981.

Pediatric Passenger Trends in Seatbelt Use and Injury Patterns, Hoffman et al, The Journal of Trauma, Sept. 1986

Performance Evaluations of Child Dummys and Baboons in Child Restraints in a Systemized Crash Environment, S. Bacagis, et al.

Performance Evaluation of Child Restraint Systems, DOT NHTSA, PB 83-219154, Oct. 1982.

Performance Measurements of Three-Year-Old Test Dummy Heads, NHTSA, PB 805207934.

Performance of Child Restraints in Serious Crashes, Melvin, Weber and Lux, American Association for Automotive Medicine, Proceedings, Oct. 7-9, 1980.

Performance of Lap Belts in 26 Frontal Crashes, National Trans. Safety Bd., W.D.C. 20594 ATSB/SS-86103

Performance of Lap/Shoulder Belts in 167 Motor Vehicle Crashes, (Volume I), W.D.C. 20594 National Transportation Safety Board NTSB/SS-88/02.

Performance of Lap/Shoulder Belts in 67 Motor Vehicle Crashes, (Volume 2), W.D.C. 20594 Nat'l. Trans. Safety Board NTSB/SS-88103

Preparing a Case Involving a Defective Child Restraint, Products Liability Law Reporter, Carla L. Harcourt, Vol. 11, No. 6, p. 125, July 1992.

Prevention of Pedestrian Injuries to Children: Effectiveness of a School Training Program, Rivara, Booth, Bergman, Rogus and Weiss Pediatrics, Vol. 88, No. 4, Oct. 1991.

Proceedings of the 20th Conference of the American Association for Automotive Medicine, Editor Donald S. Huelke, Atlanta, GA, Nov. 1-3, 1976.

Prospectives for and Problems Related to Protection of Children in Child Restraints, Bertil Aldman, Dept. of Traffic Safety, Chalmers University of Technology, Gotoborg, Sweden.

Protecting Our Own and Community Child Passenger Safety Programs, Second Edition (1982).

Protecting Our Own—Community Child Passenger Safety Programs, Second Edition (July 1990).

Protection for Five-Year-Old Children, Morris, NHTSA.

Protection of Child Occupants in Automobile Crashes, Melvin and Stalmaker, Highway Safety Research Institute, University of Michigan and Bineshmohan Research Department Insurance Institute for Highway Safety.

Rearward Facing Infant Restraints: Optimum Reclining Angles for the Design of Safer, More Protective and Comfortable Restraints, Quinton H. McDonald, American Association for Automotive Medicine Proceedings, Oct. 3-6, 1979.

Renting and Selling Child Car Safety Seats: A Community Service Project, Questor, Shinn and Associates, 1983.

Restraint System Usage in the Traffic Population 1. Automobile Safety Belts, 2. Child Restraint Seats, 3. Motorcycle Helmets, PB 83- 237032, USDOT NHTSA, May 1992.

Restraint Systems for the Prevention of Injury to Children in Automobile Accidents, Robert G. Sherz, American Journal of Public Health, Vol. 66, No. 5, May 1976.

Safe Passage, Quest for Juvenile Furniture Company, 1801 Commerce, PIQUAOH 45356.

Safety Acceleration of Infants and Car Crashes, Heinrich F. von Wimmersperg.

Safety Belt Usage Among Drivers, Benjamin M. Phillips, Use of Child Restraint Devices, Passenger Safety Belts and Position of Passengers in Cars. US DOT 145-7-01-736 May 1980.

Safety Belts, Airbags, and Child Restraints, Special Report 224, Transportation Research Board, National Research Council, Washington, D.C. 1989.

Safety Study—Child Passenger Protection Against Death, Disability and Disfigurement in Motor Vehicle Accidents, DOT NTSB, PB 83-917005, Sept. 1983.

Safety Study—Child Passenger Safety Symposium: Ways to Increase Use and Decrease Misuse of Child Restraints, NTSB, PB 85-917013, Sept. 1985.

Safety Study—Child Passenger Safety Symposium: Ways to Increase Use and Decrease Misuse of Child Restraints, US NTSB (1985).

Safety Study—Performance of Lap Belts in 29 Frontal Crashes, (1986), NTSB PB 86-917006.

Safety Study—Performance of Lap-Shoulder Belts in 167 Motor Vehicle Crashes, Volume 2, US NTSB, US Dept. of Commerce, NTIS (1988).

Sascathewen Kids Get Belted, A. Carl Shilis.

Statistical Evaluation of FMVSS 213 NHSTA, PB 83-178509 June 1982.

Statistical Evaluation of the Effectiveness of Child Restraints, NHTSA, PB 81-152225, Sept. 1980.

Step Child of American Pediatrics: Child Transportation Safety, Seymour Charles, Pediatrics Annals (sp?) Vol. 6, No. 11, Nov. 1977.

Study of Methods for Increasing Safety Belt Use, Transportation Research Board, National Academy of Sciences.

Sudden Impact—An Occupant Protection Fact Book, U.S. Department of Transportation, National Highway Traffic Safety Administration, (July 1991).

Survey of Infant Restraint Usability, Kathleen Weber, American Association for Automotive Safety, Proceedings, Oct. 7-9, 1980.

The Case for Seat Belts, Experimental and Statistical Evidence, USDOT, NHTSA (1973).

The Efforts of National Highway Traffic Safety Administration in the Development of Advanced Passive Protection Systems in Child Restraints Systems, Charles E. Strother & Richard M. Morgan, NHTSA

The Efforts of the National Highway Traffic Safety Administration in the Development of Advanced Passive Protection Systems and Child Restraint Systems, Strauber and Morgan

The Restraint of Children in Car Impacts Using Booster Cushions and Adult Seatbelts, C. Ashley,

The State of the Art of Child Passenger Safety Legislation in North America, Elaine W. Lawless and Teresa A. Siani.

The Use and Accuracy of Child Restraint Devices: The Tennessee Experiments, 1982 and 1983, Michael D. Decker and Robert H. Hutcheson, Jr., The Journal of the American Medical Association, Vol. 252, No. 18, Nov. 9, 1984.

The Use of Infant's and Children's Occupant Safety Devices in Motor Vehicles: An Observational Study, Smith and Berkline, Hawaii Medical Journal, Vol. 39, No. 11, Nov. 1980.

Toward a Uniform Child Restraint Law, The Journal of Family Law, Vol. 21 No. 2, 1982-83

Traffic Accidents Concerning Child Epidemiology—Mechanism and Means of Prevention, Romieu and Biel.

Usage of Adult Belts in Conjunction with Child Safety Systems as a Means to Optimize Convenience, Waldemar Czernakowski.

Warning: In Cars, Children May Be Hazardous to their Parent's Health: The Role of Restraints in Preventing Collisions, Hall et al, American Association for Automotive Saftey Proceedings, Oct. 7-9, 1980.

Warning: In Cars, Parents May be Hazardous to Their Children's Health, The Hazards of Infant Travel, by Allan F. Williams, 1978.

"70% by '92", Safety Belt Program Idea Sampler, U.S. Department of Transportation, National Highway Traffic Safety Administration, January 1992.

Periodicals

"AAA Sorts Out State's Varied Laws," The Washington Times, p. G17, April 24, 1992.

Adler, "FAA Is Looking Into the issue of Child Safety; Airlines: A Proposal that would require airlines to allow passengers to use child restraint seats, such as those used in cars, is now being prepared," Los Angeles Times, October 22, 1989, p. 25.

Adler, "The Cost Of Using Child Safety Seats On Planes," Los Angeles Times, January 19, 1992, p. 19

"Air Transport Association," Aviation Daily, January 8, 1993, p. 36.

"Airline Infant Safety Seats Required," Aviation Week and Space Technology, February 5, 1990, p. 17..

Allison, Malorye, M.A., "Metabolic Effects of Brain Injury," Head-lines, January/February 1993.

American Automobile Association, "Children In Traffic: Why Are They Different?," Safe Ride News, Fall 1992.

"An Atlanta Journal-Constitution Investigations; Last In A Seven-Part Series; Georgia's Dui Scandal; Programs That Battle Drunk Driving; Strategies Range From Special Jails To Ignition Locks; Prevention; Operation Prom/Graduation," The Atlanta Journal and Constitution, p. 12, November 10, 1991.

Anderson, "Cabs Must Carry Child Seats, But Some Driver's See Problems," The New York Times, p. 2, November 17, 1991.

Antonio, "Sizzling Weather Likely for Holiday," The Hartford Courant, p. C1, May 22, 1992.

"Auto Vehicle Child Safety Topic of Hearing," Proprietary to the United Press International, Regional News, February 3, 1983.

Barbour, "The New American Driver," p. 1, July 26, 1992.

Barbour, "U.S. Highways — Fewer Drunks, More Women; Safety: Roads Are Becoming Safer, But Female Motorists Are Found To Be Younger, More Agressive, And More Likely To Suffer High-Speed Fatal Accidents," p. 5, June 28, 1992.

Berry, "Parents: Make Sure Car's Seat Belts Fit Properly; Restraint Injuries Are On The Rise Among Children," The Washington Post, p. Z17, May 12, 1992.

Beyers, "Straight, Inc. Gets The Go-Ahead for Md. Drug Program," The Washington Post, p. C1, September 17, 1991.

Bond, "Require Safety Seats For Our Littlest Fliers," USA Today, March 1, 1990, p. 10A.

Borcover, "Travelin' Trends Where Tourists Will Be Heading This Fall," Chicago Tribune, October 4, 1992, p. 2.

"Boy Killed in Wreck," The Houston Chronicle, p. 34, November 16, 1991.

Boyer, "4 Children, Adult Die in 2 Crashes," Los Angeles Times, p. 1, August 5, 1991.

Bradsher, "The Crash of Flight 52," The New York Times, January 28, 1990, p. 29.

"British Airline to Offer Child-Safety Seats," UPI, January 16, 1992.

"Buckle Up In Pasadena," The Houston Chronicle, p. 16, June 16, 1992.

"Buckle Up The Kids Right Away," Star Tribune, p. 1M, February 9, 1992.

Bunch, "What You Should Know; When Danger Is In The Air; Area's Major Airports Cited for Hazards," Newsday, p. 5, March 29, 1992.

"Car-Seat Fines Raised," Newsday, p. 18, May 15, 1991.

"Child Restraints Sought on Airliners," The Washington Post, November 14, 1983, p. A15.

"Child Safety Seats," The New York Times, March 29, 1992, p. 24.

"Child Safety: parents pay," Flight International, April 1, 1992.

"Child Safety Seats," Consumer Reports.

"Child World TV Spots Win at Clios Comeback," p. 35, September 16, 1992.

"Children In Flight," St. Petersburg Times, September 26 ,1992, p. 14A.

"Clinton Will Change Regulatory Climate," The National Law Journal, November 23, 1992, p. 17.

Coben, Larry E. "The Product Liability Crisis: The Truth—Corporate Irresponsibility."

"Collector Cars Seen as Bargain," Chicago Tribune, November 17, 1991.

Consumer Reports, "1993 Buying Guide," Volume 57, No. 13, December 15, 1992.

"CPSC Seizes Banned Baby Bath Seats," Products Liability Law Reporter, Volume 11, No. 9, November 1992.

Craig, "Hospitals Lend Child Car Seats," Detroit Free Press, February 21, 1992.

"Date Moved Up," The Atlanta Journal and Constitution, p. 3, April 10, 1992.

Daunt, "Probe Criticizes Procedures Used At State Hospital; Behavior: Auditor General Says Some Children At Camarillo Were Physically Restrained Without Required Approval," Los Angeles Times, p. 3, May 10, 1991.

Daunt, "State Audit Criticizes Camarillo Hospital; Mental Health: The Survey Questions The Use Of Restriants On Some Retarded Children. A Patients' Advocate Defends The State Facility," Los Angeles Times, p. 1, May 10, 1991.

Davis-Tokarz, "Car Lap Belts For Children Are Unsafe, Study Finds," Chicago Tribune, p. r, June 19, 1992.

Dellios, "Ryan Hopes Car Seat Program Will Cut Child Fatalities," Chicago Tribune, p. 4, September 4, 1991.

Diamond, "Reducing Risk to Children on Planes, Buses," Los Angeles Times, August 11, 1989, p. 1.

Dornheim, "FAA Flight Tests To Measure Synthetic Vision Performance," Aviation Week and Space Technology, January 20, 1992, p. 41.

Downey, "Buckling Up Baby," The Atlanta Journal and Constitution, November 11, 1991, p. 1.

"Drivers Urged to Use Their Seat Belts More," Chicago Tribune, Nobember 27, 1991.

Dugger, "Wide Use of Force on Disturbed Children is Found," The New York Times, p. 9, February 13, 1992.

Dunne, Rosemary G., M.S., Kenneth N. Asher, Ph.D., and Frederick p. Rivara, M.D., M.p.H., "Behavior and Parental Expectations of Child Pedestrians," Pediatrics, Volume 89, No. 3, March 1992.

Eldridge, "FAA: Airlines Must Allow Child Seats," Gannett News Service, September 14, 1992.

Evans, "Casts Record Two Broadway Hits," The Houston Chronicle, p. 10, February 23, 1992.

"FAA Allows Safety Seats," The Hartford Courant, September 15, 1992, p. A7.

"FAA'S Final Rule Won't Make Infant-Restraint Usage Mandatory," Air Safety Week, September 21, 1992, Volume 6.

"The FAA Has Decided," Aviation Week and Space Technology, September 21, 1992, p. 17.

"FAA Plebiscite," Aviation Week and Space Technology, December 18, 1989, p. 15.

"FAA Proposes To Require Airlines To Allow Child Seats," PR Newswire, February 22, 1990.

"FAA Requires Airlines To Allow Child Safety Seats," Aviation Daily, September 15, 1992, p. 460.

"FAA Requires Airlines To Allow Child Safety Seats," Reuters, September 14, 1992.

"Father Cleared In Daughter's Death," The Washington Times, p. A6, May 6, 1991.

Field, "FAA's Refusal to Require Safety Seats Faces Battle," The Washington Times, September 16, 1992, p. C3.

Finnegan, "Fasten Your Seatbelt! Western Airports are Flying Into The 21st Century; Includes Related Articles Cover Story," Sunset, November, 1992, p. 74.

"Flight Attendants List Safety Goals For 1990," Aviation Daily, December 14, 1989, p. 489.

Forrest, "Mother Dies in 2-Car Crash; Girl, 2 in Coma; Wasn't Strapped In," Newsday, p. 24, May 13, 1992.

Gaines, "Filler Device Needed," The Atlanta Journal and Constitution, p. 2, April 10, 1992.

Gaines, "Misuse Can Be Hazardous," The Atlanta Journal and Constitution, p. 2, April 10, 1992.

Gaines, "Safe But Not Simple Choosing the Proper Car Seat for Baby is Far From Child's Play," The Chicago Tribune, p. 1, January 19, 1992.

Gardner, "Courts, Conscience Put Parents On Trial," The Christian Science Monitor, p. 13, May 14, 1991.

Gehorsam, King, "Use of Child Safety Seats is Rising But So Are Fatalities," The Atlanta Journal and Constitution, p. 3, August 30, 1991. The Washington Post, May 12, 1992.

Gellene, "Forget Those Booster Seats When Flying," Los Angeles Times, August 28, 1992, p. 3.

Gellene, "Making Air Travel Safe For Baby:. . . .," Los Angeles Times, December 7, 1989, p. 1.

"Getting Around Houston," The Houston Chronicle, p. 4, August 16, 1992.

Gogarty, "Safety Has a Price," The Daily Telegraph, January 25, 1992, p. 107.

Greenberg, "A Traveler's Election Agenda; Savvy Traveler," The Plain Dealer, November 1, 1992, p. 2I.

Greenberg, "DOT, FAA In Dire Need Of An Overhaul," The Buffalo News, November 1, 1992, p. 5.

"Group Buys Child-Car Seats To Loan With Safeco Grant," The Seattle Times, p. F3, March 24, 1992.

Haas, "Don't Kid Around With Business of Protecting Your Baby," The Atlanta Journal and Constitution, p. 19, November 22, 1991.

Haberstroh, Norton, "Tot Survives Tumble Out Of Car—Boy Unhooks Seat Belt, Falls In Rush Hour," The Seattle Times, p. B1, September 2, 1992.

Haralson, Dale. "Atla Advocate," Networking, p. 12, March 1993, Volume 19, No. 3.

Harcourt, Carla L. "Preparing A Case Involving A Defective Child Restraint," Products Liability Law Reporter, Volume 11, No. 6, July 1992.

Henderson, "Safety Agency May Press For Airliner Infant Seats," Los Angeles Times, November 4, 1989, p. 2.

Hernandez, "Orange County Focus: Garden Grove; Police Will Use Grant To Hire 4 Officers," Los Angeles Times, p. 2, May 7, 1991.

"Infant's Death Is Third From Saturday Crash," The Seattle Times, p. C2, June 3, 1991.

Irick, "The Plane Truth," The Washington Post, March 22, 1992.

Jacobsen, "Helmet Provisions May Alarm Cyclists," The Washington Times, p. G8, December 27, 1991.

Johnson, "Airlines Ask FAA To Require Infant Seats," Los Angeles Times, February 23, 1990, p. 24.

Johnson, "Snellville Woman, 77, Dies In Crash," The Atlanta Journal and Constitution, p. 4, June 27, 1991.

Kim, "Seats Aplenty for Precious Cargo; Safety: Trauma Society and the Easter Seal Society Hold Giveaway of Car Baby Carriers for Low-Income Families at Choc.," Los Angeles Times, p. 3, February 16, 1992.

Kleiman, "Employers Change With Family Times," Chicago Tribune, November 15, 1991.

Kuczka, "2nd Man Guilty In Inverness Slaying," Chicago Tribune, p. 1, May 12, 1992.

Landsberg, "Legislators Toady to Chickens, Marmots," Los Angeles Times, p. 25, March 11, 1990.

Lehman, "Car Seats for Children Often Used Improperly," The Boston Globe, p. 18, May 12, 1992.

"Lessons to be learned," Flight International, October 31, 1990.

Levey, "A Pair of Gaps in D.C. Seat Belt Law," The Washington Post, p. B22, September 3, 1992.

"Lightfoot Press Child Seats," The Washington Post, September 16, 1992, p. A19.

Loupe, Laccetti, "Man Charged with DUI in Death of Infant Boy Cobb Hit-Run Suspect Had Suspended Driver's License," The Atlanta Journal and Constitution, p. 1, February 25, 1992.

Loupe, "Didn't See Car, Says Driver in Fatal Wreck," p. 2, The Atlanta Journal and Constitution, p. 2, February 27, 1992.

Loupe, "Seat Would Have Saved Him," The Atlanta Journal and Constitution, p. 1, February 26, 1992.

Mason, "Tendernes Takes Telluride," The Christian Science Monitor, p. 12, September 13, 1991.

Mateja, "Cars of the Year: 1 is Not Enough," Chicago Tribune, p. 1, February 9, 1992.

Mateja, "Child Seats Help Bottom Line Chrysler Minivans With Fold-Down Restraints Popular," Detroit Free Press, March 5, 1992.

Mateja, "Chrysler Leads Campaign To Win Built-In Market For Safety Seats," Chicago Tribune, p. 5, January 19, 1992.

Mateja, "Driving $80,000 Worth of Power," Chicago Tribune, p. 1, October 20, 1991.

Matja, "It's No Stretch To Say Plymouth's '92 Grand Voyager Long On Function," Chicago Tribune, p. 9, November 11, 1991.

Mateja, "Technology Molds Theme For '92's: It's Safety First," Chicago Tribune, p. 3, February 9, 1992.

McClintock, "Stricter Belt Law Goal of Activists," The Washington Times, p. B3, May 23, 1991.

McMahon, "Quarrel Ends With Man Dead," Chicago Tribune, p. 1, October 10, 1991

"Metro & Georgia in Brief; Extension Service Workers Get Notices," The Atlanta Journal and Constitution, p. 2, October 1, 1991.

Metzler, "Grief and Liability Collide Under Laws," p. A1, April 1, 1992.

"Millions of Child Seats Unsafe, Group Says," Chicago Tribune, Saturday, December 16, 1989.

Minter, "Distracted Motorist Is Charged In Head-On Collision In Clayton," The Atlanta Journal and Constitution, p. 2, July 29, 1991.

Mollison, Husted, "Child Auto Fatalities Up, Group Says," The Atlanta Journal and Constitution, p. 3, June 18, 1992.

Monroe, "Cobb On Police Blitz List in Crackdown Showdown," The Atlanta Journal and Constitution, p. 2, May 17, 1991.

Monroe, "Grounding A Seat Belt Violator For Life Might Have Saved Hers," The Atlanta Journal and Constitution, p. 02, May 26, 1991..

Monroe, "Teens Learn Driving Skills By Watching The Experts," The Atlanta Journal and Constitution, p. 2, August 7, 1991.

Monson, "Families of the '90's Adopt the Minivan," The Seattle Times, p. 4, November 3, 1991.

"Nation In Brief FAA Says Child Safety Seats Must Be Available on Flights," The Atlanta Journal and Constitution, September 15, 1992, p. 8.

"New Child Seat Approved In U.K.," Aviation Europe, January 29, 1992, p. 4.

"New Generation of Safety," The Seattle Times, p. B2, October 20, 1991.

"New Seat For Children's Use in Aircraft," Origin Universal News Services, January 15.

Newman, "Westchester Car-Van Crash Injures 14," Chicago Tribune, p. 2, August 5, 1991.

"Newsbriefs", The Houston Chronicle, p. 3, July 30, 1992.

O'Mara, "Kids Deserve Safety Seats on Airplanes," Star Tribune, September 23, 1992, p. 23A.

Opdyke, "AAA Members: Toughen Container, Seat-Belt Laws," The Atlanta Journal and Constitution, p. 2, December 22, 1991.

"Other Firms Following Suit," The Atlanta Journal and Constitution, p. 3, April 10, 1992.

"Other News," Los Angeles Times, p. 2, December 12, 1991.

Ott, "Seat Manufacturers Seek Ways To Meet New Criteria," Aviation Week and Space Technology, November 23, 1992, p. 99.

"Patrols Poised for Pursuit of Safe Holiday," The Atlanta Journal and Constitution, p. 2, July 4, 1991.

Perkins, "Simplified Fares May Be Discontinued," Chicago Tribune, October 4, 1992, p. 5.

Phillips, "Child Safety Seat Rule For Planes Rejected," Los Angeles Times, September 15 ,1992, p. 4.

Phillips, "FAA Won't Mandate Child Safety Seats....," The Washington Post, September 15, 1992, p. A1.

"Pilots Blamed in Crashed of Musicians' Planes," The New York Times, September 16, 1992, p. 22.

"Police Arrest Man After 17 Are Hurt in Collision," Los Angeles Times, p. 6, April 27, 1992.

"Police Arrest 89 in Driver Crackdown," Chicago Tribune, p. 3, September 9, 1992.

"Q&A On The News," The Atlanta Journal and Constitution, p. 2, May 24, 1991.

"Ralph Nader Kicks-Off Barrister's Ball Activities," The Pillar, Volume 33, No. 3, February 11, 1993.

Poling, "FAA Refuses to Adopt Child Safety Restraint Requirement," Travel Weekly, September 21, 1992, p. 5.

Product Safety & Liability Reporter 114, "Amrhein v. Quaker Oats Co.," DC EMo, No. 89-1023-C(5), 12-29-90.

Ramsey, J. "Motor Vehicles — Safety Standards," U.S. Law Week Digest of 8-16-90 Opinion, (September 14, 1990).

Ramsey, J. "State Common Law Tort Action Alleging That Manufacturer Negligently Designed Child Car Seat is Not Pre-Empted By Manufacturer's Compliance with Child Restraint System Safety Standard Promulgated Under National Traffic and Motor Vehicle Safety Act," 59 U.S.L.W. 2163 (September 18, 1990).

Ramsey, J. "Welsh v. Century Products, Inc.," DC Md, No. R-86-192, 8-16-90.

Rehkopf, "Buckle Up Your Little Turkey; Health Department is Behind Safety Push," The Atlanta Journal and Constitution, p. 2, November 28, 1991.

Rivara, Frederick P., M.D., M.P.H., "Child Pedestrian Injuries in the United States," AJDC, Volume 144, June 1990.

Rivara, Frederick P., M.D., M.P.H., Cathryn L. Booth, Ph.D., Abraham B. Bergman, M.D., Lisa W. Rogers, and Jean Weiss, "Prevention of Pedestrian Injuries to Children: Effectiveness of a School Training Program," Pediatrics, Volume 88, No. 4, October 1991.

Routhier, "Federal Grant Will Help Boost Weekend Patrols in 43 Towns," The Hartford Courant, p. D11, September 4, 1992.

"Safety and Technology Out Next: Built-In Safety Seat For Kids," The Atlanta Journal and Constitution, p. 3, April 10, 1992.

Samuels, "Taking a Trip Overseas With the Kids," The New York Times, January 24, 1988, p. 21.

Sarra, "Police Beat," Newsday, p. 9, April 19, 1992.

Sarra, "Police Beat," Newsday, p. 9, January 12, 1992.

"Seat Belt Use Debated in Driver's Acquittal," Chicago Tribune, p. 3, January 29, 1987.

Scruggs, "Felony Charge Against Bus Monitor is Reduced in Slapping of 7-Year-Old," The Atlanta Journal and Constitution, p. 2, October 24, 1991.

Scruggs, "Monitor Accused of Hitting Child Has Charge Reduced," The Atlanta Journal and Constitution, p. 6, October 23, 1991.

Sharp, "5-Year-Old Teaches Lesson That Seat Belts Save Lives," The Atlanta Journal and Constitution, p. 2, May 10, 1991.

Shenefelt, "AA Baby Can Become a Flying Missile," UPI, January 13,1984.

Shifrin, "Do It Right! Proper Auto Restraints Can Save Children's Lives," The Seattle Times, p. K4, June 7, 1992.

"Show To Have More New-Display Cars," The Washington Times, p. G4, December 26, 1991.

Sivesind, "Traveling With Junior," The Christian Science Monitor, August 24, 1987, p. 21.

Sloan, "Barney lumbers to Universal Parks," USA Today, March 30, 1993, p. 6D.

Smith, "Tragedies Spark Renewed Calls for Child Car Safety; Driving: This Month, The County Saw The Largest Number of Deaths and Injuries to Children Who Were Not Restrained in Seats or By Belts in Recent Memory," Los Angeles Times, p. 1, January 27, 1992.

Soble, "CHP Urges Manslaughter Charge Under Car-Seat Law; Crash: The Child Had Been Sitting On Her Father's Lap. State Officials Recall No Such Prosecutions Since the Statute Was Adopted," Los Angeles Times, p. 1, September 21, 1991.

"South King County Races—Contested Races in South King County," The Seattle Times, p. C4, October 31, 1991.

Studley, "Hyannis Infant Killed In N. Dartmouth Crash," The Boston Globe, p. 25, August 15, 1992.

Sullivan, "The Risks of Poor Parenting; Health: Government Programs Aren't Enough; Parents, Community Must Do Their Part," Los Angeles Times, p. 7, October 2, 1991.

Sweeney, "Despite Pressure, FAA Won't Require Airplane Baby Seats," The Christian Science Monitor, October 15, 1992, p. 8.

Szczesny," Automakers Pushing Service, Peace of Mind Over Cash Rebates," Chicago Tribune, p. 17C, October 13, 1991.

Szczesny, "There's More to Vans Than Minis," Chicago Tribune, p. 170, October 13, 1991.

"Take A Seat," The Washington Post, September 22, 1992, p. A20.

Thelin, Carl F. "Child Car Restraints," Experts-at-Law, Car and Driver, May-June 1990.

"Thief Takes Idling Car and Sleeping Baby for a Joyride," Star Tribune, p. 1A, December 12, 1991.

"3 Killed, 1 Hurt in Head-On Crash," Chicago Tribune, p. 3, August 10, 1992.

"Toddler Dies in Vt. Car Crash," The Boston Globe, November 16, 1991.

Torpy, "Authorities Out In Force For Speeders In Cobb," The Atlanta Journal and Constitution, p. 9, May 23, 1991.

"Trains, Planes, and Automobiles—Collision Course," Trial, February 1991.

"Transportation Litigation—Road to Safety," Trial, February 1993.

Transportation Research Board, "Improving School Bus Safety," 1989.

Tucker, "Face Facts: Prevention is Cheaper Than Cure," The Atlanta Journal and Constitution, p. 13, November 13, 1991.

"Unemployed Driver Saves Tot, Lands Job," The Washington Times, p. A7, February 12, 1992.

"U.S. Won't Require Infant Seats on Planes," The New York Times, September 15, 1992, p. 18.

"Use of Automobile Safety Seats for Tots Declines in California," Chicago Tribune, p. 7, June 24, 1992.

Vartabedian, "Safety Is Not Locked Into Child Restraint Seats," Los Angeles Times, p. 7, July 18, 1991.

Washburn, "Child-Restraint seats urged on U.S. Airlines," Chicago Tribune, November 4, 1989, p. 3.

Washburn, "It's Time To Get Out Of Fast Lane," Chicago Tribune, p. 1, June 28, 1991.

White, "Danforth Critical of China, Supports MFN Trade Status," Gannett News Service, September 18, 1992.

Whitely, "Seat Belts Especially Important For Children," The Seattle Times, p. E2, May 1, 1992.

Woessner, "Crash Course on Kids' Safety Seats," USA Today, p. 4D, February 10, 1992.

FAA Articles

Adler, "FAA Is Looking Into the issue of Child Safety; Ailrines: A Proposal That Would Require Airlines To Allow Passengers To Use Child Restraint Seats, Such As Those Used In Cars, Is Now Being Prepared," Los Angeles Times, October 22, 1989, p. 25.

Adler, "The Cost Of Using Child Safety Seats On Planes," Los Angeles Times, January 19, 1992, p. 19.

"Air Transport Association," Aviation Daily, January 8, 1993, p. 36.

"Airline Infant Safety Seats Required," Aviation Week and Space Technology, February 5, 1990, p. 17.

Bond, "Require Safety Seats For Our Littlest Fliers," USA Today, Martch 1, 1990, p. 10A.

Borcover, "Travelin' Trends Where Tourists Will Be Heading This Fall," Chicago Tribune, October 4, 1992, p. 2.

Bradsher, "The Crash of Flight 52," The New York Times, January 28, 1990, p. 29.

"British Airline To Offer Child-Safety Seats," UPI, January 16, 1992.

"Children In Flight," St. Petersburg Times, September 26 ,1992, p. 14A.

"Child Restraints Sought on Airliners," The Washington Post, November 14, 1983, p. A15.

"Child Safety: Parents Pay," Flight International, April 1, 1992.

"Child Safety Seats," The New York Times, March 29, 1992, p. 24.

"Clinton Will Change Regulatory Climate," The National Law Journal, November 23, 1992, p. 17.

Diamond, "Reducing Risk to Children on Planes, Buses," Los Angeles Times, August 11, 1989, p. 1.

Dornheim, "FAA Flight Tests To Measure Synthetic Vision Performance," Aviation Week and Space Technology, January 20, 1992, p. 41.

Eldridge, "FAA: Airlines Must Allow Child Seats," Gannett News Service, September 14, 1992.

"FAA Allows Safety Seats," The Hartford Courant, September 15, 1992, p. A7.

"FAA'S Final Rule Won't Make Infant-Restraint Usage Mandatory," Air Safety Week, September 21, 1992, Volume 6.

"FAA Plebiscite," Aviation Week and Space Technology, December 18, 1989, p. 15.Downey, Buckling Up Baby, The Atlanta Journal and Constitution, November 11, 1991, p. 1.

"FAA Proposes To Require Airlines To Allow Child Seats," PR Newswire, February 22, 1990.

"FAA Requires Airlines To Allow Child Safety Seats," Aviation Daily, September 15, 1992, p. 460.

"FAA Requires Airlines To Allow Child Saftey Seats," Reuters, September 14, 1992.

Field, "FAA's Refusal To Require Safety Seats Faces Battle," The Washington Times, September 16, 1992, p. C3.

Finnegan, "Fasten Your Seat Belt! Western Airports Are Flying Into The 21st Century," Includes related articles Cover story, Sunset, November, 1992, p. 74.

"Flight Attendants List Safety Goals For 1990," Aviation Daily, December 14, 1989, p. 489.

Gellene, "Forget Those Booster Seats When Flying," Los Angeles Times, August 28, 1992, p. 3.

Gellene, "Making Air Travel Safe For Baby:. . . .," Los Angeles Times, December 7, 1989, p. 1.

Gogarty, "Safety Has A Price," The Daily Telegraph, January 25, 1992, p. 107.

Greenberg, "A Traveler's Election Agenda; Savvy Travler," The Plain Dealer, November 1, 1992, p. 2I.

Greenberg, "DOT, FAA In Dire Need Of An Overhaul," The Buffalo News, November 1, 1992, p. 5.

Henderson, "Safety Agency May Press For Airliner Infant Seats," Los Angeles Times, November 4, 1989, p. 2.

Irick, "The Plane Truth," The Washington Post, March 22, 1992.

Johnson, "Airlines Ask FAA To Require Infant Seats," Los Angeles Times, February 23, 1990, p. 24.

"Lightfoot Presses Child Seats," The Washington Post, September 16, 1992, p. A19.

"Lessons To Be Learned," Flight International, October 31, 1990.

"Nation In Brief FAA Says Child Safety Seats Must Be Available on Flights," The Atlanta Journal and Constitution, September 15, 1992, p. 8.

"New Child Seat Approved In U.K.," Aviation Europe, January 29, 1992, p. 4.

"New Seat For Children's Use in Aircraft," Origin Universal News Services, January 15.

O'Mara, "Kids Deserve Safety Seats On Airplanes," Star Tribune, September 23, 1992, p. 23A.

Ott, "Seat Manufacturers Seek Ways To Meet New Criteria," Aviation Week and Space Technology, November 23, 1992, p. 99.

Perkins, "Simplified Fares May Be Discontinued," Chicago Tribune, October 4, 1992, p. 5.

Phillips, "Child Safety Seat Rule For Planes Rejected," Los Angeles Times, September 15 ,1992, p. 4.

Phillips, "FAA Won't Mandate Child Safety Seats....," The Washington Post, September 15, 1992, p. A1.

"Pilots Blamed in Crashed of Musisicans' Planes," The New York Times, September 16, 1992, p. 22.

Poling, "FAA Refuses To Adopt Child Saftey Restraint Requirement," Travel Weekly, September 21, 1992, p. 5.

Samuels, "Taking a Trip Overseas With the Kids," The New York Times, January 24, 1988, p. 21.

Shenefelt, "A Baby Can Become A Flying Missile," UPI, janaury 13, 1984.

Sivesind, "Traveling With Junior," The Christian Science Monitor, August 24, 1987, p. 21.

Sloan, Barney lumbers to Universal Parks, USA Today, March 30, 1993, p. 6D.

Sweeney, "Despite Pressure, FAA Won't Require Airplane Baby Seats," The Christian Science Monitor, October 15, 1992, p. 8.

"Take a Seat," The Washington Post, September 22, 1992, p. A20.

"The FAA Has Decided," Aviation Week and Space Technology, September 21, 1992, p. 17.

Washburn, "Child-Restraint seats urged on U.S. Airlines," Chicago Tribune, November 4, 1989, p. 3.

White, "Danforth Critical of China, Supports MFN Trade Status," Gannett News Service, September 18, 1992.

"U.S. Won't Require Infant Seats on Planes," The New York Times, September 15, 1992, p. 18.

Newspaper List

"A Special Place for Special People," The Washington Post, March 14, 1993; p. C8.

"A Wiz of a Book," St. Petersburg Times, February 17, 1992; Pg. 1D.

Adair, "Are You A Car-Crash Survivor? If So, You Should Be Thanking A Dummy Rather Than Your Lucky Stars," The Ottawa Citizen, March 24, 1992; Pg. F5.

Adair, "These Dummies Make Cars Safer," St. Petersburg Times, March 16, 1992; Pg. 1A.

Adler, "Consumer Report: FAA is Looking Into the Issue of Child Safety; Airlines: A Proposal That Would Require Airlines to Allow Passengers to Use Child-Restraint Seats, Such as Those Used in Cars, is Now Being Prepared," Los Angeles Times, October 22, 1989; Part L; Pg. 25; Col. 1.

Adler, "Consumer Report: The Cost of Using Child Safety Seats on Planes," Los Angeles Times, January 19, 1992; Part L; Pg. 19; Col. 1.

"Air Transport Association," Aviation Daily, January 8, 1993, p. 36.

Boghdady, "Maryland's Views on the Car Safety Debate," States News Service, June 19, 1992.

Borcover, "Travelin' Trends Where Tourists Will Be Heading This Fall," Chicago Tribune, October 4, 1992, p. 2.

"Boy," United Press International, July 5, 1988.

"Bush Nominates Marion C. Blakey DOT Safety Chief," Inside DOT & Transportation Week, August 7, 1992; No. 21, Vol. 3.

"Car Seat Case Settled," The National Law Journal, January 11, 1993, For the Record; Legal News Briefs, Massachusetts; Pg. 6.

"Car Seat Recall," The Atlanta Journal and Constitution, April 23, 1991; Section B; Pg. 03.

"Car Seat Travel Tips From Century Products," PR Newswire, June 16, 1992; Lifestyle Section.

"Car Seats," United Press International, September 20, 1983.

"Car Seats," United Press International, January 14, 1984.

"Car Seats Save Babies, Not Adult's Lap," Study, Reuters, Ltd., July 5, 1992.

"Car Seats That Fall Short," Newsday, December 18, 1993; Pg. 47.

"Century Initiates 3,000/5,000 Ste. Retrofit Program," PR Newswire, October 1, 1992, Domestic News Section.

"Century Issues Repair for Child Seat Model," The Toronto Star, March 28, 1992; Pg. H5.

"Century Products Company Announces 3000 Ste and 5000 Ste Car Seat Retrofit Program," Canada Newswire, October 28, 1992, Domestic News.

"Century Products Launches 3000/5000 St. Notification Program," PR Newswire, June 14, 1991.

"Century Products Sends Notice to all Century 5000 STE Models 4450 GD, 4460 DT, 4460 FE and 4475 GA Car Seat Owners," Business Wire, March,l 1990.

"Charges Filed in Baby Death," United Press International, April 28, 1988, April 28, 1988.

"Charges Recommended in Car-Seat Death," United Press International, BC Cycle, March 6, 1990.

"Child Car-Seat Maker Settles for $4 Million," The Chicago Tribune, December 24, 1992, Pg. 8, Zone: N.

"Child Car Seats Are A Must," Chicago Tribune, August 17, 1988; Pg. 4.

"Child Car Seats Defective," The Houston Chronicle, July 9, 1992; Section A; National Briefs; Pg. 17.

"Child Car Seats Failing," Newsday, December 16, 1989, Pg. 9.

"Child Car Seats Going to Low-Income Families," The Dallas Morning News, October 15, 1992; Pg. 26A.
December 24, 1992 (North Sports Final Edition); Pg. 8; Zone N.

"Child Deaths in Car Crashes - News Conference by the Institute for Injury Reduction," Federal News Service, June 17, 1992.

"Child Health Week 1991 Focuses on Injury Prevention," PR Newswire, October 8, 1991.

"Child Passenger Safety Week/Sunday May 5," Los Angeles Times, April 23, 1991, Part B; p. 2; Col. 1.

"Child Restraint Law Reduces Traffic Injuries by 27%," United Press International, October 19, 1986.

"Child Restraint Seat Developed," Aviation Week and Space Technology, December 20, 1983; Pg. 32.

"Child Safety Seats," The Washington Post, October 20, 1983.

"Child Safety Seats," Consumer Reports, January, 1992; Vol. 57, N:o. 1; Pg. 16.

"Child Safety-Seats - Your Cut-and-Keep Guide," The Straits Times, May 22, 1992; Pg. 23.

"Child Seats in Cars Must Still Be Belted Up," The Straits Times, May 22, 1992; Pg. 23.

"Child Traffic Deaths Increase Despite Child Restraint Seats," Copyright 1991 Reuters, August 29, 1991.

"Chrysler's Child Seat Wins Design Award," United Press International, October 12, 1992; Financial Section.

"Chrysler's Integrated Child Seat Wins German Technology and Design Award," PR Newswire, October 12, 1992, Financial News Section.

"Chrysler Shows Integrated Child Seat for Minivans," United Press International, May 15, 1991.

"Chrysler Unveils Integrated Child Seat for Minivans," PR Newswire, May 15, 1991.

Clary, "Charges Dismissed for Father In Car Seat Trial; Traffic Safety: He was Accused in the Death of His Daughter, Who Sat Unrestrained in Mother's Lap. Judge Clears Him Before Jury Was To Get Case," Los Angeles Times, May 4, 1991; Part A; Pg. 2; Col. 1.

Clary, "Father on Trial in Death of Girl Not Riding in Car Seat; Law: Prosecutor Says that He 'Abandoned His Responsibilities.' The Vehicular Homicide Case is Thought to be the First of its Kind to go to Court," Los Angeles Times, May 3, 1991; Part A; Pg. 4; Col. 1.

"Company Brings In 5,000 Child Restraints for Rent," The Straits Times, June 18, 1992; Pg. 22

"Company Issues Recall for Children's Car Seat," Chicago Tribune, April 21, 1991; Pg. 17A; Zone: N.

"Consumer," Los Angeles Times, November 2, 1992, Part D; p. 2; Col. 1.

"Consumer News," Los Angeles Times, April 18, 1991; Part D; Pg. 2; Col. 1.

"Consumers; On Alert for Hazardous Baby Items," March 9, 1989; Part 5; Pg. 1; Col. 2.

Cooper, "Who Won?," National Journal, July 28, 1984; Vol. 16, No. 30; Pg. 1441.

Cote, "Mazda Explains Warranty After Prodding," The Ottawa Citizen, March 24, 1993, p. D4.

"Child Restraint Seat-Wrongful Death," Massachusetts Lawyers Weekly, August 3, 1992; Trial Reports; Pg. 34.

"Child Restraints Sought on Airliners," The Washington Post, November 14, 1983; First Sec.; A15.

"Child Safety; Government Action," Society of Automotive Engineers 1992, April, 1992; Vol. 100; No. 4; Pg. 65.

"Child Safety; Parents Pay," Flight International, April 1, 1992.

"Children In Flight," St. Petersburg Times, September 26, 1992, p. 14A.

"Clinton Will Change Regulatory Climate," The National Law Journal, November 23, 1992, p. 17.

Diamond, "Reducing Risk to Children on Planes, Buses," Los Angles Times, August 11, 1989, Part 4; Col. 1.

"DOT Urged to Improve 'Lagging' Child Protection Efforts for 'Safety Awarness' Week," PR Newswire, February 5, 1991.

Downey, "Buckling Up Baby," The Atlanta Journal and Constitution, November 11, 1991; Sec. F., Pg. 01.

Downey, "Cracking Down on Buckling Up; Trouble with Restraints is Seat-Of-The Pants Usage," The Atlanta Journal and Constitution, January 22, 1991; Sec. E; Pg. 7.

Doyle, "Drunk Drivers More Likely to Kill Children Riding in Own Car," United Press International, June 4, 1986.

Doyle, "Drunk Drivers More Likely to Kill Children Riding in Own Car," United Press International, June 5, 1986.

"Drive Smart Campaign Rewards Safety Conscious Dealers," Reduces Auto Injuries and Fatalities, Southwest Newswire, February 3, 1989.

"Drive Smart Campaign Rewards Safety Conscious-Dealers," PR Newswire, February 3, 1989.

"Drive Smart Campaign Rewards Safety Concious Dealers, Reduces Auto Injuries and Fatalities," Business Wire, February 3, 1989.

"Drivers Lacking Car Seats for Kids to be Ticketed," The Plain Dealer, November 13, 1992; Pg. 3B.

Duff/Glaser, "Family Clinic; Children and Seat Belt Safety," Newsday, May 27, 1989, Prt. II; Pg. 02.

Dumaine, "Closing the Innovation Gap," Fortune, December 2, 1991; Pg. 56.

Eldridge, "Car Seat Recalls Draw Low Response; System Blamed," Gannett News Service, September 2, 1991.

Epstein, "ABC's of Baby Care," St. Petersburg Times, July 13, 1992; Pg. 1D.

Evans, Orange County Digest: Countywide; "Survey Shows Greater Usage of Seat Belts," Los Angles Times, February 24, 1986; Part 2; Pg. 2; Col. 3.

"Extra Protection," Business Times, August 15, 1992; Pg. 1.

"FAA Plebiscite," Aviaition Week and Space Technology, December 18, 1989, Vol. 131, No. 25; Pg. 15.

"FAA Proposes to Require Airlines to Allow Child Seats," PR Newswire, February 22, 1990.

Faris, " 'A Social Problem'; Parents Buckle Down on Child-Seat Safety," Los Angeles Times, October 12, 1986; Part 9; Pg. 1; Col. 1.

Farris, "Committee Approves Child Restraint Bill," United Press International, January 14, 1985.

"Father on Trial in Car Accident Death," The Washington Post, May 3, 1991; Pg. A8.

"Fearing Injury, Manufacturer Recalls Children's Car Seat," Chicago Tribune, April 18, 1991; Pg. 4; Zone: M.

"Feds Approve Kentucky Highway Safety Plan," United Press International, September 28, 1984.

Field, "FAA's Refusal to Require Safety Seats Faces Battle," The Washington Times, September 16, 1993; Part C; Money; Pg. C3.

Finnegan, "Fasten Your Seatbelt! Western Airports Are Flying Into The 21st Century," Includes Related Articles Cover Story, Sunset Publishing Corporation, November 1992, Volume 189, No. 5, p. 74.

"Fisher-Price Recalls 900,000 of its Child Safety Seats," Los Angeles Times, October 9, 1992; Part D; Pg. 11.

"Five Die in Weekend Traffic," United Press International, January 12, 1986.

"Flight Attendants List Safety Goals for 1990s," Aviation Daily, December 14, 1992; Vol. 298, No. 50; Pg. 489.

Friedland, "Child Safety: Auto Devices Held Misused," The New York Times, March 30, 1986; Sec. 11NJ; Pg. 1; Col. 1.

Gable, "New Ideas Come From Young Minds," Gannett News Service, June 26, 1991.

"GEICO Suggests Safety-Oriented Gift Ideas for the Holidays," PR Newswire, November 21, 1989.

Gellene, "Making Air Travel Safe for Baby Pressure is Mounting to Make Infant Seats Mandatory on Jetliners, Airlines are Eager to Promote Family Travel But Fear a Revolt from Parents," Los Angeles Times, December 7, 19989, Part A; Pg. 1; Col 1.

Giangrasse, "High-Tech Booths Put Information at Showgoers' Fingertips," Chicago Tribune, February 7, 1993; Pg. 14; Zone: N.

Gillespie, "Sitting Tight When it Comes to Kids' Car Seats, What's Easiest for Mom is Safesty for Baby, Too," Chicago Tribune, November 13, 1985.

"Girl, 2, Killed in Crash," The Washington Post, November 2, 1992; Metro; p. B9;; Around the Region

"GM Tops NHTSA June Recall List," Crain Communications, Inc. Automotive News, July 24, 1989; Pg. 56

Gogarty, "Safety Has a Price," The Daily Telegraph, January 25, 1992; Pg. 107.

Golden, "Jury Told Failure to Buckle Up Girl Was Homocide," The New York Times, May 3, 1991; Sec. A; Pg. 19: Col. 4.

"Governor Signs Bill to Expand Use of Child Seats in Cars," The San Francisco Chronicle, March 28, 1990; Pg. A8.

Green, "Motoring: Getting Baby to Belt Up; Maralyn Green on the Problems of Keeping Children in Car Seats," September 8, 1990; Pg. 37.

Greenberg, "A Traveler's Election Agenda," Savvy Traveler, The Plain Dealer, November 1, 1992, p. 2I.

Greenberg, "DOT, FAA In Dire Need of an Overhaul," The Buffalo News, November 1, 1992, p. 5.

"Infant," United Press International, October 4, 1983.

Haberstroh/Norton, "Tot Survives Tumble Out of Car — Boy Unhooks Seat Belt, Falls in Rush Hour," The Seattle Times, September 2, 1992; Pg. B1.

Hamilton, "Fatal Level Crossing Accidents Trains Que.," The Gazette (Montreal), October 1, 1992, Pg. A3.

Hamilton, "Woman, Grandson, 2, Killed When Train Hits Car," The Gazette (Montreal), October 1, 1992; Pg. A3.

Hardy, "Homicide Trial Begins for Dad in Car Safety-Seat Case," United Press International, April 29, 1991.

Hardy, "Judge Dismisses Charges in Car-Seat Case," United Press International, May 3, 1991.

Hardy, "Judge Dismisses Charges in Car-Seat Case," United Press International, May 4, 1991.

Henderson, "Safety Agency May Press for Airliner Infant Seats," Los Angeles Times, November 4, 1989; Part A; Pg. 2, Col. 5.

"Holiday Safety: Pennsylvania Turnpike Priority; Motorists Near Breezewood Can Expect Major Delays," PR Newswire, May 19, 1992.

"Seat," Press Association Newsfile, Home News, February 5, 1993.

"How Not to Make an Automatic Safety Belt," Consumer Reports, March, 1988; Vol. 53, No. 3; Pg. 167.

Incantalupo, "Child Car Seats Undergo Safety Scrutiny," Newsday, February 8, 1990; Pg. 53.

"Infants Safer in Seats Than in Parents' Laps," The Washington Times, July 6, 1992; Pg. A2.

"Insurance Association, Allstate Join Department of Highway Safety & Motor Vehicles Campaign," Business Wire, September 25, 1990.

Irick, "The Plane Truth," The Washington Post, March 22, 1992; Pg. E3.

"Is it Murder? Prosecuting People Whose Kids Die in Car Crashes is No Way to Enforce Seat-Belt Laws," Newsday, January 26, 1991; Pg. 20.

Haines, "KidSafe Program Expands UPI Texas News Feature," United Press International, April 8, 1989.

Harlow, "Too-Hasty Reaction by Crew Caused Crippled Aircraft to Crash-Land on Motorway," The Daily Telegraph, October 19, 1990, Pg. 4.

Jennings, "Tougher Law on Child Safety Seats Takes Effect; Additional Provision Lets Officers Ticket Motorists Without Stopping Them for Other Violations," The Washington Post, October 1, 1992; p. M1.

Johnson, "Airlines Ask FAA to Require Infant Seats," Los Angeles Times, February 23, 1990; Part A; Pg. 24; Col. 4.

Jones, "Parents Can Avert Tragedy by Just Buckling Up Kids," The Toronto Star, March 7, 1991; Pg. D5.

Kahn, "Jury Rules for Hyundai in Suit Over Seat Belts," Crain Communications, Inc. Automotive News, February 17, 1992; Legal File; Pg. 58.

Kahn, "Tasks and Timetables Set as Senate Reauthorizes NHTSA for 2 Years," Crain Communications, Inc. Automotive News, August 28, 1989; Pg. 42.

Kastilahn, "Safety Village Gives 'Small Town' a Whole New Meaning," Chicago Tribune, July 16, 1986,

Katz, "Woman's Drive Into Harbor Kills Her, Child," Los Angeles Times, January 23, 1991; Part B; Pg. 8; Col. 4.

Kelley, "Lawsuit Against General Motors - Institute for Injury Reduction Press Conference," Federal News Service, August 19, 1992.

Kenen, "Father Faces Murder Trial for Death of Child in Car Crash," Reuters AM Cycle, April 26, 1991.

"Kid Restraints Pass Committee," United Press International, May 15, 1984.

"Kids' Inventions Merit Attention," USA Today, June 27, 1991; Pg. 6D.

Kim, "Seats Aplenty for Precious Cargo," Los Angeles Times, February 16, 1992; Part B; Pg. 3; Col. 3.

"Kits to Fix Defective Child Car Seats Found to be Defective," Proprietary to the United Press International, March 5, 1993, Financial

"Kolcraft Announces Safety Recall for Traveler 700 Child Restraints," PR Newswire, December 11, 1991.

"Kopplin," United Press International, March 21, 1983.

"LaBriefs," United Press International, December 15, 1984.

"Lawmaker Wants More Motorists Under Child Restraint Law," United Press International, December 9, 1983.

Lee, "Hospital Gives Babies a Safe Start With Free Seats for the Trip Home," Los Angeles Times, January 1, 1993; Part B; Pg. 1; Col. 2.

Leighty, "New Dad vs. New Baby," United Press International, July 30, 1985.

Lemke, "Tales From the Freeway: Safety Sense; Keeping Up On New Seat Belt, Helmet Laws for Riders, Drivers," Los Angeles Times, September 10, 1992; North County Focus; Pg. 2.

"Lessons to be Learned," Flight International, October 31, 1990.

Levey, "A Pair of Gaps in D.C. Seat Belt Law," The Washington Post, September 3, 1992; Sports; p. B22.

Lunsford, "Toddler Killed, 6 Others Injured in Head-On Crash in Glenn Heights," The Dallas Morning News, April 4, 1993, p. 44A.

Mahr, "Safety 'Price of Admission' For Carmakers," Chicago Tribune, February 7, 1993; Pg. 24; Zone N.

Major Leader Special Transcript, Press Conference Concerning Introduction of The Public Health and Safety Act of 1992, Federal News Service, June 26, 1992.

Malta, "Demand for Chrysler Child Seats is Strong," Crain Communications, Inc. Automotive News, October 21, 1991; Pg. 44.

"Marion C. Blakey Appointed Acting NHTSA Administrator," Inside Dot & Transportation Week, July 10, 1992; No. 28, Vol. 3.

"Massachusetts Car-Seat Suit Settled for $4.25 million," Liability Week, December 28, 1993; No. 48, Vol. 7.

Mateja, "Chrysler Leads Campaign to Win Built-In Market for Safety Seats," Chicago Tribune, January 15, 1992; Pg. 5; Zone CN.

Matthews, "Poorly-Fitted Child Car Seats Risk Lives," The Daily Telegraph, May 31, 1991; Pg. 6.

Matthews, "Car Safety & Security: Un-safety Seats for Kids Virginia Matthews on Research that Found Too Many Children's Car Seats Inadequately fixed; DIY Bodgers and Confusing Instructions Put Young Lives at Risk," The Daily Telegraph, July 10, 1991; Pg. 32.

Maynard, "In '92, Built-In Child Car Seats," USA Today, February 22, 1991; Pg. 1A.

Maynard, "Minivans Have Child Safety Seats Built In," Gannett News Service, February 22, 1991.

McCluggage, "Proper Precautions for Wee Passengers," Sacramento Bee, February 17, 1993; p. C1.

McRoberts, "Police Beef up DUI Units for Holiday Crackdown," Chicago Tribune, December 4, 1992; Pg. 3; Zone NW.

Meier, Consumer's World; "Child Safety Seats: Debate on Recalls," The New York Times, February 24, 1990; Sec. 1; Pg. 50; Col. 4.

Merry, "Buckling Up Toddlers: More States Require Car Seats for Younsters," The Christian Science Monitor, May 16, 1983; Pg. 9.

"Michigan Coalition for Safety Belt Use Celebrates Anniversary of Child Passenger Safety Law," PR Newswire, March 29, 1991.

Miller, "Infant Car Seat Law Goes Into Effect March 7," United Press International, February 15, 1983.

Millican, "Child Safety Seat Advocate Still Driven to Curtail Auto Crash Death," Los Angeles Times, December 31, 1993; Part B; Pg. 3; Col. 5.

Millican, "Child Safety Advocate Still Driven to Curtail Auto Crash Death," Los Angeles Times, January 7, 1993; Part J; Pg. 3; Col. 1.

"Millions of Child Seats Unsafe, Group Says," Chicago Tribune, December 16, 1989, Pg. 2; Zone: C.

"Mississippi," USA Today, April 4, 1990; Pg. 6A.

Mitchell, "Car Seat Saved Tot, Police Say," The Toronto Star, August 10, 1991; Pg. A15.

Monson, "Toys to Go: Making Gadgets and Gizmos for Cars is Big Business — We Buy Everything from Fuzzy Dice to Tiny TVs," The Seattle Times, November 4, 1990; Pg. 14.

Monson, "Families of the '90s Adopt the Minivan," The Seattle Times, November 3, 1991; Pg. 4.

"Most Say Seat Belts Are Good But Not Many Buckle Up," United Press International, July 2, 1987.

"Mother Won't be Charged In Crash That Killed Child," Los Angeles Times, December 12, 1991; Part A; Pg. 39; Col. 3.

"Mother of Crash Victim Charged With Not Using Safety Restraints," United Press International, June 18, 1985.

Mundy, States News Service March 15, 1990.

"NHTSA Broadens Child-Safety Rule," Crain Communications, Inc. Automotive News, February 8, 1988; Pg. 88.

"National Highway Traffic Safety Administration," Newsday, June 19, 1991; Pg. 43.

Ness, "Children's Car Seats For Rent in Florida," The Toronto Star, February 1, 1992; Pg. F12.

Neumann, "Care with Hot Drinks," Los Angeles Times, October 15, 1989; Part L; p. 20; Col. 1.

"New Child Seat Aproved In U.K.," Aiviation Europe, January 29, 1992; Vol. 2, No. 4; Pg. 4.

"New Court Decisions," U.S. Law Week, September 5, 1990.

"New Court Decisions," U.S. Law Week, September 14, 1990.

"New Court Decisions," U.S. Law Week, September 18, 1990.

"New Laws," United Press International, August 1, 1987.

"New Seat for Children's Use in Aircraft," Universal News Services Limited, 1992, January 15, 1992.

"News Conference: Campaign to Increase Use of Child Safety Seats and Seat Belts," Federal News Service, , February 11, 1992.

Nichols, "More Use Child-Restraint Car Seats; Problems Remain," September 24, 1991.

"No Charges in Infant Death, United Press International 1991," December 27, 1991.

"No More Warnings on Seat-Belt Use," Chicago Tribune, January 1, 1993; Pg. 3; Zone: N.

"900,000 Child Car Seats Being Recalled," The Dallas Morning News, October 9, 1992; Pg. 6A.

"Official Says Child Restraints Work When Used Properly," United Press International, January 25, 1987.

"One Million Child Car Seats Recalled," The Dallas Morning News, October 29, 1992; Pg. 5A.

Outerbridge, "Bungee Cord Can't Fill In for Child Safety Seats," The Washington Times, September 23, 1992, Pg. E3.

"Other News," Los Angeles Times, November 2, 1991; Part D; Pg. 2, Col 1.

Ott, "Seat Manufacturers Seek Ways to Meet New Criteria," Aviation Week and Space Technology, November 23, 1992, p. 99.

"Parents Now Have No Excuse Not to Protect Children in Cars," United Press International, February 8, 1992.

"Patrol Says Bad Weather, Poor Roads Kept Holiday Death Toll Down," United Press International, December 26, 1983.

Pearson, "Changes Sought in Seat-Belt Law, New Stress is Put on Child Safety," Chicago Tribune, April 4, 1990; Pg. 1, Zone: D.

Perkins, " 'Simplified' Fares May Be Discontinued," Chicago Tribune, October 4, 1992, p. 5.

Peters, United Press International, May 15, 1985.

Phillips, "FAA Won't Mandate Child Safety Seats; Airline Industry, Others Sought Requirement; U.S. Analysis Cites Costs," The Washington Post, First Section; p. A1.

"Police Warn 11 For Flouting New Law On Child Seats," The Straits Times, July 5, 1992; Pg. 1.

Pope, "Child-Seat Exemptions Advanced," United Press International, March 13, 1984.

"Press Conference Concerning Introduction of the Public Health and Safety Act of 1992," Federal News Service, June 26, 1993.

"Product Recalls; A Hitch In Transmissions and Defective Rear Seats," Newsay, April 24, 1991; Pg. 43.

"Product Recalls," Consumer Reports, April, 1988; Vol. 53, No. 4; Pg. 213.

"Product Recalls," Consumer Reports, May, 1989, Vol. 54, No. 5; Pg. 335.

"Product Recalls," Consumer Reports, September, 1989, Vol. 54, No. 9; Pg. 601.

"Product Recalls," Consumer Reports, March, 1990, Vol. 55, No. 3; Pg. 190.

"Product Recalls," Consumer Reports, June, 1990; Vol. 55, No. 6; Pg. 423.

"Product Recalls," Consumer Reports, January 1990, Vol. 55, No. 1; Pg. 52.

"Product Recalls: Unsafe Child Safety Seats," Newsday, September 11, 1991; Pg. 43.

"Prosecuting Parents Won't Save Kids' Lives," USA Today, May 2, 1991; Pg. 12A.

Pulver, "Ryan Renews Proposed Truck Fuzzbuster Ban," United Press International, March 30, 1992.

"Q & A on the News," The Atlanta Journal and Constitution, May 24, 1991; Section A; Pg. 02.

Raffles, "IIR Response to NHTSA Petition Denial: Seat Belts Releasing in Crashes," U.S. Newswire, Inc., November 17, 1992; National Desk.

"Recall of Child Seats," The Houston Chronicle, October 29, 1992; Section A, Pg. 18.

Reed, "The Honorable NHTSA Administrator; Jerry Ralph Curry," National Highway Traffic Safety Administration, Automotive Engineers, December 1989, Vol. 97; No. 12; Pg. 67.

Reed, "Cost of Injury," National Highway Traffic Safety Administration Report to Congress, Copyright Society of Automotive Engineers 1990, January, 1990, Vol. 98; No. 1; Pg. 71.

Reed, "Refueling Vapor Recovery; Environmental Protection Agency's Regulations Government Action," Society of Automotive Engineers 1992, October, 1991; Vol. 99; No. 10; Pg. 75.

Reed, "Side Impact Protection; New Federal Auto Side Collision Test Standard," Copyright Society of Automotive Engineers 1990, December, 1990; Vol. 98; No. 12; Pg. 25.

Reed, "Where's The Bag; Automobile Air Bags Government Action," Society of Automotive Engineers 1991, May, 1991; Vol. 99; No. 5; Pg. 61.

Reiner, "A Matter of Restraint — 'Big Kids' Still Need Protection of Booster Seats," The Seattle Times, April 28, 1991; Pg. K1.

Reinhard, "Car Seats - What is Best for Child?," Los Angeles Times, October 20, 1989, Part E; Pg. 5; Col. 1.

"Renolux Announces Recall of Child Restraint Seats," PR Newswire, August 26, 1991.

Reske, "Federal Hearing Held on Child Vehicle Safety," United Press International, February 4, 1983.

Resnick, "Car-Seat Trial Ends, Leaving A Legal Void," The National Law Journal, May 20, 1991, Exhibit A, Pg. 8.

"Restraint," United Press International, February 9, 1988.

"Restraint Seats Saving Lives of Missouri Children," United Press International, April 8, 1985.

"Restraints," United Press International, July 2, 1987.

"Retrofit Kit Offered on Children's Car-Seat Buckles," United Press International 1992, October 1, 1992; Financial Section.

Reuters, "TV is Viewed as Health Hazard," Chicago Tribune, July 6, 1992; Pg. 4; Zone: M.

Russell, "Accidents Happen-Or Do They? America Grapples With Its $158 Billion-A-Year Problem," The Washington Post, October 17, 1989, Pg. Z14.

"Safe Seats for Kids in Cars," The Washington Post, November 24, 1983; Pg. A26.

"SAFECO Grant Provides Child Car Seats for Low-Income Families," Business Wire, March 23, 1992.

"Safety," United Press International, February 9, 1987.

"Safety Seat Misuse Common," The Washington Post, December 22, 1983.

"Safety and Technology Out Next: Built-In Safety Seat for Kids," The Atlanta Journal and Constitution, April 10, 1992; Sec. T; Pg. 3.

Samuels, "Taking a Trip Overseas with the Kids," The New York Times, January 24, 1988, Sec. 10; Pg. 21; Col. 1.

San Diego County Digest: Rancho Santa Fe, Los Angeles Times, July 23, 1991; Part B; Pg. 3, Col. 3.

Scarborough, "How to Use Bike Child Carriers," The San Francisco Chronicle, January 1, 1990; C11.

Schuon, "About Cars," The New York Times, May 12, 1991; Sec. 8; Pg. 12; Col. 3.

Schwartz, "U.S. Says 26 Children Died in Six Years in Infant Carriers," Reuters AM Cycle, April 23, 1992.

"Seat," Press Association Newsfile, February, 1993, Home News.

"Seat Belt Bill Clears House Committee," United Press International, March 5, 1988.

"Seat-Belt Law Saves Lives in Michigan," Chicago Tribune, March 26, 1987; Pg. 3; Zone: C.

"Seat Belts," United Press International, March 13, 1989

"Seat Belts Being Used for Kids, But Improperly," Chicago Tribune, February 10, 1987; Pg. 4; Zone: C.

"Seat Belts Could Prevent 60 Percent of Serious Injuries," United Press International, August 23, 1985.

"Seats," United Press International, January 25, 1983.

"Seats: Group Plans to Donate Car Safety Seats Honor," United Press International, August 11, 1984.

"Seats of Safety - If Used Correctly," The Seattle Times, April 28, 1992; Pg. K2.

"Senate Approves Child Restraints," United Press International, February 6, 1985.

"Sentence," United Press International, February 27, 1985.

Shaffer, "Where They Stand on Child Car Seats," The Washington Post, January 21, 1993; p. J1; Dr. Gridlock.

Shah/Hijek, "Redefining the Line Between Life and Death," St. Petersburg Times, March 28, 1992; Pg. 1A.

Shenefelt, "A Baby Can Become a Flying Missile," United Press International, January 13, 1984.

Sherwood, "Council May Require Car Safety Restraints for Children," The Washington Post, October 6, 1982.

Shifrin, "Do It Right! Proper Auto Restraints Can Save Children's Lives," June 7, 1992; Pg. K4.

Sinclair, "Children's Car Seats," The Washington Post, December 29, 1982.

Sinclair, "What to Look for When Buying Car Seat," The Washington Post, December 29, 1982.

Sinclair, "Push is on to Require Child Safety Restraint Seats in Cars," The Washington Post, December 29, 1982.

Sinclair, "Safety Seats Misuse Common," The Washington Post, December 22, 1983; Consumer Update.

Sinclair, "Restraints Urged for Tots in Cars; Safety Board Cites Accident Statistics," The Washington Post, December 8, 1982.

Sinclair, "Child Car-Seat Problems," March 29, 1984.

Sivesind, "Traveling with Junior," The Christian Science Monitor, August 24, 1987, Pg. 21.

"Short Cuts,“ Newsday, October 29, 1992; Business; Pg. 53

"Short Cuts," Newsday, October 29, 1992; Business; Pg. 49

Sloan, Grossman, "Barney Lumbers to Universal Parks," USA Today, March 30, 1993, p. 6D.

Smith, "Experts Drive Home Need to Use Kids' Safety Seats," The Atlanta Journal and Constitution, February 7, 1993; Section E; Pg. 10.

Smith, "Tragedies Spark Renewed Calls for Child Car Safety; Driving: This Month, The County Saw the Largest Number of Deaths and Injuries to Children Who Were Not Restrained in Seats or by Belts in Recent Memory," Los Angeles Times, January 27, 1992; Part B; p. 1; Col. 2.

Smith, "Getting Around Child Seat-Belt Laws Put Police In A Bind," The Atlanta Journal and Constitution, February 14, 1993; Section E, p. 10.

Snow, "Court Ruling Expands Requirement to Wear Seat Belts," United Press International, April 12, 1984.

Snow, "Laws," United Press International, June 28, 1983.

Soble, "Charges in Death of Girl Urged," Los Angeles Times, September 21, 1992; Part B; Pg. 3; Col. 6.

"Special-Interest Signs are Not the Answer," The New York Times, August 3, 1986, Sec. 11WC; Pg. 23; Col. 1.

"State Safety Groups and New England Midas Dealers Promote National Buckle-Up Week With Toll-Free Hotline," PR Newswire, May 21, 1992.

"State's Holiday Death Toll Reaches 15," United Press International, December 1, 1987.

"Statistics Find Many Use Child Car Seats Incorrectly; Tips on Proper Use Provided in Free Brochure in Support of Child Passenger Safety Week," PR Newswire, February 7, 1992.

"Strangled," United Press International, January 23, 1989.

"State has Child Seats to Lend to Parents," The Washington Post, September 29, 1983, Pg. 8.

"State Rep. Seth Armstrong Critically Injured in Traffic Accident," United Press International, August 24, 1986.

Suderman, "Chrysler Puts Built-In Child Seats Into Minivans," Calgary Herald, October 4, 1991; Pg. F13.

"Survey: More Iowans Buckling Up," United Press International, September 11, 1984.

Sweeney, "Despite Pressure, FAA Won't Require Airplane Baby Seats," The Christian Science Monitor, October 15, 1992, p. 8.

Sweetman, "Tips to Help Create a Safe Environment for Children," The Ottawa Citizen, December 23, 1991; Pg. B3.

"Texbriefs," United Press International, May 22, 1985.

"Three Hundred More Baby Capsules Available For Rent Soon," The Straits Times, June 13, 1992; Pg. 22.

"Toddler Goes For a Short Joyride," St. Petersburg Times, November 20, 1992, Pg. 1B.

"Toddler Dies in Vt. Car Crash," The Boston Globe, November 16, 1991, p. 26.

"Traffic," United Press International, July 18, 1984.

"TRW Automotive Child Restraint Seat Recall," PR Newswire, December 21, 1984.

"Two Drown in Auto Accident," United Press International, October 30, 1987.

"Two Hundred Child Car Seats Going To Low-Income Families," The Dallas Morning News, October 15, 1992.

"Two Hundred Children Were Saved by Child-Safety Seats Last Year," PR Newswire, February 8, 1988.

"Two-year old Boy Killed in Hit-and-Run Collision," Los Angles Times, October 7, 1990, Part B; Pg. 6; Col. 3.

"USAA Announces Air Bag Incentives Package," PR Newswire, March 30, 1988.

Vander Schaaf, "Dealing with Dealers," Crain Communications, Inc. Automotive News, July, 1988; Pg. 55.

"VT-Seat," United Press International, December 30, 1983.

Warren, "Letters to the Editor: A Few Bad Men Don't Represent Law Enforcement," The Atlanta Journal and Constitution, March 16, 1993; Section A; Pg. 14.

Washburn, "Child-Restraint Seats Urged on U.S. Airlines," Chicago Tribune, November 4, 1989; Pg. 3; Zone: C.

"Washington Traffic Safety Commission Recognizes Traffic Safety," PR Newswire, January 24, 1992.

"Where Can I Check the Federal Regulation Approval On My Child's Car Seat?," Star Tribune, January 28, 1993; Pg. 9E.

Whitely, "Seat Belts Especially Important for Children," The Seattle Times, May 1, 1992; Pg. E2.

Williams, "Justice or Double Tragedy? Father Faces Trial in Girl's Traffic Death," The Atlanta Journal and Constitution, April 28, 1992; Sec. A; Pg. 12.

Woessner, "Crash Course on Kids' Safety Seats," USA Today, February 10, 1992; Pg. 4D.

Worchol, "Train," United Press International, January 21, 1987.

"Woman Charged in Scripps Accident," United Press International, September 5, 1984.

Wong, "Jury Decides Car Seat Company; Must Pay Paralyzed Boy $5.2 m," The Boston Globe, November 20, 1990; Pg. 70p.

Yingst, "6 Killed, 6 Hurt in Head-On Crash," Gannette News Service, August 2, 1992.

Index